Religion, Identity and Empire: A Greek Archbishop in the Russia of Catherine the Great

GREGORY L. BRUESS

EAST EUROPEAN MONOGRAPHS, BOULDER
DISTRIBUTED BY COLUMBIA UNIVERSITY PRESS, NEW YORK
1997

EAST EUROPEAN MONOGRAPHS, NO. CDLXXIV

Copyright © 1997 by Gregory L. Bruess
ISBN 0–88033–371–5
Library of Congress Catalog Card Number 97–60048

Printed in the United States of America

ARCHBISHOP NIKIFOROS THEOTOKIS

To
Isabela, Alexander and Elena

CONTENTS

ILLUSTRATIONS

ACKNOWLEDGMENTS

As one of the main concerns of this book is the process of creating identity, I feel compelled to relate a story concerning the "invention" or construction of part of my own identity and how it pertains to the study of religion and frontiers and a Greek archbishop in southern Russia at the end of the eighteenth century. When I was learning modern Greek I had the good fortune to attend the summer language program at the Institute of Balkan Studies in Thessaloniki. On the first day of the program, one of the instructors, Athanasios Karathanasis, asked each of us to write a short essay on why we wanted to learn modern Greek and, he added, the essay would be evaluated to determine the level of our modern Greek competency.

A quick survey of my fellow students suggested that most, if not all, were there owing to the accident of Greek ancestry. My Scandinavian appearance, however, revealed no such connection to the land of Homer. Undaunted, I produced an essay which invented a distant bond to the great Byzantine Empire. My Scandinavian ancestors, I suggested, had once been members of the Varangian Guard, the emperors' elite bodyguards. When they departed the service of the emperors and sunny Byzantium they took Greek wives with them back to Norway. Therefore, I argued, I was studying modern Greek to awaken the Greek in me. Regrettably, the essay earned me a place in the advanced literature section. A few years later, as I was working on my dissertation, I was reminded of that essay. Nikiforos Theotokis, the Greek archbishop in Catherinian Russia and a subject of this book, was rigid, severely religious and demanded moral perfection. Yet he was loving, lenient when necessary and all too appreciative of human frailties. In many respects, he reminded me of my own Norwegian grandmother, Clara Wallen. Perhaps my invented identity was not entirely illusory after all.

•••

This book began as a doctoral dissertation at the University of Minnesota, where I benefited greatly from my graduate mentor, Professor Theofanis G. Stavrou, whose infectious enthusiasm for the Orthodox world and Greek-Slavic relations in particular sparked my own interest in the Greek-Slavic world and led me to this field. His geographical and cultural conceptualization of modern Russian and Southeastern European history as an "Orthodox Commonwealth" stimulated me to think about my work within that framework.

During the writing of this book I have happily incurred numerous debts owing to the tangible and intangible support I generously received from family, friends, colleagues, and institutions. The completion of this study would not have been possible without the use of libraries and archival repositories in Greece and the former Soviet Union. My research in Greece was made possible by grants from the University of Minnesota Graduate School, the Office of International Studies, the Department of History, and the Basil G. Laourdas Fellowship in Greek-Slavic Relations from the Modern Greek Studies Department of the University of Minnesota. The majority of my research in Greece was done at the Gennadius Library in Athens. I wish to thank the staff of the Gennadius for their invaluable assistance and advice, especially, Sophia Papageorgiou, the former Gennadius librarian and Andreas Sideris, assistant librarian. Greek scholars who generously offered me advice and encouragement were Paschalis M. Kitromilides of the University of Athens and the Centre d'Etudes d'Asie Mineure, Efthymios Souloyannis of the Academy of Athens, and Athanasios Karathanasis and Konstantinos Papoulidis of the Institute of Balkan Studies in Thessaloniki.

My research in Moscow and St. Petersburg was made possible by travel grants from the Department of History and the Modern Greek Studies Program at the University of Minnesota in 1988, Summer Fellowships from the American Council of Teachers of Russian in 1991, 1992, 1993, and 1994, and two University of Northern Iowa Graduate College Summer Fellowships in 1991 and 1995. I wish to thank the staffs for their assistance at the Russian State Archive of Ancient Documents in Moscow, the Russian State Historical Archive in St. Petersburg, and the Manuscripts Division of the Saltykov-Shchedrin Public Library in St. Petersburg. I also owe special thanks to Professors G.L. Arsh and V.I. Sheremet and O.V. Sokolovskaia at the Institute of Slavic and Balkan Studies and B.L. Fonkich of the Institute of World History in Moscow for their generous counsel and support. I also greatly appreciated the assistance of Father Boris of the Synodal Library at Danilov Monastery in Moscow and wish him godspeed in the task before him.

In the United States, I benefited from the advice of Theophilus C. Prousis and Stephen K. Batalden, fellow students of Greek-Slavic relations, as well as John T. Alexander, Gerasimos Augustinos, Robin Bisha, Sara Dickinson, Louis E. Fenech, Gregory L. Freeze, David Goldfrank, David Kieft, Gary Marker, J. Kim Munholland, and Leonard Polakiewicz. I want to thank the staffs at the Russian and East European Summer Research Laboratory at the University of Illinois-Urbana/Champaign for providing a very accommodating atmosphere in which to work and profitably exchange ideas with colleagues, especially, in the Eighteenth-Century Russia Study Group. I would also like to thank my good colleague and friend, Timothy O'Connor, for his encouragement and support.

Finally, the completion of this project would never have been possible without the understanding, emotional support, and invaluable assistance of my wife, Isabela Varela. She spent hours helping me with difficult translations and proofreading and also shouldered the extra responsibilities of caring for our children, Alexander and Elena, while I was attending to Nikiforos Theotokis in Russia.

A brief note on the transliteration and translation of non-English names and titles used in this book. Russian transliterations generally conform to Library of Congress rules. Greek transliterations, with a few exceptions, follow a modified modern version approximating that used by the *Modern Greek Studies Yearbook*. Of the non-English titles used for this study only those in Greek are translated. Because of the particularly archaic form of Greek employed by most of the authors, the translation of these titles is cumbersome, to say the least. Our effort has been to render these in acceptable English. Complete translations of Greek works cited are found in the bibliography.

INTRODUCTION

There are no religions which are false. All are true in their own fashion – all answer, though in different ways, to the given conditions of human existence.

 – Emile Durkheim, *The Elementary Forms of the Religious Life*

I am drawn to studying earlier periods through individuals who are of intrinsic and representative importance. Of course there are "the broad, anonymous forces" that characterize the setting or structure of an age, but it is the interplay between these forces and actual people that allows us to recapture something of the spirit of the age.

 – Fritz Stern, *Dreams and Delusions*

In the fall of 1776, the Greek prelate Nikiforos Theotokis crossed the Russian-Ottoman frontier near the city of Jassy. Although he traversed a political boundary as he stepped on Russian soil, he, nevertheless, was still within the cultural boundaries of the Orthodox commonwealth, a modern legacy of the Byzantine commonwealth, a religious and cultural world that once bound together the peoples of medieval Russia, the Balkans and the Byzantine Empire.[1] Catherine the Great intended on erasing that unfortunate discordance, however, by expanding the political boundaries of the Russian Empire until they completely conformed with the cultural boundaries of the Orthodox East (or even classical Greece). She moved closer to realizing that goal and scored a major diplomatic triumph when Russia concluded a remarkable treaty with the Ottoman Empire in the small Balkan village of Kutchuk-Kainardji in 1774; a treaty which altered the balance of power in eighteenth-century Europe and held unforeseen consequences and opportunities for the peoples of the Orthodox East and Russia.

Within Russia, the situation was less sanguine. Russian forces, returning from a victory against the external threat of the Ottoman Empire, were quickly redeployed to confront a deeply embarrassing internal threat. Emelian Pugachev's massive peasant rebellion in southern Russia effectively revealed to the Empress the glaring inadequacies of Russian control of the sparsely inhabited, open steppe of southern and southeastern Russia. Catherine suppressed the revolt, executed Pugachev, and devised a strategy to expand Russia's southern borders at the expense of the Ottoman and Persian Empires and then, to transform the new territories (to be known as Novorossiia or New Russia) in accordance with the abstract and idealized principles of the French Enlightenment and German *Aufklärung*.[2] Catherine was transfixed by the promise of Novorossiia. It was a blank slate upon which she was free to write whatever pleased her enlightened sensibilities or piqued her imagination. Peter I had transformed the north in his quest for Western technology, Catherine sought to invent a "New Russia" in the south in her search for an Enlightened Russia and its classical heritage.[3]

Catherine was an avid student of the economic and population-ist theories of the French Physiocrats and the organizational theories of the German Cameralists. These rationalist theories simply stated that more subjects and more territory translated into more economic productivity and wealth. Furthermore, a highly centralized and uniform government was essential to tapping that wealth. Catherine planned to acquire more subjects through territorial expansion and colonization schemes directed at all Europeans but specifically at the oppressed Orthodox Christians of the Ottoman and Persian Empires. Their departures would serve two positive purposes for Russia: First, they would weaken the Ottoman and Persian economies through the loss of productive merchants while strengthening Russia's, and second, they would create a sizable community of former Ottoman and Persian subjects who aspired to gain religio-national independence for their fellow countrymen.

Catherine's religious policies, grounded in Enlightenment attitudes, reflected her belief that, although the state was responsible for the material and spiritual well-being of its subjects, the Church was instrumental in assisting the state in this task. Even though Catherine had "instrumentalized" religion, she understood that religious belief and, more important, the institutions which propa-gated those beliefs, were essential for creating and maintaining a semblance of social harmony and control. As a representative of the Orthodox Church, Theotokis, while not sharing Catherine's utilitar-ian views on religion, was able to contribute to the realization of her agenda of imperial expansion and consolidation while actively promoting the liberation of Orthodox Christians from the Ottoman Empire as an educator, scholar, and archbishop in southern and southeastern Russia in the last quarter of the eighteenth century. Although each appreciated religion differently, each understood its importance in giving meaning to life and determining identity in late eighteenth-century Russia.[4]

Accordingly, the main theme of this book is that religion (understood as interconnected beliefs and practices) was central to the construction of identity (whether social, ethnic, or individual) among the inhabitants of Russia's southern borderlands and played a significant role in the policies of the political and religious institutions attempting to consolidate and integrate the southern territories into the Russian Empire. By exploring the dynamic between religion and political and religious institutions, this study will examine the role of the state and Church as institutions promoting a universal/ecumenical program of meaning and order as it confronted Cossacks, peasants, ethnic minorities, and other social groups who created their own particular or local religious beliefs and behavior to give meaning and order to their world. The tensions between the three shaped the religious culture of the southern frontier at the end of the eighteenth century.

This book analyzes the following aspects of religious culture in the second half of the eighteenth century in southern Russia: Catherine's understanding of religious toleration and how she sought to "instrumentalize" religion to foster private morality, social harmony, and political integration in the newly acquired territories of Novorossiia; the relations between the Holy Synod, diocesan prelates, particularly Nikiforos Theotokis, and parish clergy; the continuous efforts of the Church and its representatives to "Christianize" and "enlighten" its parishioners; the existence of religious dissenters such as the Old Believers and Dukhobors as manifestations of popular religious "enthusiasm"; the relationship between religion and politics and how religion can legitimize change and subvert the existing political order; and the influence of religion on the definition and structure of community – especially among ethnic minorities. The career of Archbishop Nikiforos Theotokis in the Greek world and in Russia provides a narrative thread for the exploration of these aspects of religious culture in Catherinian Russian and his own goal of securing liberty for the Orthodox Christians of Greece and the Balkans.

••••

Theotokis was part of a wider Greek world that can best be likened to a triptych: three separate and distinct representations which taken together create a unified and coherent image. His life and career emerged from and were a product of a geographical, political, and cultural conjunction which occurred between Greece, Venice, and Russia. On the most fundamental and physical level, Nikiforos Theotokis was born on the fringes of the Venetian Republic on the island of Corfu, studied in Italy and lived in Russia for twenty-four years.

Politically, his native island of Corfu was part of a weakened Venetian Republic that was beginning to disintegrate as a result of external aggression and internal dissent. Theotokis, as a Greek, also indirectly experienced the onerous weight of Ottoman imperial oppression on mainland Greece. The Russian Empire, no supporter of political liberalization at home, was actively pursuing a foreign policy which encouraged politically liberal movements abroad in Venetian and Ottoman lands and proclaimed itself the protector of the Orthodox Christians. Culturally, Theotokis's world was a blend of "ecumenical" Eastern Orthodoxy, Neo-Hellenism, and the Enlightenment. He devoted himself to the Orthodox Church at a very early age as a means of safeguarding his Greek identity from the Catholic Venetians and pursuing an education available only through the Church during the Veneto-Turkokratia or Venetian and Turkish occupations. His Orthodoxy was ecumenical in the sense that he consistently stressed Orthodoxy's catholicity and downplayed its non-dogmatic variations in favor of harmony. He began his education in Corfu and continued his studies in Italian schools by following a curriculum that was both steeped in the Renaissance with its attention to Greek classicism and the sciences which were the foundation of the Enlightenment. After concluding his studies in Italy he returned to Corfu as an educator and cleric. His educational, ecclesiastical and scholarly activities obliged him to travel from Corfu to Constantinople, Jassy, Leipzig, Halle and Vienna. Theotokis finally was attracted to Russia and the Third Rome.

Theotokis, of course, was not the first Greek to make this intellectual and physical journey. In 1518, Maxim Grek, born in Arta in 1480 and educated in Italy, became the librarian of Tsar Basil III. Of more importance, a fellow Corfiote, Eugenios Voulgaris traveled to Russia to become the librarian of Catherine II in 1771. There is little wonder why Theotokis eventually took up residence in a country traditionally receptive to his countrymen, with an empress who proclaimed herself the protectress of all Orthodox Christians, corresponded with leading *philosophes* and was fascinated by the ancient Greek world.

Nikiforos Theotokis did not formulate Russian foreign policy nor was he in a position to give advice to Catherine on domestic affairs but nonetheless his actions as archbishop of Slaviansk and Kherson and, later, of Astrakhan and Stavropol were a reflection of Catherine's intentions in regard to religious toleration and harmony, foreign settlement of the southern provinces, economic development, and maintaining contact with the Greek East. Catherine and her principal advisor on foreign policy and Novorossiia, Governor-General Prince G.A. Potemkin, intentionally selected non-Russian Orthodox clerics to serve as diocesan heads in southern and southeastern Russia because of the ethnic diversity of that region and its proximity to the Ottoman and Persian territories inhabited by their Orthodox countrymen. Theotokis, however, was not an unthinking instrument of imperial policy. His own agenda and the aspirations and goals of those he served as spiritual adviser imparted a dynamic to the process which ultimately affected broader policy aims and created an inner tension which he needed to reconcile.

This is not the first study of Nikiforos Theotokis. He was a polymath typical of his day and his scholarly expertise and research ranged widely and extensively to include mathematics, physics, astronomy, meteorology, geography, Archimedean principles, Biblical exegeses, philosophy and theology. Consequently, some authors and scholars have concentrated on his educational activities or Biblical commentaries, while others have examined his activities in the Greek East. This book is the first intensive study which focuses on Theotokis's career as archbishop in Russia as well as his efforts to effect the liberation of his native Greece from the Ottoman Empire through the promotion and establishment of schools, the publication of textbooks critical to any generation of students seeking independence from ignorance and oppression, and his polemical writings directed at the Ottoman Empire.

••••

In recent decades, historians of medieval and early modern Europe (and more recently, modern Europe) have conscientiously refined their analyses of what exactly constitutes "popular religion" or "popular belief."[5] They have distanced themselves from the "two-tiered" model which conveniently divided religion between that which the educated elites practiced and believed and that which the ignorant masses practiced and believed. This division, according to Peter Brown, was first elaborated during the Enlightenment by David Hume, who held that the uneducated masses were incapable of comprehending the abstract notion of a monotheistic world and were, implicitly, much more comfortable in a personalized poly-theistic world inhabited by fairies, goblins, and the spirits of the dead.[6] In other words, the masses had failed to escape the dark and irrational universe of magic and superstition inherited from their pagan, pre-Christian ancestors.

In opposition to this ahistorical construction of an immutable popular religious culture, Natalie Zemon Davis, in her historio-graphical essay "From 'Popular Religion' to Religious Cultures," notes that scholars have begun to examine religion "as practiced and experienced and not merely as defined and prescribed." Instead of trying to determine what is "popular," she argues, historians should focus on the interconnected beliefs and practices which comprise religious cultures. Historians must also select a specific contextual and relational framework in which these religious cultures are examined.[7] Implicit in this new approach is the ongoing shift away from the primacy accorded to economics as the foundation for all cultural and religious behavior. The "new cultural history" argues that culture is not merely derivative of social and economic structures but acts on and gives meaning to those structures.[8] Social and cultural anthropologists have also been searching for an adequate definition of "popular religion." In a recent collection of anthropo-logical essays on "popular religion" the following definition, greatly influenced by Clifford Geertz,[9] was proffered as acceptable: "those informal, unofficial practices, beliefs, and styles of religious expression that lack the formal sanction of established church structures."[10]

The study of religion in Russia has labored under its own analog of the "two-tiered" model. The educated elites practiced reli-gion according to the precepts of the Russian Orthodox Church but the peasant masses were caught up in a world of *dvoeverie*, or "dual faith." In this religious system pagan beliefs and practices persisted alongside Christianity. The *dvoeverie* model also emphasizes conflict and hostility between the elite form of Christianity and the peasant form: a continuous struggle on the part of the True Church to inculcate the "correct" Christianity and the equally obstinate response of the peasantry to preserve pagan customs.[11] As a result, nineteenth-century Russian authors portrayed the peasants as either ignorant, superstitious, relics of the past or deeply pious devotees of an ignorant, corrupt and conservative Orthodox Church and Russian state. Later, Marxist authors discerned not peasant ignorance and attachment to an idyllic pagan past as an explanation for popular belief and religious dissent but social and economic protest against a hostile church and government occasioned by the changing economic structure of imperial society. Unfortunately, Russian and Soviet scholars were as reluctant to abandon or modify the *dvoeverie* model as a rationalization for popular religion as the peasants were reluctant to abandon their alleged pagan beliefs.

In recent years historians of Russian religion, culture, and society have undertaken the task of systematically exploring the complex and tendentious relationship between "learned" or clerical religion and "unlearned" or "popular" religion. Russianists have begun to cast the argument in terms similar to those developed by scholars of western medieval and early modern Christianity.[12] Gregory Freeze has argued that previous scholarship on the Russian religious experience was notable for its paucity of empirical research and overabundance of "a priori assumptions and the obiter dicta of Russia's urban intelligentsia." These two elements conspired to create the perception that popular belief was static and the Orthodox Church was incapable of engaging its own flock.[13] Recent studies have explored the advantages to be gained from selectively applying some of the new methods and models developed in western historiography to the study of the Old Belief,[14] to the explication of meaning in the death rituals among Russian and Ukrainian peasants,[15] and to the attempts of the Church to enforce morality through public penance.[16] The question remaining for Russian historians is, what was the significance of religious culture in Imperial Russia and how does an understanding of the religious experience better enable us to comprehend and give meaning to Imperial Russian history?

Scholars in the social sciences have devoted considerable attention to the question of identity, especially as a complement, precursor or sub-category of nationalism.[17] In this study I examine how the particular religious beliefs of different ethnic groups in southern Russia shaped their communities and how they reacted to Catherine's program of political and social uniformity and the Church's "Christianization" reforms. Using the theoretical work of Fredrik Barth and Paul Brass on ethnicity, and of Owen Lattimore on frontiers and boundaries,[18] of James Clifford on "local" peoples and of Talal Asad on power and belief,[19] we can envision each group's attempt to maintain its identity through the creation of boundaries. These boundaries, however, were elastic, in that groups adapted to the existing social and political environment, and they were permeable or porous, in that individuals crossed boundaries from one group to another. Contrary to the usual assumptions concerning ethnic or communal "purity," elasticity and permeability were essential if the different groups were to preserve their distinctiveness in the face of the integrative and assimilationist pressures of the Russian state.

The written word is of fundamental importance in the creation and the maintenance of identity. This is most certainly apparent in regard to Christianity which, as a textually based religion, possesses in the Bible, and especially in the New Testament, the objective marker of religious identity for those who call themselves Christians. In many respects the holy text itself is considered iconic and its mere possession signifies the identity of its holder. Although the Russian Orthodox Church deems the Holy Book essential to Christian identity it is not sufficient in and of itself. Without the guiding hand of the Church and its tradition it is all too easy to stray from the Truth. Thus the Church's continued efforts in the eighteenth century to educate priests in the "correct" interpretation of the Bible. The centrality of the written word to religious identity was reflected in the activities of the dissenting or sectarian religious communities in Catherinian Russia. The Old Believers, Robert Crummey argues, formed "textual communities" based on their mutual adherence to the pre-Nikonian texts and rites.[20] The multiplicity of Old Belief communities or concords (*soglasiia*), then, mirrored the various interpretations of the Holy Book and Orthodox rituals among those who had neither accepted the Nikonian reforms and the interpretive hegemony of the Russian Orthodox Church nor submitted themselves to a rival center of interpretive authority. The Dukhobors, on the other hand, defined their community by expunging all outward manifestations of Orthodoxy from their lives. Yet, the tradition of Orthodox textuality remained in the form of the "Living Book."

From the perspective of Catherine and the imperial center, the periphery had to be defined culturally and fixed geographically to reflect the identity of Russia.[21] As the recent work of Richard Wortman demonstrates, Catherine constructed scenarios of power, performed ceremonies, and commissioned literature that portrayed the expanding and multinational Russia as the equivalent of ancient Rome.[22] She was the mythic conqueror and renovator, deliverer of civilization to the new territories. Catherine was, above all, consciously continuing the reformist aspect of Peter the Great – her "reforming zeal," Falconet's "Bronze Horseman" as a memorial to Peter (and to Catherine herself?), the expansion to the Black Sea and the foundation of Ekaterinoslav as a mirror of the Baltic and St. Petersburg – and desperately seeking the legitimacy his image provided.[23] The empress undertook extended journeys (from senti-mental voyages to sacred pilgrimages), bringing the capital (St. Petersburg/Rome) to the provinces, as proof, or "a ceremonial affirmation," of this unified and consolidated empire. The grandest of these journeys was her trip to the Crimea in 1787. This study augments Marc Raeff's pioneering work on Catherine's policies in the south by examining the archival record of the periphery as opposed to examining the imperial decrees produced in St. Peters-burg.[24] More often than not, decrees directed at the southern frontier from the center underwent a significant transformation during their implementation. These adaptations reflected the dynamic relationship between the center and periphery and suggested that it was not a one-way street. The main reason the frontier was resistant to certain forms of control extending from the core or center lay in the diverse and kaleidoscopic nature of the borderlands. No clearly demarcated boundary existed between Russia and its southern neigh-bors. It can be variously described as a "double frontier zone," a "transfrontier," or a "middle ground."[25] As no easily recognizable "frontier" obtained, central policies directed at the frontier zones often conflicted with each other. Even after incorporation into the empire, when the frontier territories were no longer considered "geographically" peripheral, they at times remained obstinately "culturally" peripheral. This particular phenomenon could be exacerbated if governmental officials made too many accommodations to local conditions and, as a result, went "native." The state apparatus itself had to adjust to the changing character of its expanding empire with new institutions, departments, and juridical and religious policies. Paradoxically, the very goals of integration and consolidation demanded a certain degree of conformity to regional variations. More often, however, far less noticeable cultural exchanges occurred as the regions remained in flux and multiethnic populations moved within the middle ground itself or along the center-periphery axis. As a consequence, the periphery played an important role in its own reformation.[26]

All of this suggests that identity is not reducible to some natural essence. In the eighteenth century, the Enlightenment sought to displace shared religion and shared loyalty to a common monarch as signifiers of one's national identity with a scientific classification system built on the premise that identity is "natural" and, therefore, scientifically discernible and verifiable. In the case of Russia, Catherine enthusiastically endorsed this approach to ascertaining "Russianess" and, as a result, commissioned numerous scientific expeditions to crisscross the Russian Empire in an attempt to determine those "natural" and quantifiable qualities which made Russia's subjects Russian. What the naturalists discovered, of course, was that no one set of observable criteria or even multiple sets of criteria were sufficient to categorize and distill the rich human diversity of Russia's territory into a singular Russian essence.[27] (This "scientific" method was later modified by nineteenth-century organicists and idealists such as J.G. von Herder and J.G. Fichte who transferred the supposedly objective and "natural" aspects of ethnicity to the nation.)[28] Catherine had to content herself with a more cosmopolitan definition of a good Russian: one who, regardless of language, religion, or ethnicity, swore loyalty to her and the Russian state. And among the majority of her subjects and the subjects of subsequent nineteenth-century rulers, identity was not "national" as such until the end of the imperial period. Instead, Russian identity, as opposed to family or village allegiances, was founded on tsar and Orthodoxy.[29]

Identity, then, is best understood as an evolutionary, historical process which constantly adapts to external circumstances and internal dynamics of an ever changing world.[30] Groups, communities, individuals, and nations exert tremendous intellectual and

emotional energy in an effort to deny the reality of this process by
constructing or inventing irreducible and essentialist identities which
reaffirm the fixity of "their" identity while presuming the ephemeral
nature of "other" identities. This "invented tradition" is particularly
important in societies experiencing rapid change.[31] Further complicating an already problematic task in affixing identity was the
adoption, in both Russia and Greece, of two similar but different
terms of national identity. One term was employed to conform to
international expectations and was outer-directed; the other term was
inner-directed. For purposes of Russian identity in an international
context, all groups or individuals who were part of the Russian
Empire (center and periphery) were *rossiiskii* (in the Soviet period,
sovetskii). Within the Russia Empire itself, however, some groups
or individuals could also identify themselves as *russkii* (Great
Russian and Orthodox or center only). The great difficulty for
Russian rulers was, first, becoming conscious of the two identities,
and, second, drafting policies which were mindful of the consequences on both, whether in foreign or domestic affairs.[32]

In a slightly different fashion, modern Greek identity also was,
and continues to be, precariously balanced between two models: the
"Hellenic" and the "Romeic." In an attempt to create a uninterrupted
continuum from Ancient Greece through Byzantium to the modern
period, modern Greeks coined the term Greco-Christian
(*ellinohristianikos*). In conformity to international expectations,
whether inspired by the Enlightenment or the Romantic movement,
Greeks draped themselves in the robes of classical Greece and
became "Hellenic" in response to those expectations. Among themselves, however, Greeks were fellow Christians or *Romii*, inheritors
of the East Roman (Byzantine) tradition.[33] One identity was created
primarily by diaspora Greeks in response to western European
conceptions of classical Greece and the other was the identity of the
Ottoman Greeks who lived in Rum and were part of the Rum *millet*,
the Ottoman administrative category for all Orthodox in the Ottoman
Empire and the responsibility of the Ecumenical Patriarch in
Constantinople. Similarly, the Russian Empire of Catherine the
Great, in its foreign policy considerations and in the creation of its
identity, addressed itself to both *rossiiskii* and *russkii*.

Definitions of identity are at once extremely important,
notoriously imprecise and historically contingent. In late seventeenth-century Russia, for instance, to be a Russian (*russkii*) was to

be a Christian (*pravoslavnyi, pravovernyi* or the seldom used
khristianin). Conversely, foreigners (*inozemtsy*) were also non-
Orthodox (*inovertsy*). Peter I introduced the Latin-inspired *rossiiskii*
to reflect Russia's new status as an empire. He also introduced a new
term for foreigners (*inostrantsy*) which defined them relative to the
empire's borders. This definition proved to be exceedingly
problematic in the middle ground or transfrontier. Later, in the
nineteenth century, the government favored the term alien (*inorodtsy*
) to describe *rossiiskie* who were not *russkie* because they were not
pravovertsy. After 1870, *inorodtsy* gradually came to define only the
eastern and southeastern non-Russians. In the western borderlands,
government officials used *russkii* rather indiscriminately in
reference to Ukrainians, Russians, Belorussians, or even "non-
Poles."[34] Complicating matters further is the tendency to understand
or use terms anachronistically. The words "nation," "nationalism,"
nationality," and "national consciousness" are laden with modern
accretions yet are beneficial if used cautiously. It would be foolish to
argue that educated Russians in the eighteenth century did not possess
a national consciousness solely because nationalism as we understand
it did not yet exist.[35] In eighteenth-century documents, fatherland
(*otechestvo*) was a common designation for Russia and nation (*natsiia*
) referred to people of a different "race," e.g., *grecheskaia natsiia*
(the Greek nation). At the same time, Greeks, Serbians and
Bulgarians were co-religionists, fellow Orthodox, or *edinovertsy*.

When Greeks of the eighteenth and early nineteenth century
spoke of the nation and national liberation or independence they also
were trading in ambiguity. The contemporary Greek word for
"nation" is *ethnos*. At the time of the Greek War of Independence,
however, it was seldom used. Instead, the word most favored was
yenos which referred to all who spoke Greek, shared a common
tradition and were Orthodox. *Yenos* was both a classical Greek word
which meant "race," "stock," or "kin" and a word appropriated during the Ottoman occupation to refer to the Christian nations. *Ethnos*,
according to Adamantios Korais (1748-1833), a leader in the Greek
Enlightenment, was reserved for those nations already having a state
of their own.[36] Greeks also used the word *patrida* in reference to
their village, region, or even fatherland or "nation." Hence, proclamations of liberation or independence of the *patrida* or *yenos* were
at once localized and universal. The very ambiguity of the terms, as
George Frangos demonstrates in his study of the *Filiki Etairia*, was

beneficial to attracting a large and diverse coterie of enthusiastic liberationists. However, that very inexactitude led to divisions among the revolutionaries during the Greek War of Independence and the years immediately succeeding it, regarding the future political and social complexion of the new Greek *ethnos*.[37]

This study finally suggests a new framework for interpreting and understanding the complex interaction of popular belief, the institutions of Church and state, and society in Imperial Russia and examines the nature of imperial, ethnic and local identities. It, above all, recognizes that these identities continuously negotiated for the same contested terrain.

NOTES

1. The term "Orthodox Commonwealth" I owe to Theofanis Stavrou. Dimitri Obolensky formulated the concept of the "Byzantine Commonwealth" in his magnificent study, *The Byzantine Commonwealth: Eastern Europe, 500-1453* (London, 1971).

2. On the Enlightenment and German *Aufklärung* in Russia, see Marc Raeff, *The Well-Ordered Police State: Social and Institutional Change Through Law in the Germanies and Russia, 1600-1800* (New Haven, 1983); idem, "The Enlightenment in Russia and Russian Thought in the Enlightenment," in J.G. Garrard, ed., *The Eighteenth Century in Russia* (London, 1973), pp. 25-47; Isabel de Madariaga, "Catherine and the *Philosophes*," in A.G. Cross, ed., *Russia and the West in the Eighteenth Century* (Newtonville, MA, 1983), pp. 30-52; idem, *Russia in the Age of Catherine the Great* (New Haven, 1981), pp. 151-163; David Griffiths, "Catherine II: The Republican Empress," *Jahrbücher für Geschichte Osteuropas*, 2 (1973): 337-340; idem, "In Search of the Enlightenment: Recent Soviet Interpretations of Eighteenth-Century Russian Intellectual History," *Canadian-American Slavic Studies*, 16:3-4 (1982): 317-356. Ernest Gellner offers a thoughtful essay on Russia's inability, beginning with Catherine II, to implement equally the centralizing and liberalizing aspects of the Enlightenment in "The Struggle to Catch Up: Russian, Europe and the Enlightenment," *Times Literary Supplement* (Dec. 9, 1994), pp. 14-15.

3. On the role of travel literature in this process see Larry Wolff, *Inventing Eastern Europe: The Map of Civilization on the Mind of the Enlightenment* (Stanford, 1994) and Sara Dickinson, "Imagining Space and the Self: Russian Travel Writing and Its Narrators, 1762-1825," Ph.D. dissertation, Harvard University, 1995.

4. On the role of religion in society see Peter Berger, *The Sacred Canopy: Elements of a Sociological Theory of Religion* (Garden City, NJ, 1969).

5. A representative sampling of medieval and early modern works includes: Keith Thomas, *Religion and the Decline of Magic* (London, 1971); Natalie Zemon Davis, *Society and Culture in Early Modern France* (Stanford, 1975); A.N. Galpern, *The Religion of the People in Sixteenth-Century Champagne* (Cambridge, 1976); Peter Brown, *The Cult of the Saints: Its Rise and Function in Latin Christianity* (Chicago, 1981); William Christian, *Local Religion in Sixteenth-Century Spain* (Princeton, 1981); A.Ia. Gurevich, *Problemy srednevekovoi narodnoi kul'tury* (Moscow, 1981) and *Srednevekovyi mir: Kul'tura bezmolvstvuiushchego bol'shinstva* (Moscow, 1990). Some of the more recent modern European studies include: Thomas

Kselman, *Miracles and Prophecies in Nineteenth-Century France* (New Brunswick, N.J., 1983); Jonathan Sperber, *Popular Catholicism in Nineteenth-Century Germany* (Princeton, 1984); Suzanne Desan, *Reclaiming the Sacred: Lay Religion and Popular Politics in France* (Ithaca, NY, 1990); Caroline C. Ford, *Creating the Nation in Provincial France: Religion and Political Identity in Brittany* (Princeton, 1993); and David Blackbourn, *Marpingen: Apparitions of the Virgin Mary in Bismarckian Germany* (New York, 1994). For a discussion of new approaches to the study of the history of religion see Thomas Kselman, ed., *Belief in History: Innovative Approaches to European and American Religion* (Notre Dame, 1991).

6. Brown, pp. 13-22.

7. Natalie Zemon Davis, "From 'Popular Religion' to Religious Cultures," in Steven Ozment, ed., *Reformation Europe: A Guide to Research* (St. Louis, 1982), pp. 322-323.

8. On the "new cultural history," see Lynn Hunt, "Introduction: History, Culture, and Text," in Lynn Hunt, ed., *The New Cultural History* (Berkeley, 1989), pp. 1-22.

9. Clifford Geertz, *The Interpretation of Cultures* (New York, 1973).

10. Ellen Badone, "Introduction," in Ellen Badone, ed., *Religious Orthodoxy and Popular Faith in European Society* (Princeton, 1990), pp. 4-6.

11. See Eve Levin, *"Dvoeverie* and Popular Religion," in Stephen K. Batalden, ed., *Seeking God: The Recovery of Religious Identity in Orthodox Russia, Ukraine, and Georgia* (DeKalb, IL, 1993), pp. 31-52.

12. Works on the religious experience outside Europe are also quite useful. See Harjot Oberoi, *The Construction of Religious Boundaries: Culture, Identity, and Diversity in the Sikh Traditions* (Chicago, 1994).

13. Gregory L. Freeze, "The Rechristianization of Russia: The Church and Popular Religion, 1750-1850," *Studia Slavica Finlandensia* (Helsinki), 7 (1990): 101-102.

14. See Robert O. Crummey, "Old Belief as Popular Religion: New Approaches," *Slavic Review*, 52, no. 4 (Winter 1993): 700-712 and Roy R. Robson, *Old Believers in Modern Russia* (DeKalb, IL, 1995).

15. Christine D. Worobec, "Death Ritual Among Russian and Ukrainian Peasants: Linkages Between the Living and the Dead," in Stephen Frank and Mark Steinberg, eds., *Cultures in Flux: Lower-Class Values, Practices, and Resistance in Late Imperial Russia* (Princeton, 1994), pp. 11-33.

16. Gregory L. Freeze, "The Wages of Sin: The Decline of Public Penance in Imperial Russia," in Batalden, *Seeking God*, pp. 53-82.

17. For an excellent introduction to this subject see Geoff Eley and Ronald Grigor Suny, eds., *Becoming National: A Reader* (Oxford, 1996).

18. On the creation and maintenance of boundaries and their importance to religious, cultural, and ethnic identity see Fredrik Barth, "Introduction," in Fredrik Barth, ed., *Ethnic Groups and Boundaries: The Social Organization of Cultural Differences* (Boston, 1969), pp. 9-38; Paul R. Brass, *Ethnicity and Nationalism: Theory and Comparison* (Newbury Park, CA, 1991); and the pioneering study of Owen Lattimore, "The Frontier in History," in Owen Lattimore, ed., *Studies in Frontier History: Collected Papers, 1928-1958* (Oxford, 1962), pp. 469-491.

19. See James Clifford, *The Predicament of Culture: Twentieth-Century Ethnography, Literature, and Art* (Cambridge, 1988) and Talal Asad, *Genealogies of Religion: Discipline and Reasons of Power in Christianity and Islam* (Baltimore, 1993).

20. Robert O. Crummey, "Interpreting the Fate of the Old Believer Communities in the Eighteenth and Nineteenth Centuries," in Stephen K. Batalden, ed., *Seeking God*, p. 145.

21. On the problem of overcoming local affinities in the process of establishing political integration and ideological conformity see Raymond Aron, "On the Proper Use of Ideologies," in J. Ben-David and Terry Nichols Clark, eds., *Culture and Its Creators: Essays in Honor of Edward Shils* (Chicago, 1977), pp. 1-14 and Edward Shils, *Center and Periphery: Essays in Macrosociology* (Chicago, 1975), pp. 3-90, 111-139.

22. Richard Wortman, *Scenarios of Power: Myth and Ceremony in Russian Monarchy* (Princeton, 1995), pp. 135-139.

23. For elaboration see Cynthia H. Whittaker, "The Reforming Tsar: The Redefinition of Autocratic Duty in Eighteenth-Century Russia," *Slavic Review*, 51:1 (Spring 1992): 77-98; Nicholas V. Riasanovsky, *The Image of Peter the Great in Russian History and Thought* (Oxford: 1985); and Karen Rasmussen, "Catherine II and the Image of Peter I," *Slavic Review*, 37:1 (1978): 57-69.

24. See Marc Raeff, "The Style of Russia's Imperial Policy and Prince G.A. Potemkin," in Gerald Grob, ed., *Statesmen and Statecraft of the Modern West: Essays in Honor of Dwight E. Lee and H. Donaldson Jordan* (Barre, MA, 1967), pp. 1-51.

25. For thoughts on the "double frontier" see Alfred J. Rieber, "Struggle over the Borderlands," in S. Frederick Starr, ed., *The Legacy of History in Russia and the New States of Eurasia* (Armonk, NY, 1994), pp. 61-89; on the "transfrontier" see John LeDonne, "The Frontier in Modern Russian History," *Russian History*, 19:1-4 (1992): 143-154; on the southern steppe see William H. McNeill, *Europe's Steppe Frontier, 1500-1800: A Study of the Eastward Movement in Europe* (Chicago, 1964); and on the "middle ground" see Richard White, *The Middle Ground: Indians, Empire, and Republics in the Great Lakes Region, 1650-1815* (New York, 1991).

26. For a recent article on the Caucasus which anticipates many of the same issues concerning the frontier addressed in this present study see Thomas M. Barrett, "Lines of Uncertainty: The Frontiers of the North Caucasus," *Slavic Review*, 54:3 (Fall 1995): 578-601.

27. See Yuri Slezkine, "Naturalists Versus Nations: Eighteenth-Century Russian Scholars Confront Ethnic Diversity," *Representations*, 47 (Summer 1994): 170-195.

28. For a concise historiographical treatment of nationalism see Geoff Eley and Ronald Grigor Suny, "Introduction: From the Moment of Social History to the Work of Cultural Representation," in Geoff Eley and Ronald Grigor Suny, eds., *Becoming National*, pp. 3-37.

29. See Jeffrey Brooks, *When Russia Learned to Read: Literacy and Popular Literature, 1861-1917* (Princeton, 1985), pp. 214-245.

30. See Stuart Hall, "Ethnicity: Identity and Difference," in Geoff Eley and Ronald Grigor Suny, eds., *Becoming National*, pp. 339-349.

31. The notion that nations must be constructed discursively and are not "natural" began with Karl Deutsch, *Nationalism and Social Communication: An Inquiry into the Foundations of Nationality* (Cambridge, 1966) and Ernest Gellner, *Thought and Change* (London, 1964). Several Marxist scholars elaborated upon Deutsch's and Gellner's theory of nations as products of modernization by arguing that nations were "invented" or "imagined communities." See Benedict Anderson, *Imagined Communities: Reflections on the Origin and Spread of Nationalism* (London, 1983) and Eric Hobsbawm and Terence Ranger, eds., *The Invention of Tradition* (Cambridge, 1983). For a recent example of a teleological explanation see Liah Greenfeld, *Nationalism: Five Roads to Modernity* (Cambridge, 1992).

32. Rieber, "Struggle over the Borderlands," pp. 62-63.

33. See Michael Herzfeld, *Ours Once More: Folklore, Ideology, and the Making of Modern Greece* (Austin, 1982), pp. 3-23.

34. See Theodore R. Weeks, "Defending Our Own: Government and the Russian Minority in the Kingdom of Poland, 1905-1917," *The Russian Review*, 54 (October 1995): 539.

35. See Hans Rogger, *National Consciousness in Eighteenth-Century Russia* (Cambridge, 1960); Michael Cherniavsky, "Russia," in Orest Ranum, ed., *National Consciousness, History, and Political Culture in Early-Modern Europe* (Baltimore, 1975), pp. 118-143; Paul Bushkovitch, "The Formation of a National Consciousness in Early Modern Russia," *Harvard Ukrainian Studies*, 10:3/4 (December 1986): 355-376; and Greenfeld, pp. 189-274.

36. See Stephen G. Xydis, "Modern Greek Nationalism," in Peter F. Sugar and Ivo J. Lederer, eds., *Nationalism in Eastern Europe* (Seattle, 1969), pp. 207-209.

37. George D. Frangos, "The *Philiki Etairia*: A Premature National Coalition," in Richard Clogg, ed., *The Struggle for Greek Independence* (London, 1973), pp. 87-103.

OTTOMAN SUBJECT, ORTHODOX BELIEVER, AND ENLIGHTENED EDUCATOR: THE PROCESS OF IDENTITY

I am of the Greek race, born in Greece, raised, educated and took the monk's habit there. I have seen and spent time with the sacred patriarchs of Constantinople and Jerusalem; I have met and discussed the condition of the Church with bishops from Iberia and Dalmatia, Christian Arabs as well as with the learned, holy monks and fathers of Athos and Mt. Sinai.... I went to Bulgaria, Moldavia and Wallachia and now have the honor of being a hierarch in Russia.[1]

– Archbishop Nikiforos to the Znamenka Old

For it is self-evident that the spread of science can be accompanied, most successfully, by the spread of truth and piety.

– Leibniz

Theotokis was born on 15 February 1731 on the Ionian island of Corfu. His parents, Stefanos and Anastasia, named this fourth addition to their family Nikolaos.[2] The Theotokis were an old Corfiote family which traced its origins to Constantinople. The family fled the "City" when it fell to the Ottoman Turks in 1453. After some time, the Theotokis family tree expanded and split into six branches with one of them acquiring a title of nobility (*komitos*) in 1669. We can understand how some early biographers of Theotokis believed that his family was undoubtedly part of the ennobled branch as was only fitting for a man as famous as he.[3] However, neither Stefanos nor Anastasia (herself a member of the Theotokis family and daughter of Eustathios Theotokis) were descendants of noble lineage. The only "title" this particular branch of the Theotokis family held was *tou Aghiou* or "of the Saint" because they lived in the neighborhood near the Church of the Miracle Worker St. Spiridon, the patron saint of Corfu.[4]

By the time of Theotokis's birth the *Venetokratia* (period of Venetian occupation) was nearing its end. Corfu and the other six Ionian Islands, together with the Adriatic coast and Cerigo (Kythera) were all that remained of the once mighty merchant empire of the Venetian Republic. In the wake of the Fourth Crusade and the taking of Constantinople in 1204, the Venetians secured a number of former Byzantine territories including Corfu. Venice's newly acquired possessions in the Adriatic, the Morea and the Aegean offered its merchant and naval fleets ports to be used as way stations and defensive bases along the route to the Levant. Venetian fortunes reached their zenith in the mid-fifteenth century when its merchant ships plied the Mediterranean, Adriatic, Aegean, and Black Seas without fear. Venetian successes, however, were more a reflection of a power vacuum in the eastern Mediterranean than of their own military prowess. This became readily apparent with the rise of the Ottoman Empire in the east and the resultant slow and steady decline of Venetian mastery in the Mediterranean.

Through a series of military and naval confrontations with the Ottoman Empire in the sixteenth century the Venetian Republic lost many of its prized possessions. Treaties concluded with the Ottomans resulted in the forfeiture of Coron and Modon (1503), Nauplion (1540), and Cyprus (1573). The only gains the Venetians could claim were the Ionian Islands of Cephalonia and Zante, which they received in return for Coron and Modon. Ottoman expansion continued unchecked and in 1669 the Venetians lost Crete which they had held since 1211. Venice experienced a short burst of energy in the latter part of the seventeenth century as manifested in the Morosini campaign which ultimately resulted in the acquisition of the Morea (with Austrian help) with the Treaty of Karlowitz in 1699. The victory was short-lived, however, and the Ottomans retrieved the Morea in 1714.

The ease with which the Ottomans accomplished this act was due also in part to fundamental changes in Venetian administration of imperial possessions. Formerly, the Venetian Republic possessed the wealth and power to eschew the missionary zeal advocated by Rome during the Catholic Reformation in the mid-sixteenth century and this allowed for a modicum of religious toleration in the territories under its control. Venice's position had changed drastically by the end of the seventeenth century and it now relied on financial support from Rome and was therefore obligated to conform to Vatican dictates. This meant that the Greeks under Venetian control were experiencing less religious toleration than under the Ottomans. Venetian economic and material weakness also forced them to compound this error by attempting to fortify the Morea using money, men, and material expropriated from the native population. All of which served only to isolate the native population and cause them to look forward to the day the Ottomans would liberate them from their Venetian oppressors.

Emboldened by their success in the Morea the Ottomans endeavored to remove the Venetians from the Dalmatian coast and the Ionian Islands. This move however elicited the attention of the Habsburgs, whose armies under the command of Prince Eugene of Savoy joined forces with Venice and thwarted Ottoman designs bringing the conflict to an end with the Treaty of Passarowitz in 1718. The Venetians now held sway over only the Ionian Islands and Cerigo.

Most Venetian occupied territories suffered the same excesses and were governed in a similar manner, i.e., the native populations incurred heavy taxes, were allowed almost no self-government, were induced to convert to Catholicism, and commerce was strictly controlled.[5] The Ionian Islands, however, were virtually autonomous with only nominal control exerted from Venice through a governor general with a three-year term, who resided in Corfu, governors for each island, a grand judge, and inspectors who were sent out occasionally to keep Venice apprised of conditions in the islands. In this system Venetians and Venetian colonists occupied the most important government positions and allowed the native aristocracy to act as judges, commercial inspectors, and guild heads but only at the local level.[6] The native aristocracy was also mollified by Venetian recognition of their lands and titles and in return the aristocracy recognized Venetian rule.

After gaining firm control over Corfu in 1386, the Venetians intended to create a climate of political stability on the island through a policy of social, economic, and cultural assimilation. As we have seen above social stability was assured, at least at the highest order, by Venetian concessions to the native aristocracy. Economic stability was maintained in the same manner by allowing Corfiote merchants to continue their enterprises without too much interference. In the realm of culture the Venetians allowed the Catholic Church free rein to establish schools, monasteries, churches and engage in proselytism as long as it did not provoke local hostility and threaten overall political stability.

Education, needless to say, fell well within the Church's purview and the Church began to exert its influence quickly by sending missionaries and various monastic orders to the islands with the intention of educating Greeks in the correct manner.[7] The Catholic bishop of Corfu founded the Hierarchical School in 1568 to train priests as educators and later, in the seventeenth century, the school was opened to laymen as well. This institution along with the monastic schools established by the Augustinians and Jesuits were supported by a network of Catholic priests at the village level who acted as tutors. Once a student reached the upper schools they were prepared for advanced education at Italian universities, usually at Padua and Bologna. Even though this educational system provided an excellent opportunity for Greek students to learn mathematics, philosophy, rhetoric, and Latin, with the possibility of attending the medical or law faculties in Italy, the Greek community perceived the influence of Catholicism on their sons as inimical to their national and ethnic interests.[8]

A number of Greek intellectuals, aware of this threat to their national identity, became tutors (or better yet, *didaskaloi tou yenous*, teachers of the nation) to preserve the ethnicity of the younger generation. Beginning in the late sixteenth century the Venetians allowed Greek communities to hire one Greek teacher if they also hired one Latin teacher. The Catholic bishop of Corfu saw it as his prerogative to grant permission for the appointment of both teachers. As one can imagine disagreements arose over the appointment of desired candidates which generated complaints to the Venetian authorities from the Greek community with the result that sometime in the seventeenth century the power of appointment passed from the Catholic bishop to the governor general. Even so the level of education, apart from the Greek aristocrats, was very low especially among the clergy (the Catholics believed, correctly, that this would aid their cause) who were described as being "scandalously ignorant."[9]

••••

Theotokis began his education in this atmosphere under the guidance and stewardship of the *ieromonakh* (monastic priest)

Ieremias Kavvadias, an individual whom Theotokis would come to
regard not only as a teacher but also as a friend, co-educator, and a
provider of spiritual advice and emotional support in the years to
come.[10] Kavvadias understood the importance of preserving the
Greek Orthodox heritage and undertook to educate Corfiote children
in their own homes and in his small school. He counted among his
many previous students a leading figure in the Greek Enlightenment
and future associate and friend of Theotokis, Archbishop Eugenios
Voulgaris.[11] Kavvadias not only inculcated the young Theotokis with
a solid grammar school education but introduced him to the intellectual universe of the Neo-Hellenic Enlightenment. In this world, the
spirit of Plato held sway over that of Aristotle and the natural
sciences countered the deadening effects of scholasticism.[12]

Theotokis was an excellent student and it was not long before
Kavvadias suggested that he travel abroad to further his education.
At this time Theotokis's attraction to the Church became more
pronounced and he was taken into the Church and given the lay rank
of reader on 6 August 1745. This action in no way bound him to
serve the Church for the rest of his life but allowed him to remain
near the clerics that he admired, thereby continuing the cultivation of
those qualities thought appropriate for a young man. The Church,
however, must have exercised a powerful hold over the young
Theotokis for in 1748, at the early age of 17, he requested that he be
received into the Church as an ordained servant of the Lord. His
family was completely surprised by this announcement and his father
expressed his opposition. The allure of the Church, however, was
stronger than his father's objections and Theotokis prepared for his
ordination. Yet, the ordination did not occur for another seven
years. Church law required that a candidate for ordination be at least
25 years of age. In December 1748 the Venetian Counsel General of
Corfu granted Theotokis permission to be ordained at a minor age
provided he passed the examinations. Theotokis passed the examinations with no difficulty, but his ordination was prevented because the
Counsel General reversed himself six months later in the summer of
1749.[13] Following this blow Theotokis once again turned his full
attention to education and the prospects of travel to Italy.

In 1749,[14] Theotokis journeyed to Italy to continue his studies
at the Greek Gymnasium in Padua.[15] At the gymnasium he read
voraciously all subjects of the "new philosophy": grammar, rhetoric,
poetics, logic, philosophy, theology, mathematics, physics, and one

subject in particular at which he would become very adept: oratory. Later he transferred to the Academy of Bologna and studied physics, astronomy, and geography as well as advanced mathematics, theology, and philosophy.

The universities and schools of Padua and Bologna played a very important role in the education of Greeks who lived under either Venetian or Turkish domination. Corfu became Greece's window to the West. Greek intellectuals and scholars passed through the Ionian Islands on their way to Padua, Venice, and Bologna and the islands were also the first stop for those returning from the West carrying with them its latest philosophical, scientific, and theological advances. An interesting geographical and intellectual triangle developed in the late fifteenth and early sixteenth centuries between Venice, Padua, and Corfu (Greece). In order to better appreciate the circumstances under which Theotokis and his contemporaries learned, taught and studied we need to examine the intellectual background created within this triangle.

With the fall of Constantinople many of Byzantium's most cultivated intellectuals and scholars fled to the West and took up residence in the tiny republic of Venice.[16] Some of these scholars had either been students of Gemistos Plethon or, at least, worked in his spirit. Plethon revived the study of ancient Greece at his Academy in Mistra, Peloponnesus and became a student of the ideas of Plato.[17] Plethon himself introduced Plato, Plutarch and other classical Greek writers to western scholars while he attended the Council of Ferrara-Florence in 1438-1439. A good number of Greeks found employment at the University of Padua (where a Chair of Greek was established in 1463) lecturing on ancient Greek philosophers and contributing to the emergence of the Renaissance in the West.[18] The juxtaposition of the Council of Florence and the transfer of scholarly material concerning Plato, contributed greatly to the intellectual-political climate in which all subsequent Greek intellectual development occurred. Consequently, Greek scholars, under the aegis of the Greek Orthodox Church, were forced to confront and, if possible, to resolve an internal tension that emerged from the meeting between Greek East and Latin West: a new philosophy which promised to enrich and reinvigorate the intellectual life of Greece carried within it the potential to undermine the traditional authority of the Church and brought the Greek and Roman Churches into religious and political conflict.

While the cultivated Greeks who fled to the West enjoyed the intellectual advantages of studying and teaching at some of the leading universities of Europe, many of those who remained behind turned their backs on the Latin West and what it had to offer. Georgos Scholarios (Gennadios) was appointed to the patriarchate by the Turks soon after the capture of Constantinople because he shared their anti-Latin views. This antipathy toward the Latin West, and in particular Rome, was reflected in the education offered to the clergy who attended the Patriarchal Academy in Constantinople with its emphasis on Aristotelian ethics, dialectics, and rhetoric. Isolating itself from the West and entombed in a moribund Ottoman culture, Orthodoxy began to exhibit the same intellectual sterility and dogmatism as its Ottoman rulers.[19] The Greek Church, however, must be credited with creating and preserving an educational system independent of both the Ottomans and the West in which the traditions of Hellenism and Orthodoxy could survive; even if in an attenuated state.

Although the Church hierarchy, for the most part, maintained its anti-Latin outlook and defense of the status quo in the early years of Ottoman domination, persistent attempts by Rome and the Jesuits to convert Orthodox believers to Catholicism provoked Constantinople to turn to western ideas to combat the onslaught. Cyril Loukaris (1572-1638) was born in Venetian-occupied Crete and educated in Venice and Padua. Loukaris aroused the ire of both the Jesuits and the Porte, when as the ecumenical patriarch (1620-1638) he turned to the Protestants, both doctrinally and politically, in order to secure intellectual and diplomatic support against Rome.[20] His actions, unfortunately, led to his own death at the hands of the Turks, but more important, he opened the window to the West as reflected in his own work and his appointment of Theophilos Korydalefs (1560-1646) as head of the Patriarchal Academy.

Korydalefs was one of the first to return from the West with the "new philosophy" and the first major Greek "philosopher" since the fall of Constantinople. He was educated at Padua and directed the Patriarchal Academy for seventeen years after teaching in his native Athens. Even though he professed Neo-Aristotelianism and not Neo-Platonism he nevertheless played an important role in the regeneration of Greek learning by his rejection of scholasticism. Korydalefs wrote numerous critical commentaries on the works of Aristotle and advocated a philosophical system which was distinct from theology and recognized the autonomy of nature (i.e., rejection of final causes) from God's direct control. He differed from Aristotle, however, in his belief that matter precedes form. Unfortunately, the sheer amount of his scholarly work gave birth to a dogmatism of its own and with the unwitting aid of his disciples was transformed into a stifling canon and earned the epithet of "Korydalism."[21]

Korydalefs was also a forerunner to a greater intellectual movement that began in the mid-eighteenth century: the Neo-Hellenic Enlightenment.[22] The Greek Enlightenment covered the years from 1750-1821 and, effectively, offered a new attitude toward science.[23] This period of Greek history experienced a surge in a number of areas including the establishment of printing presses, book publication (especially non-theological),[24] and was symbolized by a greater attention to the natural sciences, experimentation and empirical studies, translations of leading western philosophers, and an overall spirit of free thinking. The number of individuals subjected to the new currents was small but other philosophers and educators followed in the footsteps of Korydalefs: Methodios Anthrakitis (1660-1749), Vikentios Damodos (1679-1752), Ilias Miniatis (1669-1714), Nikodimos Metaxas (1585-1646), and Iakovos Pylarinos (1659-1718), and Ieremias Kavvadias (1693-?), Theotokis's teacher. An interesting characteristic of these individuals was that they were all born in Venetian-occupied territories and were educated in either Venice or Padua. While in the West they were inculcated with the ideas of such leading western philosophers and scientists as Locke, Wolfe, Leibniz, Condillac, Descartes and Newton.

The Greek Enlightenment reached its acme in the second half of the eighteenth century. At this time the Neo-Aristotelianism of Korydalefs began to give way to a revival of Platonism. This was no mean achievement, however, as the tradition of classical and neo-classical thought enjoyed the sanction of religious authority. Educated men who learned and clearly appreciated the theories and methods of modern science while in the Latin West were exceedingly reluctant to make their views known publicly once they returned to the Greek East. Alexander Mavrocordatos (1641-1709), an enthusiastic student of Harvey's theory of pulmonary circulation, and Chrysanthos Notaras (1663-1731), later Patriarch of Jerusalem, who was quite familiar with the heliocentric theory of the universe, both refrained from espousing their knowledge of modern science publicly. Notaras actually used scriptural arguments to denounce the

Copernican system.[25] It was left to another enlightened cleric to proclaim the truth of the theory of the heliocentric universe for the first time in print in 1766: Nikiforos Theotokis's *Elements of Physics*.

Eugenios Voulgaris is credited with finally bringing about synthesis of Neo-Platonism (derived in part from the German *Aufklärung*) and the Byzantine tradition which served to greatly enhance the development of Greek education.[26] The educational and scholarly activities of Voulgaris introduced many others to the new spirit of toleration and the writings of Locke and Voltaire. Yet, Voulgaris still placed his conception of modern science within the traditional framework of classical learning. One of his more famous students from the Athonian Academy was Iosipos Moisiodax (c.1725-1780).[27] He differed from his teacher in maintaining that all knowledge flows from mathematics and not from metaphysics and logic. Other thinkers who made their mark on the revival of Greek thought were Athanasios Psalidas (1767-1829),[28] a student of Kant, Benjamin of Lesbos (1762-1824), who claimed mathematics to be the key to the universe, and Adamantios Korais (1748-1833).

In general, most of these individuals were polymaths and men of toleration. For those who felt the philosophical ideas of the likes of Voltaire and other French *philosophes* were too abrasive there was always the realm of science, especially, physics and mathematics. Participants in the Neo-Hellenic Enlightenment were, for the most part, educators and dedicated their lives to furthering education among the Greek people under Turkish control. Nikiforos Theotokis was among those who hoped to serve Greece in this manner.

••••

Theotokis returned to Greece in the spring of 1754. Upon his arrival he began teaching students, at first, as a tutor but later he turned his home into a small private school where he could educate the local children. He had not forgotten the Church after residing so many years in Italy and once again petitioned to be ordained before the legal age of twenty-five. One story has it that Theotokis was aided in his quest for ordination by the intervention of the Venetian naval commander stationed at Corfu, Iakovos Nani. Nani was charged with the task of improving the harbor facilities, but the depth of the water presented an overwhelming obstacle for his engineers. Theotokis was summoned to consult on the matter and resolved the problem.[29] In mid-July, 1754, Nikiforos Theotokis was ordained as an *ieromonakh* by the Archbishop Chrysanthos of Lefkada with the permission of the Venetian authorities on Corfu. Theotokis did not take up his ecclesiastical duties immediately, however, as he intended to devote all his time to the development of an education program for the Greeks of Corfu.

Owing to Theotokis's excellent teaching abilities and knowledge of the western sciences his home proved to be much too small to accommodate all the students who wished to study with him. With the assistance of his former teacher Kavvadias, Theotokis began soliciting support from the local community to establish a public school. On 11 December 1757, Theotokis and Kavvadias wrote to the Greek elders (*syndiktoi*), imploring them to establish a public school that would "cultivate the mind and spirit of the youth" and provide them with a proper building for instruction.[30] Theotokis and Kavvadias desired this so much that they offered to teach without pay. The Venetian Council (to whom the Greek elders had petitioned) was late in responding to the two teachers, but it finally gave them the approval and the school opened in a rented building opposite the church of Theotokos ton Stereoton on 1 August 1758.[31]

The new school was called the *Koinon Frontistirion Kerkyras* (Public Preparatory School of Corfu). Kavvadias was listed as its director, but Theotokis was its guiding spirit. The school was established as a means to prepare students for either the lyceum or university. Theotokis's school offered the courses that he outlined in his petition: "we will teach grammar, rhetoric, philosophy and mathematics both morning and afternoon." And in order to provide equal opportunity to all social and economic classes "students will be free of any expenses, contributions or other financial burdens."[32] Theotokis taught the new sciences of mathematics (algebra, conical sections, geometry) and physics while Kavvadias instructed the pupils in Greek grammar, classics, and metaphysics. Theotokis also offered the students empiricism in practice with classes in experimental science, i.e., laboratory work. His use of these teaching methods was possibly the first time it was attempted in Greece. This adherence to the "positive" sciences and the "new philosophy," in the face of some opposition, was one of the major attractions to the students who came to Theotokis's school from all parts of Greece. The curriculum also included Latin grammar, philosophy, and rhetoric taught by a

Venetian on demand of the Catholic Church (also the only paid staff member the first year). The fifty students (ranging in age from eight to thirty-five) attending the school the first year were assigned by their three teachers and three lecturers such diverse readings as the life of Aesop, the metaphysics of Purcozio, the myths of Nikiforos Vasilakis, and the works of Plutarch and Isocrates.[33]

In the same year that he founded the *Koinon Frontistirion* he was appointed priest (*efimerios*) at the churches of St. John the Baptist and Aghia Paraskevi. His oratorical skills combined with his mastery of the Greek language and scripture made him a preacher (*ritor*) of some renown. Greeks and Latins from Corfu, the surrounding islands and the mainland came to listen to his sermons. His other services (baptisms, weddings, funerals, etc.) were just as eagerly requested by the Orthodox faithful. Theotokis's religious and educational activities, however, were not popular with the Catholic archbishop of Corfu, Antonio Nani, and he soon faced the hostility of the Catholic Church and its propaganda department.[34] Theotokis's confrontation with the Catholic Church, not only on Corfu but with the papal nuncio in Venice, were a prelude to further difficulties he would experience with the Catholics, politically and theologically.

It was not long before Theotokis's fame both as a cleric and an educator reached beyond the Ionian Islands to Constantinople. Very much pleased with the activities of Theotokis the Ecumenical Patriarch Ioannikios (1761-63) offered Theotokis the possibility to direct the Athonian Academy (it had been closed since 1761 following Voulgaris's directorship). Grigorios Ghikas, the Grand Dragoman of the Porte, enamored with the intellectual and educational achievements of the young Theotokis also implored him to come to Constantinople. Finally, in May of 1765,[35] Theotokis did leave Corfu for Constantinople but the reasons for his departure remain obscure or at least not as straightforward as some accounts would make it. His leaving can be attributed to a number of causes: 1) opposition to his teaching activities and harassment by the Catholic Church, 2) he wanted to have his scholarly work published, and/or 3) the invitations from Constantinople were too attractive for a young and ambitious cleric to ignore.[36] Theotokis's departure from the *Koinon Frontistirion* and the island of Corfu began a period of travel that would include two visits to Constantinople, two short stays in Jassy, publishing activities in Leipzig, a brief tenure as metropolitan of Philadelphia[37] and culminated ten years later with his arrival in Russia.

••••

The Turkish-occupied territories of Greece differed markedly from those occupied by Venice. The Ottoman Empire was a theocracy and as such allowed for no distinction between religion and politics. In this situation the Ottoman Turks did not recognize an individual by race but by adherence to a religious creed. The Greek Orthodox Church, then, became the theocratic institution (*millet*) for those individuals professing Orthodoxy. The ecumenical patriarch, appointed by the sultan, thus served not only as head of the Greek Orthodox Church, but as ethnarch or head of Rum *millet* or the Greek Nation. He held the rank of vizir and was responsible for the ecclesiastical and political affairs of the Orthodox community. The patriarch's ecclesiastical privileges included the appointment, transfer and discipline of all Church functionaries and the management of all Church property. In the civil or political sphere the patriarch was charged with dispensing justice between Christian litigants (mainly those with some relation to the Church, i.e., marriage, divorce, etc.) and, as we have seen, coordinating educational activities.[38]

A small group of Greek oligarchs who resided in the Phanar district of Constantinople and known as the Phanariots exercised considerable influence over the Patriarchate. Although very few patriarchs came from Phanariot families (only two in the eighteenth century, Ioannikios Karatzas and Samuel Hantzeris),[39] the Phanariots held privileged positions in the Ottoman Empire and thus secured important lay positions in the Church hierarchy and provided financial assistance to a continually indebted Church.[40] These very capable men first entered the service of the Ottoman Empire in the mid-seventeenth century as interpreters (grand dragoman) and advisers to the sultan and the grand vizir. Apart from suffering from some of the vices associated with the corrupt Ottoman Empire, conspiring to gain the sultan's ear or laying snares for competitors, they contributed greatly to the political and cultural regeneration of the Greeks during the Turkish occupation. In 1711, the Phanariots were appointed *hospodars* to govern the autonomous Danubian Principalities of Moldavia and Wallachia, and subsequently created one of the more dynamic centers of Greek learning outside the

Ionian Islands.[41] Even though many of the Phanariots championed the regeneration of Greek learning through financial assistance, many others also contributed to it as writers and translators in their own right. One such learned Phanariot and patron of the arts was the Grand Dragoman Grigorios Ghikas who showed considerable interest in the young Corfiote cleric Nikiforos Theotokis.

Theotokis arrived in Constantinople sometime in 1765 and accepted the appointment as Grand Rhetor (ritor) of the Great Church of Christ at the behest of Patriarch Samuel II (Hatzeris). Ghikas had become *hospodar* of Moldavia in March, 1764, so he was not able to attend to Theotokis personally, but Theotokis became his son's private tutor and a friendship was formed nonetheless. Theotokis stayed only a few months in Constantinople when he accepted Ghikas's offer to direct the new-founded Princely Academy in Jassy.[42] He taught mathematics, physics, and geography but left the Academy after remaining at his post for only a very short time. He was replaced by Iosipos Moisiodax in 1765.[43] The reasons for his hurried departure from this prestigious appointment are once again obscure but he may have left on account of wanting to publish his works in the West[44] or overly hostile reaction from conservatives to his teaching. Regardless of the reason, Theotokis left Jassy sometime in late 1765 or early 1766 and traveled to Leipzig where he had the opportunity to publish some of his scholarly work.

Leipzig, since the mid-seventeenth century, had become a major trade center and hosted an annual trade fair that was known throughout Europe. Greek merchants from the Ottoman-occupied territories established branches of their businesses in Leipzig and other central European cities. By the mid-eighteenth century, when Theotokis arrived, the Greek community was very substantial and had invested money in Greek printing presses which served to further Greek education abroad and in Greece. Theotokis published three of his works in Leipzig in the nearly three years that he was there.[45] He published a two-volume textbook in 1766-67, *Elements of Physics*,[46] using the most recent scholarship available to him, and a collection of sermons entitled *Sermons for Holy and Great Lent, along with Certain Panegyrics, Proclamations, and Funeral Orations*.[47] Theotokis printed his works, especially on physics, in Greek because he wanted to provide textbooks on the new sciences to Greek students who could not read western languages.

Theotokis returned to Constantinople in the spring of 1767, where he once again accepted the hospitality of the Ghikas household, continued to tutor the young Ghikas, and conducted some studies in the rich Ghikas library. While working in the Ghikas library Theotokis found a medieval biblical commentary which he believed antedated the Frankfurt commentaries. Ghikas decided to publish the *Codex* and Theotokis undertook the task of preparing it for publication and providing his own commentaries. The work was published in 1772 as *A Series of Fifty-one Commentators in an Eight-Volume Work and about the Heavenly Kingdom* in Leipzig and was dedicated by Grigorios Ghikas to the Greek nation.[48]

Theotokis encountered difficulties with Patriarch Samuel II who had invited him to Constantinople in 1764-1765. The problem arose over Theotokis's conduct during the funeral of Eleni Ghikas, the mother of Grigorios Ghikas. In his funeral oration Theotokis praised Eleni and Grigorios Ghikas for their extraordinary service to the Greek community. Patriarch Samuel II considered the eulogy excessive and tantamount to blasphemy. He reproached Theotokis and condemned him for "exalting a mortal woman more than the Mother of God."[49] Following this episode Theotokis proffered his resignation in early 1768 and once again departed Constantinople and made his way to Leipzig.

During his second tenure in Leipzig, Theotokis published two more works, participated in the university's academic life and rejoined his fellow Corfiote intellectual and cleric, Eugenios Voulgaris.[50] Theotokis engaged the attention of many in the academic community by the diversity of his knowledge and depth of learning. Members of the theological faculty were pleased to have in their midst an Orthodox cleric to whom they could direct their questions pertaining to the present state of the Greek Orthodox Church. Theotokis also gave occasional sermons at the Orthodox church in Leipzig. His sermons were as popular and well attended in Leipzig as they were in Corfu and Constantinople. He preached an ecumenical message and drew not only Greek Orthodox to his sermons but Armenians, Slavs, Catholics and Protestants.[51] Theotokis's theological ecumenism had its parallel in his academic interests and was represented in two manuscripts he published in Leipzig in 1769 and 1770.

Theotokis translated and prepared for publication *The Golden Text of Rabbi Samuel, the Jew, Scrutinizing the Deception of the*

Jews [52] and edited and published *The Discovered Spiritual Exercises of the Holy Father Isaac Syros, Bishop of Nineveh*.[53] Theotokis published the work of Rabbi Samuel to demonstrate that it was possible for individuals of any creed to recognize and incorporate into daily life the revealed truth of God. One did not need to be Orthodox or even Christian to reap the benefits of God's revelation. In *The Spiritual Exercises* Theotokis once again turned his attention to producing a commentary on the work of an Eastern Father.[54] We know that Theotokis's reputation exceeded the boundaries of his native Greece when one notes that Patriarch Ephraim of Jerusalem commissioned him to edit and publish *The Spiritual Exercises*.[55] The projected publication of St. Isaac's works attracted the attention of a young *starets* at the Dragomirna Monastery in Moldavia, Paisii Velichkovskii. Velichkovskii had a Slavonic translation of St. Isaac's book from the time he was a monk on Mt. Athos, but it contained many ambiguous passages and he was anxious to find a copy in the original Greek for comparison and correction. A pupil of the *starets* happened to be in Constantinople in 1767/1768 and heard that Patriarch Ephraim had assigned Theotokis to publish the Greek original of St. Isaac's book and "started begging both Patriarch Ephraim and the *ierodidaskalos* Nikifor to give their blessings and to send this book to me [Velichkovskii]." During Advent of 1770 Theotokis sent Velichkovskii a copy which he accepted with "inexpressible joy."[56] Just as Patriarch Ephraim in the East was aware of Theotokis's abilities as a theological scholar and requested his services, the Greek community in Venice also recognized his abilities as a great orator and cleric and extended to him the metropolitanate of Philadelphia in 1772.

••••

Venice had the largest and most significant Greek community in the West.[57] The Greek community, numbering between four and five thousand in the mid-fifteenth century, petitioned the Venetian Council of Ten in 1456 to build a church in which they could practice their rites according to the Byzantine tradition. The Greek community, for the most part, accepted the Council of Florence and considered itself to be Uniate. This open avowal, however, grew stronger or weaker as it reflected the political currents at the time. The Council granted the community its request but the Venetian patriarch prevented the construction of a church. It was not until 1539 that the Greeks were actually allowed to begin construction of the famous church San Giorgio dei Greci. Here we see yet another example of the Venetian state extending to the Greek community rights and privileges that the local Catholic officials decried. Interference by Catholic clerics in the religious affairs of the Greek community supposedly ended with a Papal Bull by Leo X in 1514 stipulating that the Greeks be allowed a priest to conduct services according to the eastern rite without local Catholic interference and that they were to recognize the authority of the pope. The Greeks chafed sorely under the control of the Catholic Church but were finally permitted to place their church under the direct authority of Constantinople in 1577. Gabriel Severus (1577-1616), who was serving as their priest, became the metropolitan of Philadelphia one year later; a title that all successors would hold. This defeat for the Venetian patriarch can be attributed to a fear of possible Protestant inroads with a disgruntled Greek community and Venetian recognition of the importance of the young *stradioti* (Greek mercenaries) as well as Greek commercial successes to the well-being of the Venetian Republic.[58]

The Greek community of San Giorgio and the diocese of Philadelphia conducted their affairs without incident and little if any conflict with the Venetian episcopate until 1713. However, in 1713 the metropolitan of Philadelphia, Meletios Tipaldos, converted to Catholicism and was, as a consequence, quickly and unceremoniously removed from his post by Patriarch Cyril IV. Following Tipaldos' act of apostasy the Venetian episcopate felt itself strengthened enough to have the Venetian Senate reaffirm the lapsed decrees of 1534 and 1542 that required Greek priests to adhere to the Florentine Confession. Undoubtedly the apostasy of Tipaldos and the actions of the Venetian patriarch were the result of a revived militant and aggressive Catholicism owing to the holy war of 1687-1713 against the Turks. From 1713 to 1761, the metropolitanate of Philadelphia remained vacant because the Greek community refused to accept candidates chosen by the Venetian patriarch. Finally, in 1761, as a result of the changing international political climate and numerous petitions by the Greeks, the Venetian Senate once again granted the Greek community the right to hold elections to fill the vacant diocesan seat.

The new agreement the Greek community made with the Venetian Senate in 1761 did not satisfy the Ecumenical Patriarch in Constantinople and the seat remained unoccupied until 1780. During this twenty-year interim the Greek community elected a number of bishops but none of them were sanctioned by Constantinople and, therefore, did not take the seat. Theotokis was elected by the Greek community in 1772 and his difficulties in deciding whether to accept were typical of other candidates.[59] Twice, in 1761 and 1768, the Greek community elected bishops to fill the vacancy. Both accepted but were prevented from taking this esteemed post because the Ecumenical Patriarch refused to acknowledge a bishop who dared to adhere to the Florentine Confession.

Theotokis was extremely honored by the offer of the see of Philadelphia but he refused to accept the position despite the tireless efforts of the Greek community over a period of three years to change his mind. Although Theotokis had gone to school in Padua he had only ventured to Venice once and did not form any close relationships during his brief stay. Throughout the 1760s he found it best or, at least, politic not to involve himself in the imbroglio surrounding the Greek community and its election of an archbishop. One can imagine that Theotokis struggled terribly over his decision concerning this particular position given his devotion to the ecclesiastical and educational needs of all Greek people whether of the diaspora or under foreign subjugation. Theotokis's first reply to the Greeks of Venice stated that he must respectfully decline the offer unless two conditions were met: first, that the Orthodox Church be granted nothing less than complete ecclesiastical autonomy from the Catholic Church and, second, that the ecumenical patriarch confer his blessing on Theotokis's appointment.[60]

The conditions set by Theotokis were impossible for the Greeks to meet. Theotokis's demands and the resulting disarray in the Greek community also elicited a response from the Pope, who hoped to profit from the chaos and sent a letter to the Doge of Venice inducing him to force the Greek Church to submit to more control.[61] Theotokis was informed of this action and warned the Greeks to remain steadfast. In 1773, the Greeks attempted to entice Theotokis to Venice by enlisting the support of G. Nani, the former naval commander of Corfu who had worked with Theotokis on the harbor project. This also came to naught as Theotokis was adamant about his conditions. Throughout this exacting time Theotokis sought the advice and support of his former teacher and colleague Kavvadias as well as Voulgaris with whom he corresponded from Russia. He never visited Venice during the whole episode preferring to remain in Leipzig at good remove from the fray. Finally, tired of the whole affair, Theotokis offered his resignation from the metropolitanate in the fall of 1775. Theotokis's actions had one very important effect on the situation in Venice: the Venetian Senate decreed in 1780 that the metropolitan of Philadelphia would no longer need to abide by the Florentine Confession. The Ecumenical Patriarch found this decree acceptable and Sofronis Koutouvalis was elected and ordained metropolitan in 1780.[62]

••••

In the spring of 1774 Theotokis left the West for the last time. He arrived in Jassy at the invitation of *hospodar* Grigorios Ghikas in the fall of that year by way of Bratislava, Vienna, and Breslau.[63] Ghikas appointed Theotokis director of the Academy once again and Theotokis resumed his teaching duties with the same vigor as before. The students at the Academy were beneficiaries of Theotokis's recent sojourn in the learning centers of western Europe. He instructed them in physics, mathematics, geography and astronomy.[64] Theotokis's teaching, however, was not appreciated by everyone with the same level of enthusiasm displayed by the students. He encountered heavy resistance from the "conservative circles" of the Moldavian capital who did not care for his teaching of the "new philosophy" and perhaps viewed it as one more instance of Greek attempts to Hellenize the native Rumanians. In fact, the opposition to his activities was so great that Ghikas was unable to protect him and he supposedly had to flee "in the night like a thief" (*dia nyktos os drapetis*).[65]

Theotokis's flight from Jassy was undertaken with such haste that he had no destination in mind. Eventually he settled in Vienna and sustained himself by serving as a private tutor. His stay in Vienna brought him once again into territories under the political control of a Catholic power: this time Habsburg. The Habsburg lands of east central Europe as well as the Polish-Lithuanian Commonwealth adjacent to them contained a significant minority population of Slavic and Greek Orthodox who were continually assaulted by Catholic proselytizing. Catholic missionary activity reached its zenith and posed the greatest religious and political threat to the Orthodox East with the establishment of the Uniate Church in Poland by Council of Brest in 1596.[66] Previous to the Council of Brest the eastern patriarchs responded to the Catholic/Latin threat through the activities of churchmen such as Patriarch Meletios Pigas of Alexandria and Patriarch Cyril Loukaris.[67] By the beginning of the seventeenth century, however, the struggle over religious affiliation became intertwined with growing national consciousness and a sense of a distinct cultural identity on the part of Orthodox populations in the Polish-Lithuanian Commonwealth which paralleled developments in Greece. The foundation of the Mogilev Academy (largely based on Latin cultural models) in Kiev by Peter Mogila was representative of efforts undertaken by local Orthodox communities to protect themselves from Polish-Catholic encroachments.[68]

The Orthodox communities of the Polish-Lithuanian Commonwealth as well as the Ottoman Empire also received support from the main political rival of both: Muscovite Russia. With the fall of Constantinople, Muscovite Russia was the only Orthodox country not under the control of an alien power and as such would come to play a very important role in the affairs of the Orthodox East. In the sixteenth century Muscovite church leaders propounded the doctrine of "The Third Rome," and their gradual move toward ecclesiastical independence from Constantinople ended in the formation of the Moscow patriarchate in 1589. Muscovy, and later imperial Russia, maintained close relations with the ancient patriarchal sees of the East and often looked to the East for spiritual and doctrinal guidance.[69] In return the Orthodox of the Balkans and in east central Europe sought Russian political, military and financial support to, at first, maintain their Orthodox faith and, later, assist them in overthrowing their foreign rulers. It was within this context of a joint struggle against Latin and Ottoman domination that Theotokis made his important contribution to Orthodoxy and the maintenance of Greek-Slavic relations.

In this spirit Theotokis took up his pen while in Vienna and produced an anti-Latin polemic entitled *A Reply by a Certain Orthodox Christian to an Orthodox brother on the Catholic Dynastic Rule, and on who are the Separatists, the Schismatics, and the Severed Ones, and on the Barbarically Called Unia and the Uniates, and on How the Orthodox Must Respond to Catholic Tyranny.*[70] Published anonymously in Halle in 1775 (and graced with a cover

illustration depicting a militant Archangel Michael slaying an en-
chained demon – see Figure 2) this work brought Theotokis into the
long tradition of anti-Latin polemics begun by Meletios Pigas,
Theophanes of Jerusalem, and Cyril Loukaris. More immediate to
Theotokis and, possibly, a standard by which he wrote his own work
were the writings of Eugenios Voulgaris. Voulgaris published
Vivliarion kata Latinon ("Booklet against the Latins") in 1757 and
directed it to the Serbian Orthodox under the Habsburg monarchy.[71]

Theotokis's work was pastoral in nature and provided advice
to the Orthodox flock on how to counter the propaganda and
proselytizing efforts of Catholic missionaries. He held that "lies are
found everywhere in Europe" and that Orthodox believers must be
educated so they "can discern with grace and intelligence, what is
proclaimed to be true and held to be false."[72] Yet Theotokis still sincerely believed that a union between the two Churches was possible
although plagued with obstacles. He recounted the usual grievances,
that if removed, would pave the way to reconciliation: "the Catholic
Church [must] relinquish the aberrant *filioque*, the pope [must] lower
his level of arrogance and immodesty to a level of apostolic humilia-
tion and Christian modesty," and must return to the traditional
worship service and dress.[73] However, given the unlikelihood of
these events, Theotokis cautioned those of Orthodox faith to be on
their guard throughout Europe and counseled those who could flee
the Ottoman territories to seek out Orthodox countries (i.e., Russia),
but if fleeing was not a possibility, to uphold their spiritual integrity
in the face of tyranny.[74] Theotokis was to follow his own advice
when he departed for Russia in 1776.

Nikiforos Theotokis's life in the Greek East was one defined
by his activities in the realms of education and religion. His early
education and intellectual development were influenced by the fact
that his native Corfu lay within the Venetian colonial system.
Although the Venetian Republic was in decline by the time of
Theotokis's birth, the Venetians had left their imprint upon Corfiote
politics, society, and culture. Greek scholars and intellectuals who
had contributed to the flowering of the Italian Renaissance in the late
fourteenth and fifteenth centuries now brought this renewed interest
in classical Greece back to a Greece humiliated by foreign occupation. Many of these scholars originated from the Venetian-occupied
territories of Greece and their intellectual progeny continued the
practice of traveling to Italy to receive an education and then return-

ing as educators, doctors, and clerics. The Venetian presence, however, was a double-edged sword. Greeks, undoubtedly, benefited from their western educations and the intellectual milieu born from its culture, but the Venetians were not satisfied with mere political obedience, they also required nothing less than total social and cultural conformity from those under their control.

In response to these pressures individual scholars and intellectuals took upon themselves the obligation to preserve the traditions of Greece as *didaskaloi tou yenous* or teachers of the nation. It was in this atmosphere that Eugenios Voulgaris introduced Greece to the writings and ideas of the *philosophes* in the mid-eighteenth century. His unique melding of Byzantine traditions with the "new philosophy" produced what has come to be called the Neo-Hellenic Enlightenment. He incorporated Neo-Platonism with the rich religious traditions of Byzantium and introduced the study of the natural sciences of mathematics, geometry, algebra, physics and geography. Theotokis was among those to adopt and expand upon this novel approach (which ideally suited the character of an individual who was both deeply religious and convinced of the importance of the "new philosophy") and in conjunction with it realized his intense dedication to regenerating the Greek nation when he opened the *Koinon Frontistirion* on Corfu in 1758. He carried his educational activities to publishing when he produced a two-volume work entitled the *Elements of Physics* in 1766 during his stay in Leipzig. This work was path-breaking in that it unabashedly declared the scientific truth of the Copernican theory of heliocentricity. Prior to Leipzig he served as director of the Princely Academy in Jassy at the behest of Prince Grigorios Ghikas, *Hospodar* of Moldavia.

If Theotokis had restricted himself to education alone he would have made a significant contribution to the proliferation of learning in Greece during the Venetian and Turkish occupations. Yet a fundamental attribute of his personality was the force of his religious conviction. Theotokis became *rhetor* when he was just fourteen and was ordained as a priest at the early age of twenty-four. As a preacher at the Church of St. John the Baptist he drew hundreds to his sermons which ranged from discourses on the Scriptures to lessons on morality. He delivered his sermons in a simple and easily understood manner that endeared the parishioners to his informal style. The enduring quality of his sermons led him to publish some of them in 1766. His reputation as an exceptional speaker earned him the highest honor attainable by a preacher in the Greek East, an invitation to become Grand *Rhetor* in the Great Church of Christ in Constantinople. During his extended stay in Leipzig in the late 1760s and early 1770s he once again exhibited his fine oratorical abilities by attracting Orthodox Greeks, Slavs, and Armenians as well as Catholics and Protestants to his sermons.

Two incidents in Theotokis's life in the Greek East further illumine Theotokis's personality and permit one to draw some tentative conclusions about his intellectual and social identity. The funeral of Eleni Ghikas, the mother of Grigorios Ghikas, placed Theotokis in a rather uncomfortable position. His eulogy for the departed woman was a paean to the philanthropy of this particular Phanariot family. Patriarch Samuel II, a member of a Phanariot family himself, was offended by Theotokis's excessive praise and reprimanded him. Theotokis confronted a dilemma because he was obligated to both Ghikas and the Patriarch as his benefactors. In this instance, he satisfied the man who would continue to serve as his patron in the future. He also respected the office of the patriarch and resigned his position as requested. The other incident was the three-year struggle over his acceptance of the metropolitanate of Philadelphia in Venice. He refused to accept the metropolitanate unless the see would be completely autonomous in ecclesiastical affairs (from Catholic influence) and the ecumenical patriarch would sanction his appointment. This action reflected genuine respect for the Orthodox tradition and his interpretation of the apostolic succession and the ecumenical patriarch as the supreme representative of the true faith. The intervention in this episode of papal intermediaries in Venice and the pope himself was reminiscent of Theotokis's conflicts with the Catholic Church on Corfu over his school and sermons. Theotokis had the greatest respect for the civil authorities of Venice and Corfu but he refused to submit to the relentless pressure exerted by the Catholics.

These events can also be interpreted in another light. Theotokis left Corfu in 1758 when conditions were possibly becoming intolerable for him. His confrontation with the ecumenical patriarch unnerved him. He was circumspect to say the least in his dealings with the Greek community in Venice. Apart from the lofty motives discussed above Theotokis could have rejected the metropolitanate for the simple reason that the Greek church in Venice was in a troubled and weakened condition and the responsibility of operating an Orthodox church in the face of unremitting Catholic hostility was too much of a challenge for him at that time. Out of his confrontation with the Catholics he produced a distillation of his thoughts on Catholic-Orthodox relations, the Uniates, and a Greek-Latin reconciliation in *A Reply*.... This work, with its emphasis on understanding and education, reflects the Enlightenment's spirit of toleration and rationalism which provided a basis for Theotokis's future dealings with those outside the fold of Orthodoxy. And, indeed, this would be the case in Russia.

NOTES

1. K. Dyovouniotis, "Logoi anekdotoi kai epistolai Nikiforou tou Theotoki," *Ieros Syndesmos* (15 September 1915): 5.

2. He had six brothers and sisters: Ioannis (1718-68), Andreas (1728-?), Ilias (1729-?), Efstathios (1732-79), Athanasia (who entered the service of the Church as a nun), and Irini (wife of Count Spyridon Theotokis).

3. Among the numerous published accounts of Theotokis's life in the Greek East, the most helpful are L. Vrokinis, *Viografika Shedaria*, vol. I, (Corfu, 1884); E. Koukkou, *Nikiforos Theotokis (1731-1800)* (Athens, 1973); and Z. Mourouti-Gkenakou, *O Nikiforos Theotokis – (1731-1800) kai i Simvoli aftou eis tin Paideian tou Yenous* (Athens, 1979).

4. Vrokinis, p. 2; and Koukkou, p. 22. Titles of this nature are used by people with common surnames to distinguish them from families with identical names and, generally, are derived from a recognizable landmark.

5. L.S. Stavrianos, *The Balkans Since 1453* (New York, 1958), pp. 113-4.

6. *Istoria tou Ellinikou Ethnous*, vol. X (Athens, 1974), p. 220.

7. See S. Theotokis, "Peri tis Ekpaidefseos en Eptaniso," *Kerkyraika Hronika*, vol. V (1956): 9-142, for a survey of education during the Venetian occupation.

8. Mourouti-Gkenakou, pp. 74-5.

9. Drummond, *Travels* (London, 1754), p. 96.

10. On Kavvadias, see *Megali Elliniki Enkyklopaideia*, vol. XIII (Athens, 1930), p. 426.

11. For an excellent account of Voulgaris's career in the Greek East and Russia see S.K. Batalden, *Catherine II's Greek Prelate Eugenios Voulgaris in Russia, 1771-1806* (Boulder, 1982).

12. Koukkou, p. 24. On the Neo-Hellenic Enlightenment, see Konstantinos Th. Dimaras, *La Grèce au temps des lumières* (Geneva, 1969); idem, *Neoellinikos Diaphotismos*, 3rd ed. (Athens, 1983); Raphael Demos, "The Neo-Hellenic Enlightenment, 1750-1821: A General Survey," *Journal of History of Ideas*, 19:4 (October, 1958): 523-41; and Alkis Angelou, *Platonos Tyhai* (Athens, 1963). On the "conflict" between science and the Orthodox church in Greece, see Vasilios N. Makrides, "Science and the Orthodox Church in 18th and early 19th Century Greece: Sociological Considerations," *Balkan Studies*, 29:2 (1988): 265-82. On Greek science in the eighteenth century see G. Kara, *Oi Fisikes-Thetikes epistimes ston elliniko 18o aiona* (Athens, 1977).

13. Vrokinis, p. 23. This episode also sheds some light on the ecclesiastical structure allowed the Greek Church by the Venetians. Under pressure from the Catholic Church, ordination was to be permitted only to maintain a constant number of priests and bishops. This was enforced by not allowing bishops the right to ordain priests in most Venetian possessions, but this injunction did not apply to all Ionian Islands. For this reason, Theotokis traveled to Lefkada and was ordained by the bishop of Lefkada in the spring of 1748 and not by a prelate on Corfu.

14. The details regarding Theotokis's stay in Italy are obscure. For a complete discussion of the scholarly debate see Mourouti-Gkenakou, pp. 3-7.

15. Most scholars agree that Theotokis studied in Bologna, but disagree over whether he also studied in Padua, e.g., Vrokinis. However, Theotokis himself, claims in his *Stoiheia Physikis* (Elements of Physics) that he studied in Padua. Cited in Mourouti-Gkenakou, p. 5. The other possibility is that he studied not at the University of Padua but at the Greek Gymnasium. This would explain why his name has not been included in G. Ploumidis's on-going study of Greek students in Padua, "Ai Praxeis Engrafes ton Ellinon Spoudaston tou Panepistimiou tis Padouis (Meros B': Legisti, 1591-1809)," *Epetiris tis Etaireias Vyzantinon Spoudon*, 38 (1971).

16. Leandros I. Vranousis, "Post-Byzantine Hellenism and Europe: Manuscripts, Books, and Printing Presses," *Modern Greek Studies Yearbook*, 2 (1986): 1-71; M.I. Manoussacas, "The History of the Greek Confraternity (1498-1953) and the Activity of the Greek Institute of Venice (1966-1982)," *Modern Greek Studies Yearbook*, 5 (1989): 321-94; Deno J. Geanakoplos, *Greek Scholars in Venice: Studies in the Dissemination of Greek Learning from Byzantium to Western Europe* (Cambridge, MA, 1962); idem, *Greek East and Latin West: Two Worlds of Christendom in the Middle Ages and Renaissance* (Oxford, 1966); and idem, *Interaction of "Sibling" Byzantine and Western Cultures in the Middle Ages and Italian Renaissance (330-1600)* (New Haven, 1976).

17. Plethon's contribution to the Western Renaissance is analyzed in C.M. Woodhouse, *Gemistos Plethon: The Last of the Hellenes* (Oxford, 1986).

18. On these individuals and their activities see Geanakoplos, *Greek Scholars in Venice*.

19. William H. McNeill, *Venice: The Hinge of Europe, 1081-1797* (Chicago, 1974), p. 117.

20. For a discussion of the debate over whether Loukaris became a Protestant as he himself seems to indicate see George A. Hadjiantoniou, *Protestant Patriarch: The Life of Cyril Lukaris (1572-1638), Patriarch of Constantinople* (Richmond, 1961).

21. Demos, p. 531. On Korydalefs see Cleobule Tsourkas, *Les Débuts de L'Enseignement Philosophique et de la Libre Pensée dans les Balkans: La Vie et L'Oêurve de Théophile Corydalée, 1570-1646* (Thessaloniki, 1967).

22. The earliest Greek scholars to examine the issue of the revival of Greek thought were Konstantinos N. Sathas, *Neoelliniki Philologia* (Athens, 1868) and Andreas Papadopoulos Vretos, *Neoelliniki Philologia*, 2 vols. (Athens, 1854-57).

23. This dating is taken from Demos, *op. cit.* Other dates fall within the same general scope. Some have suggested 1766 or 1774 as the starting date and others, Dimaras, for example, have proposed that the period be extended to the mid-nineteenth century.

24. Dimaras, p. 121.

25. Paschalis M. Kitromilides, "The Idea of Science in the Modern Greek Enlightenment," in P. Nicolacopoulos, ed., *Greek Studies in the Philosophy and History of Science* (Kluwer, 1990), pp. 189-90.

26. For a discussion of this in the broader context of Greek learning under the Turks see Angelou and Batalden, p. 6.

27. See Paschalis M. Kitromilides, *Iosipos Moisiodax* (Athens, 1985) and *The Enlightenment and Social Criticism: Iosipos Moisiodax and Greek Culture in the Eighteenth Century* (Princeton, 1992).

28. See L. Vranousis, *Athanasios Psalidas: O Didaskalos tou Yenous* (Ioannina, 1952).

29. Vrokinis, p. 28.

30. From Theotokis's letter to the Council. Cited in full by Vrokinis, p. 35.

31. Vrokinis, p. 38.

32. Letter to Greek elders, cited in Vrokinis, p. 35.

33. Mourouti-Gkenakou, p. 95.

34. For an analysis of the Catholic attempts to remove Theotokis see Mourouti-Gkenakou, pp. 102-117. She bases her account on sources found in the Archivio della Propaganda di Santa Fide, S.C. Greci.

35. Koukkou, p. 40.

36. Mourouti-Gkenakou, p. 11.

37. The Byzantine city of Philadelphia fell to the Turks in 1390 and the seat of the diocese of Philadelphia was eventually transferred to Venice to serve the Greek population in northern Italy.

38. On the Greek Orthodox Church during the Turkokratia see Steven Runciman, *The Great Church in Captivity* (Cambridge, 1968) and Th. Papadopoulos, *Studies and Documents Relating to the History of the Greek Church and People under Turkish Domination* (Brussels, 1952).

39. Both of whom sent letters to Theotokis requesting his presence in Constantinople.

40. On the Phanariots, see K.Th. Dimaras, "Peri Phanarioton," *Arheion Thrakis*, 34 (1969): 117-140; Runciman, pp. 360-384; and an interesting essay by Cyril Mango, "The Phanariots and the Byzantine Tradition," in Richard Clogg, ed., *The Struggle for Greek Independence* (London, 1973), pp. 41-66.

41. On the cultural renaissance in the Danubian Principalities see A. Camariano-Cioran, *Les Académies princières de Bucharest et de Jassy et leur professeurs* (Thessaloniki, 1974).

42. The exact dates of Theotokis's sojourns in Constantinople, Jassy, and Leipzig between 1764 and 1766 are impossible to verify with any certainty. Mourouti-Gkenakou reviews the various interpretations and refutes Vrokinis and therefore, Koukkou, with archival materials. See Mourouti-Gkenakou, p. 12.

43. Kitromilides, *Moisiodax*, p. 76.

44. As he states himself in the introduction to his *Stoiheia Physikis*, vol. I. Cited in Mourouti–Gkenakou, p. 12, n. 62.

45. On the Greek diaspora communities of Europe and their role in generating and maintaining a Greek national consciousness see Deno J. Geanakoplos, "The Diaspora Greeks: The Genesis of Modern Greek Consciousness," in N. Diamandouros and J. Petropoulos, eds., *Hellenism and The First Greek War of Liberation (1821-1830): Continuity and Change* (Thessaloniki, 1976), pp. 59-78; Apostolos Vakalopoulos , *Istoria tou Neou Ellinismou*, vol. 2 (Thessaloniki, 1964), pp. 466-486, and vol. 4 (Thessaloniki, 1973), pp. 157-236, 457-463, 586-590, 736-737; Konstantinos Tsoukalas, *Eksartisi kai Anaparagogi* (Athens, 1974), pp. 269-371; and D. Zakythinos, *The Making of Modern Greece from Byzantium to Independence* (London, 1976), pp. 115-139.

46. N. Theotokis, *Stoiheia Physikis, ek neoteron syneranisthenta*, 2 vols. (Leipzig, 1766-67).

47. N. Theotokis, *Logoi eis tin Aghian kai Megalin Tessarakostin, meta kai tinon Panagyrikon, Epifonimatikon kai Epitafion* (Leipzig, 1766).

48. The work was entitled *Seira enos kai pentikonta ypomnimatiston eis tin oktatefhon kai ta ton Vasileion idi proton typois ekdotheisa axiosei men tou*

evsevestatou kai galinotatou igemonos pasis Oungkrovlahias kyriou kyriou Grigoriou Alexandrou Gkika, 2 vols. (Leipzig, 1772). For a full description see Mourouti-Gkenakou, pp. 14-16.

49. See Alexander Stourtzas, *Anamniseis kai eikones. Evgenios Voulgaris kai Nikiforos Theotokis* (Athens, 1858), pp. 12-14. Some biographers maintain that this episode happened to Voulgaris and not to Theotokis. Both Stourtzas and Vrokinis, however, support the Theotokis version.

50. Voulgaris's sojourn in the West lasted seven years, from 1764-1771, which he divided between stays in Leipzig and Halle.

51. Mourouti-Gkenakou, p. 19 and Stourtzas, p. 17.

52. N. Theotokis, *Ponima hrysoun Samouil Ravvi tou Ioudaiou exelenghon tin ton Ioudaion planin. Proton men, ek tis Aravikis eis tin Latinida metafrasthen. Nyn de ek tis Latinidos eis tin koinin ton Ellinon dialekton* (Leipzig, 1769).

53. N. Theotokis, *Tou osiou patros imon Isaak episkopou Ninevi tou Syrou, ta evrethenta Askitika axiosei men tou makariotatou theiotatou kai sofotatou patriarhou tis aghias poleos Ierousalim kai pasis Palaistinis kyriou Efraim epimeleia de Nikiforou ieromonahou tou Theotokou idi proton typois ekdothenta* (Leipzig, 1770).

54. Saint Isaac of Syria (or Isaak Sirin, Isaac Syros, or Isaac of Nineveh) was a hermit and bishop in the late sixth century who wrote on mysticism and theodicy. Theotokis's work was one of many at this time that represented a renewed interest in mysticism within Eastern Orthodoxy (particularly Russian Orthodoxy) in the late eighteenth century.

55. Mourouti-Gkenakou, pp. 19-20.

56. S. Chetverikov, *Starets Paisii Velichkovskii: His Life, Teachings, and Influence on Orthodox Monasticism* (Belmont, MA, 1980), pp. 147-149, 227-228. *Starets* Paisii Velichkovskii did not begin his translation of St. Isaac of Syria's *Spiritual Exercises* until late 1786 (by which time, according to him, he had sufficiently mastered the Greek language) and completed it in 1787. Feodor Dostoevskii owned an edition of this translation and used it as a source for Father Zossima's religious beliefs in *Brothers Karamazov*. See Victor Terras, *A Karamazov Companion* (Madison, 1981), pp. 22-23.

57. See I. Veloudis, *Ellinon orthodoxon apoikia en Venetia* (Athens, 1893) and Deno J. Geanakoplos, *Greek Scholars in Venice*.

58. Geanakoplos, *Byzantine East and Latin West*, p. 121.

59. M. Paranikas, "Nikiforos o Theotokis kai I en Enetia Ekklisia," *Ellinikos Filologikos Syllogos Konstantinoupoleos*, 20 (1891): 109-126. This work is based on the correspondence between Theotokis and the Greek community.

60. Paranikas, p. 112.

61. *Ibid.*, p. 118.

62. *Ibid.*, p. 124.

63. Ghikas's term as prince of Moldavia began in September, 1774, immediately after the Russian occupation ceased as provided by the Treaty of Kutchuk-Kainardji.

64. Mourouti-Gkenakou, p. 40.

65. I. Moisiodax, *Apologia* (Vienna, 1780), p. 81. Cited in Mourouti-Gkenakou, p. 40.

66. See O. Halecki, *From Florence to Brest, 1439-1596* (New York, 1958).

67. Batalden, p. 8.

68. On Mogila, see S.T. Golubev, *Petr Mogila, Mitropolit Kievskii*, vol. I (Moscow, 1887). For a general overview of these developments see W.K. Medlin and C.G. Patrinelis, *Renaissance Influence and Religious Reforms in Russia* (Geneva, 1971). For the latest addition to this field see Frank Sysyn, *Between Poland and the Ukraine: The Dilemma of Adam Kysil, 1600-1653* (Cambridge, 1985).

69. See discussion of Greek travelers to Russia in Chapter 2.

70. N. Theotokis, *Apokrisis orthodoxou tinos pros tina adelfon orthodoxon peri ton tis Katolikon Dynasteias kai peri tou tines oi Schistai kai oi Schismatikoi kai oi Eschismenoi. Kai peri tis varvarikis legomenis Ounias kai ton Ouniaton kai peri tou pos dei tous Orthodoxous apantan ti ton Katolikon tyrannia* (Halle, 1775).

71. Batalden, p. 10.

72. Theotokis, *Apokrisis*, p. 44 and p. 7. Cited in Mourouti-Gkenakou, p. 42.

73. Theotokis, *Apokrisis*, p. 38. Cited in Mourouti-Gkenakou, p. 44, n. 243.

74. Theotokis, *Apokrisis*, p. 71. Cited in Mourouti-Gkenakou, p. 43. *Apokrisis* was reprinted a number of times after 1775 (Corfu, 1851; Athens, 1853; Vienna, c. 1790) and was even paraphrased by a Rumanian nationalist in 1829 in Bucharest.

2

THE ORTHODOX COMMONWEALTH: THEOTOKIS AND THE WORLD OF GREEK-SLAVIC RELATIONS

If you desire to come here [Novorossiia] and settle, you will find many brothers from many places. You will find that we will do all that we can to assist and help you.[1]

– Archbishop Voulgaris's invitation to Nikiforos Theotokis

Theotokis had maintained contact with Eugenios Voulgaris throughout his long ordeal over the metropolitanate of Philadelphia in Venice. Voulgaris was kept apprised of Theotokis's misfortunes since leaving Vienna and sent him a letter in Jassy from Moscow or Poltava sometime in 1776. In his letter, Voulgaris offered this description of his diocese in Novorossiia: "my diocese...is a welcome refuge from the tyranny of the Ottomans to the oppressed, tormented, and unfortunate Greeks, Wallachians, Moldavians, Serbs and others; a privilege granted by the most excellent Empress."[2] Keeping in mind Theotokis's position he added "if you desire to come here and settle, you will find many brothers from many places. You will find that we will do all that we can to assist and help you."[3] Theotokis had hoped that he could return to his native Corfu to continue his activities there but that was not possible and his early advocate and protector, Grigorios Ghikas, was not able to shield him from the conservative elements in Jassy.[4] The only option remaining was Voulgaris's invitation to Russia; which he accepted in late 1776.

••••

When Theotokis crossed into Russian territory in the fall of 1776 he joined a long tradition of Greeks traveling to the north and demonstrated the existence of the Orthodox commonwealth. Russia's conversion to Christianity in the tenth century placed it securely within a religious and cultural world centered in Constantinople and known as the Byzantine commonwealth.[5] Greeks, Balkan Slavs, and the Rus' were united through a common attachment to Orthodoxy.

Early Greek travelers to Kievan Rus' and, later, Muscovy were prelates of the Orthodox Church sent to administer the new territories in the name of the Ecumenical Patriarch of Constantinople. Even with the fall of Constantinople in 1453, the religious and cultural ties that had been an integral part of the Byzantine commonwealth persisted as Greek clerics, merchants, and intellectuals fled to Russia or were invited there by the Grand Princes of Moscow.[6] Many of the Greeks who took up residence in Russia shared a common set of characteristics: 1) most were Orthodox clerics and were valued for their expertise in Greek Orthodox doctrine, 2) they were interested and active in education, 3) they were generally learned men and introduced into Russia variants of western humanism, and 4) they all attempted to secure financial or other assistance for the Orthodox Church and, later, the nascent Greek independence movement. Four influential Greeks who served in Russia and possessed the characteristics mentioned above – Maxim Grek, Arsenios the Greek, and the Leikhoudis brothers – offer a representation of Greek activities during the Muscovite period.

Maxim Grek's life parallels Theotokis's to an extent.[7] He was born Michael Trivolis in Arta, Epirus in 1470 and then traveled to Italy via Corfu to obtain an education. While in Italy he worked closely with the grammarian John Lascaris in Florence and then edited Greek manuscripts for the printer Aldus Manutius in Venice. He was educated in the humanist tradition of the Renaissance and was imbued with the writings of Plato. The execution of Savonarola in 1498, however, shocked him so deeply that he underwent a severe spiritual crisis and exchanged his humanist cloak for a monk's cassock. After beginning his religious life as a Dominican he returned to Orthodoxy in 1505 and resided on Mt. Athos where he studied the Greek Fathers. In 1516 Tsar Basil III of Moscow asked the ecumenical patriarch to send him a "translator of Greek books" to resolve some major disputes that were plaguing the Russian Church on account of inaccuracies that had crept into the service books over the years of separation from Constantinople. Maxim arrived in Moscow in 1518 and assiduously occupied himself with the translation of Greek texts into Slavic via Latin. Later he was charged with revising liturgical books, which eventually led him to apply humanist literary criticism to spurious apocryphal works. Maxim also involved himself in the Possessors/Non-Possessors dispute (i.e., whether or not the Church should possess land) which was dividing the Russian Church. Citing Byzantine tradition he sided with the non-Possessors led by Nils Sorskii. This act earned him the ire and opposition of Metropolitan Daniil of Moscow and led to his eventual trial in 1525 and imprisonment until 1551. Maxim did not cease his activities while imprisoned but increased his output of writings on a variety of topics and counted among his students Fedor Karpov, Andrei Kurbskii and Ermolai-Erazm.[8] Maxim did not forget his home and was possibly the first Greek to plead for Russian support on behalf of the Balkan Christians against the depredations of the Turks as is seen in the preface to his translation of the *Psalter*.[9] Although the immediate Russian response (apart from the Tsar and other like-minded elites) to Maxim's writings and Neo-Platonism was hostile and tinged with xenophobia, his revisions of Russian service books greatly influenced a number of later Russian churchmen and, one in particular, Patriarch Nikon, whose ecclesiastical reforms in the mid-seventeenth century split the Russian Church.[10]

As the spiritual inheritor of Maxim's early and significant attempts at conforming the Russian liturgy to the original Greek, Nikon needed to continue translating Greek texts into Slavonic and he was assisted in this task by Arsenios the Greek. Very little is known of Arsenios's early life except for what has been gleaned from the depositions used in his trial for heresy in Moscow in 1649.[11] Arsenios was born in central Greece in the early sixteenth century and was educated in the humanist tradition of his time when he attended the Greek College in Venice, the theological College of St. Athanasius in Rome, and graduated from the University of Padua with degrees in philosophy and medicine. His career became quite complicated when he returned to Greece as a bishop on the island of Carpathos only to be captured and imprisoned by the Turks on charges that he was a spy. He converted to Islam to avoid the severe torture promised him by his Turkish captors, then escaped to the Danubian Principalities and eventually settled for a short time in Kiev. While in Kiev he taught at Peter Mogila's Academy (incredibly on the recommendation of the King of Poland whom he had cured of a kidney disorder in Warsaw)[12] and then was invited to accompany the Patriarch of Jerusalem, Paisios, to Moscow in 1649 as his interpreter. For reasons unknown Paisios, upon returning to Jerusalem, sent a letter to Tsar Alexis condemning Arsenios for heresy and apostasy. As a result of these charges, he was tried and imprisoned in

Solovetskii Monastery, but was unexpectedly befriended by the metropolitan of Novgorod and future patriarch of Moscow, Nikon, who secured his release in 1652. It was after his released from prison that Arsenios made his significant contributions to Russian education and religious culture by translating Greek texts into Slavonic and Russian,[13] revising ecclesiastical and liturgical works which brought upon him anathemas from the Old Believers, and creating the short-lived Greek-Latin school (based on the liberal arts curriculum used by Mogila in Kiev) in Moscow in 1652-1653.

In 1685, not more than twenty-five years after Arsenios's academy began to wane following his arrest in 1662, two Greek cleric-educators, Ioannikios and Sofronis Leikhoudis, arrived in Moscow to teach at the Slavonic-Greek-Latin Academy in the Zaikonospasskii Monastery.[14] The early life of the Leikhoudis brothers imitated in part the lives of their preceding countrymen. They were born on the Ionian Island of Cephalonia and received an education in Venice and doctorates at the University of Padua. Following a long stay in Constantinople, they traveled to Moscow by way of Poland. At the Academy they taught physics and prepared school manuals in the Scholastic tradition. The Slavonic-Greek-Latin Academy was emblematic of Russia's struggle with the West in the last quarter of the seventeenth century.[15] The name of the Academy itself attests to an attempt on the part of church and secular leaders to reach a compromise in the realm of education. The Church was not yet ready to accept the concept or practice of secular education and thus, we see an academy which is Latin in form, language, and theological inquiry, yet, oddly enough, strictly Orthodox in dogma. Indicative of the turbulence in Moscow at this time were the attacks leveled at the Leikhoudis brothers by anti-Western, pro-Greek elements in the Church who supported the teaching of religious or "free" wisdom; and pro-Western, anti-Greek educators who advocated secular or "external" wisdom. The Leikhoudis could find no escape from this dilemma and were removed from their positions in 1694.[16] The Leikhoudis brothers, however, played a significant role in the development of the ideal theological academy, which taught its students Orthodox dogma and acquainted them with the scholastic tradition of argumentation and inquiry which in turn allowed them to actively defend Orthodoxy against Catholicism and Protestantism.

Apart from the clergymen-educators who traveled to Russia hoping to find sanctuary from the Ottoman Turks and seeking the support of Russia against the same Turks, other Greeks traveled to and resided in Russia who were not involved in educational or ecclesiastical affairs. Those Greeks not in the service of the Church were to be found in court circles as state treasurers and diplomats or actively engaged in trade. Two Greek families, the Rhallis and Trachaniotis, were valued by the Muscovite court owing to their familiarity with Byzantine court practice and their commercial ties with Europe and the Mediterranean which allowed them to advise Moscow on diplomatic and trade matters in those regions.[17] These families and others like them provided a conduit through which ideas and information flowed to and from Russia in the years after the fall of Constantinople.

••••

The understandable attraction which the Greeks displayed for Russia in their hopes for deliverance from Ottoman tyranny was reciprocated, in a manner, by the Russians toward the end of the seventeenth century and beginning of the eighteenth century. Initially, Russian attention was directed to the south for reasons other than the salvation of Orthodox Greeks and Slavs. The Russians were concerned with more immediate problems arising on the southern steppes caused by the Cossacks and the Crimean Tatars.[18] The Cossacks were a proud and independent people –who inhabited the vast steppe bounded on the north by Poland and Russia and on the south by the Ottoman Empire. The Zaporozhian Cossack Host deeply resented Russian territorial gains in the Ukraine as a result of the Treaty of Andrusovo with Poland in 1667 because it effectively split the Host in two with one half of its population on the left bank of the Dnieper under Russian control and the other half on the right bank under Polish control. Consequently, Cossack leaders constantly endeavored to reunite the Cossack peoples by offering their allegiance to the power most capable of assisting them in attaining unity. Unfortunately, offers of assistance by the powers were often accompanied by a *quid pro quo* which threatened the Cossacks with vassalage. As a result of this maneuvering, Russia, Poland and the Porte each feared that one of them was gaining at the expense of the other two thus engendering a friction which ultimately led to war in 1676. The Crimean Tatars, for their part, continually harassed Russian efforts to expand into the fertile southern Ukraine by encouraging Cossack intransigence and executing their own raids on Russian settlements, taking prisoners (who were sold into slavery), and demanding annual tribute. In response to these pressures, the regent of the Tsars Ivan V and Peter I, Sophia, in alliance with Poland, dispatched her trusted favorite V. Golitsyn on two occasions in 1687 and 1689 to the south to cure the Tatars permanently of their penchant for embarrassing Russia.[19] Golitsyn's campaigns failed miserably, mostly on account of grave logistical errors, and the task fell to the young tsar, Peter I, to recoup Russia's military reputation.

Peter the Great acquitted himself masterfully in his campaigns against the Tatars when he adopted a strategy which aimed at seizing the Turkish fortress at Azov not by storming headlong into the Crimea as his predecessors had attempted but, instead, by besieging the fortress from the sea with his new navy. Peter's initial progress in the south slowed and eventually ended temporarily due to the vicissitudes of international politics and the appearance of a much greater threat looming in the north in the form of Sweden and its adolescent king Charles XII. The withdrawal of Poland, Austria, and Venice from the Holy Alliance, to which Russia was only loosely tied, forced Peter to seek a truce with the Turks at Karlowitz. The tantalizing possibility of relieving Sweden of some of its southern Baltic possessions caused Peter to abandon briefly his plans in the south and to sign the Treaty of Constantinople in 1700 thereby securing his southern flank. The Treaty of Constantinople was remarkable for two reasons: first, Peter declared his intentions that Russia would never again accede to Tatar demands for tribute, and, most important, Peter secured for the first time Russian diplomatic representation at the Porte.

In 1711, Peter felt confident enough after his victory over Charles XII at Poltava in 1709 that he cast his eyes once again in the direction of the Crimea with disastrous consequences. It was in connection with this campaign that Russia made its first appeals to the Orthodox population of the Balkans to overthrow their Turkish lords. In the Treaty of Constantinople, Peter had put forward claims on behalf of Orthodoxy when he insisted on the right of Russian pilgrims to free passage to the Holy Land, the return of the Church of the Holy Sepulcher to the Greeks, and guarantees of religious freedom in the Ottoman Empire. He was successful on the first, failed on the second (one of the causes of the Crimean War 150 years later), and the outcome of the third would await Catherine the Great.

Peter was also the first Russian tsar to establish permanent diplomatic missions in leading European capitals. In 1711, Venice became the location for his second consul after Amsterdam. Demetrios Bozis, a Greek educated in Venice, was Peter's selection as first consul.[20] Although Bozis and his colleagues were unsuccessful in their attempts to obtain Venetian assistance against the Turks at this time, the idea of using Greeks or other Balkan nationals to man diplomatic posts would become fully developed under Catherine the Great with more dramatic results. Peter now made direct representations, in particular, to the princes of Moldavia and Wallachia to join him in his struggle against the Ottomans. Prince Kantemir of Moldavia came to Peter's aid after he crossed the Pruth River, but contributed very little and subsequently fled to St. Petersburg. Prince Brancoveanu of Wallachia vacillated, fearing Turkish retribution and gave Peter's supplies to the Turks after they crossed the Danube.[21] Serbs and Montenegrins revolted with no success.[22]

Peter's defeat at the Pruth in July 1711, resulted in the loss of all the gains he had made in 1700. He lost Azov, Taganrog, the Dnieper forts, and his fleet. Peter's loss also had two other major repercussions: He had excited the expectations of the Balkan Christians who now, more than ever, looked to the north for their salvation. Phanariots were appointed *hospodars* of the Danubian Principalities in place of the native Rumanian nobility whom the Ottomans now distrusted owing to the defections of Kantemir and Brancoveanu. The activities of Peter the Great helped to foster and cultivate a myth of Russian liberation. Emblematic of the apocryphal proportions the myth attained was a collection of prophesies written in the mid-eighteenth century and published as the propaganda pamphlet, *Agathangelos*.[23] The prophesies were a contemporary rendering of the Apocalypse and connected to the expression of "the blonde nation" (*to xanthon yenos*), which would deliver the Greek Orthodox from their bondage.[24] The time for direct Russian intervention and Orthodox deliverance, however, would have to await the establishment of a secure Russian military presence on the northern Black Sea littoral; something not to be accomplished until the reign of Catherine the Great.

The years immediately following the death of Peter the Great witnessed a cessation of hostilities against the Turks not to be resumed until the reign of Empress Anna Ivanovna and the First Russo-Crimean War (1736-1739) which pitted Russia and Austria against France and the Ottoman Empire. Before we examine Anna's military successes in the south we should direct our attention to another essential component of Russian expansion in the eighteenth century: Poland. During the seventeenth and eighteenth centuries Poland was in a period of decline. Internal political dissension and a debilitated central authority allowed foreign powers to intervene freely in the selection of its king and in a variety of other domestic matters. One such domestic issue, which would serve as a pretext for Russian and Prussian intervention in the 1760s, was the alleged mal-treatment of religious Dissidents (namely, Protestants and Orthodox) by the Catholic majority. The fates of Poland and the Ottoman Empire were bound inextricably together, at least, in the eyes of their European neighbors. Each possessed an oppressed Orthodox population, central authority was in decline, and their territory was coveted by the other powers. How the European powers responded to this situation is known as the Eastern Question.[25]

Empress Anna and her foreign policy advisors formulated a policy based on the recognition of this linkage between Poland and the Ottoman Empire. With the conclusion of the War of the Polish Succession (1733-1735) and the selection of a pro-Russian king, the Russian military carried out a two-pronged attack aimed at Azov and the Crimea. The initial successes and the addition of Austria as an ally in 1737 prompted Marshal Münnich to present his "Oriental Project" before the empress. Münnich had sent agents to Epirus and Thessaly to stir the Greeks to revolt against the Turks and assured Anna that as a result of his actions they would rise up in support of her and open the road to Constantinople.[26] This was not to be, however, as disaster struck while Münnich's army was holding the Moldavian capital of Jassy and preparing to move into Bessarabia. Austria, suffering terrible defeat at the hands of the Turks and distrustful of Russian advances into the Danubian Principalities, sued for peace at Belgrade in September 1739. The Russians, compelled to protect their flank, sought terms a few weeks later. The Russians relinquished their gains in Moldavia and the Crimea, maintained a non-fortified Azov, received the land between the Donets and Bug rivers, and earned the right to trade on the Sea of Azov and the Black Sea. These gains, while not impressive, did establish Russia as a power of no small importance in the Balkans. Despite the failure of Münnich's "Oriental Project," the Balkan Christians looked to the north with hope and anticipation.

••••

By the time Theotokis arrived in Russia in 1776, Catherine the Great had ruled for over fourteen years and had, without doubt, become in her own eyes the embodiment of an enlightened and "loving" monarch who professed toleration, reason, and a love of classical Greece.[27]Her coronation medal portrayed her as a militant Minerva and the dramatist A.P. Sumarokov celebrated her name day with the following ode: "Minerva is on her throne,/Bounty reigns!/Astraea has descended again from the heavens/Has returned to earth/In her former beauty."[28] Catherine and her court were enamored of Greek classicism and partook of a "philhellenism" that appeared in Russia considerably earlier than in the West.[29] Mikhail Lomonosov, the eighteenth-century Russian intellectual, was convinced that the Russian language was the distant heir and successor to Ancient Greek via Koine (New Testament) Greek and Old Church Slavonic.[30] Given Russia's traditional religious ties to the Greek world through the Orthodox Church, Catherinian Russia stood apart from the other eighteenth-century European powers in its passion for Greece and its heritages, i.e., both classical and Orthodox Byzantine. This contemporary interest in Greek affairs led Russia to take an active part in the liberation of Orthodox Greeks from the Moslem Turks. Thus, Theotokis, as Voulgaris before him, seemed to have found an intellectual and spiritual home in Catherinian Russia.

Catherine's fascination with the classical world was representative of a Russian court attracted to a classicism as received through the French *philosophes*. Catherine conducted a correspondence with such leading luminaries of the Enlightenment as Voltaire, Diderot, and Grimm. She rescued Diderot from penury when she purchased his library from him, discussed matters of policy with Voltaire who fortified her with the intellectual underpinnings for her political actions in Poland and against the Porte, and confided in Grimm when the others turned against her. Catherine transformed the barracks-like atmosphere of the court created by Peter III into a showcase of culture for all Europe to envy. She promoted theater, music, journalism, and the translation of foreign works.[31] Catherine, following Elizabeth's example, turned Petersburg into a repository of neo-classical architecture. The Greek influence was also a motif at court masked balls. In some instances the classical ambiance became so overwhelming that one English traveler was moved to remark, "I think often I can trace Grecian features among the females of this country and the subtle wit of the Greeks in the men...."[32]

Catherine the Great ascended the throne in the summer of 1762 through a coup d'état directed against her unsuspecting husband Peter III with the aid of a group of young guards officers who later would advise Catherine on both domestic and foreign policy matters. Peter III, in the brief span of six months as emperor, had accomplished nearly the impossible by alienating the three mainstays of any Russian monarch: the Church, the guards, and the nobility.[33] Upon her accession Catherine immediately moved to mollify all the injured parties. For our purposes and at this time, we need only be aware of her declared role as "Protectress of the Orthodox Church" and its consequences for the Orthodox Greeks.

The first indication that Catherine the Great would act on behalf of the Greeks under Ottoman rule came in the years immediately preceding and during the Russo-Turkish War of 1768-1774. Catherine firmly believed that the formulation and execution of foreign policy was her *metier* and skillfully played the competing factions (or parties) in the Russian government against each other to her satisfaction; adhering neither to Nikita Panin's "Northern System" of alliances nor to Foreign Minister Bestuzhev's more pro-Austrian policies she slipped the bounds of traditional statecraft.[34] Through clever diplomatic maneuvering and with the assent of Frederick the Great of Prussia, Catherine secured for her former lover, Stanislaus Augustus Poniatowski, the throne of Poland in August 1764. Catherine hoped now to have the ability to exert considerable influence over the events in her unstable neighbor to the west.

Catherine's policies in regard to Poland throughout the last quarter of the eighteenth century exhibited all the characteristics of the workings of an "enlightened absolutist." Poland found itself in the difficult position of deciding which path of the Enlightenment it would take: the path to constitutional monarchy or enlightened absolutism. The country, unfortunately, was located between the territories of three enlightened absolutists and they would make the decision for Poland. The condition of Poland was a topic of great discussion in the 1770s among diplomats and *philosophes*. Some, Voltaire and Diderot among them, favored the actions of Catherine and Frederick in forcing religious toleration upon the fanatical Catholics in accordance with natural law and in bringing an end to the unseemly anarchy that had rent the country apart for decades.[35] Others, including Voltaire's protagonist Rousseau, condemned the

activities of the enlightened absolutists and felt that it was the right
and privilege of the Poles to resolve their own difficulties without
foreign intervention. Poniatowski sincerely wanted to create a more
stable Poland by abolishing the debilitating practice of *liberum veto*
and by establishing a strong central executive power in the monarchy. Catherine's demands for granting religious toleration to the
Orthodox and Protestant "Dissenters" as well as a restoration of their
former rights, liberties and privileges seriously compromised
Poniatowski's dealings with the devout Catholic nobility in the Polish
Diet. A combination of Catherine's insensitivity to the Poles' strong
sectarian views, imposition of Russian troops on Polish soil to ensure
the implementation of her agenda, and her refusal to allow a complete political reform to strengthen Poland led to an outbreak of
hostilities between a faction of the Polish nobility called the
Confederation of Bar and Russian forces in the fall of 1768.[36]

The Ottoman Turks kept a watchful eye on the developments
in Poland and were joined by the French and Austrians in their
shared concern for the well-being of the Polish population and the
possibility of Russian territorial gains in Poland. Turkish dissatisfaction with Russian aggression was not aroused by this incident alone
but also by an increase in Russian agitation among the Christian
Balkan population which had begun once again in the early 1760s.
Catherine, it seems, was intent on profiting from anti-Turkish
sentiments in the Balkans just as she was exploiting the Dissident
situation in Poland. She did so by planting agents in Montenegro and
Greece with the hope of creating a diversion on the Turkish flank
while planning to move into the steppe north of the Black Sea.[37]
Catherine's attempts to incite revolt in the Greek lands of the
Ottoman Empire eventually led to a Russian naval expedition to the
Peloponnesus under the command of Alexei Orlov and the defeat of
the Turkish fleet at Chesme in 1770. The insurrection of the native
Greek population against the Turks and the social conditions which
fostered it have subsequently been referred to in Greek historiography as *Ta Orlofika*.[38]

In the early 1760s, an unsuccessful Greek merchant from
Siatista in Macedonia by the name of Georgios Papazolis abandoned
his native land and traveled to St. Petersburg. There he made the
acquaintance of the Orlov brothers and became an artillery officer in
the Russian military. With the assistance of two other native Greeks
from Cephalonia, Marinos Harvouris and Petros Melissinos,[39]

Papazolis's recitations of Turkish atrocities against the native Greeks excited the passions of the Orlovs who conjured up images of the noble classical Greeks defending themselves from the Persians. The Orlovs were moved to accept the idea of inciting the Greeks to revolt against the Ottomans for the greater glory of Greece and Russia.[40] Papazolis was certainly unaware that his hopes for Greek independence coincided with Catherine's plans. The Orlovs attired their idea in classical garb and presented it to Catherine who readily agreed that sending an expedition to the *spartanskii narod* (Spartan nation)[41] of Greece to ascertain the inclination of the people to revolt was indeed beneficial to Russia; and it was doubly useful in that it also served Catherine's purposes at Court in her attempt to obstruct Nikita Panin's ambitions for supreme control of Russian foreign policy with his "Northern System" of alliances.

In October 1763, Papazolis and another Greek, Emmanouil Sarros (who returned to Russia in May 1765), embarked on a three-year mission to Greece as agents of Grigorii and Alexei Orlov to examine the state of the revolutionary movements in various regions of that country.[42] In Trieste the two agents met with clerics, *armatoloi*, and other members of the Greek elite from different Greek regions and dispersed money granted to them from Catherine the Great to underscore her serious intentions in regard to the possible insurrections and future liberation from Turkish control. Papazolis then traveled through Epirus and Akarnania were his "sermons" were received with "great enthusiasm" by the local chieftains.[43] In the Mani, Papazolis met with some resistance (which Sarros, who preceded him by almost two years, had not perceived owing to the execution of the local metropolitan and several prominent leaders after their implication in a recent revolt) but he assured the Maniates that "Catherine II, protector of the Orthodox, was resolute in her decision to free the Greeks and that all the European states had promised that they would not interfere in the dissolution of the Ottoman Empire."[44] After departing Mani Papazolis went to Kalamata were he was welcomed by the local archon, Panayiotis Benakis, a person whose power the "Turks recognized and respected." Benakis called together a secret gathering of other local elite and they pledged their support for a revolt as soon as the Russian fleet appeared off their coast.[45]

Sarros had already returned to Russia by May 1765 and given his report to the Orlovs. Papazolis returned to Trieste in late 1767 and immediately sent his findings to Grigorii Orlov outlining the explosive conditions in Greece, especially in northern Epirus and the Peloponnesus (Kalamata, Mani, Sparta). Needless to say, the reports of Sarros, Papazolis, and other agents of the Russians in Greece such as Vasileios Tamara, a Ukrainian-born Greek who supplied St. Petersburg with lengthy reports filled with details on Greek and Turkish military strength, were colored with excessive optimism and only partially reflected the real situation.[46]

As the Orlovs received this information from their various agents, delegates and deputies they became more and more enthralled with their plan for insurrection in Greece and decided that two of them, Alexei and Fedor, should travel to Italy and take measure of the situation themselves. Alexei and Fedor traveled to Venice in the fall of 1768 under the assumed name of Ostrovov using the pretext of seeking the curative waters for some infliction they suffered. In Venice they met with their agents, surmised that what they had been told previously was correct and began laying plans for a general insurrection.

In the meantime, Grigorii Orlov was occupied with the broader aspects of the war with Turkey which had begun 30 September 1768. The notion of sending a Russian fleet to the Mediterranean as a diversionary force had been spoken of wistfully a number of times in the first days of the war, but during the month of November, Grigorii Orlov brought the subject before Catherine's War Council twice, on 6 and 12 November. On 12 November the Council decided to send an expedition "to the Morea, Dalmatia, Georgia, and to all the people of our religion, who live in the Turkish territories,"[47] especially in light of the letters that Catherine and Grigorii had received from his brothers in Italy stating that "[We] have found here many people of the same faith, who would like to serve under our command in the present conflict with the Turks."[48] Within a few months, on 29 January 1769, Catherine appointed Alexei as the commander of the Mediterranean expedition in a general proclamation to the subject Orthodox populations.

Alexei Orlov was the overall commander of the naval expedition to the Mediterranean but his knowledge of marine matters was woefully inadequate and fleeting at best. Alexei and Fedor continued on in Italy where their "revolutionary" activities-meetings with Greek and South Slav leaders and stockpiling materiel for the fleet were considered much too excessive for the Venetian authorities, who desiring to remain on good terms with the Ottomans, forced them to abandon Venice and continue their operations from the Tuscan city of Pisa. Meanwhile, the assemblage of the fleet at Kronstadt was under the nominal direction of Admiral Spiridov with the expert assistance of Samuel Karlovich Greig, a Scotsman in the service of the Russian state who eventually was killed in battle in 1788.[49] The first squadron departed Kronstadt in July 1769 and was the talk of Europe. Catherine's naval expedition, the first time a Russian fleet sailed outside the Baltic let alone through the Straits of Gibraltar and into the Mediterranean, was a startling development for most Europeans. It was certainly no surprise to most European governments for her diplomats already had made known her plans to friendly powers along the route from the Baltic to the Mediterranean; the British even offered to serve as a badly needed way station to effect repairs and supply additional crew members and junior officers. Voltaire, tucked away at his hermitage in Ferney along the Swiss border, knew of the Russian squadron and drew the appropriate classical parallel in a letter to Catherine: "I am not privy to your secrets: but the departure of your fleet fills me with admiration. [I]t is the finest venture that has been seen since Hannibal."[50] (Certainly unknown to Voltaire a Hannibal, Ivan Abramovich Gannibal, was a brigadier in the fleet. Gannibal was the son of "Peter the Great's Arab" and Pushkin's uncle.[51]) Catherine, of course, reveled in the attention that her "novel" expedition was attracting and hoped that "Europe [would] judge it only by the end result."[52]

After an abortive attempt to incite rebellion in Montenegro in late 1769, the Spiridov squadron sailed on to the southern tip of the Morea and put ashore at Vitilo at the end of February 1770 (during this trip the mere passing of his squadron by the Ionian Islands roused many Greeks to rise up against the local Venetian authorities)[53] where it was assumed that the Russian forces would be joined by a large contingent of native Greek legions. The Greeks, however, were stunned when they became fully aware of just how few Russian ships and soldiers had appeared off their coast. They had expected at least 10,000 troops from the Russians and the Russians, in turn, had been led to believe from exaggerated field reports that the Greeks would number in the tens of thousands. Both sides were extremely disillusioned and accused each other of deceit, betrayal, and cowardice. A small contingent was finally assembled under the command of Fedor Orlov with elements provided by Benakis and the

Mavromihalides. The group was strong enough to take Kalamata and the old Byzantine city of Mistra from the Turks in mid-March. The Greek population of the Peloponnesus responded with jubilation at news of the victory but their hopes for continued success were dashed when the same force met with defeat at the strongly held fortress of Tripolitsa. After suffering a minor setback when the siege of Koroni failed, the Russian fleet and Greek forces besieged Navarino and successfully took it in April 1770. Counting Navarino as their only major success in the face of numerous failures, the inevitable occurred when the Russian and Greek alliance collapsed under the overwhelming weight of mutual recriminations.

The Turks recovered quickly from their momentary defeats and swept down upon the Greek revolutionaries with Turkish and Albanian forces. Within a few months of the outbreak Albanian troops drove the Russian legions from the mainland and crushed those Greeks who failed to escape to the Ionian Islands. The entire Peloponnesus fell under the control of the Albanians who exacted their revenge and could not be removed by the Turks until 1779. Alexei Orlov's squadron sailed out of Navarino as the Albanians descended upon it and headed into the Aegean Sea and joined the Russian fleet. On 26 June/7 July 1770, Orlov encountered the Turkish fleet at the port of Chesme and sank it. News of Orlov's victory was greeted with exultation in St. Petersburg where Catherine ordered a *Te Deum* sung at the Cathedral of SS. Peter and Paul and conferred upon Alexei Orlov the title of Chesmenskii. Not wishing to miss the opportunity to imbue the Orlov expedition with classical motifs, the classical poet Mikhail M. Kheraskov celebrated the naval victory in his poem *Battle of Chesme* (*Chesmenskii boi*, 1771).[54]

••••

The Russian fleet remained firmly ensconced in the Aegean Archipelago until the end of the Russo-Turkish War in 1774. No longer would the Russians look to the warriors of the Morea to do battle against the Ottomans but to the seamen, fishermen, and merchants of the islands. Catherine and her ministers, as well as other European leaders, began to speak of the Aegean and its surrounding coastlines as the "Russian Levant." Voltaire was so taken by the sudden and surprising victory at Chesme that he believed Catherine's fortune to be unlimited and spurred her on to further action when he wrote her that "the time has now come for the finest and most noble historical achievement since the conquests of the first caliphs."[55] Further victories in the "Russian Levant" were not to be, however, as Catherine concentrated her attentions on gaining territories in the Danubian Principalities and along the northern littoral of the Black Sea and gave up any notions of taking the Peloponnesus or mainland Greece. Her strategy of diverting Ottoman attention from the north was successful, not in the manner she had expected, but successful nonetheless. The empress's passion for Greek culture did not diminish once her strategic interests had been met, but continued unabated as attested by a masked ball held in St. Petersburg in honor of Prince Henry of Prussia with Apollo, the Four Seasons, the Twelve Months, and Diana in attendance.[56]

The Russo-Turkish War drew more Greeks not only into the Greco-Russian cultural orbit but into Russian service or, at least, Russia itself.[57] On 27 July 1771, Eugenios Voulgaris was ushered in to appear before Catherine and delivered a prepared statement of introduction:

> Slaviano-Bulgarian by origin, Greek by birth, Russian by inclination, a servant most humble in fitting obedience and devotion; before Your Imperial Majesty, as to me is commanded, I present myself in person bearing even unto the grave my most lowly and servile submission.... It is the most precious moment of my life in which I am favored to pay my most profound respect toward the devout, Christ-loving divinely invincible Great Empress of the Russians (would that Ye be also of the Greeks!)....[58]

Voulgaris had come to the attention of the Russian court sometime in late 1769 or early 1770. In 1768, Voulgaris translated, from French into Greek, and published in Leipzig Voltaire's (whom he met in Leipzig) essay, *On the Dissensions within the Churches of Poland*. Voulgaris attached an essay of his own detailing the plight of the Eastern Orthodox believers in the Polish lands of eastern Europe and how their suffering paralleled that of their Orthodox brethren in Ottoman lands. Voltaire invited Voulgaris to Frederick the Great's court in Berlin where Frederick was much taken with Voulgaris's abilities and suggested to Catherine that she commission Voulgaris to translate her *Great Instruction* or *Nakaz* into Greek.[59]

Voulgaris was probably already known at the Russian court by this time because of his stay in Leipzig, where a good number of Russian youth received educations. Among those in Leipzig at the same time as Voulgaris (and Theotokis) was Alexander Radishchev, the famous philosopher and radical, who began a translation of Antonio Ghikas's *Supplications of the Greek Nation to Christian Europe*.[60] Voulgaris undertook the translation of the *Nakaz* from a French copy into Greek (he knew little or no Russian) and appended a dedication to Catherine and an introduction for Greek readers. In his dedication, Voulgaris lavished Catherine with praise and suggested that the worthy principles of the *Nakaz* be applied to the case of the "enslaved" Greeks and other nations of the same faith.[61] An interesting point regarding the invitation to Voulgaris to come to St. Petersburg was the group and milieu from which it originated. Undoubtedly the invitation was issued under the name of Catherine but her personal secretary Grigorii Kozitskii and Count Semon Naryshkin were responsible for recruiting him. Kozitskii was a graduate of the Kievan Theological Academy (formerly, the Mogilev Academy) and translator of the classics into Russian. His more immediate tie to contemporary Greece and her problems was his translation from modern Greek into Latin of an anti-Latin (i.e., western) track by a Greek bishop in the Peloponnesus, Ilias Miniatis (1669-1714).[62] Naryshkin and Kozitskii, aware of Russia's position in its war with the Ottomans and the importance of the Greek front, believed that Russia needed a learned man, such as Voulgaris, "for the sake of philhellenism."[63] Thus, Voulgaris's proposed service in Russia was to be mutually beneficial: Voulgaris would serve as a publicist of Russian aims in the "Levant" and as a spokesman for the Greek cause of liberation in St. Petersburg.

During his first few years in Russia, Voulgaris received numerous commissions to translate a variety of pamphlets, tracts, and essays pertaining to the Russo-Turkish War. He continued to translate the works of his acquaintance Voltaire and he translated from Italian the Ghikas tract.[64] Ghikas was another Greek who entered Russian service for the express purpose of hastening the movement toward a free Greece. Ghikas was born in Albania and was very prominent in the liberation movement in that region. He was given officer rank by Alexei Orlov and joined that expedition to the Morea. He maintained close ties with the Russians after the Battle of Chesme and at the end of the war visited Petersburg with General

Gannibal. In 1777-1778, he was nominated and confirmed in the post of councilor of the Russian embassy in Naples.[65] In a similar manner many other Greek Russophiles from Corsica to Corfu came to serve the interests of Russia and Greece.[66]

Voulgaris was also engaged in scholarly work of his own at this time and his essay, *Considerations on the Truly Critical Condition of the Ottoman Porte*, is regarded as his most noteworthy. *Considerations* was an analysis of a weak and declining empire, whose decay, according to Voulgaris, posed a serious "security" problem for the other European powers. Voulgaris's solution for this problem was the creation of an independent Greek principality which would be " 'a contribution to the balance of Europe'."[67] In this proposition the Phanariot dream of a renewed and reconstituted Byzantine Empire is quite visible, a vision with which Voulgaris was very familiar from his service in Constantinople. Unfortunately, the Phanariot dream was not to be realized anytime soon.

The conclusion of the Russo-Turkish War in July 1774, found Eugenios Voulgaris once again in the role of publicist. He published an ode celebrating the glorious peace of Kutchuk-Kainardji, a peace which proved so favorable to the Russians and to the Christian population of the defeated Ottoman Empire. Voulgaris's scholarly inclination was put to other uses as well by the Russian court. In the fall of 1774, Catherine was developing plans for the creation of a Greek Gymnasium in St. Petersburg which would educate and train the children of the Greek participants in the Orlov expedition for Russian service; and she seemed to have Voulgaris in mind as the school's director. The genesis of the school deserves a brief mention. Following the Battle of Chesme, Catherine established a Greek school on the island of Naxos, in order to combat the presence of a strong Catholic influence, in the Aegean[68] and in the Tuscan city of Pisa.[69] The termination of hostilities with Turkey in 1774 and the departure of the Russian fleet from the Mediterranean precipitated the removal of the two schools as well. The students presently attending the two gymnasia were transferred to Petersburg where they continued their studies and were subsequently joined by many others. Voulgaris, although he did not become director of the Greek Gymnasium, was involved in its curricular development. The students were to study Russian, German, French, Italian, Turkish, modern Greek, religion, arithmetic, algebra, geometry, geography, history, and even dancing.[70] As one can see, the proposed curriculum was in accordance with the precepts of an enlightened education and very similar in nature to that adopted by Theotokis in Greece. The school, which eventually came to be called the Corps of Foreigners of Like Faith, became very popular, had its own printing press, and was, for a time, directed by Grigorii Potemkin.

Voulgaris did not remain long in St. Petersburg. By the summer of 1775, Catherine was anxious to begin settling and incorporating Russia's newly acquired territories in the southern Ukraine which it had gained as a result of the Russo-Turkish War. Part of Catherine's plan to extend Russian control to this territory involved the establishment of new Russian Orthodox dioceses. Among the settlers of this area known as Novorossiia were thousands of Greeks who were fleeing the Ottoman Empire after the war. Catherine responded to their requests for a Greek prelate and offered Voulgaris the opportunity to serve Russia in the southern Ukraine along the northern shore of the Black Sea. Voulgaris grudgingly accepted the offer from Catherine which gave him the ecclesiastical rank of archbishop and necessitated his departure for Moscow to begin preparations for his duties in the new diocese of Slaviansk and Kherson. Voulgaris arrived at the headquarters of the new diocese in Poltava in October 1776 and within a month or two he was joined by his compatriot, Nikiforos Theotokis.

••••

On 21 July 1774 at the small Bulgarian village of Kutchuk-Kainardji "one of the most famous and important treaties in the history of European diplomacy" was signed by Russian and Turkish representatives.[71] The Treaty of Kutchuk-Kainardji was hastily ratified by Catherine in St. Petersburg in August 1774 but the Ottomans found the agreement not completely to their liking and delayed ratification at the instigation of the French without effect until January 1775. The treaty was not significant or notable for its territorial provisions but more so for the future implications of the concessions granted by the Porte in the realms of trade and religion.[72]

The Russians secured only a morsel of land situated between the Bug and Dnieper rivers but this area included the mouth of the Dnieper on the Black Sea. The Russian Empire now held, for the first time since Kievan Rus', land which touched the Black Sea. The

Ottoman Empire also ceded to Russia the Kuban and Terek areas east of the Black Sea, the fortress of Azov and the two fortresses which guarded the straits between the Sea of Azov and the Black Sea, and agreed to give its vassal state, the Khanate of the Crimea its independence. In return, the Russians withdrew from the Danubian Principalities and restored them to Turkish suzerainty with the stipulation that Russia would remain the guarantor of the two Principalities' political and religious privileges. Russia, however, evidently did not relinquish complete political control to the Ottomans because it was able to return the Greek Phanariot and former *hospodar* of Wallachia, Grigorios Ghikas, to the throne of Moldavia in September 1774. Ghikas spent most of the war years in St. Petersburg after his "capture" at the Battle of Chotzim in 1770.[73] We already know Ghikas as the patron of Theotokis and Voulgaris while he was Prince of Moldavia and later Wallachia, so little doubt need be entertained as to his ultimate loyalty in the Russo-Turkish struggle.

The appointment of Ghikas as prince of Moldavia represented a projection of Russian political influence into the Greek East that would be furthered by the establishment of Russian consulates to assist Russian merchants in the Ottoman Empire. Ghikas, as a Greek Phanariot, and other Greeks appointed to the new consulates as "interpreters," surely shared with the Russian court a vision of the Levant as a reinvented Greek empire. The commercial provisions of Kutchuk-Kainardji transformed the Black Sea from an Ottoman "lake" into a body of water that served equally the two signatories. Merchants were allowed to travel freely throughout Ottoman dominions and consulates and vice-consulates were established "in every place where the court of Russia may consider it expedient" to assist them.[74] The consulates gave Russia a measure of influence in the Ottoman Empire that it had never had before. Russia gained another notable concession when the Ottomans accepted Articles VII and XIV which allowed for the construction of a church of the "Greco-Russian" rite in Constantinople which would be under the protection of the appropriate ministries of the Russian Empire and the above ministries would have the right to remonstrate on behalf of the new church. These two articles would be liberally interpreted by Russia and serve as a pretext for subsequent Russian diplomatic intervention on behalf of not only the church in Constantinople but for the entire Christian population of the Ottoman Empire.[75] Taken together the commercial and religious clauses of Kutchuk-Kainardji set the stage

for expanded Russian involvement in the Greek East. The right of
Russian merchants to sail the Black Sea was the first step for future
Russian requests, demands, and threats to gain access to the Mediter-
ranean through the Bosporus and Dardanelles. And the Danubian
Principalities could serve as a springboard to deeper Russian political
and military forays into the Balkan Peninsula. All of the above were
ingredients for continued conflict between the Ottoman and Russian
Empires.

Although the Russian Empire failed in its half-hearted attempt
to liberate the Balkan Christians and abandoned its earlier demand
for an Aegean island to serve as a permanent naval base, the Russians
attempted to assuage the Orthodox Christians in the Balkans by
adding a number of beneficial provisions to the treaty. In two
separate articles, the Christian population of the Principalities and
the Greek Archipelago were to be free from Turkish retribution,
oppression, and taxes. Those individuals who believed that their
participation in the events surrounding the Russo-Turkish War
endangered them and their families were free to leave within the
next year and settle in lands outside the Ottoman Empire for a period
of one year.[76] Thousands of Greeks, Albanians, and Serbs already
had fled the Ottoman Empire and now thousands more departed for
the newly acquired lands of southern Russia to seek refuge from
Turkish retribution. It was these Orthodox Christians, mainly
Greeks, for whom Voulgaris had been called upon to minister in
Novorossiia in 1775.

••••

The settlement of foreigners itself on Russian soil was not an
eighteenth-century development, but the intensity at which it
proceeded distinguished it from its antecedents. Beginning with the
reign of Ivan the Great in the fifteenth century foreigners were
invited to Muscovy to lend technical advice and assistance in those
areas Muscovites were deficient and develop commercial contacts
with the West and East. The foreigners were restricted geographically to the "German Suburb" in Moscow and a few other trading
cities. By the middle of the seventeenth century Moscow directed its
attention to the needs of its southern border regions.[77] Following the
Union of Pereiaslavl (1654), which recognized a "union" between
Muscovy and the Ukrainian Cossacks, and the Treaty of Andrusovo

(1667), Muscovy became exceedingly involved in the affairs of the Cossack Hetmanate (eventually undermining and dissolving it)[78] and concerned about a new frontier under its protection which extended even farther to the south and abutted the Crimean Tatar territory. For the Muscovites, then, the Union with the Ukraine opened new vistas for economic growth, brought it closer to the Black Sea and presented Moscow with an intractable security problem for its expanding southern borderlands. The borderlands presented Russia with certain conditions which persistently affected not only foreign policy but domestic policy as well. One of these conditions was a permeable or porous frontier on the periphery of the empire's power, which can be defined as a "double frontier."[79] That is, the borderlands were ethnically mixed and presented no clear demarcation of "Russian" and "non-Russian" absolutes. Political boundaries, arbitrarily drawn, reflected nothing more than the workings of distant tsars and sultans. Even colonization efforts proved problematic because the colonists were not always or only Russian.

Muscovite and Ukrainian authorities encouraged the growth of foreign communities in eastern Ukraine basically for the same reasons as mentioned above: commercial development and technical assistance. However, other considerations deemed important in deciding whether to accept certain merchants were religious and political. Because of the volatile political situation in the Ukraine in the late seventeenth century and its proximity to Catholic and Uniate Poland and the Muslim Porte, it was extremely important that merchants and traders who provided connections with western markets not be anything but Orthodox. The Greek Brotherhood (*bratstva*) of Nezhin, which emerged as a major commercial group in the 1680s, was acceptable to the authorities because of its trade contacts with the West, its travel privileges within the Ottoman Empire and its adherence to Orthodoxy.[80] The importance of the Greek Brotherhood and other similar associations in fostering economic growth in the Ukraine was exhibited by their receipt of fiscal and political privileges to ensure their continued presence.[81]

The precedent of encouraging foreign settlements of co-religionists in the southern Ukraine in the seventeenth century for commercial purposes made future settlements of foreign military units seem not the least unusual. The Serbs who had joined Peter the Great in his failed Pruth campaign of 1711 were granted the right to settle as a military colony in the southern Ukraine.[82] By the early

1750s, three regiments of "Serbs" were employed along the southern borders.[83] On 11 January 1752, Empress Elizabeth granted a charter to the Serbian major-general Ivan Khorvat of Austria and his regiment of Serbs, Macedonians, Wallachians, and Bulgarians, all of the Orthodox faith. The decree allotted land to them for the creation of military colonies on the Zaporozhian "Free Lands" on the right bank; territory, which was for the first time, called Novoserbiia or New Serbia.[84] The empress also took care to protect her new immigrants physically and spiritually. The Tatars represented a serious threat to the new settlers so a fortress was to be built in Novoserbiia named after the protectress herself, St. Elizabeth. The Orthodox faithful were to be protected spiritually by provisions which called for the presence of Orthodox priests and the construction of churches and schools.[85]

The apparent success and good fortune of the Khorvat colony attracted the attention of other like-minded Habsburg subjects the following year.[86] In 1753, two other ethnic Serbs in the service of the Habsburg Empire expressed their desire to settle in the southern Ukraine to the Russian ambassador in Vienna. Ioann Shevich and Raiko Preradovich and their followers were accorded similar treatment by the Russian Senate when they were granted the right to settle as military colonists on the lands on the left bank of the Dnieper to be known as Slavianoserbiia with an administrative center in Bakhmut.[87] The military effectiveness of the colonies has been a contentious issue between Russian and Ukrainian scholars. Russian historians claim that the colonies provided satisfactory protection in the borderlands and they contributed regiments for the Seven Years' War. Ukrainian historians call into question the effectiveness of the military colonies and argue that their main purpose was to disrupt and destabilize Ukrainian society (Khorvat was exiled in the early 1760s for his lawless activities) thereby requiring additional Russian intervention.

Still other new settlements continued to follow the old practice of serving as commercial and business centers with contacts in the West and the Greek East. In 1754, a number of Greek merchants and businessmen formed a community in the area immediately surrounding the fortress of St. Elizabeth or Elizavetgrad. The community numbered around fifty with most of the inhabitants coming from Macedonia and a few from the Greek Archipelago, Constantinople, Venice and Nezhin. The small community was given permission to construct its own church and was granted limited autonomy in ecclesiastical and civic matters.[88] The Greek community was self-governing and had an elected town council but its authority was circumscribed by the mayor who was appointed by the fortress commander.

The allowance of limited autonomy at the local level was indicative of the means by which the Ukraine as a whole was administered. The hetmanate had lapsed in 1734 but was restored in 1751 by a decree issued by Elizabeth which placed Kyrill Razumovskii in the post of hetman. This act was intended to mollify the Ukrainian and Cossack elite or *starshiny* by giving them the ostensible appearance of political autonomy, yet the "election" of Razumovskii was engineered by Elizabeth and the hetman existed by her sufferance. Thus, Russia was beginning to bring order and its own brand of control to the southern borderlands through the office of the hetmanate and the Ukrainian elite who supported it, the creation of foreign military colonies among the indigenous Ukrainian population, and the continued growth of commercial settlements.

Parallel to the incipient political integration of the Ukraine in the 1750s was the movement toward ecclesiastical hegemony by the Russian Orthodox Church. This, also, was a continuation of an evolving policy begun in the late seventeenth century when the Left-Bank clergy and Metropolitan Gedeon of Kiev agreed to transfer the Ukrainian Orthodox Church from the jurisdiction of the patriarch of Constantinople to the patriarch of Moscow in 1686. At the root of this action was the fear of further losses to the Polish Uniates who exercised control over the Right Bank. In the mid-eighteenth century Elizabeth endeavored to secure more direct ecclesiastical control over the colonists by transferring their churches to Russian dioceses. Novoserbiia initially was under the jurisdiction of the metropolitan of Kiev, but was moved to the Russian diocese of Pereiaslavl in 1756. Likewise, the territory of Slavianoserbiia was subject to the Russian diocese of Voronezh.[89] It was also important to St. Petersburg that the new colonists not only be loyal Orthodox subjects but that they conform to the existing diocesan structure. Khorvat, exhibiting his independence, wished to create his own Serbian diocese in 1760, but his petition was rejected by the Holy Synod on the grounds that there were too few inhabitants to warrant a new one.[90] The empress and her government were not about to tolerate extraterritorial control or limitless autonomy within the realms of religion or local government.

With the accession of Catherine to the throne, the two new settlements of Novoserbiia and Slavianoserbiia were subject to the same programs of centralization and uniformity which Catherine initiated for all Russia in the early 1760s. Catherine, in particular, was concerned with the degree of autonomy exercised by the border-land regions of the Baltics and the Ukraine.[91] Compelled by a desire and need for security, administrative efficiency and economic productivity Catherine, true to her enlightened ideals, introduced measures, in accordance with the cameralism and mercantilism of her day (i.e., "to maximize society's economic and cultural potential, so as to expand its wealth and power"), to bring greater social and cultural uniformity to the diverse Russian Empire.[92] Thus, the hurried attempts of hetman Razumovskii in 1763 to secure the hetmanate as hereditary in the Razumovskii family and establish Little Russia as an autonomous, separate land in dynastic union with Russia ran contrary to Catherine's goals. In early 1764, Catherine forced Kyrill Razumovskii to resign from the office of hetman, abolished the hetmanate (which had been under the College of Foreign Affairs) and created the Little Russian College under the presidency of P.A. Rumiantsev in late 1764. Catherine's first move against the territorial integrity of Little Russia took place in early 1764 at the same time she was trying to remove Razumovskii. In June 1764 the province of Novorossiia was created by integrating the settlements of Novoserbiia and Slavianoserbiia with Slobodska Ukraine.[93] The creation of this province was part of a plan by A. P. Mel'gunov and the Panin brothers to rid themselves of the trouble-some Khorvat and to stabilize this sensitive border area by allowing for more settlement.

Catherine continued the program begun under Elizabeth to reduce the autonomy of the Ukrainian Orthodox Church while advancing the interests of the Russian Orthodox Church (really Catherine's interests masquerading as the Church's). At times this happened in a rather circuitous manner. For example, when Catherine resuscitated the dormant issue of secularizing monastic estates in November 1762 she encountered some resistance. The most vocal critic of Catherine's attempt to reintroduce Peter III's secular-ization program was the metropolitan of Rostov, Arsenii Matseevich, who was born in Ukraine and educated at the Kievan Academy.[94]

Arsenii's vociferous opposition to the proposed secularization was founded on his objection that the clergy would become nothing more than paid servants of the state and the loss of personal property or serfs (the metropolitan possessed no less than 16,000 souls.).[95] The forces arrayed against him (secular and ecclesiastical) were great but he persisted in decrying the Church's involvement in such matters as teaching philosophy, mathematics and astronomy when it should be teaching the word of God. He even suggested that Ivan Antonovich (imprisoned at the mere age of one by Empress Elizabeth in 1741) was the rightful heir to the throne. Ultimately, he was found guilty of *lèse majesté* and sentenced, at first, to monastic confinement and, ultimately, a prison where he died in 1772.[96] Ever cognizant of the value of symbol and performance, Catherine was compelled to punish the archbishop precisely because his attacks were only "verbal" denunciations. She chose this moment as the opportune time to undertake a pilgrimage (by foot!) to Rostov to pray at the recently opened shrine of the miracle-inducing remains of St. Dmitrii of Rostov. Catherine's pilgrimage was a grand performance clearly intended to demonstrate her religiosity and love for the people as well as symbolize the imperial reach of the center.[97]

Catherine interpreted the ugly incident with Arsenii as an expression of Little Russian reluctance to reject the "Latin" concept of separation of church and state which places the church in the dominant position and, subsequently, began systematically removing ethnic Ukrainians from high episcopal office and replacing them with Great Russians.[98] Catherine did refrain from secularizing Church lands in the Ukraine until late in her reign (1786) but in the mean time she wished no semblance of an independent ecclesiastical structure to remain for long in the Ukraine. In a related matter, Arsenii Mohylian'skii, the Kievan metropolitan, was embroiled in a dispute with the Holy Synod in the early 1760s over his right to retain the title "Metropolitan of Kiev and all Little Russia" and he encouraged the idea of an autonomous "Little Russian Church." The Synod ruled against Metropolitan Arsenii and forbade him to include "Little Russia" in his title.[99] Catherine's secular and sacred encroachments on Ukrainian and Cossack autonomy were certainly emblematic of a long-term program of imperial expansion and consolidation which did not bode well for an independent Ukraine or free Cossacks, but which was deemed essential if the southern steppe was to be secured.

••••

The conclusion of the Russo-Turkish War in 1774, followed by the quelling of the peasant revolt and capture of Pugachev in late 1774, allowed Catherine once again to concentrate on domestic matters. The intensity and breadth of the Pugachev revolt profoundly affected Catherine and dramatized for her the necessity of more domestic reform to integrate the empire and stabilize the border-lands.[100] Catherine had planned to reform local government since her accession and now the opportunity presented itself. Aided by able advisers such as Jacob Sievers, Governor of Novgorod, she drafted and issued the decree on the Institution of the Administration of the Provinces of the Russian Empire in November 1775.[101] Catherine not only intended to enhance local government by sending more centrally appointed officials to the provinces but also to enlist the local nobility in their own self-governance. The new administrative system was divided into 41 provinces (*gubernii*) with each *guberniia* led by a governor who was assisted by appointed officials in such areas as civil, criminal, financial and social administration. Gentry assemblies elected local officials (*kapitan- ispravnik*) who received a salary and rank and dealt with public welfare, fiscal, police and judicial matters at the district (*uezd*) level. The decree also promised doctors and pharmacies for each district in the province.[102]

Catherine hoped the provincial gentry would, by their involvement in the new institutions, gain an appreciation for justice and virtue, and, in time, reflect her own desire to work for and en-hance the general welfare of all her citizens. The provincial reforms were also another example of Catherine taking on the role of Minerva and bringing the benefits of reason and improved material life to the periphery. Each provincial capital reproduced the imperial capital. The governor-general (*namestnik*), who was usually respon-sible for two to four provinces, was Catherine's personal emissary to the provinces. His arrival was an occasion for festivals and celebra-tions. As the provincial nobility formed a ceremonial bond with the court at St. Petersburg, Catherine extended her reform program and her concept of Russia into the provinces.[103]

NOTES

1. Cited in Mourouti-Gkenakou, p. 41.
2. *Ibid.*
3. *Ibid.*
4. Paranikas, p. 111.
5. Dimitri Obolensky, *The Byzantine Commonwealth: Eastern Europe, 500-1453* (London, 1971); idem, *Byzantium and the Slavs: Collected Essays* (London, 1971); and idem, *Six Byzantine Portraits* (New York, 1988)
6. On Greek-Slavic relations in the post-Byzantine period, see B.L. Fonkich, *Grechesko-russkie kulturnye sviazi v XV-XVII vv: grecheskie rukopisi v Rossii* (Moscow, 1977); idem, "Russia and the Christian East from the Sixteenth to the First Quarter of the Eighteenth Century," *Modern Greek Studies Yearbook*, 7 (1991):439-61; N.F. Kapterev, *Kharakter otnoshenii Rossii k pravoslavnomu vostoku XVI I XVII st.* (Moscow, 1885); B.N. Floria, ed., *Sviazi Rossii s narodami Balkanskogo poluostrova. Pervaia polovina XVII v.* (Moscow, 1990); idem, "Greki-emigranty v Russkom gosudarstve vtoroi poloviny XV-nachala XVI v. Politicheskaia i kul'turnaia deiatel'nost'," in *Russko-balkanskie kul'turnye sviazi v epokhu srednevekov'ia* (Sofia, 1982), pp. 123-43; idem, "Vykhodtsy iz balkanskikh stran na russkoi sluzhbe (konets XVI-nachalo XVII v.)," *Balkanskie issledovaniia*, 3 (1978): 57-63; Iaroslav Isaievych, "Greek Culture in the Ukraine: 1550-1650," *Modern Greek Studies Yearbook*, 6 (1990): 97-122; Gustaf Alev, "Diaspora Greeks in Muscovy," *Byzantine Studies*, 6 (1975): 26-34; Robert Croskey, "Byzantine Greeks in Late-Fifteenth- and Early Sixteenth-Century Russia," in Lowell Clucas, ed., *The Byzantine Legacy in Eastern Europe* (Boulder, 1988), pp. 33-56; M.N. Tikhomirov, "Greki iz Morei v srednevekovoi Rossii," *Srednie veka*, 25 (1964): 166-75; Theofanis G. Stavrou and Peter R. Weisensel, *Russian Travelers to the Christian East from the Twelfth to the Twentieth Century* (Columbus, OH, 1986); and N.K. Storozhevskii, *Nezhinskie greki* (Kiev, 1863).
7. N.V. Sinitsyna, *Maksim Grek v Rossii* (Moscow, 1977); Hugh M. Olmsted, "A Learned Greek Monk in Muscovite Exile: Maksim Grek and the Old Testament Prophets," *Modern Greek Studies Yearbook*, 3 (1987): 1-73; and idem, "Maxim Grek's 'Letter to Prince Petr Shuiskii': The Greek and Russian Texts," *Modern Greek Studies Yearbook*, 5 (1989):267-319.
8. James H. Billington, *The Icon and the Axe: An Interpretive History of Russian Culture* (New York, 1966), pp. 90-91.
9. Medlin and Patrinelis, p. 44.
10. The nineteenth-century Russian historian, bibliophile, and traveler to the Greek East, A.N. Murav'ev, places the *raskol* or schism entirely within the context of the Greek East in his *Raskol' oblichaemii svoeiu istorieiu* (St. Petersburg, 1854). He makes a direct link between Maxim Grek's activities and the controversial reforms of Nikon in the opening pages of his book and concludes it with an analysis of Theotokis's initiation of *edinoverie* (i.e., union in faith between the Old Believers or Schismatics and the Church).
11. For a recent biography of Arsenios see Christos P. Laskaridis, *O Arsenios o Graikos kai i Mosha (17os Aionas)* (Ioannina, 1988) and the article by Maria Kotzamanidou, "The Greek Monk Arsenios and His Humanist Activities in Seventeenth-Century Russia," *Modern Greek Studies Yearbook*, 2 (1986): 73-88.
12. Kotzamanidou, p. 75.
13. For a listing of the more important works see Kotzamanidou, pp. 83-84.
14. On the latest biographical information, see B.L. Fonkich, "Novye materialy dlia biografii Likhudov," *Pamiatniki kul'tury. Novye otkrytia* (Moscow, 1987), pp. 61-70.

15. For a history of the Academy, see Sergei Smirnov, *Istoriia Moskovskoi Slaviano-Greko-Latinskoi Akademii* (Moscow, 1855).

16. Vucinich, p. 24.; Billington, pp. 164-168.

17. Robert Croskey, 33-56.

18. For an introduction to this period in Russo-Turkish relations see B.H. Sumner, *Peter the Great and the Ottoman Empire* (Hamden, 1965).

19. One of the East's most trenchant commentators and defenders of Orthodoxy, Patriarch Dositheos of Jerusalem, leveled this salvo at the Russians: "The Crimean Tatars are but a handful and they boast that they receive tribute from you. The Tatars are Turkish subjects, so it follows that you are Turkish subjects. Many times you have boasted that you will do such and such, but...nothing in fact is done." Cited in Sumner, p. 17.

20. Franco Venturi, *The End of the Old Regime in Europe, 1768-1776. The First Crisis* (Princeton, 1989), p. 5.

21. On the domestic decisions leading to the Principalities actions see Peter F. Sugar, *Southeastern Europe under Ottoman Rule, 1354-1804* (Seattle, 1977), pp. 113-132.

22. Some later entered the service of Elizabeth as military colonists in "New Serbia." A precedent followed by Greeks after the failed Orlov expedition of 1770 (see below).

23. This work is attributed to Theokletos Polyeides (c. 1690-c.1759) an Athonite monk, who traveled extensively in central Europe, where he founded the Greek Orthodox church in Leipzig, and Russia. *Agathangelos* was reprinted in *Eranistis*, VII, 42 (1969): 173-192.

24. For an intriguing analysis of the emergence of this myth and its subsequent transformation from a universalist vision to an ideology for modern Greek nationalism patterned after the Russian experience see John Nicolopoulos, "From Agathangelos to the Megale Idea: Russia and the Emergence of Modern Greek Nationalism," *Balkan Studies*, 26:1 (1985): 42-56.

25. For the early period of the Eastern Question see Albert Sorel, *The Eastern Question in the Eighteenth Century: The Partition of Poland and the Treaty of Kainardji*, English edition (London, 1898). For a general survey of subsequent events see M.S. Anderson, *The Eastern Question, 1774-1923* (New York, 1966) and V.A. Georgiev, et al., *Vostochnyi vopros.*

26. Sorel, p. 10.

27. On eighteenth-century Russian interest in classicism see Stephen L. Baehr, "From History to National Myth: *Translatio imperii* in Eighteenth-Century Russia," *The Russian Review*, 37:1 (January 1978): 1-13; idem, *The Paradise Myth in Eighteenth-Century Russia: Utopian Patterns in Early Secular Literature and Culture* (Stanford, 1991); Harold B. Segel, "Classicism and Classical Antiquity in Eighteenth- and Early Nineteenth-Century Russian Literature," in John G. Garrard, ed., *The Eighteenth Century in Russia* (Oxford, 1973), pp. 48-71; P.N. Cherniaev, *Sledy znakomstva drevne-klassicheskoi literatury v veke Ekateriny II* (Voronezh, 1906); idem, *Rossiiu svedenii ob antichnom mire* (Voronezh, 1911); and Wortman, *Scenarios of Power*, pp. 84-146. Most of the authors cited above conclude that Russians consciously adopted a classical Roman approach to literature and empire. For interpretations which suggest that Russians were more thoroughly committed to the classical Greek tradition see Theophilus C. Prousis, *Russian Society and the Greek Revolution* (DeKalb, IL, 1994), pp. 84-88 and Boris Gasparov, "Russkaia Gretsiia, russkii Rim," in Robert P. Hughes and Irina Paperno, eds., *Christianity and the Eastern Slavs. Volume II: Russian Culture and Modern Times* (California Slavic Studies, XVII, Berkeley, 1994), pp. 245-285.

28. Cited in Wortman, p. 110.

29. Batalden, pp. 23-4.

30. Gasparov, pp. 249-253.

31. Her courtiers translated several articles from the *Encyclopédie* which dealt directly with Greece. For a short list see Batalden, p. 24.

32. Elizabeth Lady Craven, *A Journey through the Crimea to Constantinople* (London, 1789), p. 132.

33. For a revisionist account of Peter III and how his reputation suffered abysmally at the hands of Catherine, see Carol S. Leonard, "The Reputation of Peter III," *The Russian Review*, 47:3 (July 1988): 263-292 and *Reform and Regicide: The Reign of Peter III of Russia* (Bloomington, IN, 1992).

34. For an excellent analysis of "party" politics in Catherinian Russia see David Ransel, *The Politics of Catherinian Russia: The Panin Party* (New Haven, 1975).

35. Voulgaris made apparent the connection between the religious persecution of Orthodox believers in Poland and the Ottoman Empire when he published a translation from French into Greek of Voltaire's *On the Dissensions within the Churches of Poland* in 1768 in Leipzig. Batalden, p. 16.

36. On Poland at this time see Herbert Kaplan, *The First Partition of Poland* (New York, 1962) and Norman Davies, *God's Playground: A History of Poland*, 2 vols. (New York, 1982).

37. On the strange events in Montenegro see Michael B. Petrovich, "Catherine II and a False Peter III in Montenegro," *Slavic Review*, 14:2 (April 1955): 169-194.

38. Tasos A. Gritsopoulos, *Ta Orlofika* (Athens, 1967). Also on Greek involvement in the Russo-Turkish War of 1768-1774 see P.M. Kontoyiannis, *Oi Ellines kata ton proton epi Aikaterinis B' rossotourkikon polemon, 1768-1774* (Athens, 1903); E.V. Tarle, *Chesmenskii boi i pervaia ekspeditsiia v Arkhipelag, 1769-1774* (Moscow, 1945); S.S. Dmitriev, *Chesmenskaia pobeda* (Moscow, 1945); and V.I. Sinitsa, " Vosstanie v Moree 1770 i Rossiia," *Voprosy novoi i noveishei istorii* (Minsk, 1974): 12-21.

39. Harvouris is credited with bringing the material for the base of Falconet's statue of Peter the Great to Russia from Cephalonia. Petros Melissinos was the "remaker of the Russian artillery and leading member of the Masonic movement in St. Petersburg." See Venturi, pp. 69-70.

40. *Istoria tou Ellinikou Ethnous*, vol. ia', p. 59.

41. Grigorii Orlov's expression; Solov'ev, vol. 28, p. 284.

42. In Gritsopoulos and *Istoria tou Ellinikou Ethnous*, Papazolis is considered an agent of Grigorii Orlov and Sarros an agent of Alexei Orlov, however, Batalden has found archival material that indicates that both were agents of Grigorii. See Batalden, p. 118, n. 57.

43. *Istoria*, p. 60.

44. *Ibid.*

45. For a listing of some of the individuals present and their later service in the Russian diplomatic corps in the Mediterranean, see Batalden, p. 26.

46. *Istoria*, p. 61.

47. Solov'ev, v. 28, p. 284.

48. *Ibid.*, p. 304.

49. See A.G. Cross, "Samuel Grieg, Catherine the Great's Scottish Admiral," *Mariner's Mirror*, 60 (1976): 251-266.

50. Voltaire to Catherine, 30 October 1769; Cited in Antony Lentin, ed., *Voltaire and Catherine the Great. Selected Correspondence* (Cambridge, 1974), p. 69.

51. Venturi, p. 45, n. 10.

52. Catherine to Voltaire, 9 November 1769; Lentin, p. 70.

53. Venturi, p. 40.

54. Prousis, p. 88.

55. Voltaire to Catherine, 25 October 1770; Lentin, p. 90.

56. Catherine to Voltaire, 4/5 December 1770; Lentin, pp. 93-4.

57. In many respects, the incorporation of foreign elites into Russian service is a continuation of the Byzantine practice of co-opting local leaders as the first step in the long process of integrating newly acquired territories and their inhabitants. See Obolensky, *The Byzantine Commonwealth.*

58. Batalden, pp. 22-3.

59. The *Nakaz* already existed in German, French, English and Latin translations. Wortman, p. 122.

60. D.M. Lang, *The First Russian Radical, Alexander Radishchev, 1749-1802* (London, 1959), p. 61. The Radishchev version was published only after his death, but an earlier Russian translation by Pisarev was published in the 8 August 1771 edition of *Sanktpeterburgskie vedomosti*, supplement to #65. See Venturi, p. 103 and Batalden, p. 120, n. 71.

61. Batalden, p. 19.

62. *Ibid.*, p. 20.

63. Excerpt from a letter from Naryshkin to Kozitskii, cited by Batalden, p. 21.

64. *Ibid.*, p. 29.

65. *Sbornik imperatorskogo russkogo istoricheskogo obshchestva* (hereafter *SIRIO*), vol. 154, pp. 410-11.

66. For a general discussion of the response of the southern European countries to the Greek revolt see Venturi, pp. 74-153.

67. Batalden, p. 30.

68. *Istoria*, p. 80.

69. Venturi, p. 104.

70. *Ibid.*, p. 104, n. 6; Batalden, p. 30-1.

71. M. S. Anderson, p. xi.

72. On the religious clauses see Roderic Davison, "'Russian Skill and Turkish Imbecility': The Treaty of Kuchuk-Kainardji Reconsidered," *Slavic Review*, 25, no. 3 (1976): 463-484.

73. William Richardson, *Anecdotes of the Russian Empire* (London, 1784, repr., 1968), pp. 309-13. Richardson was quite impressed by Ghikas, especially by his linguistic erudition and his noble stature. It was Richardson who believed that Ghikas was a captive of the Russians and commiserated with him over his position as a Greek in service to the Sultan. Richardson also showed diplomatic prescience when he commented that "perhaps the sovereigns of Russia would not be sorry to see...the ancient provinces of Dacia erected into what they might be pleased to term independent Dukedoms or Principalities."

74. E.I. Druzhinina, *Kiuchuk-Kainardzhiiskii mir* (Moscow, 1955), Appendix #3, p. 353, Article XI.

75. *Ibid.*, pp. 352-354, Articles VII and XIV.

76. *Ibid.*, pp. 354-5, Articles XVI and XVII.

77. For studies on the frontier in earlier periods, see Michael Khodarkovsky, *Where Two Worlds Met: The Russian State and the Kalmyk Nomads, 1600-1771* (Ithaca, 1992); Joseph L. Wieczynski, *The Russian Frontier: The Impact of the Borderlands upon the Course of Early Russian History* (Charlottesville, VA, 1976); Judith Pallot and Denis J.B. Shaw, *Landscape and Settlement in Romanov Russia, 1613-1917* (Oxford, 1990), pp. 13-78; and *Russian History*, 19:1-4 (1992), which is entirely dedicated to "The Frontier in Russian History."

78. On the varied interpretations of this Union see Orest Subtelny, *Ukraine: A History* (Toronto, 1988), pp. 134-6.

79. For elaboration on these persistent conditions see, Alfred J. Rieber, "Persistent Factors in Russian Foreign Policy: An Interpretive Essay," in Hugh Ragsdale, ed., *Imperial Russian Foreign Policy* (New York, 1993), pp. 315-359; and idem, "Struggles Over the Borderlands," in S. Frederick Starr, ed., *The Legacy of History in Russia and the New States of Eurasia* (Armonk, NY, 1994), pp. 61-89.

80. The brotherhoods also established schools which assisted the Orthodox revival in Ukraine and created a bulwark against Catholic and Protestant advances. See Ol'ga B. Strakhov, "Attitudes to Greek Language and Culture in Seventeenth-Century Muscovy," *Modern Greek Studies Yearbook*, 6 (1990): 123-156; Iaroslav Isaievych, *op. cit.*; and K.V. Kharlampovich, *Zapadnorusskie pravoslavnye shkoly XVI i nachala XVII v.* (Kazan, 1898).

81. These privileges were reconfirmed by successive political leaders in the Ukraine and in Russia. On 7 May 1775 Catherine issued an ukase doing just that. N.V. Storozhenko, "K istorii nezhinskikh grekov," *Kievskaia starina*, 29 (1890:6): 541.

82. A.A. Skal'kovskii, *Khronologicheskoe obozreniie istorii Novorossiiskago kraia*, vol. I, pp. 15-16.

83. "Serb" is descriptively inclusive of almost all Balkan Christians whether Slav or Greek.

84. N.D. Polons'ka-Vasylenko, "The Settlement of the Southern Ukraine, 1750-1775," in *Annals of the Ukrainian Academy of Arts and Sciences in the U.S.*, vols. IV-V (New York, 1955): 45.

85. N. Nevodchikov, *Evgenii Bulgaris: Arkhiepiskop Khersonskii i Slavianskii* (Odessa, 1875), pp. 16-17.

86. According to a report filed by the Russian Ambassador Obreskov from Constantinople on 22 June 1752 the excitement was not restricted to Habsburg lands: "One cannot depict the joyous exclamation with which the news of New Serbia has been received among all the Orthodox Christian nationalities." Cited in Roger P. Bartlett, *Human Capital: The Settlement of Foreigners in Russia, 1762-1804* (Cambridge, 1979), p. 271, n. 25.

87. Skal'kovskii, p. 25.

88. V.N. Iastrebov, "Greki v Elisavetgrade, 1754-1777," *Kievskaia starinia*, 2 (1884): 673-4.

89. Skal'kovskii, p. 32.

90. *Ibid.*

91. On the Baltics see Edward C. Thaden, *Russia's Western Borderlands, 1710-1870* (Princeton, 1985) and on the Ukraine see Zenon Kohut, *Russian Centralism and Ukrainian Autonomy* (Cambridge, 1988).

92. Marc Raeff, "Uniformity, Diversity, and the Imperial Administration in the Reign of Catherine II," *Osteuropa in Geschichte und Gegenwart: Festschrift für Gunther Stokl zum 60. Geburtstag* (Cologne, 1977), pp. 98-9. On the colonization, stabilization, and integration of the southern borderlands see Marc Raeff, "The Style of Russia's Imperial Policy and Prince G.A. Potemkin," in G.N. Grob, ed., *Statesmen and Statecraft of the Modern West: Essays in Honor of Dwight E. Lee and H. Donaldson Jordan* (Barre, MA, 1967), pp. 1-51; idem, "Patterns of Russian Imperial Policy Toward the Nationalities," in E. Allworth, ed., *Soviet Nationality Problems* (New York, 1971), pp. 22-42; E.I. Druzhinina, *Severnoe prichernomore v 1775-1780 gg.* (Moscow, 1959); Dmitrii I. Bagalei, *Kolonizatsiia Novorossiiskogo kraia i pervye shagi po puti kul'tury* (Kiev, 1889); Roger P. Bartlett, *Human Capital*; V.M. Kabuzan, *Zaselenie Novorossii (Ekaterinoslavskoi i Khersonskoi gubernii) v XVIII-pervoi polovine XIX veka, 1719-1858 gg.* (Moscow, 1979); John LeDonne, *Ruling Russia: Politics and Administration in the Age of Absolutism, 1762-1796* (Princeton, 1984), pp. 289-304; G.G. Pisarevskii, *Iz istorii inostrannoi kolonizatsii v Rossii v XVIII v.* (Moscow, 1909); E.A. Zagorovskii, *Ekonomicheskaia politika Potemkina v*

Novorossii, 1774-1791 (Odessa, 1926); idem, *Organizatsiia upravleniia Novorossii pri Potemkine* (Odessa, 1913); idem, *Voennaia kolonizatsiia Novorossii pri Potemkine* (Odessa, 1913); and James A. Duran, Jr., "Catherine II, Potemkin, and Colonization Policy in Southern Russia," *The Russian Review*, 28 (January 1969): 23-36.

93. Skal'kovskii, pp. 62-4.

94. I. Znamenskii, *Polozhenie dukhovenstva v tsarstvovanie Ekateriny II i Pavla I* (Moscow, 1880), pp. 45-7.

95. Many Ukrainian hierarchs considered themselves to be nobles, contrary to the Russian notion that all churchmen belonged to the clerical estate. See Kohut, pp. 162-166.

96. A. Kartashev, *Ocherki po istorii russkoi tserkvi* (Paris, 1859), p. 478; and de Madariaga, pp. 113-117.

97. Wortman, pp. 121-122.

98. K.A. Papmehl, *Metropolitan Platon of Moscow* (Newtonville, MA, 1983), p. 21.

99. Kohut, pp. 222-3.

100. Unfortunately, Catherine failed to recognize that the problems with the borderland populations were, for the most part, a manifestation of popular resentment engendered by her earlier centralizing reforms. See Marc Raeff, "Pugachev's Rebellion," in Robert Forster and Jack Greene, eds., *Preconditions of Revolution in Early Modern Europe* (Baltimore, 1970), pp. 161-202.

101. *Polnoe sobranie zakonov rossiiskoi imperii* (hereafter *PSZ*), no. 14,392 (7 November 1775). On Sievers see Robert E. Jones, *Provincial Development in Russia: Catherine II and Jacob Sievers* (New Brunswick, NJ, 1984).

102. Robert E. Jones, *The Emancipation of the Russian Nobility, 1762-1785* (Princeton, 1973),pp. 244-272.

103. Wortman, p. 130

3

REDEMPTION AND EDUCATION ON THE SOUTHERN FRONTIER

There is a school in Poltava in which the youth are able to remove the fat of ignorance and implant in themselves the first roots of education.[1]
– Archbishop Nikiforos to the Taganrog Greeks

One of Catherine's first acts in regard to the southern border-lands after 1774 was to name Prince Grigorii A. Potemkin as viceroy or governor-general (*namestnik*) of Novorossiia *guberniia* in 1774 and then, governor-general of the newly created *guberniia* of Azov in 1775. With the conclusion of the Russo-Turkish War and the acceptance of the Treaty of Kutchuk-Kainardji, Russia took the opportunity to dissolve the Zaporozhian Cossack Host, long a buffer between Russia and the Crimea. The now independent Crimea no longer posed the looming threat it had previously and thus Catherine could afford to eliminate the Host in 1775. The former lands of the Zaporozhian Host were absorbed by Governor-General Potemkin into Novorossiia as part of the reorganization and consolidation of the southern borderlands as were the recently acquired former Turkish territories between the Bug and the Dnieper rivers. Potemkin also believed strongly that "it is essential to strengthen the defence of [the boundaries] by the addition of such a number of troops as not only should provide protection for the settlement of Azov and Novorossiia *gubernii* **by people of different nations...**," but defend the borders from attack as well.[2] Potemkin and Catherine intended to reinforce the political and military con-solidation of the new provinces by placing them within a single ecclesiastical jurisdiction.[3] The single spiritual jurisdiction would serve to unite the "people of different nations" because, even though they differed ethnically and linguistically, they shared a common faith: Orthodoxy.

One group of foreign colonists that Potemkin undoubtedly had in mind when he was considering the organization of Novorossiia was the Greeks. In accordance with the germane articles of the Treaty of Kutchuk-Kainardji, Greeks who had served with the

Russian forces in the Archipelago were allowed to emigrate to Russia for their own protection. In the summer of 1774, the so-called Spartan Legionnaires sent a deputation to Alexei Orlov, then residing in Pisa, to lay before him their plight. Orlov responded to them by letter on 2 September 1774 that "those among you who desire to continue in the service of Her Imperial Majesty and to migrate to Russia" can do so. And he added that the Russians would never forget the service rendered to them during the war.[4] The legionnaires reciprocated by sending another delegation, led by a member of the Mavromihalis family, to St. Petersburg to secure the terms for their emigration and settlement. The provisions allotted the Greek legionnaires on 28 March 1775 were well within the general guidelines established by Catherine in her 22 July 1763 Manifesto on Foreign Colonists.[5] The Greeks were to settle in the cities of Kerch and Enikale (taking full advantage of Greek traders and merchants who plied the Black Sea) or the surrounding lands in Azov *guberniia* (Taganrog); they received the usual temporary dispensation from taxes and conscription (for the non-military colonists); were granted limited autonomy in local government; were encouraged to build schools at Imperial expense; and were given the right to practice their religion as they so pleased and "build themselves up Churches with steeples for Bells, and keep as many Parsons and Clergy-men as will be needful" and this would be funded by the Imperial treasury.[6] The Manifesto of 1763 allowed for flexibility of terms to meet the needs of various colonists and the Greeks were offered a very special provision in the 28 March 1775 decree: they were to have not only clergymen but a Greek archbishop to see to their needs.[7]

As we know, Catherine already had decided to appoint Voulgaris as the archbishop to serve the small Greek settlement of approximately five thousand. In preparation for his appointment, Voulgaris traveled to Moscow in early August 1775 and was ordained *ieromonakh*, monastic priest, at the end of that month. On 9 September 1775 Catherine signed a decree establishing the new diocese of Slaviansk and Kherson in the provinces of Novorossiia and Azov and mandating the appointment of the Greek *ieromonakh* Voulgaris as its first archbishop.[8] The choice of a Greek archbishop indicated that Catherine and Potemkin were aware of both the multi-ethnic character of the new inhabitants and their uniform faith. The name of the new diocese also suggested the diverse composition and history of the new provinces. Slaviansk was meant to appeal to the

Slavs who settled in southern Russia and to confirm that "Russian history holds that our people is of one tribe while also being a branch of the ancient Slavs." Kherson was in reference to the place (Crimean Peninsula) where Prince Vladimir was baptized and accepted the Christian faith for the Russian people in 988.[9] The name of Kherson also recalled the ancient Greek city of Chersonesus (Greek for peninsula), thus not only re-establishing a connection between the Russia of the Enlightenment and the Greece of the classics but also re-creating Hellenic antiquity in the south. Russia, in Catherine's view, was not encroaching on unknown territories, but restoring physical ties, as such, with classical Greece and the Greek Orthodox East.

Yet another indication of the importance which Catherine attached to Novorossiia and the diocese of Slaviansk and Kherson was the diocesan category in which the episcopate was placed. When Catherine initiated the reorganization and "rationalization" of the Church by secularizing its lands in 1764, she also restructured the existing dioceses in order of importance to determine the amount of money to be budgeted for each, now that they were dependent of state funds. The decree of 26 February 1764 established that of the twenty-six bishoprics only three would comprise the first category: St. Petersburg, Novgorod, and Moscow. The second category comprised eight bishoprics: Kazan, Astrakhan, Tobolsk, Rostov, Pskov, Krutitsk, Riazan and Tver. The third category comprised the remaining fifteen bishoprics. The diocese of Slaviansk and Kherson was added to the second category behind Tver and, of some importance, was ranked above its neighbors.[10]

Ieromonakh Eugenios Voulgaris was consecrated archbishop on 1 October 1775 at the Greek Nikol'skii Monastery in Moscow. Catherine and members of her court were present, as were the leading Church hierarchs led by Metropolitan Platon of Moscow who conducted the ceremony.[11] In Voulgaris's thanksgiving for the appointment to the empress, he once again accentuated her relationship to "the whole estate of the Eastern Church," and placed her among the "Constantines and Theodosiuses, the Justinians and Vladimirs, the Elenas and the Irenes, the Theodoras and the Olgas."[12] Voulgaris was not to depart for Poltava, the capital of the diocese, until the fall of 1776. In the interim, he occupied himself with scholarly pursuits and administrative duties.

In order to acquaint himself with the administrative system of the Russian Church and because of scholarly interest, he undertook to translate from Latin to Greek Feofan Prokopovich's *Dukhovnii reglament* or *Spiritual Regulation*. Prokopovich wrote *Spiritual Regulation* to serve as the ecclesiastical basis for the Russian Holy Synod, established by Peter the Great in 1721. The archbishop also attended to the task of assembling his diocesan staff and determining, what seemed to be an intractable problem, the exact size and composition of the new diocese. The Holy Synod appointed Theoktist (Mochulskii) as his diocesan administrative assistant and Archimandrite of the Krestovozdvizhenskii Monastery. This assistant would administer the diocesan consistory and help Voulgaris with the Russian language. Voulgaris was also appointed a secretary knowledgeable in Greek and Latin. The remaining staff appointments (he was allowed twelve) he decided to fill once he was in the diocese with local and ethnic clergy. The difficulty in ascertaining the composition of the new eparchy was two-fold: first, the Holy Synod did not possess accurate information on the number of churches, parishes, etc. in the newly acquired territories; and second, diocesan boundaries now, by imperial decree, were to coincide with provincial boundaries. This required the absorption of portions of Voronezh, Kiev, Belgorod and Pereiaslavl spiritual jurisdictions which overlapped the province of Novorossiia. Many of these matters were still unresolved when Voulgaris departed for Poltava on 5 October 1776 to take up his new position in a region of great importance to Russian security.[13]

The episcopal duties that Archbishop Voulgaris proceeded to fulfill after his arrival in Poltava were a combination of the traditional duties of a member of the "Apostolic Succession" and those required by the exigencies of the state since the time of Peter the Great. The Orthodox Church is hierarchical in nature and the bishops are an integral part of its structure.[14] Upon consecration a bishop is bequeathed with three powers: ruling, teaching, and celebration of the sacraments. The main duty of the bishop is to guide and rule over the members of his diocese in all matters relating to faith and morals. Of particular importance to the guidance of his flock is his teaching of the true faith to his flock and his assistance to them in maintaining that faith. He is empowered to act as a teacher of the faith through the receipt of a gift or *charisma* from the Holy Spirit. This special gift does not confer on him infallibility in teaching, which would reject his humanity, and any errors in teaching will be corrected by the Church as a whole. Finally, it is through the bishop or one of his delegates (e.g., priest) that the holy sacraments are celebrated. Thus, the bishop is an integral part of the hierarchy and history of the Church, but he does not exist apart from the main body of the Church which is his flock. Only in union with the laity does the bishop become whole.[15]

The Russian Orthodox Church during the Synodal Period (1721-1917) elaborated upon the traditional threefold powers of a bishop to make the position more amenable to the Russian situation as initially perceived by Peter the Great. The standard duties of a Russian Orthodox bishop in the eighteenth century were quite simple but this did not mean that they were easy to fulfill. A bishop was required to reside in his appointed diocese (that this was a listed requirement suggests that one could expect not to find the bishop in his diocese at any given moment), make regular visitations to the parishes in his diocese (this often times proved impossible given the sheer number of churches in the central dioceses and the poor road systems in the extensive outlying dioceses), oversee diocesan administration, open seminaries (when the money was available), and submit annual reports to the Holy Synod on the condition of the diocese. As part of the bureaucratic and administrative rationalization of Russia embarked on by Peter I and continued by his successors, the boundaries of any particular diocese came to mirror those of its secular equivalent: the province. Just as the governor-general was responsible for all subjects in his province and was in turn responsible to the emperor, the bishop was responsible for all members (i.e., priests, monks, laity) of the Church residing within these boundaries and reported to the Holy Synod. This applied equally to all ecclesiastical establishments including seminaries, parish schools, monasteries, churches, and other church buildings with one exception: *stavropigial'* monasteries. *Stavropigial* monasteries, for a variety of historical reasons, fell under the jurisdiction of distant ecclesiastical bodies, usually the Holy Synod in St. Petersburg or the Ecumenical Patriarch in Constantinople.[16]

Even the limited duties enumerated above would require of the bishop more time than he possessed.[17] The bishop was assisted in the execution of these prescriptions by a diocesan administrative and advisory body known as the consistory (*konsistoriia*). The consistory was established by the Holy Synod to provide orderliness and continuity in the governance of the dioceses without necessarily being dependent solely upon the administrative skills of the incumbent bishop. The consistory was a collegial board consisting of five to seven clerics who were appointed and dismissed by the Holy Synod upon the advice of the governing bishop. The members of the consistory staff were, for the most part, priests, archpriests, abbots and deacons from the local area. Their familiarity with the conditions of the diocesan clergy aided the bishop in his evaluation of day-to-day affairs. Bishops, as part of the black or monastic clergy, were not especially sympathetic to the plight of the parish clergy; the consistory staff, however, was more receptive to their grievances and was an effective sounding board for their problems. The head (*nachal'nik*) of the consistory was the secretary. The secretary was the official recorder of diocesan affairs and was expected to be fully knowledgeable of Church and Synodal law. This expertise was called upon often to settle disputes among members of the consistory staff over the proper response to clerical misdeeds and petitions which came before them. The bishop, however, was the final arbiter of all diocesan decisions and resolutions. All financial matters fell within the purview of the consistory regardless of whether it pertained to monasteries, schools, or other ecclesiastical establishments. The secretary was also responsible for implementing all decrees issued by the over-procurator (*oberprokuror*) of the Holy Synod.[18]

The combined staffs of the bishop and the consistory were still not capable of adequately governing the large dioceses of Russia. In the very populous dioceses of northern and central Russia and in the expansive dioceses of southern and eastern Russia, the bishop and consistory reduced their bureaucratic burdens by delegating administrative tasks to the local spiritual districts or ecclesiastical councils (*dukhovnoe pravlenie*). This was particularly appropriate in the geographically large new diocese of Slaviansk and Kherson. This region covered approximately 84,000 square miles, roughly the size of Minnesota.[19] The spiritual districts consisted of one or two abbots and one archpriest and governed a relatively small area which usually included forty or fifty churches.[20] The council and its staff were responsible for disseminating information from diocesan headquarters to the parishes, filing reports, and trying to settle as many disputes as possible at their level without forwarding them to the consistory or bishop.[21] The diocese which Theotokis inherited in 1779 included twelve district boards: Kremenchug, Poltava, St.

Elizabeth, Kobeliakakh, Slaviansk, Mirgorod, Kriukovsk, Ekaterinoslav, Ekaterinsk, Bakhmut, Novorostovsk, and Alexandrovsk.[22]

At the local level, superintendents (*blagochinnye*) assisted the
bishop in overseeing the parish clergy and parishioners. The superintendents or ecclesiastical supervisors were first used by Moscow's
Metropolitan Platon in the 1750s; he later tranformed them into
appointive agents of the bishop as defined in his 1775 publication,
Instruction to the Ecclesiastical Supervisors.[23] The superintendents
oversaw the behavior of the clergy and the parishioners, made
certain the clergy were fulfilling their clerical duties and conducting
services correctly, inspected church maintenance and examined
parish finances.[24] This was accomplished during biannual visits to
the parishes in their district. The bishop was kept apprised of the
conditions in the parishes through written reports submitted to him
following each visit. The superintendents, as representatives of the
bishop, possessed substantial power and acted with his implicit
authority. This permitted them to evaluate the situation in a parish
and act immediately without first seeking episcopal approval. The
superintendents could censor sermons and catechism lessons as well
as rectify other misdeeds and deviations among clergy and parishioners. The position of superintendent was not created to harass the
white clergy (a common complaint heard from parish priests) but to
initiate a return to correct liturgical practices and a semblance of
moral decency were it was found lacking.

••••

Nikiforos Theotokis arrived at the Krestovozdvizhenskii
Monastery – the seat of eparchial administration- sometime in late
1776, within a month or two of Voulgaris's own arrival in late
October. The monastery was situated atop a hill overlooking the
Vorskla River at some remove from the city of Poltava and was
isolated from ecclesiastical control in distant St. Petersburg and the
regional civil authority in Kremenchug.[25] Theotokis's arrival in
Novorossiia, so soon after his receipt of Voulgaris's letter, suggests
that he was anxious to remove himself as quickly as possible from an
unpleasant situation in Jassy. He immediately began learning the
Russian language and, according to one biographer, attained fluency
within one year. The biographer attributed this to the possibility that
Theotokis already possessed a rudimentary understanding of the

language before his arrival in Russia because Theotokis had cited a
Russian source in one of his works in Leipzig.[26] Archbishop
Eugenios understood the difficulties inherent in not having sufficient
command of a new language in a new setting and, subsequently,
chose not to place Theotokis in a responsible position for a number
of months. However, Eugenios was already considering a position
for Theotokis in the troubled area of diocesan education.

Theotokis's views on the social and moral benefits of education
coincided with those of Catherine. She initially favored Locke's
philosophy of education and believed that education had the power to
cast model citizens and create ideal human beings. Her principal
educational adviser and fellow pedagogical idealist was I.I. Betskoy,
whose *General Plan for the Education of Young People of Both
Sexes* was published in 1764. According to Betskoy, children were
to be separated from their parents and placed in a more salutary
environment from age 5 to 21 where they would be molded into
perfect citizens and free from the baneful effects of corporal punishment. Education would occur through example and persuasion.[27]
Apart from Betskoy's Moscow Foundling Home, the Smol'ny School,
and specialist boarding schools in the two capitals, Catherine's early
educational efforts actually reached very few people.

This changed in 1775 when Catherine issued the Statute on
Provincial Administration which was intended to unify, consolidate,
and integrate her vast empire in reaction to Pugachev's revolt, the
acquisition of the new southern territories, and the incorporation of
new ethnic minorities. In the statute, schools were just one of eight
institutions the provincial boards of social welfare were to establish
in order to foster social stability and cohesion.[28] Still, there is very
little evidence to suggest that the local boards possessed the financing
or the inclination to comply.[29]

The turmoil of the mid-1770s and the more pronounced multi-
ethnic character of the empire not only convinced Catherine of the
need for a structurally uniform state but also forced her to abandon
the "natural" educational philosophies advocated by Locke and
Rousseau and adopt a system favored by the central European
monarchies which stressed discipline and order. In 1782, F.I.
Iankovich de Mirievo, recruited from Austria, became Catherine's
educational adviser. Iankovich drew heavily on his experiences as a
participant in the Austrian educational reform movement under
Joseph II. In short, Iankovich's curriculum offered subjects which

had practical applicability, which were intended to produce "internally happy persons" content with their position in a "static, hierarchical society."[30]

In 1786, Iankovich's reforms culminated in the Russian Statute of National Education which provided for a system of high schools and primary schools in the provincial capitals and primary schools in district towns for everyone regardless of social standing.[31] The language of instruction was to be Russian throughout the empire. Modern languages, other than Russian, could be possible subjects but not languages of instruction. The primary schools concentrated on the four "R's" (reading, writing, arithmetic, and religion), and basic Russian grammar while the high schools offered geometry, physics, history, geography, drawing, mechanics, architecture, morality, Biblical history, and foreign languages.[32] The Russian educational reform was very similar to its Austrian counterpart in many respects but differed from it markedly in one notable area: whereas the Austrians intentionally excluded the Church, the Russians actively enlisted the Russian Orthodox Church in the educational effort, a policy initiated with the reforms of Peter the Great.[33] Of course, education in Russia had always been the provenance of the Church and, for practical reasons, neither Peter's or Catherine's educational policies could be instituted without the Church. However, a sound philosophical justification for this close relationship emerged during Peter's reign and continued into Catherine's, when Leibniz argued (for Peter's benefit), that "it is self-evident that the spread of science can by accompanied, most successfully, by the spread of truth and piety." Christianization or "rechristianization" was equivalent to education which was essential to creating a uniform and consolidated empire of Russians.[34]

When Archbishop Eugenios arrived in Poltava he was dismayed at the absolute neglect of education in the diocese and the low level of learning. Most troubling to him, however, was the absence of a seminary to train the children of the clergy and the clergy themselves. He moved to remedy one facet of the problem by charging his diocesan administrator, Theoktist, on 24 January 1777, with the establishment of a small school in the Krestovozdvizhenskii Monastery for ten choir boys who already could read and write. The young boys were to be instructed in introductory Latin and other foreign languages, catechism, arithmetic, geography and history.[35] Voulgaris thought the matter of inadequate educational facilities could be rectified easily by writing to the Holy Synod and requesting permission and funds to establish a small diocesan seminary.[36] His request was most appropriate and in accordance with the *Spiritual Regulation* in which it decreed that each diocese should have a seminary to combat clerical ignorance.[37] Archbishop Eugenios sent a letter to the Holy Synod on 4 February 1777 requesting funds for a diocesan seminary but a reply was not forthcoming. He obviously suspected that the Holy Synod would act lethargically to his request for aid and endeavored to find financial sources on his own. In March he sent a letter to Count Kyrill G. Razumovskii, the former hetman of Little Russia or Ukraine, then residing in his palace in Baturin, inquiring about the use of one of his houses, near Preobrazhenskii Church in Poltava,[38] for the site of a future seminary. Voulgaris possibly knew of Razumovksii's earlier support of education in the former hetmanate and that he had even attempted to establish a university at Baturin in the late 1750s.[39] The building was not a great concession as it lacked windows, doors, floors, and stoves, but it was adequate for the short term.[40] Evidently, Razumovskii granted Voulgaris's request because the archbishop later borrowed five hundred rubles from the monastery and solicited funds from local supporters of education and learning whom he called "lovers of learning" (*liubiteli nauk*), to rehabilitate and restore the building.[41]

The delay in receiving a reply from the Holy Synod did not deter Archbishop Eugenios in his effort to promote the establishment of diocesan education. A broad educational system was needed to create an enlightened population which was both more civic-minded and freed from baneful, superstitious beliefs. General ignorance was even pervasive among the ordained clergy as one eighteenth-century traveler remarked, "they are, in general, very ignorant.... No more learning is usually required of common officiating parish priests, or popes, as they call them, than they be able to read the old Russ or Sclavonian [sic] language."[42] The seminary would be the center of the educational system. It would accept primarily the sons of the clergy, but also the nobility and other lower classes who had passed through the parish or district schools (*dukhovnoe uchilishche*) and, then, return these educated youth to the parishes as teachers and priests or they would enter monasteries, ecclesiastical administration, or government service.[43] A seminary, as envisioned by Prokopovich and Peter the Great, was to provide a number of functions. First, it would train young men in the liturgy and holy offices in a correct and uniform manner. In theory, a bishop could not ordain an individual who had not attended a seminary without incurring the wrath of the state. Second, a skilled and educated priest could counter two of the church's major threats in the eighteenth century: Old Believers from below and Westernization from above. Third, the educated and "learned" graduates of seminaries would lend respectability and status to the ecclesiastical hierarchy.[44] Of course, the seminary also was to serve the interests of the state as mentioned above.

In May 1777, Archbishop Eugenios circulated an official document recommending that *ieromonakh* Nikiforos Theotokis become superintendent of diocesan schools and instruction. Eugenios's choice of Theotokis indicated the high regard in he held Theotokis and his experience in education and the importance he attached to the proper and efficacious development of diocesan education. The document announced the appointment of Theotokis and outlined Voulgaris's concerns for education, giving an indication of the scarcity of educational establishments and the implicit role of the Church, through its bishops and priests, in bringing enlightenment to the minds of the inhabitants of Novorossiia.

> Our duty concerning the instruction in the "liberal arts" (*svobodnikh naukakh*) of the youth of our diocese must occupy a place among the very first cares of our office. And as we, with various others, according to our pastoral calling, are burdened with other matters, so we also have proposed to appoint for this charge a worthy and able man, who having entered into such a responsibility, according to our instruction and direction, would discharge it respectably and would be a superintendent and overseer over all the schools of our diocese – however many either exist or are being founded both in the local city of Poltava, where according to Her Imperial Majesty's Royal favor we presently reside, and in other cities and small towns. Of such abilities and qualities is regarded by us the commanding deacon in our Poltava Monastery, the ieromonakh Nikiforos Theotokis, a purposeful man with both integrity of morals and superlative training, to whom we entrust the designated task.[45]

The archbishop concluded the announcement with a request that everyone should consult with Theotokis and abide by his advice on all educational matters.

For the sake of this, to each and everyone, to all the people
of our diocese in the spiritual districts (*dukhovnikh
pravleniiakh*), and in the administrations of the above mentioned, to the ordained clergy and churchmen[46] found in
them, also to the abbots of the monasteries and the ordained
monks and monks comprising their administration; likewise it
will be known to all the dvorianstva (nobility), schlachty
(Polish/Ukrainian nobility), and citizens who are found in our
diocese: that where there has been established only a school
of liberal learning or in our diocese there is to be established,
everywhere, the most honored ieromonakh Theotokis has
been acknowledged as the superintendent of it [the school];
in everything relating to education we have demanded
advice of him and, in this, we have obeyed his instruction
and charge.[47]

The Razumovskii house was not expected to be completed for
another year, owing to the absence of a Holy Synod response for
funding so Voulgaris resorted to opening a small temporary
"seminary" on 24 November 1777. Within one year, 27 November
1778, Voulgaris opened the renovated Razumovskii house and
dedicated it as the new diocesan school building.[48] Nikiforos transferred the choirboys' school and the small "seminary," which had
been created the year before, to the new building. Because of the
success of Voulgaris's solicitations for donations to help support the
school enough funds existed to allow the new building to house seven
orphans as well.[49] Apart from the choirboys who were simply transferred to the new school, the school accepted students of eight to
fourteen years of age from the clerical as well as non-clerical estates.
A few interesting conditions were attached to the admissions process:
the children should not have any diseases or disorders, they should
possess a rudimentary knowledge of reading and writing Russian,
and, those with "good high voices," between eight and ten years of
age, would be admitted immediately.[50] Students who were from
Poltava could live at home with their parents; students who were not
from the city were obliged to rent quarters near the school, or, if
extremely poor, they were given room and board at the school.
Thus, the school began to acquire the characteristics, under
Theotokis's direction, of an advanced preparatory school (*nizshaia
shkola*).[51] The preparatory school was intended to instruct students
in Russian reading and writing. Students were supposed to have
received this part of their education at home prior to their entry into

a district school but allowances were made for those who had not as well as for orphans who would not have had the opportunity. Students also were introduced to the catechism and music.[52] Theotokis's school also included the first stage of the elementary Latin school which involved an introduction to Latin reading and writing.

Voulgaris continued to solicit funds for the general upkeep and maintenance of the new school. He donated some of his own money and accepted gifts from the diocesan clergy. Voulgaris also must have considered that some churchmen (*tserkovnosluzhitely*) were to derive greater benefit from the new school than others and that they should pay for the benefit through a levy. Many clergy gave voluntarily to the new district schools so their children could attend a school locally rather than travel to a distant seminary.[53] A son sent to a seminary far from home imposed a double burden on the already financially pressed parish clergy as the clergy needed to pay the student's room and board expenses at the seminary and manage without an extra worker at home. The assessment of levies on the clergy and the donation of the fines collected by the consistory from misbehaving clergy were commonly used to maintain the school and pay the salaries of the faculty.[54] If the above is an accurate description of Voulgaris's actions, the financial circumstances of the diocese were dire and paralleled the situation in the more populated and wealthy central dioceses.[55]

Theotokis, circumscribed by the diocese's financial predicament, assembled a very small teaching staff for the new school. Grigorii Bogunovskii, the chancellor of the consistory, was appointed by Theotokis in the fall of 1778. The appointment of Bogunovskii probably saved the diocese the expense of the small salary (about fifteen rubles per annum) usually paid to a teacher because he was already a member of the consistorial staff. Petr Stanislavskii, the son of the *namestnik* of Poltava, Ivan Stanislavskii, left his position as teacher at the Krutitsk Seminary to join Theotokis's staff. The new school, as already mentioned, did not restrict enrollment to the sons of the clergy and nobility, but allowed all citizens (*grazhdane*), including merchants (*kupechestvo*), to enter if they met the minimum qualifications. The merchants showed their appreciation by providing a bookkeeper, Petr Theodorovich Paskevich, citizen of Poltava, for the school.[56]

Theotokis's diminutive teaching staff and the lack of Synodal approval and funding for a seminary in Poltava precluded him from developing an adequate school to meet the educational needs of the diocese. For over a year Theotokis and Voulgaris continued to petition the Holy Synod for permission to open a seminary. Finally, on 22 September 1779, while Theotokis was in St. Petersburg following his consecration ceremony as the new archbishop of Slaviansk and Kherson, the Holy Synod and Catherine decreed that the College of Economy was to provide 2,000 rubles annually for the establishment and maintenance of a seminary in Poltava.[57] Upon his return to Poltava at the end of October, 1779, Archbishop Nikiforos found it prudent to secure again from General-Field Marshall Kyrill Grigorievich Razumovskii a letter stating that he had indeed given one of his houses in Poltava to the diocese for the purpose of accommodating a seminary.[58]

In the fall of 1779, the diocesan seminary was opened by Archbishop Nikiforos with great fanfare, bringing to concrete form what he and Voulgaris had long imagined. Immediately evident was the increased funding manifested in the new curriculum. The seminary now offered courses covering the entire Elementary Latin and Advanced Latin levels – from Latin grammar to rhetoric – and still attended to the orphans.[59] Students who completed the five-year Latin curriculum were steeped in classical culture and supposedly could compose freely in Latin.[60] The intended effect of a heavy Latin curriculum was to internationalize the clergy (Latin was still thought to be the language of learned individuals in early eighteenth-century Europe, but it was beginning to lose ground to national languages later in the century) and create an elite group of ecclesiastics who could consider themselves the equal of the nobility. However, Latin usually was an insuperable academic burden for the majority of seminarians, and those who did pass and graduated from the seminary found themselves further alienated from the Russian peasant they were supposed to serve.[61] The Poltava Seminary attracted students not only from its own diocese but advanced students from the Kievan Academy, Kharkov Collegium, and Pereiaslavskii Seminary. The seminary had not been in existence long enough to have developed a sufficient reputation to lure students from other institutions so their presence possibly can be explained as a simple transfer to a seminary close or closer to home. Theotokis also continued to foster education for all social classes by admitting children of the nobility and merchants who lived in the Novorossiia and Azov *gubernii*.[62] His choice as rector of the seminary was a member of the diocesan consistory in Poltava, Archpriest Ioakim Ianovskii. Ianovskii later left his position at the seminary and became the archimandrite of the first-category monastery at Novgorod-Seversk where he took monastic vows and assumed the name Ieronim.[63]

In 1780 Archbishop Nikiforos added a number new subjects to the seminary curriculum including Greek, French, German, arithmetic and drawing. These additions clearly indicate that Theotokis was at the forefront of ecclesiastical education. Metropolitan Platon of Moscow, considered to be the leader of educational reform in the seminaries and academies in Catherinian Russia, did not introduce the instruction of modern languages at the Moscow Academy until 1781. Theotokis's educational experience in the Greek East, with its emphasis on both the sciences and theology, coincided with Catherine's notion of an enlightened education. His understandable inclusion of Greek in the curriculum preceded Catherine's edict of 1784 which placed it above Latin in all seminaries.[64]

••••

Archbishop Nikiforos was acutely aware of the importance of a solid education in developing skills for social improvement and perpetuating traditions and customs. His educational career in the Greek East and especially on his home island of Corfu reflected Theotokis's fervent desire to assist his "nation" in preserving its identity. His ardor for learning was no less passionate in Russia than it was in Corfu, Constantinople or Jassy. Theotokis was particularly anxious that the Greek immigrants to Russia should maintain their identity as well as show their appreciation to the "most revered and just Empress" by becoming well-educated and productive citizens. Just as the archbishop never tired of admonishing his priests to be moral exemplars to the flock, he preached the necessity of schools and education to steel oneself against corruption and moral decay.[65]

In a 1781 letter to the Greeks at Taganrog, Theotokis stated that "because of the absence of schools, the youth not only remain blind and do not progress, but the resultant idleness will also corrupt valued customs (*hrista ithi*) – 'all things bad come from idleness'."[66] But there was hope for the youth, continued Theotokis, because the empress had established a school in Petersburg for the Greek nation (*yenos*) where many fellow Greeks have been educated and now hold high social and government positions. If this was too far for the children, Theotokis wrote, "there is a school in Poltava in which the youth are able to remove the fat of ignorance and implant in themselves the first roots of education." Theotokis considered education to be the greatest treasure a parent could give to his child, even greater than money and the community would benefit as well. He finished his lesson on education by exhorting the leaders of the Taganrog community to give travel support to eligible children and he, for his part, would gladly write letters of recommendation for those who wanted to attend the school in Petersburg.[67]

Archbishop Nikiforos believed schools to be a top priority and went to great lengths to ensure the construction of schools in the Greek communities of southern Russia. In August and September 1786 Theotokis sent two letters to the Greeks of Mariupol in which he used all his ability to persuade them to establish a school in that city.[68] Following a general pastoral introduction, Theotokis informed them that education leads to the salvation of man's soul just as the Apostle Paul wrote to Timothy, "you are acquainted with the sacred writings which are able to instruct you for salvation." Therefore, "my fist advice to you…is that you build a school in Mariupol in which all your children can learn two languages, Greek and Russian." He reiterated that only those who are educated will find success. This success would be available to everyone, for the school would accept the poor and orphans and it would educate, feed, and clothe them. Just as he told the Greeks of Taganrog, the best students would be chosen for further education in more languages, general knowledge and science at the eparchial school in Poltava. Some students would go on to become priests and teachers while others would become judges and receive government positions. "For these reasons," he concluded, "we consider this affair sacred, heavenly and very useful not only for your soul but for your life."[69]

Archbishop Nikiforos announced that he had chosen the trustees (*epitropes*) of the school and they included besides Archpriest Trifillii, Hadji Mikhail, Hadji Panayiotis, Pitzakzi Stefanos and Tat Savvas. "But how can the trustees accomplish anything with empty hands (*me adeiana ta heria*)," asked Theotokis. The school needed a building, books, salaries for teachers, and bread and clothes for the destitute students. Theotokis knew of four ways to achieve these objectives. First, as the construction of the monastery of St. George could not be done because it violated Catherine's 1764 *ukase* disallowing new monastery construction, the money collected for this monastery could be turned over to the trustees of the school. Furthermore, all money, silver vessels, animals and other such goods could be collected by the trustees on an annual basis and dedicated to the school in the name of St. George, the liberator of prisoners and protector of the poor.[70]

Second, donation boxes could be placed in each church and on each Church holiday the parishioners could give money for the salvation of their souls and the good of the community. From those boxes the trustees could take money needed by the school every six months. Third, anyone who donated money to the school could have their name recorded for posterity in a "book" and their names read every Sunday at St. Kharalampiia. Fourth, the income from the Church of St. Kharalampiia could be divided three ways: for the church, for the school, and for the poor. Theotokis instructed the trustees to maintain a thorough account of the money received and spent to prevent charges being leveled against them for embezzlement. From this fund they were to pay the teacher, Brother Agathangelos. Theotokis also mentioned that he had written to the nephew of Metropolitan Ignatii requesting the donation of a building for the school.[71]

Theotokis sent a second letter to the Mariupol community at the end of September 1786. He was pleased to hear that Ivan Gozadinov, the nephew of the former metropolitan, had agreed to "donate" the money and goods collected for the proposed monastery to the new school. This, unfortunately, occurred only after the community took him to court in Kremenchug when he refused to comply with its request. Theotokis encouraged the community to put the whole legal affair behind them and concentrate on the school. He instructed the trustees to carefully inventory all materials received from the monastery fund and send the list to the consistory in Poltava. The animals were to be sold immediately and the proceeds kept in a safe with three locks (one of the keys must be kept by Trifillii at all times). Trifillii was to inform the consistory of all major financial transactions affecting the school, such as the purchase of a building (Gozadinov was not required by the courts to "donate" one).[72]

••••

Theotokis expanded his seminary faculty commensurate with the addition of the new courses. Archpriest Ivan Svietailo, treasurer (*kliuchar'*) of Preobrazhenskii Church in Poltava and a member of the consistorial staff, was to teach Greek. Grigorii Bogunovskii, who also had taught at the earlier school, was the new instructor of rhetoric. A native Frenchman, Pierre Anton, taught French. The international and academic quality of the staff was broadened by the addition of Voulgaris's own personal friend from Leipzig University, Professor Theodore Schall, who was to teach German and mathematics. A retired military officer, Lieutenant Karl von Rotkirche, was the instructor for drawing. In 1782, Theotokis hired him to teach arithmetic, geography, mathematical sciences, and German for which he would received one hundred and fifty rubles per annum.[73] The assembled staff of the seminary reflected the professionalism of Theotokis and differed from other seminaries in that its faculty was competent and proficient in the courses it taught. In September 1783 the seminary offered for the first time a course in philosophy.[74] Philosophy, with theology, constituted the last stage of the four-stage seminary educational system. The introduction of philosophy indicated that Theotokis was moving toward a complete seminary curriculum; only theology still eluded him.

The new instructor of philosophy and Greek was Gavriil Banulesko-Bodoni.[75] Bodoni was yet another example of a prelate from the Greek East who entered Russian service with the hope of improving conditions in his homeland. Bodoni was a Moldavian who attended the Kievan Theological Academy and later learned Greek at the Phanariot-endowed academy on the island of Patmos. He then accepted a position at the Jassy Academy in 1776 where he taught for a short time with Nikiforos Theotokis. Archbishop Nikiforos summoned Bodoni to Poltava in 1782. He returned to Jassy in 1784 and served in the Rumanian Church hierarchy until 1787 when he fled to the Ukraine and Poltava after the outbreak of the second Russo-Turkish War. He returned to the seminary and became the rector as well as the Greek instructor.[76] He subsequently was to play an important role in his ecclesiastical positions as metropolitan of Moldavia (1792) and exarch of Moldo-Vlachia (1808-1812) in the continuing struggle between the Russian Holy Synod and the Ecumenical Patriarchate of Constantinople over jurisdictional control of the Danubian Principalities.[77]

Three years after the addition of the philosophy course Theotokis fulfilled the seminary curriculum when he added a course in theology. The new course was accompanied by great fanfare and a celebration on 21 September 1786. The ceremony was convoked in Uspenskii Cathedral in Poltava during the Vespers which were celebrated by Archpriest Ivan Stanislavskii. Archbishop Nikiforos gave a sermon in Latin to the assembled students and faculty. He admonished them on the importance of a well-trained clergy (i.e., those who have had the benefit of theological instruction), for the spiritual salvation of their flock. "Blessed are the people who have among them zealous clergy," he began his sermon.[78] For when a man falls into sin it is only the morally upright clergy who can save him. A clergyman who leads a good Christian life "illuminates the heavenly world" for the people, saves souls, and serves the fatherland (*otechestvo*); all which is pleasing to God. By the same token, a flock who is served by a negligent and debauched clergy will suffer greatly. He reminded the clergy that it is the purpose of their calling to save Christian souls and they would be answerable for this to God on Judgment Day (*strashnii den'*). Theotokis was well aware of clerical misdeeds and chided the priests and future priests before him not to commit the most common of them all: extorting money from good Christians who seek absolution. A priest's early education did not always prove sufficient and he sometimes lapsed into corruption. If this was the case he would receive two warnings from his fellow clerics and bishop. A priest who did not correct his behavior immediately was subject to the commensurate punishment and fines (*istiazati po zakonom i shtrafovat'*).[79]

Following Archbishop Nikiforos's sermon, the newly appointed instructor of theology and prefect of the seminary, Archpriest Ivan Bashinskii, spoke glowingly of the benefits of theology classes to the workings of the Church.[80] The students then dutifully sang praises to the empress, her family, and to the Holy Synod. Most of the students attending the seminary were Ukrainians as were most of the instructors. Among the students at the seminary on 21 September was a young man who was to become a leading Russian classicist and a translator of Greek classics: Ivan Ivanovich Martynov. Martynov's background and his activities at the seminary allow us a glimpse at Theotokis's educational system from a student's perspective.

Martynov was born in 1771 in Poltava *guberniia* into a clerical family with tenuous connections to a past nobility. His mother taught him basic Russian grammar and he also read church liturgical works. At the age of nine he entered the diocesan school in Poltava and even became acquainted with Voulgaris (he continued to reside in the city following his retirement from the archbishopric), who initiated his interest in Greek and later would support his career in Petersburg.[81] He was an outstanding student and very often received rewards for his academic achievements. On one occasion Theotokis examined him in the Greek language and rewarded him with a prize of a few silver rubles and two books: a New Testament in Greek/Latin parallel text and a copy of Friedrich Christian Baumeister's textbook *Physics*, in Russian translation, for his success in philosophy.[82] The presence of the Moldavian *hospodar*, Alexander Mavrocordatos, at Martynov's examination suggests that the Poltava Seminary was a recognizable center of Greek learning. Apart from the activities and presence of Voulgaris, Theotokis, and Banulesko-Bodoni, the short-term visits of Mavrocordatos and Athanasios Psalidas at the Poltava Seminary testify to its importance in the Neo-Hellenic Enlightenment.[83]

It was customary in seminaries, both as an economy measure and a teaching practicum, to use advanced seminary students as instructors. Martynov, while he was still in the rhetoric class, began teaching Russian and Latin grammar. Eventually the rector bestowed on him a very special honor by allowing him to move from the dormitory to his own apartment. In his apartment he received students for instruction and solicited fees from them to support himself. His teaching career advanced further when the rector, Archimandrite Gavriil, became quite ill and gave up his Greek language class. The archbishop appointed Martynov as Gavriil's successor when the boy was only sixteen years old and still in the Theology course. Finally, owing to his excellent record, the archbishop sent Martynov to Petersburg to continue his studies at the Academy where his poetry and translations attracted the attention of Catherine.[84]

The archbishop was responsible for organizing and monitoring the daily activities of the seminary staff and its students. Each of the academic levels followed a daily plan of instruction. Theology students were usually in their mid-twenties. The Theology course lasted two years and began on the first day of September. In the morning of every school day except Saturday, the instructor gave a lecture and led a discussion on the works of Feofan Prokopovich supported, if necessary, by reference to other theologians. After the lecture on Mondays, he read from the Scriptures in the original or from a proper translation and discussed them. On Wednesdays he taught church history from the Old and New Testaments. On Fridays he read the *Spiritual Regulation* or the Nomocanon (*kormchaia kniga*) with commentaries. On Saturdays, he engaged the Theology students in mock debates (*disputy*), asking them questions on selected theologians. On Sundays, students took turns giving short sermons to gain some practical pastoral experience. The students participated in public debates three times per year: at Christmas, Easter and just before vacation. These debates became a social occasion at which the bishop or archbishop displayed his seminarians' knowledge of theology to the local notables. The average age of the Philosophy student was early twenties and the course was two years long. On every day but Saturday, the instructor lectured and discussed Frederick Christian Baumeister's *Philosophy*. On Monday, Wednesday and Friday afternoons he lectured on the history of philosophy and read from the works of the ancient philosophers: Cicero, Seneca, Plutarch, Plato, etc. On Saturdays, the instructor scheduled debates in which the students demonstrated their knowledge of a pre-selected philosopher. Each student continued his debate from the pulpit until he could do so with "perfect pronunciation" (*c prilichnim proiznosheniem*). The Philosophy students also participated in the same public debates as the Theology students three times per year, but appeared after them and replied to questions on philosophy.[85]

Students in poesy (*piitika*) learned the finer arts of Latin grammar, composition and verse. They discovered the iambic pentameter, the alexandrine, elegiac couplets, and other forms of versification. The students also studied the Russian classicists Trediakovskii and Baibakov. On Mondays, Wednesdays and Fridays they read Virgil and Ovid as well as Sumarokov and Lomonosov. The students memorized many of the verses and recited them repeatedly on Saturday mornings from the pulpit until they achieved perfection. The rare student who attained the final year of Latin found himself in rhetoric. These students finished the abridged version of Baumeister's *Logic*, delved into the rules of rhetoric according to Vratislavskoi and absorbed the edifying and moralistic lessons of Latin and Russian authors. On Monday, Wednesday and Friday afternoons the rhetoric instructor gave lectures on Cicero's speeches with special attention to the penetrating logic and pure style of Latin. The instructor read the speeches and sermons of Lomonosov and required the students to memorize portions of them. On Saturdays, the instructor assisted each student deliver, in an appropriate manner, what they had memorized. The instructor was to attempt to correct "unseemly body movement and voices which were unmoving, monotonous and hurried." The students wrote their own Latin and Russian compositions. Instructors in both poesy and rhetoric were required to write reports on their students' progress and account for any absences from class.[86]

The instructions the archbishop prescribed for the teachers of the lower classes placed more emphasis on maintaining discipline and order in the classroom. The instructors of Russian, Greek, German and various levels of Latin grammar sent reports to the prefect at the end of each month detailing the progress of their students, the number of days of class they attended and the reasons for absences. The instructions placed great pedagogical importance on the continuous use of whichever language the students were learning. The instructors were to ask questions, discuss issues and encourage conversations among the students in grammatically proper Russian, Greek, German or Latin. The students translated from the respective foreign language to and from Russian at varying degrees of difficulty. In the Latin classes the instructors taught from Kamenskii's grammar. In the Beginning Latin course, Saturday mornings were dedicated to lessons in Russian grammar from Lomonosov's text to supplement their Monday, Wednesday and Friday Latin lessons. The Advanced Latin class read and translated Cicero and Erasmus on Tuesday, Thursday and Saturday mornings. All translations were done at home and returned to class the next day for correction. Both Latin classes occupied Saturday afternoons by studying the catechism. The students memorized sections of the catechism over the weekend and took quizzes on it on Mondays. Of course, much of the students' time in the Latin classes was used to memorize rules, declensions, conjugations and vocabulary. The students in the Greek class read the New Testament, the Scriptures and "pagan" (*iazycheskie*) or ancient Greek authors.[87]

The prefect of the seminary was, in essence, the principal. According to the list of responsibilities enumerated in 1787 at Ekaterinoslav Seminary the prefect's primary duties were of an overseeing nature. The faculty members were to be in their classrooms the entire time stipulated in their respective contracts and not to leave the seminary premises unless they had permission. Those who violated these rules too frequently were fired. The prefect reviewed the monthly reports of the faculty and visited their classes monthly. He was charged with keeping a watchful eye on the students and their class attendance. The prefect employed a "censor" (*senior*) to monitor the students when they were not in class. The censor also assisted the prefect in ensuring student attendance at church services and their correct behavior during church feasts and fasts. Each morning the prefect directed the students to be awakened and then led to the church where they took assigned places before the divine procession. The censor searched each dormitory room after the students left for stragglers. The prefect was also responsible for imbuing the students with proper personal behavior and character; and those students who exhibited any type of defect were referred to him immediately. Finally, the prefect was to tour the dormitories and dining hall at least each week to observe that all was in order.[88]

The seminary initiated by Voulgaris and developed by Theotokis was the paradigm of diocesan education as envisioned by Catherine and praised by later scholars.[89] The two hierarchs drew on their own educational experiences in the Greek East and were convinced of the importance of an enlightened populace for the good of a nation. As clerics both men naturally believed that the primary educator was the local priest. If the village priest did not possess a moral disposition how could he direct by example the lives of his parishioners. Voulgaris was shocked at the absolute ignorance of the local clergy and church officials and doubted their ability to lead and enlighten: even the "educated" clergy knew only a few Russian letters and signed their names with the greatest difficulty. The young men who did venture away from home to attend the seminary at Pereiaslavl or the Kievan Academy rarely returned.[90] Theotokis and Voulgaris did not restrict access to the seminary to members of the clerical estate alone. All citizens of the diocese could attend the seminary from Cossacks to merchants.[91] In 1788, of the 259 students attending the seminary only fifty-nine were not the children of churchmen. In 1792, of the 327 students enrolled, that number increased to eighty-one. In 1785, the Ekaterinoslav *namestnichestvo* recruited thirty students from the seminary to staff its various offices and departments and established a policy to repeat the process periodically.[92] Apart from serving as the primary educational institution for all subjects, the main purpose of the diocesan schools and seminary was to produce enlightened priests and monks by moral persuasion whose deeds would be pleasing to both God and state. The seminary attracted numerous faculty members who went on to respectable careers in the Russian Church and it produced a few notable students.[93] However, without further study, the overall effect of the seminary is difficult to judge.[94]

••••

In the late spring of 1779 Archbishop Eugenios wrote to the Holy Synod requesting that he be relieved of his administrative duties in the diocese of Slaviansk and Kherson and that Nikiforos Theotokis be appointed as his successor. He cited reasons of advancing age (he was sixty-three) and numerous ailments which precluded him from conducting himself in an efficient and capable manner. He also missed the time to devote to his scholarly work. Nor could his minimal command of the Russian language have made his tenure an easy one. Catherine granted Voulgaris's petition for retirement in a letter she sent to the Holy Synod on 5 May 1779. The letter also directed the College of Economy to bestow upon Voulgaris a yearly pension of 2000 rubles, a 500-ruble increase over his 1771 allowance.[95]

On 10 May, the Holy Synod compiled a list of two candidates for the vacated seat in Poltava and sent it to the empress. The report appended to the list drew attention to the large number of recent inhabitants of the diocese that did not speak Russian, but adhered to the Greek faith. For this reason the Synod chose Voulgaris as the first archbishop of this diocese and the Synod concurred that the successor ought to speak a foreign language, but especially Greek. The first on the list was Theotokis and the Synod reported that "currently in the diocese of Slaviansk is ieromonakh Nikiforos, also a Greek, who as the Synod knows is a good teacher and knowledgeable of other languages as well as Greek. He works diligently on sermons, serves as the rector and inspector of the diocese, and is currently on the consistory staff."[96] The second candidate was Archimandrite Kassian of Bratskoi Seminary in Kiev. He was born in Little Russia, taught Latin and Greek and was rector at the Kievan Academy and a member of the consistory. On 10 May 1779 the Synod sent its report to Catherine strongly suggesting that Nikiforos be appointed the new archbishop because "in the diocese there is not a small number of foreign inhabitants who do not know the Russian language." The report concluded, however in the usual manner, with the statement that the Synod would appoint whomever Her Imperial Majesty deigned appropriate.[97] On 13 May, Catherine indicated her choice as the successor to Voulgaris by making a marginal notation on the Synod report next to the name Theotokis "this one;" she also added that he should be consecrated archbishop in Petersburg.[98] A.A. Bezborodko informed the Synod of the empress's wishes the next day and the Synod issued an *ukase* announcing Theotokis's selection.[99]

Catherine's decision was acted upon immediately by the Holy Synod which drafted two decrees: one confirming the resignation of Archbishop Eugenios; the other, naming Theotokis as his successor. The diocesan consistory received the decrees on 9 June, and within a few days Theotokis departed for Petersburg accompanied by such a large contingent of ecclesiastical and secular notables that one source was led to quip that the diocese of Slaviansk and Kherson had "become a widow."[100] Prince Potemkin, who had supported Theotokis's candidacy, was charged with the honor of informing Archbishop Gavriil of Novgorod that he would celebrate the rite of consecration for the new archbishop on 6 August.[101]

On 28 July Archbishop Gavriil conferred on Theotokis his archiepiscopal name which remained the same as the name taken for holy orders: Nikiforos. On 6 August, the feast day of the Transfiguration (*Preobrazhenie*) of our Lord, Ieromonakh Nikiforos entered the Preobrazhenskii Sobor (Cathedral of the Transfiguration) of the Preobrazhenskii light-guards regiment in St. Petersburg and was escorted to the elevated altar by two deacons.[102] There, the Archbishops Gavriil of Novgorod and Innokentii of Pskov performed the ordination ceremony and invested him with the office of bishop and rank of archbishop of Slaviansk and Kherson in the presence of Catherine and members of her court. Also present were two Greek prelates then residing in Petersburg, the Metropolitans Ignatii of Gottha and Kefa and Venediktos of Nauplion.[103]

Archbishop Nikiforos then delivered an ode of thanksgiving to Catherine in Greek. The speech was later translated into French and Russian by L. Sechkarev', one of the Holy Synod's translators, and published in St. Petersburg that year.[104] Nikiforos's speech was customary to the extent that all newly consecrated bishops were required to express their gratitude for the honor. His ode, however, did contain references to the situation in Greece and Russia's role therein. He was obviously aware that Catherine and her court had explicitly adopted the classical world as the model by which they would renovate Russia. Catherine imagined herself as the legislatrix, the philosopher king, who improved her subjects' welfare through rational and universally valid laws.[105] Theotokis began correctly by praising the empress's famous laws (the *Great Instruction* or *Nakaz* of 1767) which, he declared, truly demonstrated to all people the breadth of her intelligence and the philanthropy of her heart.[106] He continued by commenting that Catherine's greatness and spirit of generosity were like swift flowing streams which could not possibly be stemmed by the boundaries of her own empire but would affect countries far removed from Russia's borders. By the strength of her words alone, he opined, Catherine could maintain a peaceful balance as if using victorious arms against the enemies of the faith. And this, he said, was particularly beneficial to "that once glorious civilization, which today is the oppressed Greek people whom you gladly protect."[107]

Theotokis continued by exclaiming that Russia had attained a level of honor not even occupied by ancient Greece or Rome owing to the "inimitable wisdom and perspicacity" of its empress. Catherine received the greatest praise and honor from the "universal church of Christ" for her defense of its interests. He also proclaimed that the recent birth of Catherine's grandson had passionately inflamed all Greece and fulfilled a prophetic expectation for he shared a common name with the last Byzantine emperor Constantine.[108] Theotokis concluded his speech by beseeching God to shower upon the empress, her son and daughter-in-law, and her grandsons, the abundant grace of heaven. Thus, two points deserve comment: First, Theotokis was exceedingly grateful to Catherine for her struggle on the part of the Orthodox Church against those that would harm it, namely, the Ottoman Turks. Second, he was a tireless supporter of the Greek cause and foresaw the possible benefits to Greek liberation of Catherine's activities in the Greek East, hence his mention of her second grandson Constantine Pavlovich.

Theotokis's ordination as archbishop in the late summer of 1779 represented a turning point in his career. One can not help but be struck by the contrast in reactions by Theotokis to the offer of an episcopal see in Russia and his previous offer, seven years earlier, in Venice. Although the see of Philadelphia was a highly honored position Theotokis refrained from accepting due to the imposition of excessive Catholic control which circumscribed his ability to act in accordance with his office. Theotokis could not abide a situation in which he was in direct confrontation with secular authorities; especially if those authorities adhered to a faith inimical to his own. He did not shrink from confrontation with those in authority if he considered his actions justified on religious grounds (e.g., the Ghikas funeral), but was loath to expend time and energy to fight superior forces. The situation in Russia was perfect for him. Catherine was the self-proclaimed protectress of the Orthodox faithful and her country was a secure haven for all those seeking refuge from the Ottoman Empire and those conspiring to realize a liberated Greece. Theotokis threw himself into his duties with the vigor of a man who slipped his chains. The atmosphere of Russia must have seemed extremely liberating to an individual who had always faced opposition to even his smallest deeds. Now, the state would sustain and nurture his agendas for education, faith and foreign policy. The state would not always support his projects with limitless resources but, more important, the state was not an impediment to him. Thus, Theotokis found his niche in Novorossiia in the last quarter of the eighteenth century.

NOTES

1. Emmanuel Ioannidis Amorginos, "Anekdotoi epistolai Nikiforou tou Theotoki arkhiepiskopou Slavoniou kai Hersonos," *Ellinikos Filologikos Syllogos Konstantinoupoleos*, 18 (1861-1886), p. 105.

2. *PSZ*, XX, 24 December 1776, no. 14522. Cited in Kohut, p. 118.

3. Nevodchikov, *Evgenii Bulgaris*, p. 19.

4. S. Safonov, "Ostatki grecheskikh legionov v Rossii, ili nineshneie naseleniie Balaklavy," *Zapiski odesskogo obshchestva istorii i drevnostei* (hereafter *ZOOID*), I (1844), pp. 209-211.

5. For the official English-language version see Bartlett, *Human Capital*, pp. 237-242.

6. Safonov, pp. 212-214 and Bartlett, p. 239.

7. *Ibid.*, p. 213.

8. *PSZ*, 9 September 1775, no. 14366.

9. Batalden, *Catherine*, p. 43.

10. *PSZ*, XVI, no. 12060.

11. On Platon's career see K.A. Papmehl, *Metropolitan Platon*. Platon and Voulgaris were indicative of the new enlightened prelates whom Catherine was promoting within the Russian Church in the late eighteenth century. Platon, as Voulgaris with his tract, caught Catherine's attention when she heard him give his sermon at the memorial service marking the Russian victory over the Turks at the Battle of Chesme

at SS. Peter and Paul Cathedral in St. Petersburg. His sermon was later passed on to Voltaire who remarked that it surpassed the works of the Greek Plato. In this manner, the West was learning of the enlightened prelates in the employ of the enlightened monarch.

12. Quoted in Batalden, p. 45.

13. *Ibid.*, pp. 46-49.

14. In the Eastern Orthodox Church the hierarchy consists of four offices of differing status but equal hierarchical or episcopal rank. In a descending order of status the offices are patriarch, metropolitan, archbishop and bishop. A particular diocese confers on its officeholder a title requisite to the status of the diocese. Thus, the bishop of Moscow holds the title of metropolitan and the bishop of Constantinople holds the title of ecumenical patriarch, and, of course, the bishop of Rome is the pope.

15. Timothy Ware, *The Orthodox Church* (London, 1963), pp. 252-3.

16. Krestovozdvizhenskii Monastery, the location of diocesan headquarters in Poltava, was a *stavropigial'* monastery. This was obviously of some significance because in Theotokis's episcopal correspondence he or his staff closed letters with the date and the address *Stavropig. Moni.*

17. On diocesan administration see Gregory L. Freeze's "Introduction" to I.S. Belliustin, *Description of the Clergy in Rural Russia: The Memoir of a Nineteenth-Century Parish Priest.* Translated with an Interpretive Essay by Gregory L. Freeze (Ithaca, 1985), pp. 15-29.

18. I.S. Berdnikov, *Kratkii kurs' tserkovnago prava* (Kazan, 1888), pp. 168-9.

19. Donald Lynch, "The Conquest, Settlement and Initial Development of New Russia (the Southern Third of the Ukraine): 1780-1837." Ph.D. dissertation, Yale 1965, p. 4.

20. In Slaviansk and Kherson, the largest district council included 73 churches and the smallest held seven. The smallest district council was located in the city of Alexandrovsk in Azov province and the seven churches were widely dispersed (between sixteen and 309 verst from Alexandrovsk). In contrast, the district council of Kobeliakakh in Novorossiia contained 31 churches located two to 38 verst from the council. I.M. Pokrovskii, *Russkiia eparkhii v XVI-XIX vekakhy, ikh otkrytie, sostav i predely* (Kazan, 1897-1913), Supplement, vol. 2, p. 33.

21. Freeze, p. 18.

22. Pokrovskii, Supplement, pp. 32-3.

23. Papmehl, p. 55.

24. Berdnikov, pp. 170-1.

25. Batalden, p. 51.

26. Solov'ev, p. 571.

27. Among the many works on Catherine's educational reforms see J.L. Black's *Citizen for the Fatherland: Education, Educators and Pedagogical Ideals in Eighteenth Century Russia* (Boulder, 1979), pp. 70ff.; Max J. Okenfuss, "Education and Empire: School Reform in Enlightened Russia," *Jahrbücher für Geschichte Osteuropas*, 27:1 (1979): 41-68; Isabel de Madariaga, *Russian in the Age of Catherine the Great* (New Haven, 1981), pp. 488-502; Pavel N. Miliukov, "Educational Reforms," in Marc Raeff, ed., *Catherine the Great: A Profile* (New York, 1972), pp. 100-112; and D.A. Tolstoi, *Gorodskie uchilishcha v tsarstvovanie Imperatritsy Ekateriny II* (St. Petersburg, 1886). For an essay which critically examines the receptivity of Catherine's educational policies as well as the paradoxical consequences of their "failure" as vehicles of Enlightenment universality, see Gary Marker, "Who Rules the Word: Public School Education and the Fate of Universality in Russia, 1782-1803," *Russian History*, 20:1-4 (1993): 15-34.

28. Okenfuss, "Education," p. 61.

29. Janet Hartley, "The Boards of Social Welfare and the Financing of Catherine II's State Schools," *Slavonic and East European Review*, 67:2 (April 1989): 211-227.

30. Okenfuss, "Education," p. 60.

31. On the uniqueness of Catherine's introduction of a "classless" educational system see Max J. Okenfuss, "From School Class to Social Caste: The Divisiveness of Early-Modern Russian Education," *Jahrbücher für Geschichte Osteuropas*, 33:3 (1985): 321-344.

32. Black, pp. 142-3.

33. Okenfuss, "Education," pp. 65-66. On the Austrian reform program and Iankovich's role in it see Philip J. Adler, "Habsburg School Reform Among the Orthodox Minorities, 1770-1780," *Slavic Review*, 33 (1974): 23-45.

34. Cited in Slezkine, "Naturalists versus Nations," p. 179.

35. Gavriil,"Otryvok poviestvovaniia o novorossiiskom kraie iz original'nykh istochnikov pocherpnutyi," *ZOOID*, 3 (1852), p. 107.

36. Nevodchikov, p. 40.

37. James Cracraft, *The Church Reform of Peter the Great* (Stanford, 1971), p. 262.

38. Solov'ev, p. 573.

39. Kohut, pp. 119-120.

40. Gavriil, p. 109.

41. Nevodchikov, p. 41.

42. Richardson, p. 62.

43. The ecclesiastical education system, since its establishment by Peter the Great, was never intended to serve only the interests of the church, but also to train young men for state service. See Gregory Freeze, *The Russian Levites: Parish Clergy in the Eighteenth Century* (Cambridge, 1977), pp. 79ff.

44. *Ibid.*, p. 79.

45. Gavriil, pp. 109-110.

46. The ordained clergy and churchmen comprised the white or parish clergy of the Russian Orthodox Church. The ordained clergy could administer sacraments and consisted of three ranks: archpriest, priest and deacon. The churchmen or sacristans were charged with care taking duties, bell-ringing, and assisting in church services; they were not ordained but were confirmed in their position by the bishop. See Freeze, pp. 3ff.

47. Gavriil, p. 110.

48. Nevodchikov, p. 41.

49. *Ibid.*, p. 42.

50. Gavriil, pp. 110-111.

51. Solov'ev, p. 577.

52. P.V. Znamenskii, *Dukhovnye shkoly v Rossii do reformy 1808 g.* (Kazan, 1881), p. 436.

53. Freeze, *Russian Levites*, p. 89.

54. Gavriil, p. 111.

55. Metropolitan Platon of Moscow also gave from his own pocket to help support the five seminaries in Moscow as well as giving them the proceeds from the sale of icons and equipment from demolished churches, rents from ecclesiastical property, and private donations. Papmehl, pp. 65-66.

56. Gavriil, p. 111.

57. *Ibid.*, p. 119.

58. Solov'ev, p. 578.

59. Gavriil, p. 120.

60. Znamenskii, pp. 445-447.

61. Of course, the liturgy in the Russian Orthodox Church was not conducted in Latin nor did the village priest need to converse with his parishioners in Latin, but, as Lotman and Uspenskii have suggested, the priests who did finish the Latin curriculum became part of a culturally "bilingual" world and thus separated from the world of the majority of Russian subjects. See Iurii M. Lotman and Boris Uspenskii,

"Binary Models in the Dynamics of Russian Culture (to the End of the Eighteenth Century)," in A.D. and A.S. Nakhimovsky, eds., *The Semiotics of Russian Cultural History* (Cornell, 1985), pp. 30-66.

62. During the second half of the eighteenth century a seminary education was, for the most part, gradually restricted to the children of the clerical estate (*soslovie*) due to space limitations as a result of inadequate funding. The fact that Theotokis was admitting non-clerical children indicated the paucity of churchmen in the new provinces.

63. Gavriil, p. 120.

64. *PSZ*, XXII, nos. 16047, 16061.

65. Theotokis avidly sought financial support to construct schools and teachers to staff them. He even looked beyond the boundaries of Russia to find adequate teachers as attested by his letter to *Starets* Paisii Velichkovskii requesting monks to teach in city schools. S. Chetverikov, *Starets Paisii*, p. 324

66. Ioannidis Amorginos, p. 105.

67. *Ibid.*

68. V.V. Latyshev, *K nachal'noi istorii g. Mariupoliia* (Odessa, 1914), pp. 14-24. Latyshev published the letters in Greek with a Russian translation. The letters were found among the private papers of Archpriest Trifillii Karatsoglu. The original letters sent by Theotokis were not among his papers, instead Trifillii made Tatar (with Greek letters) translations (with the facing page in Greek) for the parishioners. Although the Mariupol Greeks had been in Russia since the emigration of Crimean Christians in 1779 they were not under the spiritual jurisdiction of Archbishop Nikiforos but that of Metropolitan Ignatii. With Ignatii's death in February 1786 all those formerly under his jurisdiction passed to Theotokis. On the Greek community in Mariupol see F.A. Braun, "Mariupol'skie greki," *Zhivaia Starina*, 1 (1890): 78-92; I.I. Sokolov, "Mariupol'skie greki," *Trudy instituta slavianovedeniia AN SSSR*, 1 (1932): 297-317; and Viron Karidis, "The Mariupol Greeks: Tsarist Treatment of an Ethnic Minority ca. 1778-1859," *Journal of Modern Hellenism*, 3 (1986): 57-74.

69. *Ibid.*, pp. 14-15.

70. *Ibid.*, pp. 15-16.

71. *Ibid.*, pp. 16-17.

72. *Ibid.*, p. 18.

73. A copy of Rotkirche's contract is found in "Dokumenty otnosiashchiesia k istorii Ekaterinoslavskoi dukhovnoi seminarii," *Letopis' Ekaterinoslavskoi Uchenoi Arkhivnoi Komissii*, 8 (Ekaterinoslav, 1912): 191-192. The contract stipulated at what times during the week he was to teach his classes and the length of the classes. The contract was for a period of two years and he was obliged to inform the rector of the seminary at least three months in advance if he did not wish to renew his contract. Likewise, the rector was obliged to notify him at least three months in advance if he was no longer needed after two years.

74. *Ibid.*

75. *Ibid.*

76. *Rossiiskii gosudarstvennyi istoricheskii arkhiv* (hereafter, *RGIA*), *fond* 796, *opis'* 71, *god* 1790, *delo* 144, *listy* 1-3.

77. Stephen K. Batalden, "Metropolitan Gavriil (Banulesko-Bodoni) and Greek-Russian Conflict over Dedicated Monastic Estates, 1787-1812," *Church History*, 52:4 (1983), pp. 470-473.

78. Gavriil, p. 121.

79. *Ibid.*, p. 122.

80. He was the son of a Ukrainian priest in Slaviansk and attended Kharkov Collegium from 1771 to 1782. He served briefly as a secretary in the bishop's residence before transferring to the school at the local foundling home where he taught Russian grammar and mathematics. In 1784, he returned to the seminary to teach rhetoric and Russian poetics. *RGIA*, f. 796, o. 71, g. 1790, d. 144, ll. 3-4. Bashinskii

later became rector of the seminary when it was moved to Ekaterinoslav in 1804. N.M. Murzakevich, "Eparkhial'nye arkhierei Novorossiiskago kraia: I. Eparkhiia slovenskaia i khersonskaia," *ZOOID*, 9 (1875), p. 297.

81. E. Kolbasin, "I. I. Martynov," *Sovremennik*, 56 (1856), pp. 3-4.

82. Kolbasin, p. 4. The Baumeister textbook replaced Aristotle in the philosophy courses in the late eighteenth century and was particularly noted for its response to the skepticism of the Enlightenment. See Freeze, *Russian Levites*, p. 94.

83. Batalden, *Catherine*, p. 54.

84. Kolbasin, pp. 5-6.

85. "Dokumenty," pp. 192-193.

86. *Ibid.*, pp. 194-196.

87. *Ibid.*, pp. 196-200.

88. *Ibid.*, pp. 201-203.

89. Znamenskii, p. 512.

90. Nevodchikov, p. 34.

91. The archival sources contain lists of all instructors and students at the seminary in Ekaterinoslav for 1789, 1793 and 1797. The majority of students were the children of churchmen: ranging from 100% of the theology class to 60% of the Russian course. The non-clergy parents were primarily military (from soldiers to colonels) but a few were merchants, pharmacists, civil servants, Cossacks, and nobility. Enrollment dates were as early as 1779 when Theotokis established the seminary in Poltava. The average age of students in Theology was 27, in Philosophy - 22, in Rhetoric - 16, in Advanced Latin (II) - 14, in Elementary Latin (I) - 14, and in Russian - 12. The oldest student in the seminary during this time was 31 and the youngest was 8. The number of students who remained in the course the entire year was dependent such factors as job opportunities for Theology and Philosophy students or simply falling ill. The number of students enrolled in different schools and classes. Figures in () represent children of churchmen.

Year	Theo.	Philos.	Rhet.	Poesy	Latin II	Latin I	Russian
1789	9 (8)	20 (16)	84 (66)		59 (44)	45 (33)	58 (35)
1793	18 (17)	35 (28)	63 (53)	46 (32)	65 (49)	54 (37)	28 (15)
1797	14 (14)	25 (24)	77 (67)	30 (22)	49 (34)	50 (36)	74 (66)

Sources: *RGIA*, f. 796, o. 71, g. 1790, d. 144; f. 796, o. 75, g. 1793, d. 522; f. 796, o. 78, g. 1797, d. 982.

92. Dokumenty otnosiashchiesia," p. 186.

93. For profiles of the teaching staff see *RGIA* f. 796, o. 71, g. 1790, d. 144, ll. 1-6 *RGIA*, f. 796, o. 74, g. 1793, d. 568, ll. 2-6.

The 1789 seminary staff:

Faculty	Positions Held	Ethnicity & Father's Rank	Education
Gavriil Banulesko-Bodoni	Rector & Greek	Moldavian - Drabant	Kievan Academy
Ivan Bashinskii	Prefect & Theology	Ukr.- Priest	Kharkov Collegium
Iakov Artemov	Philosophy	Ukr.- Merchant	Kievan Academy
Ivan Stanislavskii	Rhetoric & Poesy	Ukr.- Archpriest	Kharkov
Grigorii Savurskii	Advanced Latin	Ukr.- Deacon	Kharkov
Fedor Krulianskii	Elementary Latin	Ukr.- Cossack	Kievan Academy
Matfee Tisarevskii	Russian	Ukr.- Archpriest	Kharkov
Andrei Peigii	German	Hungarian - Land Judge	Uni Seminary

The 1793 seminary staff:

Faculty	Positions	Ethnicity & Father's Rank	Education
Ivan Bashinskii	Prefect & Theology	Ukr.- Priest	Kharkov
Iakov Artemov	Philosophy	Ukr.- Merchant	Kievan Academy
Daniil Samma	Rhetoric & Poesy	Ukr.- Archpriest	Kharkov & Ekaterinoslav
D. Stefanovskii	Math, History, Geography	Ukr.- Deacon	Kharkov, Ekater., Alex. Nevskii
Petr Kunetskii	Greek & Ad. Latin	Ukr.- Priest	Ekaterinoslav
S. Zaushkevich	German	Polish - Priest	Kanev, Poland
G. Matveevskii	Elementary Latin	Ukr.- Priest	Ekaterinoslav
Anton Tregudov	Russian	Ukr.- Priest	Ekaterinoslav

94. For a brief discussion of this see Gary Marker, "Faith and Secularity in Eighteenth-Century Russian Literacy, 1700-1775," in Robert P. Hughes and Irina Paperno, eds., *Christianity and the Eastern Slavs, Vol. II: Russian Culture and Modern Times* (Berkeley, 1994), pp. 3-24.

95. *RGIA*, f. 796, o. 60, g. 1781, d. 188, l. 2.

96. *Ibid.*, l. 2ob. Also see Potemkin, "Pis'ma svetleishago kniaza Grigoriia Aleksandrovicha Potemkina-Tavricheskago," *Russkii arkhiv*, 7 (1880): 1597

97. Ibid., ll. 10 -10ob.

98. "Pis'ma," p. 1599.

99. *Ibid.*, ll. 11 -12ob.

100. Gavriil, p. 118.

101. "Pis'ma Potemkina," p. 1597. The announcements of Theotokis's ordination were sent out on 26 July 1779. The top half was in Russian and the bottom half in Greek. His official acknowledgment of the new post was printed in the same way as was the list of attendees: Catherine, Paul and Maria Feodorovna, Alexander Pavlovich and Constantine Pavlovich and members of the Holy Synod. *RGIA*, f. 796, o. 60, d. 188, ll. 38-40.

102. Gavriil, p. 118. This was the regimental church of the Grenadier Company of the Preobrazhenskii Guards Regiment commissioned by Elizabeth Petrovna to commemorate the regiment's support for her successful coup in 1741.

103. Solov'ev, p. 575.

104. N. Theotokis, *Prosfonima ti evsevestati, theostepto, sevasti, trismegisti kai filanthropotati avgousti kyria Aikaterini Aleksiadi, aftokratori pasis Rosias* (St. Petersburg, 1779). A manuscript copy of the Greek version is located in the Manuscript Division of the Szechenyi Nationalbibliothek of Budapest. See Robert Benidicty's transcription in his "Eine unedierte Rede von Nikiphoros, Metropolit von Cherson," in Johannes Irmscher and Marika Mineemi, eds., *O Ellinismos eis to Exoterikon* (Berlin, 1968), pp. 289-295.

105. Wortman, *Scenarios of Power*, pp. 122-128. For an explicit treatment of Catherine as legislatrix see O.A. Omelchenko, *"Zakonnaia Monarkhiia" Ekaterina II* (Moscow, 1993).

106. Theotokis ingratiated himself solidly with the Empress in the opening sentence when he praised Catherine's *Nakaz* and thereby produced, in effect, the image of her as an enlightened monarch who was completely deserving of admiration such as his. It is worth remembering that his well-regarded predecessor, Voulgaris, translated the *Nakaz* into Greek.

107. Solov'ev, p. 576.

109. Catherine's second grandson, Constantine Pavlovich, was born in 1779 and immediately became an integral part of Catherine's plan to revive the Greek Empire of which he would be the emperor.

4

Consecrating the Land/Constructing an Empire: Religion and Ethnicity

It gives us great pleasure to see our own countrymen act
with such zeal to build a church and because of this we give
without reservation our permission to do so.[1]

    – Archbishop Nikiforos to Taganrog Greeks

Every temple or palace – and, by extension, every sacred city
or royal residence – is a Sacred Mountain, thus becoming a
center.

    – Mircea Eliade, *Cosmos and History*

Following his 6 August consecration, Archbishop Nikiforos
remained in St. Petersburg until mid-September before beginning his
return journey to Poltava where he was to undertake his new diocesan responsibilities.[2] Theotokis used his time in St. Petersburg to
good purpose by relentlessly imploring the empress and her staff to
grant the funds needed to establish a new seminary in the diocese of
Slaviansk and Kherson. This was an annoying but necessary task that
Theotokis would often find himself repeating; he and his staff in the
diocese were constantly soliciting funds for projects begun under
Voulgaris but for which he received none little if any during his
brief tenure as archbishop. His request was finally granted and when
he set out for Poltava he carried with him the imperial edict
proclaiming the foundation of the Poltava Seminary and the requisite
funds from the College of Economy. Upon arriving in Poltava
Theotokis, by order of the Holy Synod, was given complete control
and direction of the Krestovozdvizhenskii Monastery, which would
continue to serve as the diocesan headquarters until a separate administrative building was constructed. Theotokis's initial delight with his
new position and duties was more likely than not tempered appre-
ciably when he learned that the diocesan administrative assistant had
elected to resign effective immediately. Archimandrite Theoktist had
accompanied Voulgaris to Poltava from Moscow in 1776 and was an
invaluable asset through his dealings with the Holy Synod and

in his management of the day-to-day bureaucratic matters eschewed by Voulgaris.[3] Theoktist received a stipend of five hundred rubles per annum and resigned his monastic as well as diocesan administrative position at the end of October 1779 just a few days after Theotokis arrived in Poltava[4].

••••

Even though the archbishop was thrust into this predicament without the services, initially, of a competent and experienced administrative assistant, it was not as if he was completely unaware of his new surroundings. Theotokis had resided in Poltava since 1776, had quickly learned the Russian language, and served capably under Voulgaris as rector of the little school in Poltava as well as inspector of all diocesan schools. The added episcopal responsibilities were, however, new to him and he moved with alacrity to begin meeting them until that time when, as he said to the empress in his thanksgiving address, "there is no breath left in me and my life will have reached its end."[5]

Of primary concern to Russian rulers since the time of Peter the Great was the adequate education of parish priests. If the majority of Russian subjects lacked the fundamental ability to read and write it would be nearly impossible to enlighten them according to the principles set forth by each monarch. As we have seen in regard to Theotokis's educational activities in the diocese, the burden of "enlightening" the masses was delegated to the Church, sometimes with, but usually without the requisite funds. The bishop was responsible for the education of his priests and was to assure himself and civil authorities that they understood their duties and were competent to exercise them. As a teacher of the true faith the bishop was to combat superstition, heresy, schismatics, and independent priests or, "wanderers," by educating them and directing them to the correct and true path. This also served the purposes of the state by eliminating the anti-Orthodox, anti-social elements which duly disrupted social stability. The bishop was head of the local seminary and in this capacity he appointed the rector and prefect and gave final approval to the curriculum, the hiring of instructors, and the discipline or promotion of faculty. Sometimes the bishop, if so inclined as was Theotokis, would teach a class in theology for the final year students. Spreading the faith to the broader population of the diocese required churches and the bishop was responsible for the construction of new churches where they were needed and closing churches that had fallen into disuse.[6]

••••

One problem which proved to be exceptionally difficult to overcome for Voulgaris during his brief tenure as archbishop of Slaviansk and Kherson was the inadequate number of churches and staffs for the growing population of his diocese. Initial Synodal reports made available to Voulgaris in 1776 informed him of the small number of existing churches in the new diocese. One report stated that no more than 293 churches were present in the *guberniias* of Novorossiia (115) and Azov (178).[7] Subsequent published accounts indicate how imprecise the figures on churches in the recently acquired southern territories were owing to St. Petersburg's ignorance of the conditions in Novorossiia. Nevodchikov, in his nineteenth-century biography of Voulgaris, provided a another set of figures: 344 churches (excluding monasteries) with 232 in Novorossiia and 112 in Azov.[8] Regardless of the discrepancies in the two reports the most significant fact is common to both: the relatively low number of churches in the southern reaches of the diocese. Areas of recent immigration by ethnic Greeks and others especially suffered from a lack of churches. In a report to the Holy Synod dated 21 December 1778, Voulgaris noted that three districts (*uezdy*), with a total population approaching four thousand, did not even have one church between them.[9] The Holy Synod reported that it knew of one church in Taganrog on the Sea of Azov, but if a church existed in Kerch, located on the peninsula between the Sea of Azov and the Black Sea, it was not aware of it.[10]

Church construction or the creation of "sacred" space was of fundamental importance to Catherine and to the Orthodox Church if they were to populate and to consecrate the landscape of Novorossiia.[11] The uncultivated lands and "desert" steppes needed to be filled with objects, both secular and sacred, that represented the presence of man and the divine sanction of the act of colonization. The construction of churches, chapels, cathedrals, monasteries and even the consecration of portable altars in military regiments were clear manifestations of a spiritual universality which connects those assembled in or around the sacred space to an experience which transcends local time and space. As metaphor, the religious sites are the saving grace of God in the godless deserts of the unbeliever. They are also a recreation of celestial temples. On a more mundane but no less significant level, the churches become an extension of the center into the periphery. The new lands are joined through the ritual act of church construction to the imperial center in St. Petersburg. The center is not bound by geography or time because it can recreate itself and, thereby, establish a universal empire. The problem, of course, is that just as believers can stray from the True Church and its sacred representations so can subjects stray from the True Monarch or True Empire and its provincial representations of the center.

Archbishop Eugenios moved to correct the situation as quickly as he could. In February 1777 he wrote to the Holy Synod informing it about a number of difficulties confronting the new diocese and made particularly clear the unusual multiethnic composition of the southern Ukraine and the dearth of available buildings to serve as churches. He requested that he be able to initiate directly the construction of new churches and ordain immigrants with the appropriate languages and religious training to staff the new churches.[12] This request came at a time when Catherine had decided to address the chronic problem of excess churches in the central provinces by placing restrictions on new church construction and contemplating ways to eliminate superfluous clergy and make them available for more productive tasks of benefit to the state. The desire to stabilize and develop quickly the southern regions, along with Governor-General Potemkin's endorsement of his request, worked in Voulgaris's favor and freed him from the restrictions obtaining in the central dioceses. On 27 March 1777 the Holy Synod issued a decree which granted Archbishop Eugenios the permission to establish churches for communities in need and to appoint non-Russian clergy to parishes provided they were examined and found capable of performing their duties and that they accept Russian citizenship.[13]

Voulgaris began touring his diocese in the summer of 1778 in order to determine better the needs of various communities. As a result of his visitations and his desire to meet the spiritual needs of the communities under his charge, Voulgaris decreed that churches be constructed in numerous cities and villages. During his three-year tenure as archbishop he granted permission for the establishment of many churches but relatively few were actually constructed while he was in office due to a variety of delays. For example, Archbishop Eugenios decreed the construction of four churches in Taganrog on the Sea of Azov in the summer of 1778, but the petitioning process was not completed until the arrival of Theotokis. He also received a positive response from the Holy Synod to his request that churches be established in the areas of Kherson and Novopavlosk in January 1779.[14] In another instance, representatives from the village of Konskovodovki sent a request to build a church to the Pavlovsk district council in July 1778. Their village of 120 households had already collected five hundred rubles toward church construction, building materials, bells, wax, candles, oil, communion wine and bread, and had set aside the land on which the priest and his family would live. Archbishop Eugenios reported all of this to Potemkin's assistant in the Azov *guberniia* chancellery, V.A. Chertkov, and he also approved the construction of a church in Konskovodovki. However, even though the approval was given at the end of July 1778, the village did not open its church until January 1781. The first delay was bureaucratic in nature: information on the ethnic composition of the petitioning village and the surrounding villages and hamlets was required by Synodal decree. Once this was done the village faced still further delays because they could not attract a qualified priest for two years.[15]

In late October 1778, the Elisavetgrad district council in Novorossiia began studying a petition sent to it by the second mayor of Pantazievka. Either the Elisavetgrad council was better staffed than Pavlovsk or the presence of immigrants (Wallachians and Serbians) in the petitioning village was a priority because Pantazievka laid the foundation stone of its church in June 1780, only three months after the council had delivered its report to the consistory in Poltava, and not even two years after the initial petition. In a rather curious case from the same period we see that the investigation of petitions by district councils was warranted and was more than perfunctory. In August 1778 court councilor (*nadvornii sovetnik*) and doctor, Ivan Poletika, sent a petition to Archbishop Eugenios requesting permission to construct a church. He wrote that he had recently settled near the Bazabluk river where he had also surveyed land for a village. A number of houses were already present in the village and not a few Zaporozhian Cossacks lived in the area. Poletika was rather concerned that because of the distance to the nearest church his villagers and the Cossacks would not receive the religious rites and education they needed. He had already gathered material for the new church, including church vessels and priestly vestments from his own resources, as well as set aside land for the priest and churchmen. Both the archbishop and the governor of Novorossiia approved the request and put in motion the investigative apparatus of the district council. The Slaviansk district council sent a superintendent, Father Grigoriev, to the village of Poletika in June 1779. Grigoriev reported that he counted only five huts in the village and a total of eighteen only if he went a considerable distance from the village.[16] He did not see any materials for church construction nor could he find Doctor Poletika anywhere. Grigoriev concluded his report by stating that at such a time when the village has the requisite number of households, land set aside for the priest and churchmen, and ample building supplies available for church construction then the consistory could grant a permit. The doctor petitioned the consistory twice again in August 1779 and July 1781, appealing to first Eugenios's, and then, Theotokis's "episcopal mercy," but to no avail.[17]

The appointment of clergy and churchmen to the newly created parish churches was, in many ways, more formidable than the act of constructing the church itself. Voulgaris was aware that he did not suffer the same "embarrassment of excess" clergy as his counterparts in the central provinces.[18] The absence of an established clerical estate in Novorossiia as well as the lack of an adequate ecclesiastical educational system together made it very difficult for the archbishop to find qualified clerics in the new region. Occasionally, students from the seminary in Pereiaslavl or the Kiev Academy would wander into Poltava and be appointed to the appropriate positions. But for the most part, parish positions remained vacant for a year or more, or worse yet from the viewpoint of the hierarchy, a Pole or Wallachian of doubtful credentials would fill the position.[19]

Voulgaris and Theotokis also were alert to the activities of religious pilgrims who frequented the southern Ukraine with no intention of becoming a priest in a new parish.[20] Many of these wandering clergy or fugitive priests came from Moldavia, Wallachia, Mt. Athos or other areas within the Ottoman Empire. Some came to Russia on legitimate missions to collect alms for monasteries and shrines under Ottoman control. Not all, however, had permission, in the form of a passport, to do so.[21] As a result, this was not only a concern of the ecclesiastical authorities but of the state as well. The governor-general of Little Russia, Field Marshall P.A. Rumiantsev, wrote in a letter to Archbishop Eugenios to beware of "pilgrims who under the cover of monastic garb" attempt to defraud the parishioners.[22] All migrating clergy were to be detained, interrogated to learn their intentions, and then either granted permission to stay or be sent back across the border.[23] Clergy who were allowed to stay were usually given the single option of entering a monastery to live out their days. Some found this life too constricting and fled, seeking safety wherever they could find it.[24]

••••

When Archbishop Nikiforos arrived in the diocese in the fall of 1779 he also made use of the Synodal decree of 1777 regarding the construction and consecration of new churches. As we have seen, many of the construction projects initiated by Voulgaris extended well into Theotokis's term of office. So, we already have a sense of what he confronted in determining the appropriate places for new parish churches and then trying as hard as possible to move toward a quick conclusion of the petitioning process. Archbishop Nikiforos embarked on his own four-month tour of the diocese, leaving Poltava in April 1780 and returning in July.[25] According to material collected by Pokrovskii, Theotokis was successful in substantially increasing the number of parish churches and staffs in southern Russia. Pokrovskii offers two sets of numbers which indicate that the number of churches in the diocese of Slaviansk and Kherson had increased dramatically by 1784. The total for the individual district councils was 388 and his figure for the two *gubernii* was 424.[26] Either figure provides compelling evidence that the number of churches did increase between twenty-five and thirty-five percent.

Church construction in the diocese of Slaviansk and Kherson during Theotokis's tenure fell into one of four categories: 1) new parishes in recently established villages or towns; 2) rebuilt or remodeled churches in already existing communities; 3) additional churches in a rapidly expanding village or town, and; 4) churches constructed for the special needs of a particular segment of a community, e.g., parishes established for an ethnic group. Of the approximately 180 churches constructed in the diocese from 1779 to 1787 the highest percentage would belong to the categories of new churches in new villages and additional churches for growing communities (ninety percent). Only two percent of churches were constructed for an ethnic community and the remaining eight percent were considered rebuilt churches.

The suburb (*sloboda*)[27] of Znamenka was founded by the vice governor-general of Azov, Chertkov, in late 1779 in order to "improve and ease" communications between the cities of Novoselitsoe and Matveevkoe in the district of Novomoskovsk.[28] In a very short time, owing no doubt to the position of its founder and benefactor, Znamenka was populated by "many manufacturers and the well-to-do." Two large noble estates and their peasant settlements sprang up around Znamenka within a few months of its establishment. A good number of the new inhabitants of Znamenka were colonists as Chertkov refers to population figures he received from land captain Alexandrov (*zemskoi komisar kapitan*) in his letter to Theotokis requesting permission to construct a church in the suburb. Znamenka and its surrounding settlements had a total population of 755 souls, Chertkov reported to Theotokis in his 3 November 1780 letter, but the residents lacked a priest who could administer the rites of the church they so badly needed. Chertkov respectfully informed the archbishop that the villagers already had in mind a former priest with the Rostov military regiment, Theodore Zelenskii, to serve their future parish. The consistory in Poltava instructed the Ekaterinoslav Spiritual District on 22 December 1780 to investigate the situation in Znamenka, i.e., see that it is indeed settled; determine the size of the population and to which parish, if any, the people belong; ascertain whether the people want a church and if so whether they have the means to construct one and support its churchmen; and, finally, give an appropriate recommendation. The investigation found that the population had increased to 1016 from 755 and concluded that everything was in order. On 27 January 1781, Archbishop Nikiforos charged Zelenskii to report to Znamenka to serve as a parish priest in a temporary building until the church was constructed.[29]

For most of the following year, the parishioners of Znamenka and the two peasant settlements used the church in the neighboring village of Novoselko for ceremonies, such as weddings, which could not be celebrated in the temporary building. The trips to the church in Novoselko became rather tiresome and the inhabitants of Znamenka decided in February 1782 to construct a temporary chapel in which these services could be held. Not too long after this the village was surprised by the charitable largesse of a former Light Guards Regiment priest near Orel. Father Kyrill Tarlovskii told the assembled villagers that "he would take them under his patronage and build for Znamenka a wooden church at his own cost (*na ves' svoi kosht*)." All he required of the village was that it supply the oak for the foundation, 120 desiatin of land for church maintenance, choose the location for it, and provide for any miscellany needed during construction.[30] A committee of eight parishioners, formed at the suggestion of Tarlovskii, wrote to Chertkov at the end of February requesting permission to take sixteen oaks from state land for a foundation, claim 120 desiatin for church maintenance, and asked for assistance in gaining an episcopal letter to begin construction of a church. The Chancellery of Azov Guberniia agreed to grant the parishioners the oaks and land and sent a letter to Archbishop Nikiforos on 6 April 1782 seeking permission for construction of a church in his diocese. On 25 April 1782 Theotokis granted the episcopal permission and in nearly a year, on 25 May 1783, the foundation stone was laid and blessed. On 1 March 1785 Archpriest Alexei Handeleev of Novomoskovsk consecrated and inaugurated the Church of Krestovozdvizhenskaia for services.[31]

Overall the parishioners of Krestovozdvizhenskaia Church in Znamenka were very fortunate that the founder of their suburb was the assistant to the governor-general of the province and that a "well-known charitable person" took them under his patronage. Chertkov was anxious to appease the inhabitants of his suburb and worked on their behalf to secure for them a priest within months of their request for one. This was amazing given the absolute shortage of qualified priests and churchmen in the southern provinces. That he was transferred to Znamenka also attests to the influence Chertkov exercised with the archbishop of Slaviansk and Kherson, Nikiforos Theotokis. Still, Theotokis did not grant the suburb permission to construct a church when first approached in 1780, but suggested that the church in the next village serve it as well. The appearance of the ex-Light Guards priest, Kyrill Tarlovskii, and his desire to assist the people of Znamenka in acquiring a church of their own is hard to explain. The southern frontier region was blanketed by numerous military regiments each with a priest, so it was no surprise that an individual like Tarlovskii appeared. However, one wonders by what manner a member of the white clergy came to possess a quantity of money enabling him to offer patronage in the construction of a church, and allegedly to have done so on previous occasions as well.

The archbishop's consistory received many simple requests which were resolved quickly. This was the case with a petition from the small Cossack state suburb of Alexandrovka in Pavlograd district just outside the city of the same name. This particular petition also touched upon the enactment of Catherine's decree to create a new province in southern Russia. In 1783, the two *gubernii* of Novorossiia and Azov were combined to form the *namestnichestvo* or lord lieutenancy of Ekaterinoslav (Glory of Catherine) and Prince Potemkin appointed as its *namestnik* or governor-general. Catherine created Ekaterinoslav *namestnichestvo* according to the Statute of 1775 on local administration even though its population fell short of the required number of inhabitants for a lord lieutenancy. This reflected the political importance of the southern province to both Catherine and Potemkin.[32] The new province comprised fifteen *uezdy* or districts whereas the total number of districts of the two *gubernii* had been twenty-one. This meant that some districts expanded and others disappeared. The petition submitted to Archbishop Nikiforos in May 1785 from the inhabitants of Alexandrovka dealt incidentally with this matter of changing districts.

The six-man committee from Alexandrovka wrote to Archbishop Nikiforos on 10 May 1785 requesting that their parish be allowed to transfer to another church. With the creation of Ekaterinoslav *namestnichestvo* their village was now in the district of Pavlograd and their parish was assigned to Uspenskii Church in the capital of the district, Pavlograd. This was posing some problems for the parishioners, however, because Alexandrovka was seventeen *versty* (eleven miles) from Pavlograd and it was only with great difficulty that they were able to attend services at Uspenskii or summon a priest to administer the "Christian rites when in the most extreme need."[33] The obvious solution to this unbearable situation was soon proposed by the petitioners: just down the road, only three versty away, was the village of Troitskaia with its own church and priest. It would be much easier for the parishioners of Alexandrovka to attend the church in Troitskaia than the one in Pavlograd, reasoned the petitioners, and thereby ensure adequate exposure to the Christian teachings and rites. The only problem was that Troitskaia was in the *uezd* of Novomoskovsk while Alexandrovka was in Pavlograd *uezd*. The petitioners wanted Theotokis's permission to transfer from one church in one district to another church in another district. The archbishop acted on the petition the following day by granting the request and sent word to the appropriate authorities in the affected jurisdictions of Pavlograd and Novomoskovsk Spiritual Districts.[34]

In some instances, as in the case above, the requests and petitions sent to Archbishop Nikiforos reflected not only the desires and needs of the immediate community but also the constantly and rapidly changing demographics and political situation of the southern frontier. In mid-July 1782 Theotokis received a petition from Colonel Ivan Petrovich Kasparov, commandant of the Taganrog fortress, requesting permission to begin construction on a new cathedral to replace the rotted and dilapidated Church of the Archangel Michael. In a manner, the fortune of churches in Taganrog mirrored the overall success or failure of Russian foreign policy initiatives along the northern Black Sea littoral and the Sea of Azov in particular.[35]

The first church in the Taganrog fortress, Holy Trinity, was constructed by command of Peter the Great after his victory over the Tatars at Azov in 1696. In 1711, Holy Trinity was transferred to Bakhmut following the razing of the fortress in accordance with the Pruth negotiations. Another church did not appear in Taganrog until 1769 when the fortress was retrieved from the Turks and Archangel Michael was built. This was the church to which Colonel Kasparov referred in his letter to Archbishop Nikiforos. Given the conditions of southern Russia in the years immediately following the Russo-Turkish War of 1768-1774, it would have been no surprise if the church in Taganrog had been constructed hastily with little thought given to its suitability as a permanent structure. On his visit to Taganrog in July 1778 Archbishop Eugenios found a church constructed "of pilings, with a covering of bast ... in which no more than two hundred could fit" and a movable or campaign field altar (*pokhodnaia podvizhnaia antimins'*).[36] Voulgaris suggested that until a new church was constructed services for feast and great feast days be held in the larger Church of St. Nicholas located in the wharf district of Taganrog nearby. At the time of Kasparov's letter to Archbishop Nikiforos the church was in such a deteriorated condition that it was no longer considered safe enough to conduct in it any services at all.

The diocesan consistory ordered the Novorostov Spiritual District to look into the affair and report back to it. In a report dated 24 August 1782, the investigating superintendent stated that the church was "indeed extremely decayed" and presented too great a danger for services to be held in it, but he was also quite impressed by the local parishioners' desire to construct a new church, in fact, one with a stone foundation.[37] The regimental commander, three battalion staffs, merchants and *raznochintsy* comprised the parish and all had given signed assurances that the means to build a new church were available. The parish, according to the superintendent's report, had already collected five hundred rubles, and was obtaining items for the divine service such as oil, wine, incense, etc. Arrangements for the financial security of the clergy and churchmen had already been made and posed no problem. As the church was to be located inside the fortress the priest and churchmen would not receive financial recompense from the parish but salaries from the commissariat instead: two priests at one hundred rubles each, one deacon at sixty rubles, two *diachoki* and two *ponomari* at twenty rubles each.[38] This was quite adequate considering the possible of size of the parish: three battalions of 1393 men, accompanied by two hundred women, supported by two hundred in artillery and engineering units brought the total number of those living inside the fortress to nearly 1800. Merchants living just outside the fort added another two hundred.[39]

The consistory responded favorably to the superintendent's report and on 24 September 1782 granted permission to begin construction of the new Church of the Archangel Michael. On 14 October, Archpriest Andreev of Novorostov consecrated the ground and construction commenced inside Taganrog fortress. Archpriest Stefan Razoretskii of the Mariupol Spiritual District sent a memo to Archbishop Nikiforos on 3 February 1783 stating that all was functioning well in the new church and that vestments, relics, icons, bells, and books had been successfully transferred to it from the decaying old church. He requested that the archbishop send his blessed approval to open the church for holy services and the sanctified communion cloth to place on the altar. This was done within a few days of receipt of the letter and the church of Archangel Michael began services in March 1785.[40]

Taganrog's population lying outside the walls of the fortress was expanding and changing as rapidly as it was inside the fortress itself. By 1775, the ethnic composition of Taganrog was beginning to reflect the recent influx of immigrants to southern Russia.[41] In fact, just two years earlier, in 1773, the commandant of the fortress declared that a particular area outside the fortress would be known as the "Greek Quarter" due to the increasing number of Greek merchants in the region.[42] The Greek population in Taganrog surged with the arrival of the two-hundred-strong "Spartan Legionnaires" or "Albanian Regiment" in 1775 and a large number of civilians. The settlement of both military and civilian Greek contingents in the aftermath of the Russo-Turkish War exhibited Catherine's and Potemkin's joint concerns of defense and economic development of the southern frontier. The soldiers were placed in newly constructed barracks near Pavlovskii fortress overlooking the harbor of the Mius River southwest of Taganrog. The regiment was also given the right to choose its own commanders: the first were General Dmitriades and Captain Alferakis of the naval detachment.[43] The civilian population settled within the fortress at first, but later moved into the city proper and took up residence near the port. Many of them were merchants and the majority of their shops were located along one street which was called "Greek Road" (*Graikiki agiia*). The civilian community counted among its more prestigious citizens members of the families of Alferakis, Holiaras, Drakos, Astlan,[44] Karayiannis, Gerodimatos, Palamas, Pogonatos, Stasas, Anastasis, Foumilis (Foumelis), and Flouttis.[45]

The Greek population of Taganrog was large enough by 1777 that some members of the community decided that it was appropriate and necessary to recruit a Greek-speaking priest to Taganrog to administer the sacraments and conduct the holy liturgy. They contacted Gerasim Balysh of Constantinople who agreed to come and serve as their priest. *Ieromonakh* Gerasim was to conduct services in the Church of the Archangel Michael just as the other local priests. When Archbishop Eugenios was visiting Taganrog in the summer of 1778 he discovered that Gerasim had not answered his call or appointment. Voulgaris promised the Greeks that he would appoint the Greek *ieromonakh* Epifanios to fill Gerasim's place and, at the same time, advised the community to think about constructing their own church.[46]

The Greek community responded enthusiastically to his suggestion and immediately turned their attention to the creation of a committee charged with laying the plans for a Greek church and parish in Taganrog. The first committee moved to obtain from the government of Taganrog land on which to build the church.[47] Having accomplished this the committee, on 20 December 1780, sent a petition to Archbishop Nikiforos apprising him of what had transpired up to that time in regard to creating a parish in Taganrog and seeking ecclesiastical permission to construct a church.[48] The petition began with a note of thanksgiving to Catherine for offering her patronage to the Greeks who came to Taganrog "from various places of the Archipelago." And that as foreigners to a new land the Greeks did not understand the Russian language and therefore were unable to attend the church services. The community sought to rectify this problem by constructing a Greek church in honor of the SS. Constantine and Eleni and recruiting a Greek-speaking priest. Preparations were already under way with an eight-member committee made up of the "most honorable" men of the community. The committee was divided equally among those who had lived in Taganrog for a few years and those who had recently taken up residence.[49] This committee had already collected nearly one thousand rubles through voluntary donations and building materials necessary for construction. The question of maintaining the salary allowance for the priest and the churchmen as well as annual expenses for oil, candles, incense, etc., was to be solved in an enterprising manner peculiar to a merchant community. A type of levy or surcharge would be imposed on all transactions involving the use of weights and measures and containers for making butter (*eisprattosin (en eidei forou) merida tina ek ton emporikon stathmon, metron kai leviton, en ois analiousi to voutiron*).[50] This, the committee hoped, was sufficient for Archbishop Nikiforos to give his episcopal permission (*blagoslovitel'naia gramota*), send to them a book in which to record the money collected for the church and a consecrated communion cloth. One final request was, in fact, a reminder that the community desired a Greek priest and that if one could not be found in Russia that they be allowed to call one from Greece (*ek tou Arhipelagous*) with the permission of his local bishop.[51]

An internal memo drafted by the secretary of the consistory, Vasilii Kervinskii, and sent to the archbishop on 18 February 1781 summarized the petition of the Taganrog Greeks. The consistory informed the committee that once construction began it was to submit a report in Russian to the archbishop providing a very detailed account of the dimensions of the altar and the holy sanctuary (*ieron vima*) to ensure the consistory that they were within the guidelines. In regard to securing a Greek-speaking priest for the parish, the consistory ruled that if one could not be found in the diocese by the archbishop, then the community would be allowed to choose from among them one to be ordained or if already ordained to be sent to Poltava to be examined and, if adjudged worthy, to be ordained. Finally, the consistory would notify the Novorostov Spiritual District as to its decision, appeal officially to the governor-general of Azov to grant the land for the church and its servants, and send the record book to them.[52]

Archbishop Nikiforos replied to the community in Taganrog by letter on 18 February 1781 (the same day as Kervinskii's memo to the archbishop). Nikiforos began his letter by stating that "it gives us great pleasure to see our own countrymen act with such zeal to build a church and because of this we give without reservation our permission to do so." He then addressed the question of obtaining a Greek-speaking priest for the parish: the first appointed priest, Archpriest Konstantin Tyrlinskii, unfortunately had died on 10 January 1781 and now was resting with the Lord (*kekoimitai en Kyrio*), but another priest, *Ieromonakh* Ieremia Grammatikopoulos from the Greek Church of St. Vladimir in Elisavetgrad, had been appointed to take his place.[53] This priest, Theotokis wrote, "will attend to your salvation by practicing the divine liturgy and will, by word and deed, exhort everyone to follow the road of virtue." The career of Ieremia is enlightening as it represents fairly well the experiences of other Greek churchmen who left their native land and sought refuge in Russia. According to the interrogation report sent to Theotokis, he was born on an Aegean island to Greek Orthodox parents, received the tonsure in 1768, went to Athos in 1769 and remained there until 1779. In that year he traveled to Constantinople where he received a passport from the Russian consul, Stakhiev, which gave him permission to proceed to Kinburn in the province of Azov. Ultimately, he made his way to Poltava. Theotokis, pleased to have a Greek priest, requested that the Holy Synod allow him to send Ieremia to a Greek regiment under the command of Brigadier Iakov Repinskii.[54] The Holy Synod failed to respond to his request. In November 1779, Theotokis sent a three-page letter to the Synod complaining about the Synod's reluctance to attend adequately to the spiritual needs of good Christians. He argued that children were not

baptized, the dying were without confession, and no one was receiving Holy Communion.[55]

The archbishop's letter produced results. The Synod, on 27
January 1780, ruled that it would accede to Nikiforos's requests but
it also set forth guidelines for the recruitment and acceptance of
priests from abroad. The priests were allowed into Russia *only* to
serve the new settlements where they spoke Greek or other foreign
languages. The appropriate civil authorities and the archbishop
would supervise the new priests and examine them in matters of faith
and doctrine. The Synod would allow new church construction for
the non-Russian speaking communities only if they possessed enough
members per church. The archbishop would assume responsibility
for supervising the priests' performance of the rites. Metropolitan
Ignatii was solely responsible for the Crimean Christians of the
Greek rites. Finally, Nikiforos was responsible for finding and
appointing the priests either from among the colonists themselves or
among Russians who spoke Greek.[56]

In his letter to the Taganrog Greeks, Nikiforos next addressed
the matter of parish finances. The archbishop was quite explicit
about maintaining "very detailed" records of all manner of revenue
and expenditures. As we have seen above the diocesan administrators
were constantly on the alert to detect possible fraudulent actions
which would reflect poorly on the Church. Theotokis seemed especially concerned that the Greek parish should appear to be
completely without corruption and above reproach. With this is
mind, the consistory also decided to send a second book in which
would be recorded all offerings collected by the church besides the
book used to record transactions relevant to actual church construction. The archbishop then strongly advised the committee to "put all
church money in a strongbox and put it in a safe place making sure it
is locked two or three times."[57] A memo sent to Archbishop
Nikiforos by the consistory secretary Kervinskii a few days later,
elaborated upon the necessity of adopting measures to maintain
financial integrity at all costs and assured Theotokis that this had
been expressly communicated to the Greek representative, Gounalis.
The committee was allowed to continue to solicit donations from
individuals and the names should be recorded properly in the book.
Conduct yourselves appropriately, warned the secretary, for the
tiniest scandal (*paramikrotaton skandalon*) inevitably leads to fines
and punishment. And once the church was constructed the book of

donations was to be placed in the church as a memorial to those who gave.[58]

On 24 March 1781 the foundations of the Church of SS. Constantine and Eleni were consecrated by Archbishop Neofitos Zarnatis.[59] The construction of the church proceeded rapidly and on 27 January 1782 the committee sent a letter to Archbishop Nikiforos requesting that he send the inaugural letter and the consecrated communion cloth so the church could open. The archbishop responded to the request on 8 February 1782. He praised the committee for the manner in which the funds were raised and the church constructed (all without scandal). He, however, had a request to make of the community which he hoped would not be too burden-some or difficult: parts of all the divine services and holy liturgies should be conducted in Russian. In Theotokis's attempt to persuade the parish to allow this he cited a number of reasons why this should be done. First, it was just (*dikaion*) that the Greeks should show their appreciation for all that they had received from the Russian state and nation. Second, out of necessity (*anangkaion*), the Russians who lived in the Greek quarter would attend the Greek church until they built one of their own. Third, it would be beneficial (*epofeles*) to the church if more attended its services. Fourth, it would bestow a great honor (*timion*) on the parish to have the leaders [Russians] present among the subjects [Greeks]. Finally, it would foster mutual feelings of protection and love (*prostasias kai agapis*) between the two communities.[60] Archbishop Nikiforos closed his letter by gently entreating the parish to collect money for "our brothers the poor" at each church meeting and then have the parish representative disburse the charitable contributions each Saturday according to the wishes of the priest.

The Church of SS. Constantine and Eleni was officially conse-crated and opened for holy services and divine liturgy on 13 March 1782. The amount of attention Archbishop Nikiforos devoted to his flock in Taganrog did not diminish after the inauguration as parish problems concerning staffing, ecclesiastical jurisdiction and finances continued to arise until his departure from the diocese in the fall of 1786. The problems the Greek community had in keeping priests in its parish seemed never to end. In early 1782 the parish took it upon itself to find a Greek priest and recruited the Archpriest Nikita Agurosa from the island of Paros.[61] By the end of that same year, in December 1782, the parish decided it needed a second priest and sent to Theotokis a candidate they had chosen for ordination. This candidate obviously did not satisfy the requirements which the archbishop established upon assuming his diocesan seat for the priest was rejected and unceremoniously returned to the community.[62] A few months later, in March 1783, Theotokis wrote to the parish in Taganrog and informed them that he had found a priest for them and that they should not bother to send any more candidates for examination. Archimandrite Nikolaos Priftin joined the parish in the spring and the income of the church was to be divided equally between Nikolaos and Nikita. However, in matter of rank Nikolaos, as an archimandrite, was to be superior to Nikita, who was an archpriest.[63] One year later, Archpriest Nikita returned to Paros and was replaced by Konstantin Pavlov Scholarios, a Greek who previously had worked in the Azov Provincial Chancellery, served as a secretary in the Mariupol court or tribunal (*sud'*), and a teacher in the Greek school.[64] Thus, once again we can see how the conditions in southern Russia were so entirely different from those obtaining in the central provinces that parishes and bishops were allowed an amount of latitude in the election or appointment of clergy and churchmen that was contrary to Synodal law. Of greater interest, however, is the notion that Orthodox immigrants from the Balkans would not have regarded the situation as anomalous because, traditionally, Orthodox parishes were allowed to elect their own priests and only an eighteenth-century decree by the Russian Holy Synod enjoined bishops alone to make appointments in order to reduce the number of supernumerary priests and churchmen.

Questions of ecclesiastical jurisdiction and parish finances from the parish of SS. Constantine and Eleni demanded Archbishop Nikiforos's attention in 1784. As already noted above, the two provinces of Novorossiia and Azov were subsumed into the newly created *namestnichestvo* or lord lieutenancy of Ekaterinoslav in 1784. The parishioners of the Greek church in Taganrog were no less concerned about the ramifications of this change than were there counterparts in the tiny settlement of Alexandrovsk and, as a result, sent their representative to Poltava in July 1784. Theotokis assured the representative of the parish, Ioannis Pogonatos, that the clergy and churchmen were still responsible, as before, to the consistory in Poltava in all spiritual and pastoral matters. Annual reports and financial accounts, however, should be given to Archpriest Stefanos Razoretskii of the Novorostov Spiritual District who will carry them to Poltava.[65] This alone did not seem serious enough to warrant a journey to Poltava by Pogonatos, however, the content of a letter written by Theotokis on 9 July reveals the primary purpose.

Pogonatos was concerned about the financial situation of the parish especially the maintenance of the clergy, churchmen, and expenses incurred through the practice of holy services and divine liturgy. Originally, the parish intended to meet these maintenance obligations by imposing a users' fee or surcharge on certain commercial transactions involving weights and measures. Unfortunately, the revenue earned from these fees was insufficient to cover the annual expenditures. Pogonatos explained to Archbishop Nikiforos that the parish had conceived yet another idea to resolve the problem of monetary shortfall. The parish and community established eight workshops (*ergastiria*) in the wharf commercial district known as Virzan. Not only the profits from these shops, but the shops themselves, belonged to the church to meet the maintenance requirements of the staff and to help in retiring a debt of 1800 rubles the parish expected to incur in the construction of its iconostasis. Theotokis found nothing objectionable with the project and the consistory officially decreed that this was an appropriate means to maintain the servants of the church. The parish also wanted to assure itself that this favorable condition would continue into the future and requested that the archbishop intervene on its behalf with the Ekaterinoslav government to secure for the Greek community exclusive rights to establish shops and businesses in the Virzan district. Theotokis was amenable to this idea as well and indicated that he would inform the government of the consistory's favorable position. He also stated that "we see the warmth of the community in Taganrog for its church and servants and praise its diligence and zeal."[66]

The fondness which Archbishop Nikiforos exhibited toward the Greek community in Taganrog in the summer of 1784 had completely dissipated by that November when whiffs of scandal in the parish of SS. Constantine and Eleni reached the consistory in Poltava. "Whoever has the audacity to misappropriate to himself something of the church, whether small or large, whether much or little...the soul of that miserable wretch (*trisathlios*) shall be filled with mortal sin (*thanatiforon amartian*)."[67] In this manner Theotokis began his letter of 20 November 1784 admonishing the Greek community for allowing the establishment of a grievance court in the courtyard (*avli*) of the church. Evidently some of the church leaders appropriated the small church building within the courtyard and conducted legal proceedings in it. They also took church funds allegedly to maintain the court but this money was instead "squandered by the embezzlers." The archbishop reproached them for these actions which brought scandal to the Church, "for the house and money of the church is dedicated to God," and chided them for not consulting their priest or the consistory to determine the propriety of such an act in the first place.[68] Theotokis then commanded that the community remove the court from the court-yard and force the "judges" (who were the same church elders who established the court) to surrender all the property and funds they misappropriated from the church. To prevent such a scandal from occurring again the archbishop instructed the parish to elect, accord-ing to parish rules, a responsible member of the church to be placed in charge of all church funds and he shall be held accountable for them. The scandal divided the parish horribly and threw it into a state of mutual recrimination and quarreling. Theotokis advised the parish to find peace within it and live in brotherly love, for if the fighting and quarreling does not end, he warned, the parish faced possible dissolution.[69]

Archbishop Nikiforos's subsequent relations with the com-munity in Taganrog were less stressful in his remaining years in the diocese. Later in 1784 Theotokis sent an instruction to Ioannis Pogonatos regarding the location of the parish cemetery. The parish, of course, had expressed the wish that the cemetery should be placed very near the Church of SS. Constantine and Eleni, but Theotokis cautioned them first to inquire into the required distance separating a cemetery from the church or other buildings to avoid possible viola-tions and future forfeiture of the land. Perhaps it would be wiser, he suggested, to claim land outside city limits for the cemetery and use the land next to the church at another time.[70] The last correspon-dence we have between Archbishop Nikiforos and the community occurred in early 1786 and concerned the construction of the church's iconostasis. Theotokis first praised the community for its fine philanthropic activity and then informed its representative, Ilia Oikonomou, that he was sending a skilled craftsman, Andreas Galtzounis, to Taganrog to design and construct an iconostasis for the church. Once again, Theotokis could not restrain himself from dispensing fatherly advice to his flock when he whispered the follow-ing caveat, "also, it is good to have one [the iconostasis] constructed under your own supervision."[71] And if the parish did not find the design agreeable they could return the craftsman to Poltava and owe him nothing.

••••

In the summer of 1780 Archbishop Nikiforos was confronted with a very different and perplexing problem in the realm of church construction and parish development. This dilemma did not result from the usual lack of funds or the absence of a favorable report from the local superintendent, but oddly enough, was precipitated by the recent arrival of Christian Greeks from the Crimea under the spiritual guidance and authority of Metropolitan Ignatii Gozadinov of Gottha and Kefa.[72] On 27 July 1780 Theotokis received a notice from the Pavlograd Spiritual District which reported that owing to the presence of the Crimean Greeks in the area, the campaign church (*pokhodnaia tserkov'*) of St. Nicholas on the Kal'mius River was now a Greek parish by command of Metropolitan Ignatii. The message continued by reporting that the priest of St. Nicholas, Roman Koshevskii, had been summarily removed by the same metropolitan and replaced by a priest from among the Greeks. This action brought Theotokis into a confrontation with the governor-general of Azov *guberniia*, V.A. Chertkov, over the question of ecclesiastical jurisdiction and, by extension, the interrelated problem of unquestioned state priority in all domestic matters with foreign policy implications.[73]

Archbishop Nikiforos, in a letter to the governor-general's chancellery, questioned the propriety of Metropolitan Ignatii's action as it obviously affected a church within the eparchial boundaries of his diocese of Slaviansk and Kherson. Chertkov sent him a reply on 13 August more or less telling Theotokis to accept the metropolitan's action as a *fait accompli.* He attempted to soften the effect of this statement, however, by decreeing that he would permit the parish of St. Nicholas on the Kal'mius, with its holy vessels and communion cloth, to be transferred to the newly founded city of Pavlograd on the Vol'chia River. Archbishop Nikiforos was reluctant to accept this decision, which forced Chertkov to justify his own demands and those of Metropolitan Ignatii for the church. Chertkov claimed that the original builders and members of this church were Zaporozhian Cossacks who had since fled to the Pavlograd area after the Sich' was destroyed by Potemkin.[74] Thus, in a bit of circular reasoning, it seemed eminently sensible to Chertkov that the church be transferred to Pavlograd, which had the right to demand that this church be given to it. The priest appointed to the parish will not only receive a salary of sixty rubles per annum from the Treasury, Chertkov promised, but also all profits from the church and a fine plot of land in the community. And if this were not sufficient to convince Archbishop Nikiforos, Metropolitan Ignatii informed Theotokis that Prince Potemkin himself had issued the order to Ignatii during his recent stay in St. Petersburg that the Kal'mius church be given up to the Greeks.[75] Theotokis finally accepted the situation and the parish was transferred to Pavlograd on 11 December 1780 where it did remain under his jurisdiction.

The contents of the church of St. Nicholas soon found their way to Pavlograd but were not placed in a sturdy church similar to the one on the banks of the Kal'mius. Instead the communion cloth, holy books and vessels, and icons were housed in a small wooden hut that was consecrated for holy services in April 1781. Within a few months, however, the governor-general of Azov requested that Archbishop Nikiforos give his permission to begin construction of a new wooden church in the name of the SS. Peter and Paul. Theotokis granted his permission on 4 August and in less than a year the new Church of SS. Peter and Paul was completed and consecrated on 23 April 1782 by Archpriest Feodor Pisarevskii from the Pavlograd Spiritual District.[76]

Even after its transformation into the Church of SS. Peter and Paul the little Kal'mius church was not destined to remain in the city of Pavlograd for more than two years as colonizing pressures of an extremely remarkable nature forced the parish to relocate once again. In this instance not only the church was transferred to the new colonists but all the inhabitants in the entire city of Pavlograd. On 19 April 1784 a group of Catholic colonists from Corsica were settled by imperial decree in the city of Pavlograd.[77] The presence of these colonists in southern Russia was yet another consequence of Russian foreign policy objectives in southern Europe in the 1760s and 1770s. The recently appointed Russian *charge d'affaires* in Livorno (Tuscany), Count Demetrio Mocenigo, sent five separate groups (1010 people) of Greeks and Corsicans to Russia between August 1782 and July 1783.[78] Many of the Corsicans had great difficulty adapting to agricultural life in Russia which subsequently led to flights from their original settlements. Eventually, Potemkin collected eighty-four families from various places in Novorossiia and settled those who had indicated their desire to work the land in the Pavlograd area.[79] The government then proceeded to remove all the Russians and Cossacks from Pavlograd and transfer them to Nikitskoe fortress where there was not yet a church but the priest from Pavlograd stayed with them nonetheless. The old Church of SS. Peter and Paul was simply abandoned, but the iron cross from the roof was sent to the Greek settlement in Mariupol for safekeeping.[80] Thus, we return to the original source of the discomfiture of the parish of St. Nicholas.

••••

The sudden appearance of Metropolitan Ignatii of Gottha and Kefa and the Crimean Greeks in Novorossiia in 1778-1779 must be examined in light of Russian intentions regarding the Crimea following the Treaty of Kutchuk-Kainardji. Following Crimean independence from the Ottoman Porte in 1774 there was no doubt in Europe that Catherine intended to annex it to the Russian Empire. Catherine secured the title of khan in 1777 for one of her native Tatar supporters, Shagin Girey, in order that the Crimea would be more independent from the Ottomans and more receptive to her own plans. Shagin, however, found very little support among the Muslim Crimean population because of his strong desire to implement westernizing reforms and, as a consequence, a revolt broke out against his reign in October 1777. The revolt was suppressed within a few months but only with the assistance of Russian troops under the command of Lieutenant General Prozorovskii.[81] Once the revolt had been quashed and Shagin Girey's authority was restored the Russian army prepared to leave. During this time of upheaval and suppression Field Marshall Rumiantsev instructed Prozorovskii to persuade Metropolitan Ignatii of the merits of evacuating the Crimean Greeks from the Crimea to protect them from Muslim reprisals against those Greeks and Armenians who had participated in the suppression of the revolt.[82] Ignatii actually needed little in the way of persuasion and eagerly entered into negotiations in April 1778 with the Russians to determine the privileges the Crimean Greeks would receive when they emigrated to Novorossiia.[83]

Catherine's successes in the Russo-Turkish War of 1768-1774 had the completely understandable impact of turning her attentions away from Nikita Panin's "Northern System" and increasingly toward Potemkin's southern vistas. She and Potemkin dreamed of driving the Turkish Moslems from Europe, liberating the Balkan Christians, and restoring geographical and cultural contiguity with classical Greece by creating a Hellenic kingdom. Her machinations with Shagin Girey in the Crimea were the first steps in actualizing the dream. In 1779, she christened her second grandson Konstantin, an unmistakable allusion to the first and last Byzantine emperors, and proposed that he occupy the throne of a new Greek Empire in the recovered Constantinople. The reverse side of the medal Catherine ordered to celebrate his birth, depicted the Cathedral of St. Sophia. His childhood friends, wet nurse and servant spoke Greek.[84] Potemkin laid plans to construct a kingdom comprising Bessarabia, Wallachia and Moldavia under the ancient name of Dacia. Perhaps, never certain of his tenure as Catherine's current favorite or her health, he was building a refuge from rejection or the wrath of her son, Paul. Although Catherine and Potemkin dreamed of a reconstituted Greek kingdom, it was Foreign Minister A.A. Bezborodko who drafted a document, the so-called "Greek Project," in May 1780 which gave concrete expression to the empress's (as well as Bezborodko's and Potemkin's) desires to dismember the Ottoman Empire with the assistance of Joseph II of Austria. His plan also became the foundation of a Russo-Austrian alliance in 1781 which enabled Catherine to annex the Crimean peninsula two year later.[85]

Catherine continued to forge Byzantine and classical Greek bonds with the southern region when, in 1782, she created the new Order of St. Vladimir, named in honor of the grand prince of Kiev who converted to Orthodoxy in 988 in Kherson, the city she founded in 1778. She even referred to Potemkin as "the young Colossus of Kherson!" She populated the south with classical Greek appellations: The Dnieper was rechristened the Vorysthene (the Greek Vorysthenis) and the Black Sea once again became the "Euxine." In the spring of 1783 Catherine's manifesto announcing and justifying her annexation of the Crimea belied yet again her imagined association with Minerva, the bearer of civilization, when she stated that the Tatars must surrender their freedom because their ignorance and savagery made them incapable of appreciating it.[86] The conquest of the Crimea was accomplished without much bloodshed and, more important, without an Ottoman declaration of war. In early 1784 Catherine resorted to another classical allusion when she renamed the Crimea the Tauride (allegedly the place where Agamemnon's daughter Iphigenia took refuge in Euripides's *Iphigenia in Taulis,* the comic sequel to his tragedy, *Iphigenia in Aulis*). Later that same year, Russia's civilizing mission proceeded, when Potemkin announced the foundation of a university in Ekaterinoslav (the city was moved in that same year from the Samara River to the banks of the Dnieper). Subsequently, Potemkin planned to build a theater, an academy of music, a cathedral to rival St. Peter's in Rome, official buildings, almshouses, an Exchange, and hospitals. It was also one of the first cities in Russia built according to a plan. He enhanced cultural development with the introduction of a mobile or campaign (*pokhodnoi*) press which even printed works in Greek, Latin, French and Russian.[87] Catherine very much wanted to undertake a journey to her new acquisitions and grace it with her imperial presence but the trip was postponed until early 1787.

Catherine's grand tour began on 7 January 1787 and lasted nearly seven months.[88] Her entourage included the envoys of France (de Ségur who produced an intriguing "illusory" account of the trip), Austria (Cobenzl) and Britain (Fitzherbert), leading officials of the court, her personal staff, and a few honored guests (Prince de Ligne met them at Kiev and Joseph II of Austria joined the group near Kherson) . They departed from St. Petersburg in fourteen carriages, 123 sledges and forty supporting vehicles and transferred to a fleet of seven specially designed galleys, armed with canons and orchestras, eighty support ships and three thousand troops.[89] Ostensibly, Catherine's traveling court was to see Russia and, perhaps, underscore the imperial reach of Russia attained by Catherine as she continued to advance to the south and to displace the Ottoman Empire. The traveling empress, however, also became an object of spectacle herself as she willfully projected the magnificence and glory of the center onto the periphery. Thousands of her subjects personally witnessed the great performance and marveled at the finery and brilliance of the traveling court, others kept informed through the newspapers in St. Petersburg and Moscow, and even Europeans fixed their gaze upon the expedition to the "Orient" within the "Orient." Catherine intended to display to the world her civilizing mission: the transformation of the formerly uninhabited and desert steppe of southern Russia into magnificent and fertile gardens of paradise.[90] When she arrived in Kiev she ordered the mint in Petersburg to strike a medal to commemorate the trip. On one side was Catherine's image, on the other, her itinerary encircled by the inscription "The Way to Benefit" (*put' na pol'zu*).[91]

The plans for Catherine's journey to the south had been in the making for nearly two years and Potemkin was responsible for many of the elaborate celebrations, fireworks, staged performances, and choreographed spectacles that bombarded travelers and the "objects" of their travel alike. He wanted to glorify Catherine, her empire, and her golden reign. It was a grand parade in which everyone was a participant and a spectator. All that Potemkin had accomplished in Novorossiia was on display, festively decorated in garlands of flowers and draped with colorful banners. At nearly every stop Catherine received the local nobility which allowed them to participate in the court ever so briefly and created bonds between the empress and her most prized subjects. She also extended recognition to the newest members of the empire when she met with Tatar delegations in Kremenchug and Bakhchisarai. In each community she was met by crowds of people who accompanied her and her entourage through a victory arch into town. In Ekaterinoslav, Archbishop Amvrosii, Theotokis's successor, lauded Catherine's achievements in turning "infertile deserts into inhabited villages and cities, defending this country from foes, and securing the well-being of the subjects."[92] When the empress entered Kherson, the local fortress displayed a banner proclaiming, "The Route to Byzantium." Archbishop Eugenios, now residing in Kherson, addressed Catherine in Greek and gently reminded her that she was the hope of Greece, its liberator and protector.[93] Perhaps the show of military might in the shipyards of Kherson was sufficient for Voulgaris as two ships of the line were newly launched a few days later.

Catherine and her guests entered Tauride in late May and were immediately seduced by an exoticism of their own creation. The empress stayed at the palace of the last khan during her excursion to Bakhchisarai and used his *divan* as her throne. Her fellow travelers scoured the countryside for a chance sighting of an unveiled woman. Potemkin contributed to the exoticism when he presented a surprised empress with a battalion of "Amazons," one hundred Greek women dressed in red dresses and gold turbans.[94] The visitors represented the Crimea as elusive, culturally distinct, and "oriental." They relished the escape it offered, yet recognized that the peninsula must yield to the Russian Empire and its tireless civilizing mission. It was, indeed, Catherine's voyage to the south, the imperial gaze of her retinue, which, in a sense, created the south. Her very act of visitation validated its existence. This process of invention or renovation appropriated the land, the people, and their history and made them part of Catherine's world. The numerous travel accounts and literary treatments of her grand tour reinforced the image of the Crimea's absorption into Russia. The empress and Potemkin saw Tauride not Crimea, Sevastopol not Akhtiar, Odessa not Gadzhibei, SS. Andrew and Vladimir not Genghis Khan, Novorossiia not the steppe, paradise not desert. Of course, the steppe never was an uninhabited desert. That too was an invention made necessary if a transformation where to occur. They displaced Tatar history, topography, and culture with monuments to classicism and their own achievements. The imperial theme continued on the journey home. At Poltava, Potemkin arranged a reenactment of Peter's great battle and Catherine bestowed on him the title of "Tavricheskii" (of Tauride) and the sum of 100,00 rubles. A few months later, Potemkin asked Eugenios Voulgaris to write a history of Vorysthenis:

> Even as you unite in yourself the knowledge of diverse centuries, so you are our Hesiod, Strabo and Chrysostomos. Take then the time to make a description of our historic region [Novorossiia], what it was in ancient times, where from time immemorial were the Slavs and the inhabited cities: Ol'viia, Melitopol'; the islands of Achilles, the routes and so forth. Dig up the hidden past and show the action as societies flourished there....
> The *Voristhen*, bearing on itself the fleets of the early Rus', was not so named by chance. Its banks recall also the bright path of St. Andrew, who preached salvation to our fathers.[95]

Voulgaris was never able to oblige Potemkin with a history of New Russia or the new Vorysthenis, but the request underlines his commitment to reinventing the southern steppe.

••••

The evacuation of the Christians (the Armenian community led by Peter Margos and the Roman Catholic community led by Father Iakov also fled)[96] from the Crimea was a significant step in the

ultimate annexation of the Crimea by Russia in 1783. The exodus of
the Christians was initiated by a legitimate and real concern for the
safety of the various Christian communities once the Russian army
left the Crimea. Political and economic considerations, however,
soon superseded this initial humanitarian concern. The majority of
Christians were merchants and artisans.[97] Their departure from the
Crimea would drastically undermine its economy and precipitate
political instability which the Russians could exploit to their own
benefit.[98] Furthermore, the immigration of these same merchants
and artisans into Russia would have a salutary effect on the economic
prosperity and political stability of Potemkin's Novorossiia. The only
difficulty encountered by the Russian policy-makers was a reluctance
on the part of some of the Christian population to leave their homes
and prosperous businesses behind. Many of the Greeks in the Crimea
had been there for generations and did not even speak Greek but a
Tatar or Turkic language.[99] Very few shared the urgency of their
Balkan co-religionists to leave the Muslim dominated lands because
they occupied a protected and privileged position in the Crimean
Khanate owing to their taxpaying potential.[100] As a result,
Metropolitan Ignatii's role in mobilizing the Crimean Greek population for the migration to southern Russia was significant.

In mid-summer 1778 the migration to the northern coastal
region of the Sea of Azov began under the leadership Metropolitan
Ignatii. By the end of August, 10,239 had left and by 18 September
the last emigrants crossed into Russian territory. The final number
of Crimean Christians who left was somewhere near 32,000.
Pokrovskii has broken this figure down into the component
ethnic/religious groups: 18,400 Greeks, 300 Georgians, 161
Wallachians, and 12,606 Armenians.[101] The number who actually
settled in the Azov region, however, is difficult to determine because
many died of disease during the trip and others gave up and returned
to their homes in the Crimea.[102] Curiously, Archbishop Eugenios
learned of the metropolitan's presence from Chertkov only on 20
October 1778 and when he informed the Synod of this new Greek
hierarch he received no reply from them until the following spring
on 15 March 1779, one day after Catherine's edict to the Synod
granting three provisions to Metropolitan Ignatii.[103] First, Ignatii
was to be the hierarch of the new colonists from the Crimea and
directly responsible to the Synod; and the priests who accompanied
him were to remain with their parishes and under his spiritual

supervision. Second, he was to be called metropolitan of Gottha and Kefa and occupy a place under the archbishop of Slaviansk and Kherson. Third, the College of Economy was to grant the metropolitan and his staff a yearly maintenance allowance of 3000 rubles.[104]

About one month later, on 21 May 1779, Catherine issued another decree delineating the rights and privileges of the new Crimean Greek residents. All debts owed to the khan or khanate were to be paid at the expense of the Treasury. The entire community was given the right to use the land along the *guberniia*'s rivers and coastline for fishing without paying tax. Also, merchants, traders, and artisans were allowed to settle in the cities of Ekaterinoslav and Mariupol. All were freed from taxes and any type of government service for a period of ten years and were not subject to military conscription for perpetuity. Metropolitan Ignatii was designated as the spiritual head of the community and responsible directly to the Holy Synod. The Greek community, within the general framework of Russian law, would administer the courts and police functions. All Russian laws relevant to the magistrate court would be translated into Greek. Those appointed to executive positions or elected by the community were to be paid by and responsible to the Azov *guberniia* administration. Finally, merchants and tradesmen were given full protection under Russian law to engage in both internal and international commerce and were given permission to construct whatever factories, buildings, transportation vessels or gardens necessary to their commercial ventures.[105]

Just as the decree made the new settlement an integral element in the construction of empire, it also provided for the consecration of the land. Catherine granted the Crimean Greeks the right to build a monastery in the honor of their most revered saint, St. George the Triumphant, in which they could place his relics transferred from the Crimea. The empress promised to build "a church more excellent and better than all the others and a metropolitan [Ignatii] who will make it a cathedral." She also decreed that an overseer would look after the new cathedral as well as the three other churches in the city and the new monastery.[106]

The influx of this second great immigration of Greeks into southern Russia in 1778-1779 was a pivotal point in the history of Novorossiia in more ways than one. Archbishop Eugenios submitted his request for retirement for reasons of "health and age" only one month after Catherine's decree announcing the creation of a vicariate under the jurisdiction of Metropolitan Ignatii within the boundaries of the diocese of Slaviansk and Kherson. Batalden suggests that Voulgaris's dislike for administrative detail, his desire to return to scholarly pursuits and Catherine's appointment of Gozadinov to oversee the Crimean Greek community (and his salary of 3000 rubles per year) contributed to his departure from ecclesiastical governance.[107]

Metropolitan Ignatii Gozadinov died on 16 February 1786 at the age of seventy after serving the eparchy of Gottha and Kefa for seven years. During his tenure as spiritual leader of the Crimean Greeks he oversaw the construction of numerous churches in the city of Mariupol and the surrounding Greek villages. After a fire destroyed his home in Mariupol he built a small house on some land overlooking the Kal'mius River a few miles from the city. On that land he also began preparations for the foundation of a monastery in the name of St. George. With his death, however, this plan was never realized.[108] His death also brought a significant change in the relationship between the archbishop of Slaviansk and Kherson and the territory formerly under the metropolitan's jurisdiction. Catherine's decree of 14 March 1779 granted the title of metropolitan only to Ignatii Gozadinov personally, i.e., there would be no continuation of the office of metropolitan after his death. Therefore, the bishop who succeeded Metropolitan Ignatii in February 1786 was responsible to the archbishop of Slaviansk and Kherson.[109]

Archbishop Nikiforos not only assumed spiritual authority over the new bishop of Theodosia (Kefa) and Mariupol but also responsibility for church construction and staffing within that bishopric. Two petitions sent to Theotokis in the summer and fall of 1786 represent the range of problems presented by the Crimean Christian populations in the Mariupol district. On 30 September 1786 Archbishop Nikiforos received a petition from the Mariupol superintendent, Archpriest Trifillii Karatsoglu, on behalf of a Crimean Greek priest, Boris Kiriakov-Paraskeva, who wished to be transferred from the city of Cherkassk ("because my family and I do not find it desirable to live there") and appointed to the Kefa street parish in Mariupol. In 1780, Metropolitan Ignatii gave permission for the Greeks from Kefa to build the Church of the Soldier-Saint and Martyr Theodore Tirona in Mariupol. The church burned in either 1785 or 1786 and its priest died about the same time and had not been replaced. Paraskeva wanted to replace that priest and help the community rebuild the church of St. Theodore. On 19 October 1786 Theotokis appointed Paraskeva to the parish "of the burned Church of St. Theodore" and instructed Archpriest Trifillii to apprise the consistory of the parish's progress in constructing a new church.[110]

Mariupol was the largest among the twenty-four settlements of Crimean Christians in Novorossiia. The villages around Mariupol and scattered along the Kal'mius river and the Sea of Azov bore the names of the Crimean villages the Christians had fled in 1778-1779. Metropolitan Ignatii recognized that not all immigrants were attached to specific villages in the Crimea and therefore did not have a "namesake" village in which to settle in southern Russia. Ignatii established a village in his name, Ignat'evka, specifically for these "unattached" Christians, the majority of whom were Georgians. Archbishop Nikiforos received a petition on behalf of the Georgian community and parish of SS. Peter and Paul in Ignat'evka from Archpriest Trifillii, the Mariupol superintendent, near the end of July 1786. The priest presently assigned to the parish of SS. Peter and Paul, according to the petition, was becoming quite "old and, as a result, senile." He was not able or, in some instances, willing to perform the "spiritual and worldly duties" of his calling and office.[111] The old priest, a widower, only desired to be tonsured and enter a monastery.

The essence of the petition was the question of who would replace the current priest, Konstantinov. Trifillii reported that a certain archpriest, Zakharii Trifilov (Purtskhelii), was the favorite of the parish. He was from Georgia, spoke Georgian (something the former priest did not do), and he apparently was more than capable in performing the duties required of an Orthodox priest in Russia. Superintendent Trifillii, on the basis of his own examination of Zakharii, also supported his candidacy.[112] On 9 August 1786, Archbishop Nikiforos received another plea on behalf of Archpriest Zakharii from Georgii Garsevanov, a collegial counselor at the Azov chancellery. Garsevanov informed Archbishop Nikiforos of how he originally had settled Zakharii in the village of Ignat'evka, with the approval and permission of the metropolitan, to reinforce the spiritual life of its Georgian inhabitants. He allowed Archpriest Zakharii to settle in the village based on the strength of a letter of introduction he carried with him from the Georgian Orthodox

Patriarch Catholicos Antonii.[113] Gersavanov personally vouched that Zakharii had been an archpriest in the Georgian capital of Tiflis. On 4 September 1786 Archbishop Nikiforos ruled that Archpriest Zakharii would serve as a second priest and split the salary with the old priest until Zakharii passed the diocesan examination and the old priest formally submitted his petition to retire. At which time Zakharii would become the sole priest for the parish of SS. Peter and Paul.[114]

••••

In the spring of 1780 another series of events occurred which seemed to indicate that not all the Russian plans for a smooth and successful military colonization of its southern frontier were proceeding as expected. These particular events, however, revealed the other important reason for the appointments of Voulgaris and Theotokis as archbishops in Novorossiia by Catherine: to persuade and counsel their flock, the Greek immigrants, to act in the best interests of their new homeland. Among the first Greeks to arrive in Russia at the conclusion of the Russo-Turkish War were the "Albanian" or "Spartan Legionnaires" from the Aegean Archipelago who settled in Kerch and Enikale in 1776.[115] They had come with their families based on the promises made by Catherine in her decree of 1775. In May 1776 the leadership of the Greek settlement sent a petition to Potemkin pointing out to him the utter lack of provisions and adequate housing for the military colonists as dictated in the 1775 charter.[116] Their grievances did not diminish with time but instead increased. In August 1777 the Greeks presented to Potemkin a long list of complaints ranging from inadequate provisions and no opportunity to engage in commerce to resentment directed at the Russian commander of the regiment, General Barsov, for his capricious manners. Lieutenant General Prozorovskii, under the command of Field Marshall Rumiantsev suggested in a note to Potemkin at the same time, that part of the general discontent among the Greeks possibly stemmed from the recent proposal that the regiment be transferred to Taganrog.[117] Later that fall, the same lieutenant general, however, praised the "Albanians" for their brave and admirable performance in the suppression of the recent Tatar rebellion.

Potemkin also was suitably impressed by the "Spartans" and suggested that select members of these regiments voluntarily form another regiment composed of twenty companies (grenadiers and infantry) which would have great offensive potential. "And Your Imperial Majesty would deign to name these companies after the glorious ranks of ancient Greece such as Macedonian, Epirote, Spartan and others."[118] Catherine approved Potemkin's proposed regiment on 3 August 1779. Anton Dmitriev, a Greek who spoke Russian and Greek, became the lieutenant, and later colonel, of this new regiment located in the city of Taganrog.[119] The actual formation of this honorary regiment and the possible misunderstanding that they were to be forcibly transferred to it seems to have sparked the revolt in the spring of 1780 among the Greeks of Kerch and Enikale, who already were very discontented with their situation.[120]

In a letter of 25 April 1780 the Greeks of Kerch and Enikale adamantly rejected Archbishop Nikiforos's pleas in an earlier letter to them (14 April 1780) that they remain true to the Russian Empire and vociferously declared that they were not mercenaries of any state, but were free and "neither the Asian nor the European sovereigns" would take that away from them. The Greeks sarcastically mocked the terms of their transfer to Taganrog. The Russians had offered them a one ruble bonus for enlisting in the new regiment. "How can we feed our children and wives on one ruble each?" they asked. The Greeks were on the verge of utter despair. "We will drown ourselves or return to Turkey and sacrifice ourselves to its brutality, ferociousness, and tyranny in order to liberate ourselves from our five years of suffering, sorrow, and grief." For this reason, they explained, they have sold all their possessions and bought horses for their imminent flight.[121] They proclaimed that they chose freely those they wish to serve and "if the [Russian] state gives us in Kerch and Enikale the promised privileges, then we shall be ready with loyalty to give our last drop of blood, as in the last war."[122] The Greeks would not accept any transfer to Taganrog and threatened to flee Kerch and Enikale if they did not hear that Theotokis had reached some accommodation with Potemkin before Easter or 14 May.

Archbishop Nikiforos's letter to the Greeks on 14 May was a blend of pastoral advice, cajolery, admonition, and attempts at rational persuasion. Theotokis could not understand how the Greek settlers had convinced themselves that the Russians were intent upon enslaving them. "How can the Russians, who have sought and continue to desire liberation of the Greek race, enslave that same race." He went on to admonish them for such thinking because it demonstrated not only "great ingratitude, but also much stupidity." Theotokis warned them that any thought of fleeing to the Ottoman Empire was extremely foolish and dangerous. It would also be "a lasting and great dishonor to all our race." If the lack of privileges as promised to them in 1775 was the real source of their grievance, Theotokis suggested that once they were in Taganrog they would receive the same privileges as the recently migrated Crimean Greeks and he urged them to find a copy of that charter signed by Catherine and take it with them. Theotokis pleaded with them to go to Taganrog and join the regiment because of its great importance to the present and future freedom of all Greeks.[123]

> It is [useful] in the present because the enemies of the faith [Turks], having heard that you bear arms in your hands, will stop harassing our fellow believers found under their domain. And in the future, when the timely circumstances [for liberation] shall arise, you will be able to render truly great assistance.[124]

Archbishop Nikiforos closed his letter with a reminder that Governor-General Prince Potemkin was indeed a defender and lover of the Greek people and if, upon arriving in Taganrog, the promises were not fulfilled Theotokis would intercede on their behalf with Potemkin and secure for them what they lacked.

Theotokis also informed Potemkin of his contact with the Greeks in letter to him on 15 May 1780. He included in his report a copy of the letter he received from the Greeks and a copy of his response to them. Theotokis obviously understood the gravity of the matter and stated that he was going on a tour of the diocese very shortly and would investigate the situation.[125]

Theotokis's attempt to dissuade the Greeks from their impending departure from Kerch and Enikale was not sufficient and 800 fled on 28 May 1780. On 16 June, in a letter to Potemkin, Archbishop Nikiforos reported that a deputation of the Greeks had appeared in Kherson on 15 June (a distance of 360 km.). Accompanying Theotokis's letter was a petition from the Greeks to Potemkin, and through him to the empress herself, requesting permission to receive full privileges and take up residence in Kherson. On 19 June

1780, the Greeks recounted to the commander of Kherson, General Gannibal, their reason for leaving Kerch, how they had fought loyally and gallantly for the Russians against the Turks and Tatars, abandoned their homeland, and now have been "dispersed to the four corners of the world." They pleaded with him to present they case in a positive manner to Prince Potemkin and to allow them to settle in Kherson.[126]

On 9 July, after still not having heard from Potemkin, the commander of Kherson, General Gannibal, settled the Greeks in a local fortress.[127] Potemkin finally responded to the Greek flight in a letter to Archbishop Nikiforos on 14 November. Potemkin was quick to assure Theotokis that this incident had not dampened his love for the Greek nation. He, however, had no intention of abandoning his plans for the Taganrog regiment and instructed Theotokis to inform the Greeks that they would receive all they had been promised in the charter of 1775 when they moved to Taganrog. The Greeks, according to Potemkin, would not be considered as a "regular" regiment but have special privileges. The members of the regiment would be paid and allowed to wear native dress. The regiment could develop commerce and trade in peace time. A school for boys would be built, and an "intelligent and honorable" priest would be attached to the regiment. Potemkin also outlined four benefits of Taganrog as a new home: 1) it was a very secure place; 2) it had a wonderful harbor; 3) the land was fertile; and 4) Her Imperial Majesty had given this city to them.[128]

In spite of these assurances, only a small number of Greeks finally went to Taganrog while an overwhelming majority remained in Kherson.[129] Theotokis was charged with overseeing their pacification and later, in 1781, Archbishop Eugenios was persuaded to move from Poltava to Kherson to watch over them personally. When Voulgaris departed for Kherson he was armed with copies of Catherine's 1779 charter to the Crimean Greeks mentioned by Theotokis in his 14 May 1780 letter to the rebellious Greeks of Kerch and Enikale.[130] Catherine and Potemkin now had three high-ranking Greek prelates situated in strategic positions along the southern frontier. Archbishop Nikiforos was responsible for the entire diocese of Slaviansk and Kherson; Archbishop Eugenios Voulgaris was in Kherson seeing to the needs of the Greek population in that city; and, Metropolitan Ignatii Gozadinov provided spiritual guidance to the 30,000 Christians of the Crimean exodus.

Each individual was respected by the Greek communities and imperial authorities alike. They were in an ideal position to serve the immediate spiritual and material needs of the Greek immigrants and lay the foundations for the future liberation of their homeland. Their pastoral work among the military and civilian colonists assisted the Russian government in stabilizing southern Russia for economic and political development while simultaneously serving Russian long- and short-term foreign policy objectives. Archbishop Nikiforos provided spiritual guidance and support primarily to the Greek colonists in the diocese of Slaviansk and Kherson within the broader outlines of Russian state interests, but he also became actively involved in the spiritual affairs of other colonists such as the Old Believers, once again, within the broader imperatives of the Russian state.

NOTES

1. Ioannidis Amorginos, "Anekdotoi," p. 104.

2. *RGIA*, f. 796, o. 60, g. 1781, d. 188, l. 97.

3. The Holy Synod also understood that Theoktist would be conducting most of the consistorial affairs of the new diocese owing to Voulgaris's poor command of the Russian language and gave him a salary commensurate with a diocesan administrator of the first category even though Slaviansk and Kherson was a second category diocese. Pokrovskii, p. 504.

4. Gavriil, p. 119.

5. Solov'ev, p. 577.

6. Berdnikov, *Kratkii*, pp. 164-5.

7. Batalden, *Catherine II's*, p. 48.

8. Nevodchikov, p. 26.

9. *Ibid.*

10. Cited by Batalden, p. 48.

11. On the transformation of profane space into sacred space see Mircea Eliade, *Cosmos and History: The Myth of the Eternal Return*. Translated by Willard R. Trask (New York, 1959).

12. Permission to construct and consecrate a new parish church was traditionally granted by a bishop. Peter the Great, however, concerned about "excess" churches and unproductive use of labor, temporarily relegated this duty to the Holy Synod. Bishops once again gained the authority to consecrate churches with supervision from the Synod in 1726. Freeze, *Russian Levites*, p. 112.

13. Batalden, p. 56.

14. Nevodchikov, p. 27; Batalden, p. 56.

15. Nevodchikov, p. 29.

16. This was far short of the "recommended" number of households to qualify for a parish church, which the Synod, by a decree in December 1770, had set at forty for rural areas and twenty for urban settings. Freeze, p. 113.

17. Nevodchikov, pp. 29-32. Bishops, often when petitioned by nobles, could grant permission for new church construction, even if it did not meet the official standards, by claiming the grant as an act of "episcopal mercy." Usually, in these

circumstances the bishop was convinced that the petitioner could support the new parish financially.

18. *Ibid.*, p. 34.

19. *Ibid.*, p. 35. Once discovered, these individuals were required to appear before the presiding district council and be examined over their beliefs and training.

20. Batalden (p. 57) refers to these religious pilgrims as *stranniki* or wanderers which is a problematic translation. The *stranniki*, especially in the late eighteenth century, were a radical *bezpopovtsy* (priestless) sect of Old Believers who eschewed and condemned all accommodation with Antichrist. By definition, Old Believers, even other priestless communities, who had any contact whatsoever with the Russian government (e.g., resided in villages or communities recognized by the government) or Antichrist were defiled and eternally damned. Thus, the *stranniki* were permanent wanderers who never settled for fear of becoming polluted by Antichrist.

21. For further discussion on almsgiving to the Church under Ottoman control and its regulation under the *Palestinskii shtat*, see Batalden, pp. 55-6.

22. Nevodchikov, p. 48.

23. The interrogations were recorded and kept in diocesan files to monitor both recalcitrant and obedient clergy. The interrogations provide interesting material on the permeability of the borders in southeastern Europe and the constant movement of people from one territory to another. One example which testifies to this is the story of *ieromonakh* Anthony. Anthony was arrested and detained by military police in a small village near Poltava and he gave this account of his own odyssey. He was the son of Lieutenant General Tolenov, and he himself was a captain in the service when he chose the monastic life and entered Kievomezhigorskii Monastery in 1745. In 1753, the monastery assigned him to their apiary in Poland, but he chose instead to go to Wallachia where he wandered from monastery to monastery for 13 years. From there he went to Mt. Athos and in due time was enlisted by Admiral Spiridov into the Russian navy. He became quite ill and was given leave in Italy to recover. He made his way from Italy to Constantinople and obtained a passport from the Russian consul. He eventually arrived in Poltava by way of Enikale and Taganrog. Nevodchikov, p. 49, n. 95.

24. In one instance the local authorities discovered twenty caves near the village of Brusei. The consistory ordered them destroyed to deter other "vagabonds." Nevodchikov, p. 50, n. 100.

25. Gavriil, p. 122.

26. Pokrovskii, Supplement, pp. 23, 33.

27. A *sloboda* was a village exempt from the usual State obligations and dues.

28. Feodosii, vol. I, p. 387.

29. *Ibid.*, p. 388.

30. *Ibid.*, p. 389.

31. *Ibid.*, p. 391.

32. Druzhinina, *Severnoe*, p. 148.

33. *Ibid.*, p. 530.

34. *Ibid.*, p. 531.

35. Feodosii, II, p. 166.

36. *Ibid.*

37. *Ibid.*, p. 167.

38. According to Freeze, pp. 120ff., the average salary of most parish priests rarely exceeded 40 rubles per year and only those clergy attached to wealthy district or diocesan cathedrals consistently received amounts greater than that. Archpriests and priests attached to cathedrals were the only priests in eighteenth-century Russia who received a stipend or salary from the state; and thus, were not reliant upon parish beneficence or their own labor to sustain themselves. In his study, Freeze does not mention priests who serve in churches located in fortresses, but if the material from

Feodosii is correct, we can assume that priests and churchmen attached to fortress churches can join cathedral priests in the class of state-paid clergy. The salary structures, however, do conform to the standard ratio of priest/churchmen remuneration: lower churchmen usually received 25%-40% of the priest's salary.

39. Feodosii, II, p. 167.

40. *Ibid.*, pp. 168-9.

41. See section on colonization in Chapter 2.

42. Feodosii, II, pp. 169-70.

43. Ioannidis Amorginos, p. 116.

44. The history and fortunes of the Aslan family deserve some attention. According to a petition sent to Catherine in the spring of 1783 by Ekaterina Aslanos, the family had made quite an impression in Russia and with Prince Potemkin in particular. Pavel Aslan, the husband of the petitioner, was a Greek resident of Constantinople when he decided to flee the Ottoman Empire with his family in the late 1770s. Aslan soon found himself in Poltava where he and his wife were converted from Islam to Orthodoxy and baptized into the church by Archbishop Eugenios Voulgaris. In 1780 the Aslans were invited by Prince Potemkin to one of Catherine's masked balls in St. Petersburg. While in the capital city, Potemkin conferred on Aslan the rank of ensign (*chin praporshchika*) and a salary of 300 rubles per annum. The reason for Potemkin's beneficence and relative largesse was that Aslan was in the process of establishing a "factory" in Taganrog which would produce "Turkish brocade" for the "honor and glory of the Russian Empire." The means of producing this brocade was so secret that it was unknown outside of Constantinople. Aslan received 6000 rubles from the State to purchase the requisite machinery and materials and a supplementary subsidy of 700 rubles per annum (the petition was seeking a 200 r.p.a. increase; which was granted by Catherine). The fabric was of such high quality that even Catherine ordered some. See, *SIRIO*, xxvii, pp. 257-258 and Druzhinina, *Severnoe*, p. 84.

45. Druzhinina, p. 117.

46. Feodosii, II, p. 170.

47. The members of this committee were G. Trandafilov, D. Piniyator, G. Gynii, A. Volgar, D. Palamariv, E. Kotsinakhin, Captain G. Ekonom, P. Smiril, G. Kraneot, I. Rossetii and P. Aslan. Feodosii, II, p. 170-1.

48. The petition was possibly carried to Poltava by one of the members of the construction committee, Ioannis Gounalis (Ganali). The consistory *nachal'nik* or secretary refers to him in his internal memos to Archbishop Nikiforos as if he were physically present in Poltava as a representative of the Taganrog Greeks. See Ioannidis Amorginos, p. 106.

49. Feodosii, II, p. 171. The four members who had lived in Taganrog for a few years were I. Palamaria, M. Kanitsiota, I. Ganali, and I. Pogonata. The members of more recent residency were M. Gavaly, A. Ellina, Ch. Zakintiia, and Ch. Bilina.

50. Ioannidis Amorginos, p. 103.

51. *Ibid.*

52. *Ibid.*, p. 104.

53. Ioannidis Amorginos, p. 104 and Feodosii, II, p. 172.

54. *RGIA*, f. 796, o. 60, g. 1781, d. 354, ll. 1-4.

55. *Ibid.*, ll. 10-16.

56. *Ibid.*, ll. 16-19. For an instance involving the Greeks in Kherson in August 1780 and their wish to appoint the Greek *ieromonakh* Ioannis who was born near Arta, Greece, joined the Orlov fleet as a chaplain in the Albanian Red Brigade in 1772, and settled at the fortress of St. Catherine see *RGIA*, f. 796, o. 61, g. 1780, d. 332, ll. 1-21. A similar biography accompanied the request of another group of Greeks in Kherson who had recently arrived from the Enikale. See *RGIA*, f. 796, o. 62, g. 1781, d. 499, ll. 1-3.

57. Ioannidis Amorginos, p. 104.

58. *Ibid.*, p. 106.

59. The Greek community had requested in its petition of 20 December 1781 that Archbishop Neofitos be allowed to conduct the consecration ceremony. According to Feodosii, Archbishop Neofitos Zarnatskii was living "among the Greeks in Taganrog and was of the Greek nation." The correspondence between the consistory and the Taganrog Greeks suggests that he was known by the consistory and Theotokis who called him "our brother." See Feodosii, II. p. 172 and Ioannidis Amorginos, pp. 103, 106.

60. Ioannidis Amorginos, pp. 106-7.

61. Feodosii, II, p. 173. The fate of *Ieromonakh* Ieremia is not known.

62. Ioannidis Amorginos, p. 107.

63. *Ibid.*

64. Feodosii, II, p. 173.

65. Ioannidis Amorginos, p. 108.

66. *Ibid.*, pp. 108-9.

67. *Ibid.*, p. 109.

68. *Ibid.*

69. *Ibid.*, p. 110.

70. *Ibid.*

71. *Ibid.*, p. 111.

72. A. Fisher, *The Russian Annexation of the Crimea, 1772-1783* (Cambridge, 1970); Gavriil (Rozanov), "Pereselenie grekov iz kryma v azovskuiu guberniiu," *ZOOID* (1844:1), pp. 197-204; and N. Dubrovin, ed., *Prisoedinenie kryma k rossii* (St. Petersburg, 1885).

73. Gavriil, p. 122.

74. According to P.M.K., when the Greeks arrived in the Kal'mius river area in 1779 they found about seven Cossack houses. See "Peri Marianoupoleos," *Pandora* (16):534.

75. Gavriil, p. 123.

76. Gavriil, p. 124.

77. Pokrovskii, p. 512.

78. Druzhinina, p. 159. Demetrio Mocenigo was a member of the great Venetian family of Mocenigo but came from a branch that was Orthodox. When the Russians began their propagandistic and insurrectionary activities in southern Europe to distract Venice Mocenigo participated with them because of his faith. He was in command of the port in Zante when the Russian fleet arrived during the Orlov expedition and for his services Orlov conferred on him the rank of colonel. Following the war he remained in good graces with Catherine and was awarded with the office of *charge d'affaires* in Tuscany in 1783. As *charge d'affaires* he worked diligently to settle in Russia those southern Europeans who had joined the Russian fleet during the Russo-Turkish War. Most of the Greeks in this colonization effort came from Minorca. See Venturi, pp. 52-4 and Arsh, "Grecheskaia," p. 87.

79. Many had been reduced to penury and turned to begging for alms in order to survive in Novorossiia. Of course, not all of Potemkin's plans for recruitment succeeded. At one time or another he had considered as probable colonists groups as diverse as American Loyalists and English convicts. The last of the five groups sent to Russia by Mocenigo actually mutinied in the Black Sea when they learned they were destined to become agricultural laborers. See Bartlett, pp. 127-8 and Pokrovskii, p. 512.

80. Gavriil, p. 125.

81. The" Albanian" or" Spartan Legionnaires" quartered in Kerch and Enikale participated in this action against the Tatar rebellion and were praised for their bravery by Generals Prozorovskii and Pavel Potemkin. Safonov, pp. 218-219.

82. Prozorovskii was subsequently replaced by A.V. Suvorov in the negotiations because Rumiantsev doubted whether Prozorovskii was completely supportive of the project. Fisher, pp. 100-1 and Pokrovskii, p. 515.

83. Pokrovskii, p. 514.

84. Wortman, p. 138.

85. On the Greek Project see Hugh Ragsdale, "Evaluating the Traditions of Russian Aggression: Catherine II and the Greek Project," *Slavonic and East European Review*, 1 (1988): 91-117; O.P. Markova, "O proiskhozhdenii tak nazyvaemogo grecheskogo proekta (80-e gody XVIII v.)," *Istoriia SSSR*, 4 (1958): 52-78; and the original Bezborodko memorandum is "Memorial Brigadira Aleksandra Andreevicha Bezborodka po delam politicheskim," *SIRIO*, 26 (St. Petersburg, 1879): 385.

86. John T. Alexander, *Catherine the Great: Life and Legend* (Oxford, 1989), pp. 247-249.

87. For further discussion on provincial publishing and its impact on intellectual life see Gary Marker, *Publishing, Printing and the Origins of Intellectual Life in Russia, 1700-1800* (Princeton, 1985), pp. 135-141.

88. Numerous accounts of Catherine's journey to the Crimea exist, many of them written by the travelers themselves including Catherine, the foreign envoys, Prince de Ligne, and Khrapovitskii, who was the official diarist. For some interesting descriptions and interpretations based on the original accounts of the "voyage" see A. Brükner, "Puteshestvie Imperatritsy Ekateriny II v poludennyi krai Rossii v 1787 godu," *Zhurnal Ministerstva Narodnogo Proveshcheniia*, pt. 2, vol. 162 (1872): 1-51; de Madariaga, *Russia in the Age of Catherine the Great*, pp. 370-373; Alexander, *Catherine the Great*, pp. 256-261; Wolff, *Inventing Eastern Europe*, pp. 126-141; Wortman, pp. 139-142; Dickinson, pp. 125-169. Wolff and Dickinson analyze how the more "imaginative" travel writers "represent" or "invent" Russia and the Crimea.

89. de Madariaga, pp. 370-371.

90. Stephen L. Baehr, *The Paradise Myth*, pp. 65-84.

91. Alexander, p. 258 and Wortman, p. 139.

92. Cited in Wortman, p. 141. Ironically, Theotokis was on his journey to Astrakhan at the same time Catherine was on her grand tour to the Crimea. Many nineteenth-century historians incorrectly believed that Theotokis met the empress during her tour. This error can be attributed to a letter from I.M. Sinel'nikov, the head of Potemkin's Ekaterinoslav Chancellery, to Potemkin which covered matters relating to Catherine's tour. Sinel'nikov reported that Theotokis planned a ceremony for her arrival in Ekaterinoslav at which he would deliver a speech in French. On her return from the Crimea to Petersburg she intended to pass through Poltava where Theotokis was to welcome her in Russian and then accompany her to the diocesan border and bless her remaining journey. "Pis'ma kniazu G.A. Potemkinu-Tavricheskomu," *ZOOID*, 9 (1875), pp. 281-282.

93. Batalden, *Catherine II's*, pp. 76-77.

94. A.M. Panchenko, "'Potemksie derevni' kak kul'turnyi mif," in *XVIII vek*, 14 (Leningrad, 1983), p. 96.

95. Cited in Batalden, p. 71.

96. Fisher, p. 103.

97. The skilled artisans produced knives, clay pottery, sandals, metal and copper wares, and flour. P.M.K., p. 534.

98. Suvorov believed that the Crimean Christians were responsible for supplying Constantinople with much of its food supplies and thus, the impact would be felt in the Ottoman Empire as well. Bartlett, p. 131.

99. These "Greeks" were Orthodox but the service books they used were in Tatar or Turkish and written in Greek. Batalden cites a letter from a bishop in 1794

who states that very few of his "Greek" parishioners or priests could actually speak Greek but conversed in Tatar or Russian. P.M.K. states that of the 24 settlements of Crimean Greeks established around Mariupol only 15 spoke Greek. Batalden, "Eugenios Voulgaris in Russia, 1771-1806: A Chapter in Greco-Slavic Ties of the Eighteenth Century." Ph.D. dissertation, University of Minnesota, 1975, pp. 153-155 and P.M.K., p. 534.

100. de Madariaga, p. 380.

101. Also among the Christians were Tatars who had converted to Christianity in order to leave the Crimea. This was known to Suvorov who accepted them with no difficulty. When Rumiantsev informed Potemkin of this he supposedly called Suvorov "the equal of an apostle" (*ravnoapostol'nii*). Pokrovskii, p. 515.

102. Gavriil, "Pereselenie," p. 200 and P.M.K., p. 534.

103. Batalden, "Eugenios Voulgaris," pp. 151-152.

104. Gavriil, "Pereselenie," p. 197, n.2.

105. Gavriil, "Pereselenie," pp. 198-200. Similar decrees were issued to the Armenian and Roman Catholic communities. The Greek community in Mariupol placed their decree in a silver-gilded frame.

106. *Rossiiskii gosudarstvennyi arkhiv drevnykh aktov* (hereafter *RGADA*), *fond* 16, *delo* 689, *chast'* II, *listy* 28-28ob.

107. Batalden, *Catherine II's*, p. 63.

108. See section on Mariupol Greek School in Chapter 3.

109. Gavriil, "Pereselenie," p. 203.

110. Feodosii, II, pp. 317-319.

111. *Ibid.*, p. 330.

112. *Ibid.*, p. 331.

113. The curious circumstances surrounding his presence in southern Russia deserve a brief note. The patriarchal letter stated that Archpriest Zakharii's children had been kidnapped from Georgia by some Lesghians who took them in chains to Turkey to be sold. The archpriest had fallen into debt to raise the ransom for their freedom and now he was seeking charity from "all our brothers, churches, and Christ-loving Orthodox people." The archpriest had been wandering for some time because the letter was dated 4 February 1782, but Gersavanov reported to Theotokis that he arrived in Ignat'evka "one year ago," or in 1785. Feodosii, II, pp. 329-330.

114. *Ibid.*, p. 332.

115. See S. Safonov, "Ostatki grecheskikh," pp. 205-226.

116. Batalden, p. 65.

117. *Ibid.*, p. 66.

118. Safonov, pp. 219-220.

119. Safonov, p. 220 and Batalden, p. 66.

120. Batalden was the first to discover archival evidence of this revolt and flight in 1780 and a full account of it is given by him in Batalden, pp. 65-70.

121. *RGADA*, f. 16, d. 689, ch. 2, l. 25.

122. Cited in Batalden, pp. 66-67.

123. *RGADA*, f. 16, d. 689, ch. II, ll. 19-21.

124. Cited in Batalden, pp. 67-68.

125. *RGADA*, f. 16, d. 689, ch. 2, l. 18.

126. *Ibid.*, l. 12.

127. Batalden, pp. 68-69.

128. *RGADA*, f. 16, d. 689, ch. 2, l. 29ob.; also see Batalden, p. 69.

129. This may account for the small size of the Taganrog regiment (8 companies instead of the originally intended 12). Safonov, p. 220.

130. Batalden, p. 70.

5

RELIGIOUS LANDSCAPES: BOUNDARIES OF POPULAR BELIEF AND DISSENT

Religion, like art, lives in so far as it is performed, i.e. in so far as its rituals are 'going concerns'.... For religion is not a cognitive system, a set of dogmas, alone; it is meaningful experience and experienced meaning.

– Victor Turner, *From Ritual to Theatre*

If they [the Old Believers] want union with the Church, some say, let them reunite in such a way that no differences will exist between them and us. This idea, which is very severe, I respect and esteem; I accept it in the hope that finally there will no longer exist differences between them and us, not in the use of the new books nor in the celebration of all the rites, no matter how minor. But the other idea, the idea of leniency, I praise and welcome. But if the higher powers [Holy Synod] inform me that they are not pleased, I am fully prepared to stop it [unification], prepared no longer to use and even dismantle that which is already accomplished.[1]

– Archbishop Nikiforos

It was never said that Catherine was a deeply religious person. Religion sat lightly on her. She was born and raised a Lutheran in her native Germany and converted to Orthodoxy with singular ease before her marriage to the Grand Duke Peter. Catherine exhibited a considerable amount of intellectual curiosity toward Orthodoxy and was a very adept catechism student. The ideas and notions of the Enlightenment were more attractive to her, however, than theology and she personally adopted an attitude of religious indifference which some have chosen to define as either deism or agnosticism.

Yet, as a monarch she understood the importance of religion in the promotion and maintenance of social order and public and private morality; hence her pilgrimages to several holy sites to the wide acclaim of her subjects. Her approach also reflected the ever-expanding role of the eighteenth-century European state into all realms which affected human order, both material and ideal. The state had arrogated unto itself the duty of imbuing the community with spiritual and ethical values and the Church became indispensable to the state in providing these values. The state was "the exclusive locus of the principle of unity among men" and men themselves were the loci of liberty (religious as well as intellectual) and piety.[2] The Church, in a sense, was considered an extension of the state because it provided a certain degree of unity to men in the spiritual realm just as schools provided unity in the intellectual realm. The Church was perceived as nothing more than a political institution, subject to state regulation and control, responsible for instilling in the public a degree of general social ethics.[3]

That all her subjects should hold religious beliefs and be free to practice them without fear of persecution, Catherine believed, was beneficial to the state.[4] Catherine made known her views on religious toleration in her *Nakaz* or *Instruction* to the Legislative Commission in 1767 when she stated "the human mind is irritated by persecution, but the permission to believe according to one's opinion softens even the most obdurate hearts...." She manifested particular sensitivity toward the minority religions: "In such a state as ours, which extends its sovereignty over so many different nations, to forbid, or not to allow them to profess different modes of religion, would greatly endanger the peace and security of its citizens. [T]he most certain means of bringing back these wandering sheep to the true flock of the faithful, is a prudent toleration of other religions, not repugnant to our Orthodox religion and polity."[5] Although Catherine espoused "enlightened" pieties concerning religious freedom she never confronted the issue of toleration in its totality. The closest Catherine came to issuing an "edict" on toleration was in June 1773 when she decreed that "as almighty God tolerated on earth all faiths, tongues, and creeds, so Her Majesty, starting from the same principles, and in accordance with His Holy Will, proposed to follow in the same path."[6] This particular proclamation was part of Catherine's order allowing for the construction of mosques and signaled the beginning of her "Islamic policy."

Catherine's religious toleration was tempered, however, by her insistence that all religious groups possess a leadership, preferably a hierarchy, with which she could communicate and issue decrees.[7] This was, of course, the case in regard to the Russian Orthodox Church. For those religious communities whose leadership resided or originated outside Russia or who lacked a clear hierarchical structure Catherine created one. She established the Moslem Spiritual Assembly in 1788-1789, all Catholics were subsumed under the new diocese of Mogilev in 1772, and the Protestant communities were indirectly placed under the control of the College of Justice for Livonian, Estonian, and Finnish Affairs. Catherine attempted to establish the same institutional arrangement with the Old Believers and was partially successful. Those religious communities, such as the Dukhobors, Molokane and Khlysty, however, which did not admit to any form of outward organization and even rejected the authority of the state strained Catherine's sense of religious toleration. Thus, Catherine created the climate or the "spaces" for the emergence and growth of popular beliefs that ultimately exceeded Catherine's own understanding of what constituted "acceptable" religion.

A considerable gap existed between the ideal Russian state, as envisioned by Catherine, the ideal Christian, as demanded by the Church, and the lives of the priests, monks, peasants, *odnodvortsy*, and ethnic groups inhabiting the southern borderlands. The religious beliefs held by the inhabitants of the south which gave meaning and value to their lives at times reflected the ideals of Catherine and the Church, but at other times they differed from them. Local populations accepted some universal values but also manifested their own particular beliefs. From the perspective of the Church, the sectarians and dissenters were simply individuals who, because of human weakness, had succumbed to the temptations of evil and sin. Its responsibility was to exercise its power and, if necessary, call upon the power of the state, to foster the proper environment of education, *eruditio*, and admonishment, *admonitio*, which would keep believers from straying from the "correct" path or restore them to it.[8] The ensuing struggle that erupted between popular belief and the religious and political institutions of Catherine's Russia influenced all three to some degree.

••••

The Old Believers (also known as *raskol'niki* or schismatics, *staroobriadtsy* or Old Ritualists) were Orthodox Russians who systematically rejected Patriarch Nikon's liturgical and doctrinal reforms enacted at the Council of 1666-1667 in Moscow and accepted by the Russian Orthodox Church.[9] The Old Believers soon split into two main divisions: those with priests (*popovtsy*) and the priestless (*bezpopovtsy*); and among the priestless there were two branches, the Pomorians and the Theodosians, who disagreed over the question of marriage.[10] The Council and the leaders of the Church decided that those who remained in opposition to the reforms (Archpriest Avvakum and his followers) would be condemned as heretics and excommunicated.[11] The tsar, also, was to assist the Church in its attempt to return the dissidents to the fold of the true faith by punishing those non-conformists or Old Believers who adamantly refused to admit their error. During the reign of the regent Tsarevna Sofia the punishment became quite severe: schismatics, who after repeated tortures were still recalcitrant, suffered death by fire.[12] The advent of Peter I and his appreciation of religious tolerance and the economic and social benefits which accrued to the state because of it considerably lessened the punishment meted out to the Old Believers.

Peter I's fascination with the West and his desire to recruit western technicians to bring about Russia's transformation made him a qualified champion of religious toleration. Qualified because he extended toleration to the western recruits of different faiths but not to the " 'Christian sects separated from our [Russian] church.' "[13] He did, however, remove the penalty of death as a possible consequence of holding to the Old Belief and placed greater emphasis on economic and social persuasion. Peter I decreed in 1716 that the schismatics were to register themselves annually with the local parish priest, to pay double fines if they failed to register in a timely manner, to pay double taxes, and to dress in a distinctive manner so as to distinguish them from the rest of society.[14] Eleven years earlier while Peter was moving his army through northern Russia to do battle with the Swedes he passed near the Vyg community of Old Believers. This community, located in the Olonets iron-ore region, had established a very efficient economy based on iron-ore mining. Peter recognized the advantages this production held for Russia and allowed the Vyg community to operate autonomously (with complete religious toleration) as long as it supplied the state with iron ore.[15]

Catherine II approached the problem of the Old Believers in much the same manner as Peter the Great. This was also true of her husband and predecessor, Peter III, who, in imitation of his illustrious grandfather, initiated a more tolerant atmosphere for the Old Believers by allowing them to return from abroad and live in peace in Russia. Within her own framework of general religious toleration (Voltaire, in a typically sycophantic missive to Catherine, declared "my object, from which I will not budge, is tolerance; that is the religion I preach; and you are at the head of the Synod in which I am but a humble friar...."[16]), Catherine pronounced two decrees in the first two years of her reign which affected the Old Believers. She allowed the Old Believers to return to their places of origin from the periphery of the Empire and to practice their belief freely.[17] During her reign, Catherine was indirectly responsible for the creation of the two major centers of Old Belief in Moscow at Preobrazhenskoe and Rogozhskoe. The exigencies of public health and the general welfare of the people persuaded her to consent to the establishment of Old Belief "cemeteries" during the great Moscow Plague of 1771 as yet another means to extend the quarantine and construct more pesthouses in the Moscow suburbs. The cemeteries eventually became major centers of Old Belief.[18] One Russian scholar has suggested that Catherine's policies toward the Old Believers were influenced by Grigorii Potemkin from his position as assistant procurator of the Holy Synod to which she appointed him in 1763.[19] This seems all the more probable considering his own later policies in Novorossiia.

The empress's decrees, however, carried some unforeseen consequences. Some Old Believers interpreted the new freedoms and toleration as an admission by the state that the Old Belief had been the correct faith all along and proceeded to attack Orthodox priests and devastate church and monastic property. Catherine's response to this situation was measured and she chose not to move against the Old Believers in the cruel manner of her predecessors. She charged the Holy Synod with devising a means by which the Old Believers would be enlightened sufficiently to recognize their errors and return to the mother church. This task fell to the future metropolitan of Moscow, Platon Levshin, who was then an *ieromonakh* and tutor to the tsarevich Paul.

In December 1765, the Holy Synod published Platon's *An Exhortation by the Orthodox-Catholic Eastern Church to Her Former Children Now Suffering from the Malady of Schism* or *Uveshchanie*, an abbreviated version from its Russian title.[20] Platon's work was not the first such exhortation to the Old Believers, but his enlightened approach distinguished it from earlier official treatises which censured the Old Believers for bringing grief and sickness to the church and, therefore, were deserving of the harshest punishments of torture and death. As the title suggests, Platon believed that precisely because the Old Believers were suffering from this malady they should not be tortured, imprisoned or executed. He held that the Old Believers and the Church "differed only over the superficial, but their strongest beliefs were in agreement with Orthodoxy."[21] Platon assured them that it was only out of love for them and concern for their salvation that he wanted them to return to the Church. The *Uveshchanie* of Platon went through four printings and was widely read. Later ecclesiastics addressing the issue of the Old Believers found within the *Uveshchanie* particular statements which provided support for their own policy of *edinoverie*, or "unity in the faith."[22]

Many Old Believers who returned from abroad (mostly Poland and Moldavia) or from the more distant areas of the empire chose to resettle in regions of Novorossiia set aside for them (i.e., fugitives and foreigners) by Catherine's manifesto on foreign colonization.[23] Their presence in southern Russia posed difficulties for everyone from the local parish priest to the governor-general of the province. Catherine's decrees had not removed the ambiguity which surrounded the status of the Old Believers. They were legal citizens and allowed limited participation in the social and economic life of secular Russia; problems arose, however, over the question of what type or manner of religious rights and privileges they enjoyed. An incident involving Archbishop Eugenios in 1777 helped to define the limits or extent of Old Believer rights.

••••

Archbishop Eugenios received a report in early 1777 from the Elisavetgrad Spiritual District relating to a complaint it had received from Dmitrii Smolodovich, a priest in the fortress of St. Elizabeth concerning a community of Old Believers who were erecting their own large chapel[24] (which, according to Smolodovich, far exceeded the other churches of the city in size and in the number of its bells and disgraced the city with its Old Believer cross high upon its steeple) for religious services, hiding fugitive priests and monks, and "enticing the simple people from the church of God to their own chapel with money and other confidence measures." Smolodovich requested that the authorities remove the fugitive priests and "false teachers," but allow the chapel to remain.[25]

After investigating the affair, the consistory learned from the Novorossiia provincial chancellery that at least four other schismatic chapels were in the province and that their existence was allowed by imperial decree. The area around the fortress of St. Elizabeth had a sizable community of Old Believers reaching back to its founding in 1754. Empress Elizabeth Petrovna granted pardons to the fugitive Old Believers then residing in Moldavia and Poland in 1754 and 1755 and issued formal invitations to them to settle in Novoserbiia.[26] Voulgaris inquired about this with the Holy Synod in March 1777 and he was informed that this was true and confirmed by Prince Potemkin himself. Another Synodal letter to him in July outlined the imperial decrees of 1722 and 1763 which permitted the Old Believers to practice their faith freely in Russia.[27]

Voulgaris, however, chose to act contrary to the suggestions of the Synod and instructed Smolodovich to "unite the schismatics to the church of Christ." He also wrote to the metropolitan of St. Petersburg (and member of the Holy Synod), Gavriil Petrov, to request his "brotherly advice" on the matter of returning schismatics to the Church. Petrov advised him to receive them according to established liturgical rites as written for the admonition of the schismatics. Petrov, therefore, at least as interpreted by Voulgaris, seemingly gave advice contrary to the instructions of the Holy Synod of which he was a member. The Synod had little or no choice in regard to tolerating the presence of the Old Believers in Russia on account of Catherine's imperial decrees, but neither had it moved to formulate a general policy to entice them back into the Church. The Synod's position was quite clear: if the schismatics renounced the schism and recognized the one true Orthodox Church they would be readmitted. The Church was also quite clear in that it would not accept any form of "conditional" unification, which would allow the Old Believers to keep the old liturgical books but accept the episcopal authority of the Church, except on a case-by-case basis when an Old Believer community initiated contact with the Church. The number of schismatic initiatives was increasing in the 1770s and the Synod responded to some positively and some negatively depending on the exact circumstances and conditions requested.[28] From another perspective, one could argue that Voulgaris and Petrov were not acting in direct opposition to the decrees which gave the Old Believers the right to worship freely. Voulgaris did not instruct Smolodovich to obstruct their right to worship only to work toward their unification with the

Church (the Synod had denied Smolodovich's request to have the "fugitives" removed). Smolodovich, evidently, followed his instructions thoroughly because he was credited with converting nearly one hundred Old Believers to the Church between 1777 and 1779.[29]

Archbishop Eugenios faced another problem with an Old Believer community in the village of Znamenka at the same time as the incident in St. Elizabeth. The inhabitants of the this Old Believer settlement petitioned Voulgaris to permit them to erect a church and to have a priest from among them to celebrate the divine liturgy according to the old books. Before he would act on their petition, Voulgaris first demanded of the inhabitants their disavowal of the schism and confession to the Orthodox faith. The Old Believers of Znamenka evidently failed to give sufficient proof to Voulgaris of their sincere renunciation of un-Orthodox beliefs and because of it he denied their petition.[30]

••••

The Znamenka Old Believers, however, were not deterred and submitted yet another petition, this time to the new Archbishop of Slaviansk and Kherson in Poltava, Nikiforos Theotokis. The petition contained 116 signatures and was accompanied by a recommendation letter from the governor-general Prince G. Potemkin.[31] This second petition was possibly inspired by Theotokis's pastoral letter, *Okruzhenoe poslanie*, to the Old Believers in his diocese at the end of March 1780.[32] The letter was intended primarily for the two villages of Znamenka (*popovtsy*) and Zlynka (*bezpopovtsy*) in the Elisavet-grad district and both admonished and summoned them to the Church while promising them protection of the old rites.[33] Theotokis's open letter to the Old Believers begins unequivocally declaring that it is his intention to convince them to rejoin the one true "Orthodox flock." He sees them as the Apostle Paul saw the Jews, "who had the zeal of God, but not by knowledge." Theotokis believed that it was only because of the Old Believers' "zeal that they fell away from the Orthodox Church of Christ and because of zeal they detest Orthodox Christians." Just as the Jews detested the new faith because it was an innovation and deviation from their traditional beliefs, "you leave the Church because you believe that the Russians brought innovations into the Church, that is, they added to and altered the old accepted traditions." Theotokis was not daunted by this, however, because he knew that they were not to blame as much as they simply were misled.[34]

Archbishop Nikiforos was determined to persuade the Old Believers to reunite with the Church and he used a rational and enlightened approach in much the same style as Platon Levshin had in his *Uveshchanie*. Theotokis first established his credentials and made a point of informing them of his extensive travels and experience in the Orthodox East.

> I am of the Greek race, born in Greece, raised, educated and took the monk's habit there. I have seen and spent time with the sacred patriarchs of Constantinople and Jerusalem; I have met and discussed the condition of the Church with bishops from Iberia [Georgia] and Dalmatia, Christian Arabs as well as with the learned, holy monks and fathers of Athos and Mt. Sinai, who keep in the minutest and greatest detail the practices of the old Church. I went to Bulgaria, Moldavia and Wallachia and now have the honor of being a hierarch in Russia.

In light of these travels, Theotokis told them, he did not notice the slightest difference between all of the aforementioned and the Russians in the celebration of the rites of the Church. He was, moreover, "in awe" that given the great variety of languages and geographical dispersion of the Orthodox believers that they all "adore God and rightly interpret the faith in harmony and with a unified spirit." As a matter of fact, he claimed, only the Old Believers were different from the Russians.[35]

The scholar within Theotokis came to the fore in his analysis and examination of the causes which led the Old Believers to deviate from the true path. Theotokis traced the origins of the schism back to an Armenian monk by the name of Martinos. This heretical monk had traveled extensively outside of Armenia and even had visited Rome where he was infected by the "papal pest." From Rome he journeyed to Russia where he arrived in 1150 and presented himself as a Greek Orthodox and a relative of the ecumenical patriarch. With this facade he began to preach and disseminate his heretical ideas and superstitions: Christ descended from heaven making a sign of the cross with the first (thumb) and last two fingers crossed (i.e., a two-fingered sign); at the close of the psalms only two hallelujahs are sung; face toward the west when celebrating the liturgy; and the communion bread should not have the sign of the cross on it.[36] The Orthodox Synod of the Kievan Church apprehended Martinos and interrogated him about the heresies and superstitions he was spreading among the people. Standing before the Synod he admitted that he was neither Greek nor Orthodox nor even a relative of the ecumenical patriarch but an Armenian by birth and faith. Martinos was sent to Constantinople where he was declared a heretic by Patriarch Loukas and condemned to death by fire by Emperor Manuel I Comnenus in 1166.[37] Martinos, according to Theotokis, was the first teacher of the Old Believers and he was responsible for leading them astray. False teachers, monks, and priests followed in the footsteps of Martinos. Two in the seventeenth century, an Armenian and a Hungarian Jew, introduced the heretical practice of suicide by self-immolation. If the Old Believers had been led astray by false teaching, they could be returned by true teaching.[38]

Theotokis was very sympathetic toward the Old Believers because he was convinced that it was a lack of education and improper teaching that were primarily responsible for their predicament. "You do not have schools or wise men as teachers and therefore, you ignore the meaning of the divine scriptures." Theotokis stood firm in his insistence that Scripture and the law of God can only be understood correctly and appreciated through a thorough knowledge of church history, the proclamations of the ecumenical and local synods, and the writings of the Church Fathers. The Old Believers "had lain in the depths of darkness without the sparkle or light of education" to guide them to the truth. The Orthodox, however, not only have many schools but the books of the Holy Fathers, histories, interpretations, and the learned men who study the doctrines of the Church and examine the heresies and heretics of the past and present and publish their findings.[39] Archbishop Nikiforos admonished them for not having churches such as the Orthodox whose churches are modest yet "full of life." He chastised them for allowing "the most cunning (*ponirotaton*) priests to take refuge among you with their cunning ways." Theotokis brought to their attention the variety of holy vessels and sanctified articles they lacked, ("unless you stole it or bought it from a thief"), and rites they no longer received (e.g., episcopal grace and blessing)[40] and concluded that "you are naked and indigent because you lack these divine gifts."[41] In stark contrast to their situation, the Orthodox had innumerable churches and clerics who could celebrate all the sacred liturgies and perform all the ceremonies.

Theotokis formulated six lessons from his sketch of the Old Believer situation and expounded on them for the benefit of the Old Believers in Znamenka and Zlynka. First, he hoped that it was obvious to them that they had been seduced by Satan who, transformed as the Angel of Light, planted in them the false idea that the Russian Church violated the patriarchal traditions. Satan's lies and deceits had drawn them away from the true Church through excessive false zeal just as with the Jews in relation to Jesus Christ. Second, Theotokis wrote that "I have given you my sworn testimony that the Church of the Russians does not differ in any way from the Church of all Orthodox Christians." Thus, it was now apparent to them that their zeal was mistaken. Third, their first teachers were sly Armenians and Jews who deceived their honest forbears and through deception "kidnapped them from the straight road and hurled them down the precipice of loss. You are following them outside the reasoning flock and serve as spectacle for all devout men to fear." Fourth, Theotokis argued that God's presence creates harmony and agreement, but His absence breeds disharmony and disagreement. All true Orthodox are united in the one true faith, the Old Believers, however, do not share that faith and are even divided among themselves and therefore, "God's presence and grace is not present" in them. Fifth, the Old Believers did not believe in the true celebrations and ceremonies of the Church but "took the superstitions of some ignorant old women and old fools and in small and worthless matters limited the Christian belief." Sixth, Theotokis stated that the situation of the Old Believers fills him with sadness and moves him to tears because God appointed him to tend to and restore all souls. He knows they are starved for the word of God, hunger for the sacraments, and thirst for the forgiveness of sins but they have no priests to provide for them.[42]

Along with the petition for the erection of a church and a priest to celebrate the liturgy, the petitioners sent a declaration of their faith which left no doubt in Archbishop Nikiforos's mind of their sincerity. In *Kratkoe povestvovanie* or *A Short Narrative on the Conversion of the Schismatics of the Village of Znamenka*, Theotokis wrote:

> with all their heart and with all their soul they denied all the
> schismatic doctrines and acknowledged the Greek Church as
> the true, universal, catholic, and apostolic Church; and that
> all its dogmas, sacraments, and rites are in accord with the
> word of God, the traditions of the Holy Apostles and the
> seven ecumenical councils as found in the Greco-Russian
> Church.

The petitioners later reaffirmed this when they assured him orally
that "they [were] applying to and seeking union with the Church with
a sincere heart and pure soul," and that their adherence to the old
rites and books was simply "on account of [their] infirmities and
insufficient judiciousness."[43] Theotokis was confident that what he
was about to do next had the approval of the secular authorities
(Potemkin's recommendation letter) and assumed that the ecclesiastical authorities in St. Petersburg would respond favorably as well.

Archbishop Nikiforos, after a close reading and examination
of the writings of the Apostles and Church Fathers, found that the
Church permitted and, in some instances displayed great leniency
toward, a variety of rites with the understanding that the celebrants
adhered firmly to its doctrines and traditions. He also had in mind
the Holy Synod's own publication, Levshin's *Uveshchanie*, which
expressed the view that the use of the old rites and books was
legitimate.[44] "So, I accepted them and allowed them to use the old
books published in Russia, to sing according to their own customs,
and if someone should appear worthy among them, I will elevate him
to the priesthood."[45] Theotokis acted decisively and without hesita-
tion in granting legal status to the Old Believers. He stated in his
resolution that from this moment forward no Orthodox Christians
shall dare to call them *raskol'niki* (the Schismatics who had reunited
with the Church) for they "are Christians of the true faith and we
shall honor and call them such."[46] Very soon after his decision
Archbishop Nikiforos sent the "respected and learned" Dmitrii
Smolodovich[47] to Znamenka. Theotokis instructed Smolodovich to
accept them officially into the Church once they had publicly
declared their renunciation of the *raskol* and profession of the
Orthodox faith, which they did.

The Znamenka community, now integrated into the Orthodox
Church, began construction of a new church dedicated to the Virgin
with the blessing of the foundation celebrated by Smolodovich in
early May. This was the first *edinovertsy* church in Russian history

and Archbishop Nikiforos himself traveled to Znamenka to consecrate it sometime in June. Theotokis consecrated the church in the true spirit of *edinoverie* : his clerics and choirboys sang from the choir to his right using their own books and the former Old Believers sang from the choir to his left using their old books while he performed the liturgy and delivered the sermon. The archbishop appointed as parish priest Stefan Popov, a native of Russia, born and raised in the Orthodox faith and gave him permission to conduct services according to the old rites and old books.[48] Theotokis, in the hope of creating and maintaining an atmosphere of cooperation and harmony among the former Old Believers, elected not to force their former fugitive priest, *ieromonakh* Arsenii, to abandon the village but instead permitted him to remain in Znamenka. Arsenii was allowed to stay (but not as a priest) out of respect for his assistance in bringing his flock back into the fold (his name was first on the petition) and for the influence he could exert on the other Old Believers still in schism.[49] Theotokis was convinced of the success of his action when the villagers no longer talked of returning to Moldavia, but instead, *raskol'niki* from foreign lands were coming to the village and joining the parish.

Archbishop Nikiforos was extremely elated and pleased with his acceptance of the Znamenka Old Believers into the Church in the spring of 1780. He had done so however, according to Titlinov, at great risk and peril to his own career because he had not secured any preliminary agreement to his proposed action from the Holy Synod.[50] Theotokis's first contact with the Synod was not directly with the Synod *per se* but with one of its more important members, Archbishop Gavriil of Novgorod. His letter of 3 August 1780 to Gavriil may have been an attempt to contact a Synodal member whom he believed would be supportive of his action and help to present his case to the Synod or simply the act of a newly installed archbishop writing to the high-ranking prelate who had consecrated him as archbishop almost a year earlier. Theotokis also sent a letter to another important member of the Synod, Archbishop Platon of Moscow, author of the *Uveshchanie*.

Theotokis opened his letter to Archbishop Gavriil by excitedly proclaiming that "by your holy prayers and in accordance with my most ardent wishes, a village of Old Believers, named Znamenka, has returned to the holy Orthodox Church." Theotokis did not enter into the specifics of the union but instead felt compelled to remind

Gavriil of the Church's mission to acquire eternal salvation for all souls by a variety of means such as the Apostle Paul who "not only himself worked among the Jews as a Jew, but even Timothy was circumcised (*obrezal*) although apostolic law promulgated that it was forbidden."[51] He then turned to Platon's *Uveshchanie* which advocated the use of the new books, but nowhere specifically prohibited the use of the old books, " which, up to the time of the most blessed and pious Peter the Great, the entire Russian Orthodox Church read..., and therefore, I had little difficulty in allowing them to use the old books and songs, which they were used to." In regard to the Old Believer priest, Arsenii, Theotokis admitted that he had not acted against him with the required severity but he thought he would be helpful in recruiting more schismatics to the Church if he remained in the village. Finally, Theotokis "most humbly" asked that his report of this affair be presented to the Holy Synod by Gavriil who, Theotokis believed, was favorably disposed toward him. The eminent and respected Gavriil could sway the Synod toward a confirmation of his action and enlighten the minds of the others of the value of the union. The continuity and intensity of the letter is destroyed by the last paragraph in which Theotokis requested permission from Gavriil and the Synod to publish his sermons which had been translated into Russian. Theotokis wanted to expedite the procedure of obtaining Synod approval for the use of the translation in the churches by claiming that Gavriil was familiar with the sermons even though he had not seen them. Theotokis wondered if that would be satisfactory to Gavriil and appropriate in order to clear the bureaucratic obstacles.[52]

Archbishop Nikiforos did not receive any type of answer from either prelate for over one year. The two high-ranking prelates and the Synod must have been completely bewildered by Theotokis's act of leniency toward the Old Believers. The slow response signified, if not a split within the Synod, at least some personal doubts and indecisiveness on the parts of Platon and Gavriil. Theotokis finally received a reply in the form of a letter from Archbishop Platon dated 23 September 1781. Platon began by relating to Theotokis the case of a priest in his own diocese of Moscow who was recently chosen by the newly converted Old Believers to be their priest and conduct services according to the old rites and books. This priest was considered "depraved" and the Old Believers surprised Platon by their poor choice. This was proof, according to Platon, that their conversion was not "sufficiently sincere." Platon feared that this example would become the norm for the other Old Believers who returned to the Church under the condition of retaining their old books and rites ("ignoramuses attracting ignoramuses") and this could overwhelm the Church. If they want real union, he argued, let them reunite with us without the conditions; otherwise the Church would become "lame in both knees." He ended his short letter with some remarks about not being able to find the historical works which Theotokis cited in his letter to the Old Believers and closed with a greeting to Archbishop Eugenios.[53]

Platon's letter to Theotokis amounted to an indirect reproach, but the letter he was to receive from Gavriil could be considered the Synod's unofficial response. Archbishop Gavriil wrote to Archbishop Nikiforos on 11 October 1781. Gavriil apologized for not writing to Theotokis sooner but he himself did not know, until this moment, what to write. Gavriil enjoined Theotokis to examine very carefully the edicts of the Council of 1667, Peter's *Spiritual Regulation*, and the oath that all bishops take upon assuming office; and he will see that they all forbid the type of leniency he showed to the Old Believers. The Synod, he wrote, had wanted to countermand his decision, but did not for fear of exciting greater troubles. The Synod had remained silent in the hope that he would strive to bring them "to a more sensible understanding" of and into a fuller agreement with the Church. Gavriil remarked about his reference to the Apostle Paul and the circumcision of Timothy and noted that Paul had done only what the Church required. The Synod heartily approved of Theotokis's *uveshchanie* to the Znamenka Old Believers, reported Gavriil, but they were displeased with his reference to the heretic Martinos and wanted the exact page numbers of the Honiates's text and others which covered it.[54] And finally, in regard to the translated sermons, Gavriil informed Theotokis that he must present them for approval but he would personally work for their Synodal endorsement.[55]

Archbishop Nikiforos was troubled and dismayed by the responses he received from Platon and Gavriil. He had undoubtedly expected Archbishops Platon and Gavriil (and by extension, the Holy Synod) to greet his work in the same spirit of Christian reconciliation that suffused his achievement of conditional unification. Instead, he was reproached and admonished for acting contrary to Church law and faced the possibility that his accomplishment could be reversed. He worked quickly to prepare a justification for his action in order to deter a more severe response from the Holy Synod. During October and November he wrote his tract, *Short Narrative* (*Kratkoe povestvovanie*), in defense of his Znamenka decision and sent copies not only to Platon and Gavriil but to Prince Potemkin as well in December 1781 with accompanying letters.

In the letter accompanying Gavriil's copy, Theotokis took the opportunity to respond to his previous charges. He opened by chastising himself for initially believing that Gavriil's prolonged silence on the Znamenka affair was due to his other much more important responsibilities, but he now understood that he was terribly mistaken. In compliance with Gavriil's wish that he consult the edicts of the Council of 1667 and other Church bodies on the topic of the Old Believers, he could find no clear statement which prohibited his deed in Peter the Great's *Regulation* or in the episcopal oath. Perhaps, he added, "there is something related to this in the acts of the above mentioned council, but it is not known to me." Theotokis disputed Gavriil's claim that the Apostle Paul's circumcision of Timothy (*oikonomikos*) was done according to the dictates of the whole Church, rather, he maintained, it was done only to satisfy the Jewish people among whom they traveled. As a matter of fact, Theotokis continued, shortly before Paul's act, a Church council in Jerusalem, attended by the Apostles and presbyters, ruled that circumcision was not necessary to convert a pagan to the Church. Theotokis finally adopted a more conciliatory, or perhaps a less contentious, tone after having challenged Gavriil initially. He stated that he sent the accompanying *Short Narrative* to elicit Gavriil's "wise judgment" on the matter and to present it to the Holy Synod. Gavriil, however, was not the only individual to receive a copy of his justification. In a demonstration of subtle political and diplomatic acumen, he mentioned, parenthetically, that he had also sent a copy to the governor-general of Novorossiia, Prince Potemkin, who had shown a great deal of interest in the Old Believers from Moldavia.[56] He was presenting the defense of his actions because he was confident he was correct according to Church doctrine and precedent. If, however, he was not,

> I say only that I am fully prepared to rescind and reverse, at the behest of the Holy Synod, all that I have permitted thus far and will not, in the future, permit the conversion of others;

and also I will change my thinking concerning the mentioned leniency, although it is affirmed by many principals and invested with a spirit *akriveias* (austere).[57]

Every time Theotokis suggested that he would bow to the wisdom, if not the pressure, of the Holy Synod and adopt its course in regard to the Old Believers as proof that he was still an obedient servant of the Church, he never failed to append a small rejoinder or disclaimer to voice his dissatisfaction and displeasure. Next, he provided Gavriil with specific references to the historical works which dealt with the Martinos affair of the twelfth century and closed his letter by expressing his hope that Gavriil would continue to remember him as his "servant and son in Christ," and to keep him informed about the current affair.[58]

••••

Archbishop Nikiforos began his *Short Narrative* with a brief but detailed description of the events which led to his acceptance of the Old Believers' petition and their subsequent conversion to the Russian Orthodox Church with the proviso that they be allowed to keep their old books and rites. In an attempt to counter Platon's fear that his offer of conditional union to the converts ultimately would be inimical to the Church's best interests, Theotokis reported that the *edinovertsy* in Znamenka were turning more and more toward Orthodoxy in that some now were making the three-figured sign of the cross and starting to use the new books.

Theotokis then turned to the task before him and cited nine reasons why the *edinovertsy* should be permitted to use the old books and rites. 1) Theotokis declared that no published public edicts or "at the very least, secret published edicts," exist which preclude the use of the old books and rites. 2) He claimed that the old books contain no "blasphemy, heresy, perversion of dogma, or distorted lessons on the mysteries." 3) Theotokis referred to the Holy Synod's own 1773 publication[59] which pronounced that the old books were not censured or condemned; nor did it "counsel abstaining from their use." 4) He held that the Russian Church itself has used and continues to use some of the old books, e.g., *Kormchaia*. 5) Theotokis expanded on this by mentioning that from the very beginning, since the baptism of Russia, all tsars, boyars, holy men and countless numbers of Christians have used the old books and they are still revered and honored by the Russian people. 6) He addressed the age-old issue of the use of corrected and "uncorrected" holy books which has been a point of contention since Origen first translated and corrected the Septuagint in the second century. Some churches accepted Origen's translation and others did not, but the "unity of the Church was not shattered and the use of the old publications [Septuagint], although they were not corrected, was not prohibited." 7) Theotokis again used the example of the Apostle Paul's dictum to work among the Jews and as a Jew. Paul tried to please all men, not for his own advantage, but so they might be saved. "He [Paul] himself persuaded me to do this, when he exclaimed and said, 'Be imitators of me!' "[60] 8) He held out the hope that by bringing the Old Believers into conditional union with the Church they received "the holy mysteries of which they have been deprived for so long," and some will exhibit a desire to use the new books in time. 9) Finally, Theotokis argued that the old books should be accepted because in the words of Platon's *Uveshchanie*, " 'it is not the simi-larities between the old and new books, but the evidence of purity of faith which saves us.' "[61]

Archbishop Nikiforos was intent on giving his act of condi-tional union to the Old Believers validity not only by citing reasons why the old books should be allowed, but also by citing evidence of the Church's previous acts of "leniency" toward different rites. He began by stating that the Church only required that singing be conducted in a proper manner without excessive screeching and wailing, but it did not specify or designate one form of singing as the only acceptable one. Theotokis gave eight historical examples of the Church manifesting leniency toward the practice of various rites. 1) In regard to the matter of the correct and true form of singing praises to God, St. Basil resolved this problem when he declared that we should be ashamed to argue over such trivial things. 2) Theotokis claimed that the Church has never welcomed heretics back to it on the basis of their "indispensable fulfillment of the rites..., but only by adherence to the faith, the aims of the dogma and the holiness of life." 3) He underlined the previous point by citing the example of the early Church accepting former heretics without asking about their rites. 4) Theotokis argued for the allowance of diversity by demonstrating that the two sources for the celebration of the rites, the Tipika and Evchologia, had, themselves, undergone numerous changes and existed in at least four variations and, yet, the faith has always remained the same. 5) He noted that Rome and the East used different rituals long before the schism, but it was a disagreement over dogma and faith that precipitated the division. Theotokis wrote, "It is not unity in rituals, but unity in faith which creates spiritual union of churches and believers." 6) Theotokis pointed out that very few churches celebrated the rites and rituals completely the same and they had not anathematized one another. 7) In the past attempts at reconciliation between the Lutherans and the Orthodox Church, the disagreements were over the procession of the Holy Spirit, sacraments, reverence of the icons, and other matters, but never over ritual. 8) His final illustration of Church leniency in matters of ritual was from the present: the Russian and Ukrainian Churches were one spiritually, although differences in ritual existed between them, for example, in baptism.[62]

Theotokis concluded his letter with a last attempt at fashioning a reconciliation between the Holy Synod and himself. His greatest concern was for the *edinovertsy*, but he understood that he must accept the decision of the Church leaders no matter whether he agreed with that decision or not.

> If they [the Old Believers] want union with the Church, some say, let them reunite in such a way that no differences will exist between them and us. This idea, which is very severe (*akriveias*), I both respect and esteem; I accept it in the hope –that finally there will no longer exist differences between them and us, not in the use of the new books nor in the celebration of all the rites, no matter how minor. But the other idea, the idea of leniency (*oikonomias*), I praise and welcome. But if the higher powers [Holy Synod] inform me that they are not pleased, I am fully prepared to stop it [unification], prepared to use no longer and even dismantle that which is already accomplished.[63]

Archbishop Nikiforos's decision to allow the Znamenka Old Believers into the Church on the basis of conditional union was not overturned by the Holy Synod. Ultimately, the conditions granted to the Znamenka Old Believers by Theotokis – they were permitted their own churches and priests, use of their old books and rituals, but in turn were required to accept the authority of the Church's bishops and Holy Synod – became the foundation for the policy of

Edinoverie adopted by Emperor Paul I on 27 October 1800.[64] Whether or not Theotokis's *Short Narrative* swayed the members of the Holy Synod one way or the other is not easy to determine. The initial reactions of Archbishops Gavriil and Platon to Theotokis's "excessively lenient" decision suggested that the Holy Synod's most important members were displeased and were inclined to force him to revoke his permission. This, however, would not have been consistent with the Synod's own declared position on the status of the Old Believers as manifested in Platon's tract and a position paper on the matter of accommodation with the Old Believers produced at the request of Catherine by two other Synodal members. The situation becomes even more puzzling when we know that the Holy Synod itself was engaged in discussions with the Starodub Old Believer community and its leader, Abbot Nikodim, at approximately the same time it was chastising Archbishop Nikiforos for doing precisely the same with the Znamenka community.[65] But here the distinction becomes clear: Theotokis undertook to accommodate the Old Believers without first seeking the permission of the Synod, while the Synod itself was directly responsible for the Starodub affair without the agency of an archbishop or bishop.

Theotokis presented the Holy Synod with a *fait accompli* at a time when the Synod was in the process of formulating a policy, founded on the resolution of the Starodub affair, which it hoped could be applied broadly to all Old Believer communities. This would account for both the irritability of the Synod (it had been outflanked by one of its own bishops) and its reluctance to reverse Theotokis's decision. The church historian Titlinov suggests that Gavriil and Platon were not opposed to Theotokis's action in principle but only the manner in which it was done; for that reason Gavriil argued that Paul circumcised Timothy with the "blessing of the **whole Church**." The Synod was charged with making decisions which would affect the entire Church and therefore proceeded with a greater degree of caution.[66] Theotokis's decisive and quick resolution of the Znamenka affair became a catalyst for the realization of an *edinoverie* policy. The Holy Synod had entertained ideas about *edinoverie* since Catherine's accession to the throne in 1762, but it never had reached the point where it was willing to implement them. The Znamenka case compelled the Synod to act. The position of the Old Believers in Russian society improved substantially after the events of 1781: as of 1782 they were no longer called *raskol'niki* (primarily because they were not obligated to pay the double tax); as of 1785 they could hold public office; in 1783 they were permitted to establish printing presses; and in 1785 Potemkin placed all Old Believers under the new bishop of the Crimea and founded a *edinoverie* monastery there.[67]

Still the question remains: why was it that Archbishop Nikiforos was more inclined than others to offer union and why were Znamenka Old Believers so anxious for union and ready to accept the conditions? Some observers have suggested that it was Theotokis's pastoral letter, written in an admonitory tone but suffused with spiritual love and kindness, to the Old Believers in late 1780 or early 1781 that first induced them to approach the new archbishop of Slaviansk and Kherson.[68] This explanation ascribes, perhaps, a greater amount of persuasive ability to Theotokis's writing than he possessed. It also fails to take into account the fact that the Znamenka Old Believers petitioned Theotokis's predecessor, Archbishop Eugenios, first. The motive then must lie within in the Old Believer community itself. Grekov suggests that the community, comprising mainly immigrants from Moldavia, was more inclined to seek the assistance of the local bishop because of their experience in Moldavia. According to Grekov, the metropolitan of Jassy, in his attempt to acquire a bishop for the Old Believers in Moldavia so they would not need to rely on "fugitive priests," considerably reduced the traditional hostility between the official church and the Schismatics. The Znamenka Old Believers, in light of their experience in Moldavia, thought it was only natural that they contact the archbishop of their new residence to secure from him legal right to build a church and elect a priest.[69] This interpretation places a greater emphasis on the peculiar or "local" origins of various dissenting communities and reveals the inherent limitations of a universal proposal for reunion.[70]

Titlinov argues rather persuasively that Archbishop Nikiforos was uniquely prepared to be more responsive to the Old Believers' petition for two reasons: First, Voulgaris already had informed the petitioners that until they publicly renounced the *raskol* and confessed the true faith their petition could not be accepted. Theotokis, thus, received with the second petition a declaration of their renunciation of the schism and their belief in the doctrines and traditions of the one true Church. Second, Theotokis was a Greek and had lived and traveled for most of his adult life in the Greek

East where he observed the diversity of the Orthodox experience and, therefore, perceived the development of the Nikonian reforms within a broader ecumenical context. Titlinov believed that "as a Greek...he was free of the Russian biases concerning the *raskol'niki*" and the Old Believers somehow understood this "foreignness" and accepted him as "some sort of neutral figure, a representative of ecumenical Orthodoxy, the voice of which was convincing to them."[71] And as a Greek, Theotokis was more likely to allow them to preserve their old rites and books. The irony of the entire Znamenka affair was that although Theotokis acted out of conscience (and maybe a sense that he understood Orthodox doctrine better than his immediate superiors?) and did not bother to consult with the Synod on such an important and significant matter as he should have, he nonetheless was serving the imperial interests of Catherine and Russia.

••••

Apart from dealing with entire communities of Old Believers, Theotokis and the other bishops constantly encountered individual cases involving the consequences of conversions to or from the Old Belief. Individuals moved from Old Belief to Orthodoxy or from Orthodoxy to Old Belief with stunning frequency. As St. Augustine wrote, a man's total environment is responsible for shaping matters of belief. Not too long after the Znamenka affair, Archbishop Nikiforos received a report from Elisavetgrad. It seemed that a merchant, Roman Dolganov, hurled epithets and falsehoods against the Orthodox Church and cursed at the miracle-working SS. Peter, Alexei, Job and Philip, while dispensing *raskol* literature at the entrance to the market in Elisavetgrad on the 31 July 1781.[72] The tradesmen and merchants in the market were so insulted that they reported him to the authorities immediately. When the consistory interrogated him they discovered that Dolganov had a pronounced weakness for alcohol and on the day of his transgression he had drunk enough that "he knew not what he was doing" (*vykhodit iz uma*). He denied his actions entirely and even refused to admit that he was a *bezpopovets*. The merchants, however, insisted that he was not drunk on this occasion even though he was known to drink for a month at times. The consistory ruled that his alleged drunkenness was a ruse and that he was guilty of cursing the True Orthodox Church. He was placed under moderate supervision.[73]

The ambiguous construction of the boundaries between Old Belief and Orthodoxy were highlighted in a case presented to Archbishop Nikiforos in late 1779. This particular episode reveals the fragmented and indeterminate quality of popular belief and implicitly suggests, as Robert Crummey notes, that without the arbitrary determinations of Church and state officials it would be very difficult to ascertain who was or was not a True Believer.[74] In October 1777, Anna Avromsimova met Peter Iagodov, a merchant, in Kharkov. He persuaded her to accompany him to Krylovskii *shanets* in "Turkish territory" where they married and, according to the report, lived according to *raskol'nik* ways (unfortunately, the report does not enumerate these "ways"), but Anna claimed to have been unaware of this. She only learned something was amiss when the parish priest in Kremenchug denied her access to the church because she was an Old Believer. She consulted the Kremenchug Spiritual District in August 1778 on the advice of friends. The district authorities interrogated Iagodov and he corroborated his wife's story but added that an Old Believer priest had performed their wedding ceremony. He also stated that he had not compelled Anna to adhere to Old Believer ways. The friends, however, who convinced her to contact the spiritual district, testified that he had compelled her to follow the Old Believer ways and even forbade her to attend an Orthodox church. Anna denied she was forced to do anything and only wanted to stay with her husband. The Kremenchug authorities ruled the marriage dissolved as it was performed by an illegal Old Believer priest, that Iagodov be turned over to the civil authorities on charges of impersonating an Orthodox, and that Anna be sent to a convent for one year and a half as penance. Theotokis, however, argued that the punishment was much too severe considering each had entered the marriage voluntarily, they had agreed to raise the children as Orthodox, and that they wanted an Orthodox marriage ceremony. On 14 December 1779 the Holy Synod concurred with Nikiforos's opinion that the husband should be sent to the civil authorities and judged Anna innocent of any evil deed.[75]

The movement of parishioners from Orthodoxy to Old Belief was to be expected. Undoubtedly, they did not possess the same level of erudition to keep the ignorance of Old Belief from them. How, then, to explain the facile activities of monks and priests? On 14

April 1783, Theotokis sent a report to the Holy Synod concerning the deacon Ivan Ivanov and his desire to return to the Mother Church after serving the *raskol* community in the village of Ploskoi.[76] Ivanov was the son of a priest in Kostroma and was ordained a deacon in 1772. He claimed that, in 1777, some *raskol'niki* convinced him to leave his parish with his wife and two children and accept the "*raskol* faith." After living in numerous Old Believer communities in Russia and Poland for several years, he learned of Catherine's manifesto allowing Old Believers to return to Russia, which he did in 1780. He was now requesting re-ordination as a deacon in the Orthodox Church. After examining his story, Theotokis ruled that Ivanov be allowed to return to the Orthodox Church as a deacon, but only after he maintained a good record for at least one year. Theotokis then remarked that he did this "to show his good will to all *raskol'niki* who would return from abroad."[77] Soon after this case moved through the Holy Synod in the summer of 1783, an Imperial *ukase* was issued on 6 September 1783 regarding the treatment of monks and priests returning to Orthodoxy from the Old Belief.[78] The *ukase* basically informed the bishops and diocesan staffs to expedite all returns to the Church. Archbishop Nikiforos seems to have led the way again.

Symptomatic of life in the "middle ground" or "transfrontier" was the ease with which individuals acquired or exchanged identities as a means to conform to the ever-changing religious landscape. Two cases which occurred during the tenure of Nikiforos's successor as bishop of Ekaterinoslav diocese (the name of the diocese of Slaviansk and Kherson after 1787), Metropolitan Gavriil (Banulesko-Bodoni), illustrate the transitional quality of identity in the borderlands. In 1796, the consistory received the file of Isaiah Salikov, a merchant from Kherson, who had converted to Orthodoxy from Judaism in 1788. He was reported to the local civil and religious authorities after someone witnessed him living among the city's Jews (*zhidati*) and practicing only Jewish rituals and no Christian rituals. This odd remark seems to imply that other Jewish converts to Orthodoxy possibly abided by rituals that were a mixture of Christianity and Judaism. The consistory recorded that Salikov had voluntarily strayed from Orthodoxy and returned to his "hideous Jewish customs" (*bogomerzskikh zhidovskikh predanii*). He "sincerely" repented of his transgression, however, and was prepared to undergo any form of penance. The metropolitan sentenced Salikov to one year's public penance in a monastery where a spiritual father was to monitor him and attest to his sincere return to Orthodoxy before his release.[79]

Arap Nikolai appeared before the consistory because he had converted from Orthodoxy to Islam. In his defense, Nikolai claimed that while he was living in Karasubazar (Crimea) he was held against his will for eight days in the village of Artaelli and forced to adopt the ways of Islam by Ennana, an old friend of his, and the other villagers. The entire ordeal caused him to become quite ill and he stayed in the village until Bishop Job of Feodosiia learned of his case. When the bishop attempted to interview him he fled and roamed the country until returning to the village of Artaelli. During the subsequent investigation, the bishop discovered that Nikolai was not exactly forced to convert to Islam, but was tempted to undergo circumcision by his own cupidity (*korystoliubiia*) and by the promise of gifts after the ritual. Nikolai told the consistory that he was born a Christian and that in his 31 years he had never wanted to be anything other than a good Orthodox believer. He was at great pains to insist that he had only accepted circumcision because he wanted the gifts. Nikolai was sent to Krestovozdvizhenskii Monastery for penance until that time his spiritual father judged him to be effectively repentant.[80]

••••

Archbishop Nikiforos confronted yet another sensitive religious issue soon after assuming his new position in Poltava. The empathy Theotokis exhibited toward the poor souls who had strayed from the flock as Old Believers was not duplicated in his relations with another group also separated from the mother Orthodox Church and wishing to reunite: the Uniates. In late 1779, Archbishop Nikiforos learned that a local priest, Vasilii Moiseevich Zrazhevskoi, who had been in the diocese since its creation in 1775, was not an ordained Orthodox priest but a "converted" ordained Uniate priest.[81] Theotokis immediately forbade him to conduct holy services or administer the sacraments, but allowed him to remain as an assistant. Zrazhevskoi appealed Archbishop Nikiforos's ruling and the Holy Synod addressed it in 1783. The priest argued that he was ordained in 1758 by the Ukrainian Uniate Metropolitan Filip Volodkovich because he and his family lived in lands under Polish domination and, therefore, were obliged to assume the Uniate religion outwardly even though they remained Orthodox in their hearts. In his appeal, Zrazhevskoi noted that he "converted" to Orthodoxy in 1768 (the year Catherine became involved in the "dissident" question in Poland) and had served the Orthodox Church faithfully as an Orthodox priest ever since, first in the diocese of Pereiaslavl and then in Slaviansk and Kherson. The Synod obviously did not see a problem: the important point was that he had converted to Orthodoxy and it did not matter that he had been ordained by a Uniate bishop. The Synod asked Archbishop Nikiforos to defend his action.

Theotokis presented to the Synod on 26 April 1783 a defense of his action in an essay entitled, *A Treatise Which Contains In It Reasons Which Prove That Ordination By Uniate Bishops Must Be Dealt With By The Temporal*.[82] His treatise claimed that the Orthodox Church cannot abide Uniate ordinations and still remain true to the traditions and doctrines of the Church. He also noted that if the Orthodox Church were to accept the legitimacy of Uniate ordinations performed by Metropolitan Volodkovich (who was still loyal to Rome) the Russian Church could be considered subordinate to Rome. The Synod issued a refutation of his treatise and then ruled against him in the summer of 1783. The Synod's decree reproached Archbishop Nikiforos for the patronizing and didactic tone of his treatise and for his audacity in addressing not only the spiritual aspects of the affair but its secular and political implications as well. Theotokis complied with the decree and permitted Zrazhevskoi and three other Uniate-ordained priests to conduct holy services and administer the sacraments.[83]

Archbishop Nikiforos was as adamant in his opposition to accommodation with the Uniates as he had been in his support for some form of accommodation with the Old Believers. Just as Theotokis's experience in the Greek East had conditioned him to be more responsive toward the situation of the Old Believers it also underlay his deep antipathy toward the Uniates. Theotokis's contact with the Roman Catholic Church, either in Corfu or in the see of Philadelphia, never had been pleasant and he perceived in the Roman Church the workings of an insidious force that was intent on subverting the Eastern Orthodox Church. His treatise did not elucidate the differences between the Uniates and Orthodox in matters of dogma because this was already recognized by everyone. Instead, he focused his attention on the possible dangers to which the state could be exposed if the Russian Church, whether implicitly or explicitly, acknowledged the right of bishops loyal to the pope to ordain Orthodox clergy. The idea that Russian subjects could be spiritually responsible to an institution outside the borders of Russia also greatly concerned Catherine after the first partition of Poland in 1772. To lessen this prospect she endeavored to create new Catholic and Uniate bishoprics in Russia whose bishops would be responsible to her and not to hierarchs in Poland or Rome. One year after the Zrazhevskoi affair, Catherine installed a Uniate bishop at Polotsk, Irakli Lisovsky, who was responsible for all Uniate clergy in Russia.[84] In later years, after the second partition of Poland and the integration of large population of Uniates within the borders of Russia, the Holy Synod asked Archbishop Eugenios's advice on how best to reunite the Uniates to the mother Church.[85]

••••

On 18 March 1786, Archbishop Nikiforos sent his annual report concerning the "religiosity" of his diocese to his superiors at the Holy Synod in St. Petersburg.[86] Among the thousands who settled in the south, some, like the Old Believers, were promised religious toleration in return for political allegiance to St. Petersburg, yet others (runaway serfs, religious sectarians, and deserters) sought the frontier precisely because it still lacked the political consolidation and social integration sought so avidly by Catherine. And it was just such a sectarian group that caused Archbishop Nikiforos to report that his diocese was free of superstitions (*sueveriia*) except in Pavlograd *uezd* in the *odnodvortsy slobode* of Bogdanova where there was a new settlement of Dukhobors.[87]

Nikiforos's report in March was the first of three reports he sent to the Holy Synod in 1786 concerning the presence of Dukhobors in Russia's southern borderland diocese. He reported that all three cases involved groups who erroneously had strayed from the true faith of Orthodoxy. In summarizing the three separate cases Nikiforos determined that each had the following in common: The Dukhobors rejected the sacraments of the Christian faith, the cross of Christ, and the Holy Icons. They never attended church and proclaimed that they believed only by way of their souls and prayers.[88] The first case involved the village of Bogdanova and a homesteader, Foma Razvodov (referred to as "the debauched" in the report) who was responsible for "seducing" others in the village to the beliefs of the Dukhobors. Razvodov had two previous encounters with civil and ecclesiastical authorities owing to his repudiation of Orthodoxy. In 1774 and in 1781 he had gone astray of the true path and after admonitions (*uveshchaniia*) from the local diocesan consistory had returned to the Church only to reject it both times.[89] This behavior was, in fact, quite common among Old Believers and other sectarians who had been discovered and transferred to the offices of the consistory. The local Church hierarchs would officially exhort individuals to return to the Orthodox Church and, in most instances, the individuals would relent and repent of the error of their ways and return to the Church only to renege after leaving the presence of the Church officials. The Church was actually rather understanding of this particular behavior because, as St. Augustine wrote, human beings are frail creatures who also possess the capacity of free choice.

In 1786, Razvodov and his wife, Avdotia, once again announced with solemn hearts their foolishness and declared themselves repentant and "damned in the court of God and monarch if they again erred and asked that he and his wife be united with the Church." The archbishop also ordered the local parish priest to keep them under surveillance, steadfastly instruct them in the faith of the Church and offer to them the holy fasts and sacraments. Razvodov and his wife were also guilty of converting seventeen families in Bogdanova to Dukhobor beliefs and practices. The villagers were admonished to return to Orthodoxy by the *hegumen* of the local monastery and an archpriest from Pavlograd. They pledged to resist no longer the Church secretly or openly. However, within a few months, Nikiforos received a report that all of them including a young woman had lapsed. They all went to the parish church and declared that "they have the church in their belly."[90]

The archbishop, hearing of this latest infraction, ordered the Pavlograd Spiritual District to conduct another inquiry. Razvodov was condemned as the one "who has invented this impious and blasphemous heresy." He lured the others into error and encouraged them to "sing praises to their false success." When two parents attempted to prevent their children from leaving the Church they were called *zhibovka* (little Jewess) and little devil. Another inhabitant hurled insults at the icons and called the icon of St.

Nicholas false. Yet another refused to believe that the Scriptures contained the words of God.[91]

It seems that the spiritual message of the Dukhobors was attractive to more than just odnodvortsy. Nikiforos received information that several *meshchane* (merchants) from the city of Novomoskovsk had attempted to obtain passports to move to the village of Bogdanova. In total thirteen families were sent to the consistory for admonishment. Among the leaders two had rejected Orthodoxy in the past: one had been sentenced to military service and the other sent to the island of Ezel, from where he later ran away to Kurland, and then under an Imperial amnesty of 1779 settled in the city of Novomoskovsk.[92]

The conclusion reached by the archbishop of Slaviansk and Kherson was that he did not have the ability to bring these lost souls back to the Church. The Holy Synod concurred with him and issued an *ukase* ordering the *eresenachalniki* to be removed from their homes and sent to the northern diocese of Archangelsk. This was a policy the Church had adopted in the Tambov case of 1773.[93]

In this case, the Church was not necessarily interested in the source of the beliefs held by the groups that had "fallen" from the true faith, but were more concerned with returning them to the correct path. The diocesan and synodal leadership actively strove to redeem those in error through admonishment and exhortation. This approach was founded on the belief that parishioners were simple-minded and easily seduced by false teachers who were themselves merely the victims of treacherous lies. With such assumptions, the Church believed that corporal punishment was ineffective, although civil authorities never tired of advocating it as a solution. (This method also reflected Catherine's enlightened attitude toward all aspects of her reform program.) Instead, the Church placed greater faith in instruction and surveillance by local clergy. When this failed the individual or individuals were sent to another diocese where instruction and surveillance were once again applied. The irony of this approach, of course, was that by sending the penitents to different parts of the empire, the government was unwittingly contributing to the dispersion of the heretical beliefs. This error would be corrected in the reign of Alexander I who ordered them isolated and confined to the Milky Waters along the Sea of Azov.

In late 1788, Archbishop Amvrosii (successor to Nikiforos) was informed of a group of Cossacks in the village of Bereka in

Slaviansk *uezd* who had strayed from the Church to the so-called Dukhobors.[94] On 16 July 1788, during a church service in honor of Catherine, the parish priest noticed that not all the parishioners were making the sign of the cross or genuflecting when the cross passed them. In total, twenty-one men and women were guilty of this lapse and when the priest inquired about their actions he received nonsensical answers. When taken to the diocesan authorities for admonishment only eight admitted to their errors and returned to the Church. A few years later, in 1791, the same parish priest reported that the thirteen who had refused to return to the Church had reappeared and were accompanied by another twenty-four. When members of this group admitted that they did not acknowledge the traditions of the Church they were called before the Church authorities. During the interrogation at the diocesan consistory, the archbishop learned about their beliefs and, from his perspective, their errors.[95]

In the course of the examination of the thirty-two Cossacks (fifteen men, fifteen women, and two children), Amvrosii discovered that the Orthodox Church and Dukhobors held some beliefs in common and were at variance in regard to others. At the most fundamental level the Dukhobors were Christian. They believed in the one true God and the Holy Trinity of the Father, the Son and the Holy Spirit. They acknowledged Christ as Savior. On the issue of the Mother of God, they recognized Mary as nothing more than the "mother" of God, i.e., they did not ascribe to her a measure of holiness. They revered Christ's Apostles as his disciples and the martyrs as "good people" and saints who did good deeds and believed that their acts should be imitated, but they did not believe that they were holy as only God is Holy.[96]

They accepted as Holy Scripture the books of the Holy Prophets and a few of the Psalms of David in the Old Testament and the books of Christ's Apostles in the New Testament. As these Cossacks were illiterate, like the majority of Dukhobors, most of their "texts" were obviously committed to memory, but in this case they claimed that according to Scripture "what is written on the heart, will rise to the tongue." This is the first suggestion that they rejected the externals of organized Christianity. Although they accepted portions of the Old and New Testaments they did not extend that acceptance to the Church Fathers, the Ecumenical Councils or the local councils of the Orthodox Church. They considered the Church to have been made by the hands of man and therefore accepted none its traditions, customs, rituals or, more important, none of its sacraments. They had no need of churches or the Church.[97]

Their entire life cycle was devoid of the Orthodox rituals and sacraments which accompany the great stages of life, birth, marriage, and death. They rejected the sacrament of baptism for children because children were incapable of recognizing the man-made Church's imperfections and did not know that it was not the true church of God. If an adult converted, however, he could baptize himself with the words of God: in the name of the Father, Son, and Holy Spirit. Marriage was also rejected as a man-made sacrament for married life, they held, was founded in the word and respect. Burial occurred without ceremony; the community simply sang the Psalms of David. They also rejected the veneration and worship of icons, because they were adjudged neither divine nor holy and had no bearing on salvation. In a religious community without external trappings or rituals there is hardly a need for priests, bishops and archbishops. These Dukhobors believed that Christ the Lord was the eternal bishop and the others were not necessary as they were no different from any other person. Their priest was Christ the Lord who created the heavens and the earth and blessed the entire world and endowed it with reason.[98]

Regarding their attitudes toward secular power and their own identity they held some interesting ideas. They considered themselves to be inhabitants of Russia and acknowledged the leadership of the empress of the all the Russias. They also recognized that they, by her command, were in a Cossack regiment. They had fought for Russia and would continue to serve her. However, they did not consider themselves to be hers but to be Cossacks. And if the empress allowed them to worship freely, they would swear to fight her enemies and defend her laws, her citizens, their right to worship, their families, and their homes. But if the empress denied them the right to worship as they pleased and constrained their movement, they would refuse to acknowledge the empress and her laws and refuse to take up arms against her enemies. And if their homes were destroyed they would flee with their families from place to place by the word of God.[99]

••••

Undoubtedly, the Dukhobors were a very secretive sect and were loath to provide information unless they were compelled to do so. If Archbishop Nikiforos or Archbishop Amvrosii were only concerned about spiritual matters they would not have asked them about Dukhobor history or the origins of their beliefs, if indeed they could even answer such questions. One of the early Dukhobor leaders, Silvan Kolesnikov, actually protected his followers from persecution in the 1760s and 1770s by instructing them to adopt the outward forms of Orthodoxy while remaining true to their inner selves.[100] This may account for the paucity of information gained from the Dukhobors in Ekaterinoslav, but a more likely reason was the essentially parochial or local nature of the different dissenting groups and their differing levels of education and knowledge of Dukhoborism. As an example, at the same time that Amvrosii was interrogating the Bereka group, another group was submitting a "Confession of Faith" (*Ispovedanie svoei very*) to the governor of Ekaterinoslav, Kachovskoi, which afforded the government with its first glimpse of Dukhobor beliefs and history.[101] It is from this account that most historians base their treatment of early Dukhobor history supplemented by other oral Dukhobor sources. In order to better understand the Dukhobors we need to highlight briefly the history of the Dukhobors in eighteenth-century Russia.

The standard account of Dukhobor history begins with the arrival of a literate army officer in the village of Okhotchee in the province of Kharkov in 1717 or 1718. He taught that the teachings of the Orthodox Church were corrupt and not the true words of Christ. He also preached pacifism which may have accounted for his departure from the army and his appearance in Kharkov. Silvan Kolesnikov emerged as a leading figure among the early Dukhobors in the 1750s in the village of Nikol'skoe in the province of Ekaterinoslav. He distinguished himself by his literacy and preached from his home on Sundays to the local peasants. He used the Bible as a guide, but rejected all religious and governmental authority and institutions. Kolesnikov counseled that God dwells in each man and therefore man only needs to listen to the "inner voice."[102]

Following Kolesnikov's death in 1775, another leader appeared in the village of Goreloe in the province of Tambov. Ilarion Pobirokhin was a wool merchant who traveled widely and probably came into contact with Kolesnikov and his followers and/or with another sectarian group, the Khlysty, who resided along the

Volga. Pobirokhin abandoned the Bible completely, claimed that truth could only be found in the spirit or "Living Book," proclaimed himself the living Christ, and chose twelve disciples to assist him. This dramatic departure from the teachings of Kolesnikov made the dissenters visible to neighbors, priests, and the authorities who questioned him in 1769. Pobirokhin's authoritarian manner, absolute rejection of the Bible, and his deification fomented dissension among the sectarians and convinced one of his followers, Semeon Uklein, to break away and form his own sect, the Molokane. Pobirokhin subsequently fled Goreloe and began preaching in the city of Tambov where he was apprehended and exiled to Siberia in the late 1780s. He was succeeded in Goreloe by Savelii Kapustin, a moderately educated man who arrived in the village in 1790. He was born in 1743, served as a corporal in the Guards, and at the age of forty-seven appeared in Goreloe and became the living Christ.[103]

This brief account of the emergence of the Dukhobors in eighteenth-century Russia confirms the notion that Dukhobor beliefs were fragmented and somewhat localized. The Dukhobors were too dispersed to recognize any one variant of their beliefs to be decreed the "correct" one. For that reason, even the account given above should be recognized as just one of many possible narratives.[104]

What, if anything, can the student of religion conclude about the religious domain constructed by the Dukhobors in late eighteenth-century southern Russia? What motivated individuals or groups to undertake the difficult and troublesome task of abandoning Orthodoxy and adopting a religion that inspired the ire of both Church and state? Are historians in the position to even deduce something as ephemeral as motive? Whatever did motivate peasants, Cossacks, *odnodvortsy*, and city dwellers to dedicate themselves to a relatively new religious movement must have been of considerable importance in order to attract the same uneducated masses that persistently evaded the Orthodox Church's attempts to educate them in the ways of "true" Orthodoxy.[105] It is true that, even though the Dukhobors were cast as opponents of the established Church and the Russian state, they had not rejected the dominant religious structure of Christianity in its entirety. In other words, the Dukhobors were people who were obviously discontented with certain aspects of Orthodox Christianity, but did not resort to Buddhism, Hinduism or even animism out of dissatisfaction with Orthodoxy. We cannot discount the notion that the dissenters were keeping their "enthusiasm" for religion alive by denying rituals altogether as a symbol of their faith.[106]

The power and influence of the Orthodox Church itself perhaps precluded a more dramatic departure by not allowing certain thoughts and practices (or "spaces") even to be discussed, thus leaving only some variant of Christianity as a real possibility.[107] (On the other hand, many Balkan Christians, and later, many Russian Christians in Central Asia, converted to Islam or Buddhism when they found themselves in an area where Islam or Buddhism was the dominant religion.) Dukhobor beliefs and practices were by no means alien to Christian tradition. Within the scope of European Christianity, the Dukhobors resemble the Gnostics, the Manicheans, the Anabaptists, and the Quakers, to name just a few. Therefore, it is not inconceivable that sectarian groups should arise in Russia without resorting to the belief that a "foreigner" (usually a Quaker) brought the beliefs into Russia. Within Russia, the tradition of religious dissent is also glaringly apparent in the cases of the Bogomils, the Judaizers, and the followers of Kuhlmann. Each of which rejected church ritual and advocated extra-ecclesiastical means to inner illumination.[108]

The Dukhobors developed a world view that was markedly different from that of their neighbors, parish priests, and the Orthodox hierarchs. They constructed an outer world that was bereft of references to the holy or the divine. They refused to accept or acknowledge the propriety of icons, churches, the canonical Bible, or the rituals that mark the stages of life, birth, marriage, and death, because all were man-made and therefore imperfect, undistinguished, and tainted. They constructed a "disenchanted" world in which they no longer celebrated festivals or saints' days nor did they observe fasts. In terms of religious landscape, the Dukhobors moved from the forest to the desert. They accepted no priests or hierarchs because Christ the Lord was the eternal hierarch and the first and only priest and His spirit resides in each individual. Paradoxically, the Dukhobors defined themselves, in a sense, negatively. Most belief systems possess outward manifestations or rituals of that system which signify whether one belongs to a certain community or not. The Dukhobors chose to define themselves by *not* using the rituals of their neighbors.

The Dukhobors' absolute rejection of all ritual and outward manifestations of Christian faith, as understood and practiced by the Orthodox Church, placed them squarely in the category of religious dissenters and therefore political dissenters. Catherine's reforms expanded the domain of the state into realms previously dominated or inhabited by other institutions. In effect, she was continuing the policies initiated by Peter the Great. It would be incorrect, however, to assume that their programs of state expansion were simultaneously programs of "dechristianization." Even though Catherine had "instrumentalized" religion, she understood that religious belief and, more important, the institutions that propagated those beliefs, were essential for creating and maintaining a semblance of social harmony and control. Catherinian Russia was still a deeply Christian, indeed Orthodox Christian, society. Much has been written about the necessity of Orthodoxy to Russian national identity. The Dukhobor rejection of the outward manifestations of an extremely liturgical and ritualistic form of Christianity was nothing less than a rejection of Russia itself. The Dukhobors sensed this when they suggested to the examiner that they would gladly and fiercely defend Catherine and her empire and her subjects as long as she allowed them to worship freely. The problem, of course, was that "their" freedom to worship was tantamount to a repudiation of Russia.

The Dukhobors abandoned Orthodoxy for a number of reasons, but the search for religious renewal was among them. Their rejection of all ecclesiastical ritual was a manifestation of popular "enthusiasm" not available to them within Russian Orthodoxy, but yet part of the non-canonical Christian tradition. Coincidentally, their abject refusal to recognize any form of external religious authority extended to the state and was a direct challenge to the political structure of Catherinian Russia. Their beliefs "legitimized" their quest for change and "delegitimized" and subverted political and social norms. Dukhobor beliefs also allowed for a strong sense of community for the dissenters involved. Using their religious beliefs they fashioned a democratic community which admitted no external control or circumscription of their freedoms. The Dukhobors, in effect, adopted a religious system that created a world that was spiritually and, at times, physically apart from the Orthodox world of Catherinian Russia.

••••

On 28 November 1786, by order of Catherine, Archbishop
Nikiforos was relieved of his position as head of the diocese of
Slaviansk and Kherson and transferred to the diocese of Astrakhan
and Stavropol where he was to succeed the recently deceased Arch-
bishop Antonii Rumovskii as the seventeenth bishop of Astrakhan
and Stavropol. Theotokis was replaced by Archbishop Amvrosii of
Olonets who was also elevated to a seat on the Holy Synod.[109]
Theotokis's transfer evidently was initiated by Prince Potemkin. In a
letter sent to Potemkin by A.A. Bezborodko (who had announced
Theotokis's appointment to the diocese seven years earlier),
Catherine's foreign policy advisor, Bezborodko wrote, "in
compliance with the wish of your highness the most reverend
Nikiforos (Count Theotokis) was transferred to Astrakhan...with his
former rank and salary."[110] Theotokis's simple acknowledgment of
the decree ended with the words "with the assistance of God I will
endeavor to fulfill your decree."[111] On the same day as his
announced transfer the diocese was renamed the diocese of
Ekaterinoslav and Kherson-Tavricheskii to reflect more accurately
the changing provincial boundaries and circumstances of southern
Russia.

The reasons for Potemkin's wish to have Theotokis transferred
to Astrakhan remain obscure. Nineteenth-century church historians
advanced two possible reasons for his sudden departure but neither
can be corroborated. The first postulates that Archbishop Nikiforos
was invited to a large dinner hosted by Potemkin and when asked by
the host to bless the table Theotokis reproached the assembled guests
for violating Church law by eating meat on a fast day. Supposedly,
this outburst created a great disturbance and the indignant guests
demanded that Theotokis be removed. Potemkin complied and transferred him to Astrakhan.[112] This fanciful story originated with
Aleksandr Sturdza and seems all too similar to the account of
Theotokis's flight from Jassy for offending the local dignitaries. The
event does, however, reflect vintage Theotokis: a penchant to
remonstrate all who violate the laws of the Church no matter their
rank. The second is a misunderstanding of Archbishop Nikiforos's
role in the Zrazhevskoi case. According to Solov'ev, his "excessive
pastoral zeal" in forcefully returning Uniate clergy to Orthodoxy
necessitated his removal to Astrakhan by the Holy Synod to prevent
popular unrest in his diocese.[113]

Whatever the reason for his departure from Poltava in November 1786, Archbishop Nikiforos left an indelible imprint upon the diocese of Slaviansk and Kherson in education, church construction and Church relations with the Old Believers, the Uniates, and the Dukhobors. He accomplished a great deal during his seven-year tenure and established himself as an independent hierarch whose strong convictions in matters of faith and great erudition in Church history and traditions made him an ideal ecclesiastic in the frontier region of southern Russia. Ultimately, however, he always remained a loyal and obedient son of the Church and bowed to its decisions even when he disagreed with them. And now the Church instructed him to take up duties nearly seven hundred miles to the east in the diocese of Astrakhan and Stavropol.

NOTES

1. Theotokis, "Kratkoe povestvovanie o obrashchenii raskol'nikov seleniia Znamenki, kakim obrazom oni byli priniaty v pravoslavnuiu tserkov'; izlozhenie osnovanii, po kotorym im pozvoleno bylo chitat' starinnyia knigi, izdannyia v Rossii, i pet' po svoemu obychaiu, postavit' sviashchennika iz ikh sredy, esli by iavilsia dostoinyi; mezhdu prochim i razsyzhdenie o obriadakh," *Bratskoe slovo*, 2 (1892): 138.

2. On this see Leonard Krieger, *Kings and Philosophers, 1689-1789* (New York, 1970), pp. 284-290.

3. On the issue of the subservient church, see Gregory L. Freeze, "The Handmaiden of the State? The Church in Imperial Russia Reconsidered," *Journal of Ecclesiastical History*, 36:1 (January 1985): 82-102.

4. A comparable attitude was held by the Austrian monarchy in the eighteenth century. See Grete Klingenstein, "Modes of Religious Tolerance and Intolerance in Eighteenth-Century Habsburg Politics," *Austrian Studies Yearbook*, 24 (1993): 1-16.

5. W.F. Reddaway, ed., *Documents of Catherine the Great. The Correspondence with Voltaire and the Instruction of 1767 in the English text of 1768* (Cambridge, 1931), p. 209.

6. *PSZ*, XIX, 17 June 1773, No. 13996.

7. On Catherine's religious policies, see Isabel de Madariaga, *Russia in the Age of Catherine the Great* (New Haven, 1981), pp. 111-122, 503-520; Gregory L. Bruess, "Religious Toleration in the Reign of Catherine the Great," in *International Perspectives on Church and State* (Omaha, NE, 1993), pp. 299-315.

8. Asad, *Genealogies of Religion*, pp. 34-35.

9. The literature on the Old Belief is voluminous but some standard accounts include Michael Cherniavsky, "The Old Believers and the New Religion," *Slavic Review*, 25 (1966): 1-39; Serge Zenkovsky, *Russkoe staroobriadchestvo* (Munich, 1970); A.I. Klibanov, ed., *Russkoe pravoslavie* (Moscow, 1989); V.V. Andreev, *Raskol' i ego znachenie v narodnoi russkoi istorii* (St. Petersburg, 1870); P.S. Smirnov, *Istoriia russkogo raskola staroobriadchestva* (St. Petersburg, 1895); A.P. Shchapov, *Russkii raskol staroobriadstva* (Kazan, 1859); Pierre Pascal, *Avvakum et les débuts du raskol* (Paris, 1963); and Frederick Conybeare, *Russian Dissenters* (New

York, 1921). For a review of the historiography, see Robert O. Crummey, "Interpreting the Fate of the Old Believer Communities in the Eighteenth and Nine-teenth Centuries," in Batalden, ed., *Seeking God*, pp. 144-159 and "Past and Current Interpretations of the Old Belief" (paper presented at Russia's Dissenting Old Believ-ers: An International Conference, Northfield, MN, Sept. 30-Oct. 2, 1994); N.N. Pokrovskii, "Trends in Studying the History of Old Belief by Russian Scholars" (paper presented at Russia's Dissenting Old Believers: An International Conference, Northfield, MN, Sept. 30-Oct. 2, 1994); and Roy R. Robson, *Old Believers*, pp. 3-13.

10. For a profile of the Old Belief, see Robson, pp. 14-40.

11. Standard works on the Old Believers have presented the participants in the Old Belief as socially uniform and undifferentiated in nature; a homogeneous community which coalesced around Archpriest Avvakum. For a study which challenges this interpretation by emphasizing the contingent and local nature of many of the "Old Belief" communities, see Georg Michels, "The Solovki Uprising: Religion and Revolt in Northern Russia," *The Russian Review*, 51 (January 1992): 1-15, and "Some Observations on the Social History of the Old Belief during the Seventeenth Century" (paper presented at Russia's Dissenting Old Believers: An International Conference, Northfield, MN, Sept. 30-Oct. 2, 1994). This aspect of the historicity of religious construction is a dominant theme in Harjot Oberoi, *The Construction of Religious Boundaries: Culture, Identity, and Diversity in the Sikh Tradition* (Chicago, 1994).

12. Smirnov, p. 168.

13. Cited in Cracraft, p. 73.

14. On further actions under Peter I, see Smirnov, pp. 173-196.

15. For a history of this community, see R.O. Crummey, *The Old Believers and the World of Antichrist: The Vyg Community and the Russian State, 1694-1855* (Madison, 1970).

16. Voltaire to Catherine, 13 February 1773; Lentin, p. 148.

17. Papmehl, *Metropolitan Platon*, p. 14.

18. John T. Alexander, *Bubonic Plague in Early Modern Russia: Public Health and Urban Disaster* (Baltimore, 1980), p. 181.

19. Andreev, pp. 126-127.

20. Papmehl, p. 15.

21. Smirnov, p. 200.

22. For a review of the historiography of *edinoverie*, see, V.I. Belikov, *Deiatel'nost' moskovskogo mitropolita Filareta po otnosheniiu k raskolu* (Kazan, 1895).

23. Bartlett, *Human Capital*, p. 48.

24. Yet another example of the importance of creating a transcendental "sacred" space for the maintenance and continuity of community.

25. *RGIA*, f. 796, o. 58, g. 1777, d. 134, l. 1.

26. After initially settling in the St. Elizabeth fortress area the Old Believers spread to other regions of Novoserbiia and later, Novorossiia. In one village, Klintsy, they had not only a church, but a school and printing press as well. By 1773, accord-ing to Solov'ev, their numbers reached 13,000 between Kremenchug and St. Elizabeth. Solov'ev, p. 580.

27. Nevodchikov, *Evgenii Bulgaris*, pp. 45-46.

28. B.V. Titlinov, *Gavriil Petrov, mitropolit novgorodskii i sanktpeterburgskii* (Petrograd, 1916), pp. 881-884.

29. Nevodchikov, pp. 46-47.

30. Titlinov, p. 886.

31. *Ibid.*, p. 887.

32. Titlinov gives 14 February 1780 as the date of the petition. V.A. Grekov argues for a later date sometime in early June. He believes that the Znamenka Old

Believers were motivated to renew their petition attempt only after reading Theotokis's 25 March 1780 publication "Okruzhenoe poslanie." V.A. Grekov, "Kem i kak polozheno nachalo Edinoveriiu v Russkoi tserkvi," *Bratskoe slovo*, 2 (1892): 111. Another letter to the schismatics, dated 16 July 1780, has been published by K. Dyovouniotis, "Logoi anekdotoi kai epistolai Nikiforou tou Theotoki," *Ieros Syndesmos* (15 Sept.. 1915): 4-8 and an edited version by Skal'kovskii, *prilozhenie*, pp. 275-279. There is no mention of a previous letter in Dyovouniotis and the text does not suggest that Theotokis has communicated this same material before, so it is possible that the letter dated 16 July 1780 by Skal'kovskii is identical or nearly identical to the 25 March 1780 letter cited by Grekov.

33. Solov'ev, p. 581.

34. Dyovouniotis, p. 5.

35. *Ibid.*

36. The reluctance of Old Believers to alter these rituals is convincingly explained by Roy Robson who suggests that "for the faithful, pre-Nikonian rituals *realized* rather than *represented* heaven on earth." This "process of realization" or the conception of symbols as a means to realization as opposed to mere representations, is very common in Eastern Christendom because of its emphasis on *theosis* or deification, i.e., man's salvation means his divinization. See Robson, p. 8.

37. Dyovouniotis, pp. 5-6. Theotokis cites as his source for this reconstruction the *History* of Nikitas Honiates, a late twelfth-early thirteenth century Byzantine writer. The main focus of the *History* was the Emperor Manuel I Comnenus and his relations with the Latin West. The Byzantines of the twelfth century were extremely concerned about the threat of heresy and Catholicism to the very survival of the Empire. According to Vasiliev, Manuel I Comnenus and his mostly legendary exploits were well known in Russian heroic epics. A.A. Vasiliev, *History of the Byzantine Empire*, vol. II (Madison, 1952), p. 432.

38. Dyovouniotis, p. 6.

39. *Ibid.*

40. Even the priestly Old Believer communities (*popovtsy*) were denied the full services of their priests because the clerics had not been ordained by a bishop as no Old Believer bishops existed and no Orthodox bishops would deign to do so.

41. Dyovouniotis, p. 7.

42. *Ibid.*, pp. 7-8.

43. Grekov, pp. 128-129. "Kratkoe povestvovanie o obrashchenii raskol'nikov seleniia Znamenki, kakim obrazom oni byli priniaty v pravoslavnuiu tserkov'; izlozhenie osnovanii, po kotorym im pozvoleno bylo chitat' starinnyia knigi, izdannyia v Rossii, i pet' po svoemu obychaiu, postavit' sviashchennika iz ikh sredy, esli by iavilsia dostoinyi; mezhdu prochim i razsyzhdenie o obriadakh" was originally submitted to the Holy Synod in Latin under the title "Brevis narratio." The petitioners had the opportunity to speak to Theotokis when he visited Znamenka in the summer of 1780.

44. Grekov, pp. 112-113.

45. "Kratkoe," p. 129.

46. Grekov, p. 113, n. 1. The author cites Lebedev's article in *Tserkhovnye vedomosti* (1889), p. 953.

47. Lebedev states that according to the resolution Theotokis sent Archpriest Evthimii Zavurskii of Kremenchug to Znamenka, but Theotokis claims to have sent Smolodovich in three different publications. Grekov, p. 113, n.2.

48. "Kratkoe," p. 129.

49. Grekov, p. 114.

50. Titlinov, p. 888.

51. "Pis'mo arkhiepiskopa Slavenskago Nikifora k arkhiepiskopu Novgorodskomu Gavriilu, OT 1780 goda, avgusta 3-go dnia," in Grekov, *Bratskoe slovo*, p. 121. This particular quote refers to I Corinthians XIV, 20.

52. Letter to Gavriil, 3 August 1780, pp. 122-123.

53. Platon's letter to Theotokis, 23 September 1781, (original in Latin with a Russian translation) in Lysogorskii, *Moskovskii mitropolit Platon Levshin* (Rostov-on-Don, 1905), pp. 465-467.

54. Grekov noted that such interest by Gavriil and by Platon in the Martinos heresy case suggested that the Church was beginning to question the validity of the story. Grekov, p. 117, n. 1.

55. Letter from Archbishop Gavriil to Archbishop Nikiforos, 11 October 1781, in Grekov, pp. 123-124.

56. The letter to Potemkin is reprinted in *Bratskoe slovo* by Grekov. Theotokis stated that he only had the best of intentions for the Church and for the Russian government when he permitted the Old Believers to return to the "mother Church." Instead, he writes in a shocked expression, "the Holy Synod informs me by letter...that they not only do not welcome the deed, but are even censuring it." He continued by explaining to Potemkin that he had not given him details of the matter when he first informed him of the conversion because he did not think it necessary. Now, however, events proved otherwise, and for that reason he was sending him his "Kratkoe povestvovanie." He closed by saying, "Frankly speaking, I had no other goal in this affair, except the glory of God and benefit of the community," but if he was in error he would reverse his decision in regard to the conversion. Grekov, pp. 118-119, n. 2.

57. Letter to Gavriil, 18 Dec. 1781, p. 126.

58. Letter to Gavriil, pp. 127-128.

59. The second edition of Platon's *Uveshchanie* appeared in 1773.

60. Theotokis did not cite the entire verse from I Corinthians XI, 2, which is: "Be imitators of me, as I am of Christ."

61. "Kratkoe," pp. 130-133.

62. *Ibid.*, pp. 134-138.

63. *Ibid.*, p. 138

64. Pia Pera, "Edinoverie. Storia di un tentativo di integrazione del Vecchi Credenti all'interno dell'Ortodossia," *Rivista di storia e letteratura religiosa*, II (1984): 345.

65. Smirnov, p. 209. If the Znamenka case had been rejected by the Synod in 1780 or 1781, the Starodub affair surely would have been the precedent setting case. The Starodub Old Believers and Abbot Nikodim had the firm support of the governor-general of the Ukraine, Razumovskii, and Prince Potemkin (Nikodim even was given an audience with Catherine).

66. Titlinov, p. 891.

67. Pera, p. 291.

68. Theotokis received a negative reply from a group of Old Believers in Bakhmut district entitled "Solovetsk Petition." He responded by writing a point-by-point refutation of their arguments for not accepting his offer of conditional union. He found their argumentation to be the work of "great ignoramuses" and therefore was not surprised by their refusal to reunite with the mother Church. Theotokis later published his "answers" to them in *Otvety preosviashchennago Nikifora arkhiepiskopa slavenskago i khersonskago, a potom byvshago astrakhanskago i kavalera, na voprosy staroobriadtsov* (Moscow, 1800). Solov'ev, p. 582.

69. Grekov, p. 110.

70. For example, the community of Ploskoi rejected Theotokis's proposals at the same time Znamenka was accepting them. See *RGIA*, f. 796, o. 62, g. 1781, d. 527, ll. 1-4ob. Other cases (e.g., *ibid.*, o. 62, g. 1781, d. 502 and *ibid.*, o. 64, g. 1783,

d. 226) represent a variety of responses and also suggest that individuals, and even whole communities, frequently convert and reconvert depending on the circumstances. Also see Michels, 1-15.

71. Titlinov, p. 887.
72. *RGIA*, f. 796, o. 62, g. 1781, d. 502, ll. 1-4.
73. *Ibid.*, l. 32.
74. Crummey, "Interpreting the Fate," p. 155, n. 16.
75. *RGIA*, f. 796, o. 60, g. 1779, d. 456, ll. 1-5.
76. *RGIA*, f. 796, o. 64, g. 1783, d. 226, ll. 1-1ob.
77. *Ibid.*, l. 3ob.
78. *RGIA*, f. 796, o. 64, g. 1783, d. 397, ll. 1-1ob.
79. *RGIA*, f. 796, o. 78, g. 1797, d. 198, ll. 3-3ob.
80. *Ibid.*, d. 152, ll. 1-3.
81. Batalden, *Catherine*, p. 61.
82. "Razsuzhdenie soderzhashchee v sebe prichiny dokazyvaiushchiia chto s rukopolozhennymi ot uniatskikh episkopov postupat' nadlezhit' tak kak s mirskimi." Batalden, p. 131, n.56.
83. Batalden, pp. 61-62.
84. de Madariaga, p. 515.
85. Batalden, pp. 85-87.
86. *RGIA*, f. 796, o. 67, g. 1786, d. 189, ll. 1-2.
87. Some standard accounts on the Dukhobors include Orest Novitskii, *Dukhobortsy: ikh istoriia i verouchenie* (Kiev, 1832; 2nd ed., 1882); F.V. Livanov, *Raskol'niki i Ostrozhniki: ocherki i razskazy*, vols. I-IV (St. Petersburg, 1872-3); V.A. Sukhorev, *Dokumenti po Istorii Dukhobortsev i Kratkoe Izlozhenie ikh Veroispovedaniia* (North Kildonan, Man., Canada, 1944); V.D. Bonch-Bruevich, *Materials Concerning the History and Study of Russian Sectarianism and Schism* (St. Petersburg, 1908); A.I. Klibanov, *The History of Religious Sectarianism in Russia (1860s-1917)* (Oxford, 1982 reprint); George Woodcock and Ivan Avakumovic, *The Doukhobors* (Toronto, 1968); Aylmer Maude, *A Peculiar People: The Doukhobors* (New York, 1970 reprint); and Frederick Conybeare, *Russian Dissenters* (New York, 1921).
88. *RGIA*, f. 796, o. 67, g. 1786, d. 189, l. 46.
89. *Ibid.*, l. 23ob.
90. *RGIA*, f. 796, o. 67, g. 1786, d. 189, l. 24.
91. *Ibid.*, ll. 24-24ob.
92. *Ibid.*, ll. 48ob-49.
93. *Ibid.*, ll. 55-55ob.
94. Archbishop Amvrosii is generally the Church hierarch credited with naming the adherents of this new sect the Dukhobors. In 1785, he referred to them as the people who wrestle with the Holy Spirit. He, of course, meant this to mean those who wrestled *against* the Holy Spirit. The Dukhobors, like other groups, later adopted this name for themselves but interpreted it to mean those who wrestle or struggle *with* the Holy Spirit, which resides within them. See, Novitskii, p. 1 and Livanov, vol. I, pp. 181-2. Novitskii does not offer a citation for this statement, Livanov cites Baron von Haxthausen, and nothing that I saw in the Synodal records during this period indicate that he did or did not invent the word. That the term Dukhobor antedates at least 1786 is obvious owing to Theotokis's reference to the heretics as Dukhobors in his report to the Holy Synod of that spring.
95. *RGIA*, f. 797, o. 1, g. 1792, d. 1162, ll. 3-3ob.
96. *Ibid.*, ll. 4-6.
97. *Ibid.*
98. *Ibid.*
99. *Ibid.*, l. 6.

100. Woodcock, p. 27.
101. Novitskii, p. 4. The confession of faith was, reportedly, written for the Dukhobors by Gregory Skovoroda.
102. Novitskii, pp. 18-23.
103. Novitskii, pp. 23-34.
104. A "uniform and common" narrative does eventually emerge during the nineteenth century. As the Dukhobors are often compared to the English Quakers, an interesting study which explores George Fox's creation of an unchallengeable Quaker "orthodoxy" in a religious movement begun as an overt challenge to established religions see H. Larry Ingle, *First Among Friends: George Fox and the Creation of Quakerism* (New York, 1994).
105. See Freeze, "Rechristianization."
106. For an excellent comparative analysis of sectarian movements see Bryan Wilson, *Religious Sects: A Sociological Study* (London, 1970).
107. A concept advanced by Talal Asad, "Anthropological Conceptions of Religion: Reflections on Geertz," *Man*, 18 (1983): 237-259.
108. Billington, p. 174.
109. *RGIA*, f. 796, o. 67, g. 1786, d. 534, l. 2.
110. *SIRIO*, p. 284, n. 12, 29 November 1786.
111. *RGIA*, f. 796, o. 67, g. 1786, d. 534, l. 124.
112. Solov'ev, p. 585.
113. Solov'ev, p. 585-586.

6

A New Diocese and New Challenges: Astrakhan

> God is my witness, that I wanted and endeavored, that my
> priests would be like bright lamps, enlightening through
> God's word in sermons and holy virtuous example. I wished
> and asked of God, that the soldiers always be strong defend-
> ers of the fatherland, the leaders be fathers of the nation, the
> judges be executors of justice and law, the merchants be
> useful to the community and the artists be diligent and assid-
> uous. I wished, I say, and endeavored that all my Christians
> be in agreement with and love one another, abide by God's
> commandments and be examples of the virtuous. And in this
> way you will be happy on earth and blissful in heaven.
>
> – Archbishop Nikiforos's final sermon to his parishioners
> in Astrakhan, 15 June 1792.

Archbishop Nikiforos arrived at Spasskii Monastery in the
ancient city of Astrakhan, located on the estuary of the Volga on the
Caspian Sea, on 5 May 1787 to assume his new position as the seventeenth bishop and head of the diocese of Astrakhan and Stavropol.
On the following day, he led a procession of the cross from the gates
of the kremlin to St. Nicholas Cathedral. There, before the assembled local notables and citizens of Astrakhan, he conducted the divine
liturgy, gave a sermon, and then departed for his new quarters in the
episcopal residence (*arkhiereiskii dom*).[1] Theotokis was destined to
remain in Astrakhan for slightly more than five years. He had
expended a great amount of his youthful energy during his seven-
year tenure in Poltava and the duties in the diocese of Astrakhan and
Stavropol, made more onerous by the horrible climate,[2] were to tax
him to such a degree that he requested from the Empress permission
to retire, citing reasons of poor health, at the relatively early age of
sixty in 1792. Theotokis found the diocese of Astrakhan and
Stavropol to be quite similar to Slaviansk and Kherson in that it was
large, strategically located on the fringes of the Russian Empire and
under the nominal governorship of Prince G.A. Potemkin. It differed from Slaviansk and Kherson in that it had a large indigenous
population of Islamic Kalmyks, a considerable Armenian population

and a decidedly "oriental" quality owing to its proximity to Persia
and a sizable Persian community in the city of Astrakhan itself.

Broadly interpreted, Prince Potemkin's plans for Astrakhan
guberniia, of which he was governor-general until 1783 when he was
replaced by his cousin P.S. Potemkin, closely resembled those for
Novorossiia. The settlement and economic development of Novorossiia were first and foremost the means by which Russia's southern
frontier was secured from Ottoman penetration. The first foreign
colonists were "recruited" primarily for military duty along an ever
expanding system of concentric defensive perimeters, but were also
given free land and tax privileges by the Russian government to
encourage economic growth. The port cities on the northern Black
Sea coast and the Sea of Azov, founded by Potemkin in the late 1770s
and early 1780s, served as naval bases and shipyards for Catherine's
projected Black Sea fleet and centers of commerce for the foreign
colonists who developed trade and commercial contacts with their
homelands. Once the region of Novorossiia was sufficiently developed it could be used as a possible staging area for military forays
into the Ottoman Empire and further territorial expansion. Local
and regional peculiarities demanded minor adjustments to his overall
program of settlement and development, but for the most part
Potemkin's plans were consistently implemented in all the territories
under his control marked in the west by the Bug River and in the
east by the Caspian Sea.

While Prince Potemkin was establishing Novorossiia in 1775
he emphasized the importance of a strong Orthodox presence to
unify the disparate nationalities that comprised the population of
southern Russia. This belief led him to propose the appointments of
Voulgaris and Theotokis to the episcopal see of Slaviansk and
Kherson to serve as representatives of both Russian Orthodoxy and
the Balkan Christians who were colonizing the northern Black Sea
littoral. The same concern possibly prompted the transfer of Archbishop Nikiforos to the diocese of Astrakhan and Stavropol in 1786.
Although Astrakhan had been a part of the Russian Empire since the
reign of Ivan the Terrible, Catherine's addition of the former
Turkish and Persian north Caucasus territories of the Kuban and
Karbada to the empire during the first Russo-Turkish war, opened
new lands with large non-Russian populations. This region had great
economic potential for Russia but its sparse population and precarious location precluded its efficient use. Potemkin, thus, undertook in

1777 to stabilize Astrakhan *guberniia* and to secure the north Caucasian steppe as a base for future campaigns to the south by establishing a fortified line extending from Mozdok to Azov which would replace the old Tsaritsyn line and continue the Kizliar-Mozdok line begun in 1763. Ever mindful of the implications of economic development, he also intended that those who served as soldiers on the line would engage in agricultural and commercial pursuits. Potemkin believed that "by its position, [the line] gives the opportunity to set up vineyards, silk and cotton plantations, to increase stock-breeding, stud-farms, orchards and grain production."[3] Once the soldiers secured the line Potemkin hoped to expand commercial development by attracting foreign colonists, "not excluding even Jews," who were in possession of sufficient capital, "for migration to the new Mozdok line, which abounds in everything needful for life."[4]

In the two decades following Prince Potemkin's announced project colonial settlement in the province of Astrakhan and the Caucasus proceeded fitfully and slowly. This was due in part to the inability of Russian forces to stabilize the Mozdok line until the mid-1780s and thereby provide a guarantee of security to colonists as a minimal condition of their settlement and the Russo-Turkish war which began in 1787. Potemkin was disappointed by the progress of colonization in the early 1780s and moved to remedy this deficit by issuing an Imperial decree in 1782 which granted land to all who desired it. Primarily, Prince Potemkin and, later, his successor, P.S. Potemkin, directed this decree at the *odnodvortsy* and the economic and state peasants of the overpopulated central provinces.[5] The Potemkins were satisfied with the response of the peasants to the invitation, but the resettlement of Russian colonists obviously did not advance the Empire's foreign policy interests with the same effect as the recruitment and settlement of foreign colonists.

On 14 July 1785, the Potemkins issued a Manifesto to correct the problem of insufficient foreign settlement in the Caucasus and Astrakhan *guberniia*. The Manifesto's emphasis on urban development reflected Catherine's recently issued Charter to the Towns, but it also offered the usual inducements to colonists such as freedom of religion, freedom from taxation for six years and equal rights with natives. It primarily targeted the Transcaucasian populations south of the Mozdok line, but was published in the West as well. Very few in the West heeded the call from Potemkin to settle in the Caucasus

Province or along the Volga in Astrakhan *guberniia* (a few years later, however, a faint echo of the Manifesto initiated the emigration of the Mennonites from Danzig to Russia in the late 1780s and 1790s), but sizable numbers of Armenians did accept the offer to settle in the northern Caucasus region.[6]

Thus, when Archbishop Nikiforos arrived in Astrakhan in early May 1787 he entered a diocese which had been in existence for over two hundred years and yet exhibited the economic, social and cultural characteristics usually associated with a newly established region primarily due to its fluctuating southern border and frontier status. Taking this into account, Archbishop Nikiforos confronted an array of problems which were similar in kind to those in Poltava but seemingly more intractable. His life-long passionate belief in education's ability to foster spiritual enrichment and material well-being led him to enhance the level and quality of both parish and seminary education in Astrakhan. His sincere anguish over the souls of those who had strayed from the Orthodox Church prompted his appeal to the Old Believers of Saratov for reunification with the Russian Orthodox Church. The influx of Transcaucasian immigrants obliged Archbishop Nikiforos to maintain satisfactory relations between the Orthodox and the non-Orthodox (primarily, Armenian) communities within the diocese. Finally, the archbishop was compelled to protect the property and financial prerogatives of the Church from legal actions initiated by provincial authorities.

••••

Despite the relative maturity of the diocese of Astrakhan and Stavropol, the quality and quantity of educational institutions in the diocese was substantially inferior to that of its neighbors. The diocese had a "seminary" but it was quite small and had been in existence for less than ten years. Earlier attempts were made to establish schools in the diocese going back as far as the 1720s without lasting success. Bishop Lavrentii expressed his desire to establish a school in the mid-1720s with the hope of creating "a better educated clergy."[7] At that time some children of the clergy were attending a "mathematics" school at Ivanovskii Monastery and Lavrentii proposed to transfer them to the new episcopal school (*arkhiereiskaia shkola*), but it was never created owing to the poverty of the diocese. Bishop Lavrentii then adopted a different approach which allowed him to procure money from non-ecclesiastical sources. He decided to open a parish church school for children of both the secular as well as spiritual ranks in accordance with the *Spiritual Regulation.*

A Latin School was built in 1728 in the parish of St. John Chrysostom with funds provided by a few local individuals who also requested that a reader (*ritor*), Petr Iaskol'skii, be appointed director with an annual compensation of 100 rubles, fifteen *chetverti* of rye flour and twenty meters of firewood. Ironically, only one priest's son was enrolled in the first year's class with the majority of the children coming from townspeople and house-serf families. In 1729, Archbishop Varlaam requested an instructor of Latin from the Holy Synod and it complied by sending Pavel Goroshkovskii, a philosophy student from the Moscow Academy (Slavonic-Greek-Latin Academy), in 1730. The two instructors were intent upon recruiting children of the clergy to the school, but their zealousness at times led them to resort to force. The parents responded by hiding their children and even attacking the instructors on the road.[8] In spite of this, forty-one students of all ranks attended the school in 1730 with educational levels ranging from those just learning the Russian alphabet to those studying Latin grammar.[9] The school rapidly declined after Varlaam retired to Moscow in 1730 and the merchants of Astrakhan wanted to change the curriculum to meet their needs. The merchants no longer required the services of Goroshkovskii because "the learning of the Latin dialect did not befit a merchant" and he could not teach German nor arithmetic which they did need for their businesses.[10] The school closed in 1731.

Seven years later, in December 1738, the Holy Synod took the initiative and issued a decree ordering the diocese to open a Slaviano-Latin School for the benefit of students, children of clergy, orphans and illegitimate children (*zazornykh prinosimykh mladentsev*). Bishop Ilarion responded that he had already located a teacher and that the diocese was able to support the children of the clergy in the school but that the same could not be done for the orphans and illegitimate children due to the diocese's precarious financial position. The Slaviano-Latin School opened in the summer of 1739 with twelve students and Petr Iaskol'skii as the instructor once again.[11] Bishop Ilarion funded the new school through a one-ruble levy imposed on each priest and deacon in the diocese as well as transferring to the school the profits from Trinity Monastery in Tsaritsyn. Unfortunately, the school began to disintegrate after only one year of operation when Iaskol'skii was released from his duties for drunkenness and mismanagement of school funds. The problems caused by his dismissal were compounded when the Holy Synod was not able to send a replacement instructor. The school eventually closed but another had opened at Spasskii Monastery in 1740 and was initially supported by gifts from wills. The school's success attracted the attention of the Senate which directed one hundred r.p.a. to it from the local fishery. It continued to function until 1766 when the College of Economy transferred its operating funds to seminary development (this translated into the loss of a school in Astrakhan because a seminary did not exist in the diocese).[12]

Ten years passed before the diocesan leadership was, more or less, compelled to establish yet another school (this time a seminary) by Imperial *ukase* in 1776. Some argue that a "school" did exist from 1766 to 1776 if teaching a few orphans Russian grammar and singing in monastic cells can be considered a school. On 27 August 1776, Catherine decreed that the diocese of Astrakhan and Stavropol construct a seminary in Astrakhan as the city is "clearly on the frontier and many foreigners of various ranks live there and a seminary is needed to teach them to read."[13] The College of Economy was instructed to provide 2000 rubles per year for its maintenance. By the end of October 1776, the Holy Synod ordered the new archbishop of Astrakhan, Antonii: 1) to select a location for the construction of the new seminary as soon as possible; 2) to begin recruiting students for the seminary among the children of the eparchial priests and churchmen and selecting teachers who possess a sufficient education and honorable behavior; 3) to maintain and support teachers and students from the funds provided by Her Imperial Highness except for the children of wealthy parents who will pay for themselves; and 4) to report to the Synod where and when the seminary will be constructed and who will be appointed as instructors.[14]

Archbishop Antonii, who had just arrived in Astrakhan at the end of 1776, undertook this task with "unusual zeal." By the end of January 1777 Antonii reported to the Synod that a "seminary" was now located in the Archbishop's Residence where a total of twenty students were either learning to read and write in Russian or studying basic Latin grammar from *Ieromonakh* Innokentii, who was from the diocese of Pereiaslavl (Archbishop Antonii was the former head of that diocese and he probably invited Innokentii to follow him to Astrakhan). Within a year, on 6 January 1778, the school moved from its cramped quarters in the Archbishop's Residence to more spacious accommodations in a stone building rented from the local vineyard bureau for only 150 rubles per year.[15] In its first full year, the school counted thirty-six students who were enrolled in lower form classes: four in elementary Russian, two reading the Book of Hours (*chasoslov*), one reading the Psalter, twenty-one in elementary Latin grammar, and eight in Latin grammar.

In 1780, Archbishop Antonii, to his credit, moved to improve both the academic quality of the "seminary" and its organization. His enhancement of the academic caliber of the school was an investment in the future. He sent four of the school's best pupils to study at the Slavonic-Greek-Latin Academy in Moscow at diocesan expense. At the Academy these students were to take courses in subjects which were fundamental to the core curriculum of a seminary. All four returned to Astrakhan as teachers of Greek, history, geography and arithmetic; and two of them later became prefects of the seminary.[16] Archbishop Antonii gave the school the organizational appearance of being a seminary even though it could not be considered one on the merits of its course offerings by appointing *Ieromonakh* Pavel (Petr Chudnovskii), a theology student from the Kievan Academy, to the post of prefect on 1 May 1780. The only other change introduced by Archbishop Antonii during his tenure was moving the school to a new location in 1783; again an external change as opposed to a curricular or academic change. The diocese received money from the government to construct a stone almshouse/workhouse for the indigent of Astrakhan and Antonii decided to house the school in the new buildings (it comprised four annexes).[17] Seminaries were usually arranged by "classes" or levels, but the school in Astrakhan was simply divided into two groups: older and younger students. Antonii attempted to create "classes" with examinations at the same time he established the prefecture and again when the prefect, *Ieromonakh* Pavel, resigned in September 1786. He intended to appoint a successor to Pavel and once again reorganize the school by classes when he returned from his annual tour of the diocese later that fall but he became gravely ill and died on 10 November 1786 without ever returning to Astrakhan.[18]

Archbishop Antonii, perhaps due to an unfamiliarity with the academic aspects of a seminary, directed most of his attention to the physical and organizational dimensions of the fledgling seminary. In reality the "seminary" was nothing more than a primary school (*pervonachal'naia shkola*). Apart from sending four students to study at the Slavonic-Greek-Latin Academy in Moscow and appointing *Ieromonakh* Pavel to the position of prefect (a post required of all seminaries in the *Spiritual Regulation*), Archbishop Antonii did little to improve the quality and level of education. Archbishop Nikiforos, on the other hand, was contemplating measures to improve the condition of the seminary in Astrakhan even before he arrived in May 1787. Surely apprised of the situation at the school, Theotokis, having communicated with Archbishop Theoktist of Belgorod by letter before departing for Astrakhan, recruited an individual from the Kharkov Collegium who would be the moving and shaping force in the reorganization of the seminary: *Ieromonakh* Silvester Lebedinskii.[19]

Kharkov Collegium, where Silvester taught poetics, was considered one of the finest seminaries in all Russia. Archbishop Nikiforos wanted to imitate the Kharkov program as closely as possible for the Astrakhan seminary so it was eminently sensible that he should recruit one of its better teachers to fill the recently vacated post of prefect at Astrakhan.[20] Lebedinskii also brought with him the type of experience which was appreciated at a seminary dedicated to producing well-educated parish priests and churchmen. The son of a parish priest, he was born in 1740 in the Ukraine. He began his education in parish schools, graduated from the Kievan Academy and attended the Slavonic-Greek-Latin Academy. *Ieromonakh* Silvester arrived in Astrakhan in September 1787 and immediately took up his position as prefect. On 7 January 1788, Archbishop Nikiforos selected him to be the abbot of St. John the Baptist Monastery and on 1 August 1788 he became a member of the diocesan consistory.[21]

Theotokis and Lebedinskii reorganized the curriculum and administration of the diocesan school according to the structure of the Poltava Seminary and Kharkov Collegium which, in turn, were a variation on the Kievan Academy. With these alterations and additions the school finally became the Astrakhan Seminary with a full Latin curriculum. *Ieromonakh* Silvester easily accomplished the task of dividing the curriculum into classes or levels; something which Antonii attempted to do twice without success. In the elementary school (*nizshaia shkola*) the students were expected to take *Fara*, *Infima*, *Grammatika* and *Sintaxima* classes. Next they graduated to the advanced school (*vysshaia shkola*) where they enrolled in Poetics and Rhetoric. If they survived advanced Latin (and very few did) philosophy and theology courses were capstone offerings.[22] Besides the Latin component, the Seminary offered Greek, history, geography, arithmetic and other foreign languages.

Archbishop Nikiforos added another layer of administration in July 1789 when he appointed *Ieromonakh* Parfenii, the abbot of Voskresenskii Monastery and a graduate of the Kievan Academy and Slavonic-Greek-Latin Academy, as rector of the Astrakhan Seminary.[23] Parfenii's new position as rector eased the administrative burden of the archbishop and provided another layer of oversight for a rapidly expanding educational institution. An administrative superior devoted fully to the Seminary also allowed Silvester to teach courses in philosophy and theology. In April 1790, Nikiforos recommended both men to the Holy Synod as possible successors to the post of abbot of the Spasopreobrazhenskii Monastery. The Synod chose Silvester to fill the vacancy and elevated him to the rank of archimandrite on 23 May 1790.[24] In 1791 he became rector of the Seminary and his post was filled from within by Mikhail Nilov, who was one of the four students Archbishop Antonii had sent to the Moscow Academy ten years earlier.[25]

Most of the faculty who taught the lower division classes were themselves former students of the seminary. The upper division classes were taught by teachers, like Nilov, who went on to receive more training at the Academy in Moscow after attending the Astrakhan Seminary, or those who were products of the Kharkov Collegium or the Kievan Academy.[26] Even though Archbishop Nikiforos left the diocese in the summer of 1792 the Seminary continued to operate smoothly under the direction of Silvester Lebedinskii. After 1794, when Lebedinskii was lured away to become rector of the Kazan Spiritual Academy,[27] the tradition begun by Theotokis continued as Mikhail Nilov became the rector and Nikolai Skopin, another of the four students originally sent to Moscow by Antonii, rose to the post of prefect and taught *Sintaxima* and Greek.[28] The library of the Astrakhan Seminary would not become substantial until the beginning of the nineteenth century after Archbishop Platon dedicated his personal library to the seminary. By the mid-1790s the number of students attending the Seminary reached 280 with sixty on stipends. This was a remarkable number considering the presence of numerous private schools and the "public" school in Astrakhan.[29]

Archbishop Nikiforos was nominally involved in the direction and governance of several other schools in the diocese as well. On 22 September 1788 the province of Astrakhan opened a "national school" (*glavnoe narodnoe uchilishche*) in compliance with Catherine's Russian Statute of National Education promulgated on 5 August 1786.[30] The Commission on National Schools drafted the statute and provided the initial capital expenditures for school construction to the province. The governor of the province maintained overall responsibility for the schools but a member of the local board of social welfare served as the director.[31] The school in Astrakhan was divided into three levels-primary, intermediate, and high-with each level consisting of two, three, and four classes respectively. The first two levels taught reading, writing, arithmetic, Catechism, history and geography. The last level, or high school, offered geometry, architecture, mechanics, physics, natural history, and German language. The last offering reflected the language needs of the merchant community of Astrakhan; a point made clear to the diocesan school in the 1730s when it attempted to offer Latin instead of German. This school's enrollment also expanded rapidly: in 1789, 98 boys and two girls were in attendance; in 1791, 219 boys and nine girls were enrolled.[32]

Besides the "national school" a number of private schools were located in Astrakhan. At the same time the "national school" opened in 1788, the Armenian School was founded. By 1791, there were nineteen private Russian schools with a total of 251 students attending them. These schools were strongly supported by the local communities and when the director of schools, Alexander Agathi, attempted to close them he was not in the least successful.[33] As archbishop of the diocese Theotokis inherited the directorship of a school which opened in 1777 and was located in Mozdok. The school was directly operated by the Ossetian Commission which was established in 1771 in Mozdok as part of the Russian Orthodox Church's missionary activities among the mountain people of the northern Caucasus. The teachers at the school were very well trained and Theotokis often recruited them to the seminary during his tenure.[34] The school was also quite effective in executing its duties: by 1792 nearly 8200 Ossetians were converted to Christianity.[35]

Archbishop Nikiforos was successful in opening one district school (*dukhovnoe uchilishche*) in the city of Saratov. The school was simply a lower or primary school with a Latin curriculum which did not advance beyond *Sintaxima*. What was remarkable, however, about the establishment of this particular school is that Theotokis did not order the community to open the school but instead the priests and churchmen of Saratov and the surrounding districts of Kamyshin and Petrov requested that a school be opened in their area. Theotokis made the necessary arrangements for the foundation of the school and traveled to Saratov to attend its inauguration in Spasskii Monastery in July 1790.[36] The school remained open for one or two years but reports from the Saratov Spiritual District make no mention of a school in that district after 1792.[37]

Even though the school did not become permanent, another event with greater significance occurred while Archbishop Nikiforos was in Saratov on 18 July 1790. A group of priestly (*popovtsy*) Old Believers from Irgiz approached him and presented him with a list of fifteen theological questions about *edinoverie* to which they expected Theotokis to respond. Once again Theotokis was about to be embroiled in a dispute concerning the policy of *edinoverie*.

••••

Many Old Believers fled to Astrakhan during the first half of the eighteenth century because of its sparse population and "god-forsakeness." They joined already established centers of Old Belief found among the Don Cossacks along the Terek River, in the Caucasus mountains and along the Volga near Tsaritsyn and Dubovka in the Saratov district. The city of Astrakhan itself was a gathering place for Old Believers to meet and to learn the locations of the many secret communities in the province and just beyond its borders. They were assisted by the most unlikely sources: the authorities arrested a monk in 1723 from the Spasskii Monastery in Astrakhan for aiding *raskol'niki*. In the late 1750s and early 1760s, the consistory in Astrakhan received numerous reports from the outlying districts concerning Orthodox priests who were conducting services and liturgies, attending to the gravely ill, and singing alleluias according to the old books and rites. (One priest stated laconically during his interrogation that at first he crossed himself with three fingers, but then he read Filaret's prayer-book {*trebnik*} and ever since {twenty-seven years!} he had crossed himself with two fingers.)[38]

Catherine's Manifesto of 4 December 1762 invited fugitives to return from abroad and to settle in Russia with complete religious freedom as well as certain economic privileges for a period of six years. The Manifesto made reference to several "preferred" areas for settlement by the colonists including large sections of land north and south of Saratov on the left bank of the Volga and along the Irgiz River where a large community of Old Believers was already unofficially located. Shortly after the Manifesto was issued the Old Believers along the Irgiz established three *sketes* (small monasteries) for men and two for women. The *sketes* attracted a monk from Poland in 1776 by the name of Sergii Iurshev who became a leading figure in the "flowering" of the Old Belief in Astrakhan in the second half of the eighteenth century.[39] Irgiz became the "live nerve" (*zhiznennaia nerva*) for all the Volga Old Believers.[40] Under the direction of Abbot Sergii and with money provided by V.A. Zlobin, a wealthy merchant converted by Sergii, the Irgiz *sketes* gained the status of monasteries and their elders, priests, and monks were sent to all corners of the province.[41] The Old Belief developed and expanded significantly in the late 1770s primarily due to the absence of Orthodox priests and parishes in the rural areas and to the inability of the priests who were present to counter effectively the propaganda of the Old Belief owing to their own ignorance of official Church teachings.

Archbishop Nikiforos was no doubt thoroughly familiar with the considerable presence and activities of the Old Believers in the diocese of Astrakhan and Stavropol even before his appointment. Soon after his arrival in Astrakhan Theotokis circulated throughout the diocese a pastoral letter imploring the lost children to return to the bosom (*nedra*) of the Orthodox Church. The letter was almost identical in its sincerity and impassioned tone to the appeal he had sent to the Old Believers in Slaviansk and Kherson. A copy of the letter eventually came into the possession of the Irgiz community and its leader, Abbot Sergii. The abbot composed fifteen questions concerning the similarities and differences between the Orthodox Church and the Old Belief which he then presented to Archbishop Nikiforos in Saratov in July 1790. Sergii succeeded in attracting Theotokis's complete attention when he added that "if your Highness will give us the wished for and requested by us holy church ruling and unreserved resolution, we, in the name of our community, promise before the almighty God, by resolution, to reunite with the

Greek-Russian Orthodox Church."[42] Nikiforos's response was enthusiastic and immediate. He supposedly devoted all his time, except
feast days, during the month of August to formulating his answers
(*otvety*) to the questions.[43]

Just as in the Znamenka affair in Novorossiia, Theotokis's
pastoral letter, even though well-written, was not solely responsible
for returning the Irgiz Old Believers to the Orthodox Church. The
letter provided Sergii an opportunity to do what he had wished to do
for some time: forge an understanding or agreement between the
Irgiz community and the Church. Archbishop Nikiforos's reputation
from the Znamenka incident possibly persuaded Sergii to approach
him at this time but he was also aware of the attempt made by
Nikodim on behalf of the Starodub Old Believers to return to the
fold on their own terms.[44] At home a rival, Prokhor Kalmykov, was
beginning to challenge Sergii's undisputed position as leader of the
Irgiz community and Sergii was looking for a means to forestall his
own decline. His close associate, the wealthy Zlobin, was already in
favor of reaching an accord or compromise with the Church for
social and business reasons and he easily convinced Sergii that the
notion of the Orthodox Church as a corrective for the corrupt and
degenerate fugitive clergy on whom they relied could serve as the
pretext for initially approaching the Church. Sergii proceeded cautiously and wrote the questions only in consultation with the elders of
the community and even Prokhor affixed his signature to the final
draft.[45]

The questions were simple and no different from other tracts
of this type. Sergii's intent, it seems, was to make it nearly impossible for Theotokis to reject their request for union. The first four
questions were on Church history: 1) Were all the ecclesiastical rites
and ceremonies taken directly from the Greeks during Vladimir's
conversion? Theotokis responded that all dogma and doctrine necessary to eternal salvation were borrowed directly from the Greeks at
the time of Vladimir's baptism. The actual rites and rules of the
Church however were received over a long period of time. 2) In response to a question concerning the continuity of the Orthodox faith
from Vladimir to Alexei Mikhailovich, he answered that for prudent
Russians this was indeed the case. For the imprudent, swept away by
"the rain of superstition, river of heresy and wind of *raskol*" there
were, of course, many variations. The conclusion: where there is
union there is truth; where there is division there is falsehood.

3) Have all tsars, princes, and clerics since Vladimir been Orthodox? The answer to this was to be found in the second, responded Theotokis; however, regarding clerics, all, with the exception of Metropolitan Isidore and a few wayward priests, have been Orthodox. 4) The next question asked whether Orthodoxy or another faith was sanctioned at the sixteenth-century Council of a Hundred Chapters (*Stoglav*) and whether its decrees were law. Theotokis replied that the Council did not rule on faith, dogma or heresy. Its charge was to address the failings of society in general and the clergy in particular and to establish a court for members of the clergy. But the Council allowed itself to stray from its purpose and the priests' ignorance produced "banal thoughts and mistakes." The errors of the priests were not considered heresy because they did not touch upon dogma, but those who followed its decrees (*raskol'niki*) separated themselves from the mother Church.[46]

The next six questions concerned matters of the use of the old books and the correct sign of the cross: 5) Were the Russian saints saved by the old or new books? Theotokis's rejoinder was predictable: books did not save the Russian saints but faith combined with good works. He went on to say that without a doubt the old books contained many fundamental errors, but they in no way prevented the salvation of those who read them. 6) On the question of whether the old books commanded the use of the two-fingered sign of the cross Theotokis declared that he had never seen such a teaching in any of countless Greek books, old or new. Only among the Armenians was it used. 7) Sergii expanded the previous question to include "miracle-working" icons as well. Theotokis's reply was simply that icon painters made mistakes. He then cited several other examples of factual errors found in old icons. Nevertheless, he personally had never seen a Greek icon using a two-fingered sign of the cross and the bishops Pitirim and Theofilakt made the same claim of the ancient Russian icons. 8) Another question on the sign of the cross exhibited sophisticated reasoning: did not the three-fingered sign represent the Trinity and the two-fingered the dual nature of Christ? Although this interpretation seemed appropriate it was an unwarranted digression from Church tradition by the Council of Hundred Chapters. 9) Sergii asked whether it was not true that the new books censured and hurled abuses at the two-fingered sign? No, replied Theotokis, because the Old Believers and Church were in agreement on matters of dogma and such charges were caused by misunderstandings and excessive suspiciousness. 10) Theotokis advised that the only way to escape the confusion, fostered by the *Stoglav* and fugitive priests, over which sign of the cross to use in oaths was to return to Orthodoxy.[47]

Sergii asked only two questions concerning the actual return of the Old Believers to the Church: 11) On the issue of requiring prior repentance before returning to the Church, Theotokis assured them this was required of heretics as well as *raskol'niki*. 12) Theotokis emphatically stated that it was unquestionably true that heretics who returned to the Church would be allowed into all the holy places and receive the rites. 13) Sergii again returned to the matter of the old and new books by asking about the *Stoglav*, its participants and their rulings on the new books. Some of the rulings were correct, admitted Theotokis, but others were incorrect and based on falsehoods and mistakes. "In the Gospels there is falsehood, uttered by the enemies of the Savior, but we do not reject the Gospels on this basis." 14) Theotokis assured them that *Oblichenii*, a book attributed to St. Kyrill of Jerusalem, was not written by him and was filled with lies intended to mislead the simple people. 15) Theotokis explained that services honoring the martyrs Antonii, Ioann and Efstafii (14 April) and Evfrosin of Pskov (15 May) were not included in the new books because the saints' lives about them were filled with lies and heresies.[48] Theotokis closed his letter by noting that the Old Believers lacked the three basic conditions to be part of the Orthodox Church: unity, hierarchy and sacraments. What frustrated him about the Old Believers was the obviously arbitrary manner in which they accepted some elements of the Church yet rejected others. "What is it: obstinacy, prejudice, ignorance, stupidity or all of them combined," which resulted in their separation from the Church? He ended with a lamentation from the Prophet Jeremiah.[49] Sergii reacted favorably to the *Otvety* and immediately circulated it to all who had approved of the original questions. The others did not share his overt enthusiasm for Theotokis's reply which revealed his secret hopes for reunion and he was dismissed from his post. He retreated to a remote *skete* for a year and even managed to meet with Archbishop Nikiforos in Astrakhan. During this visit, according to a later account, Theotokis could not persuade him with his erudition, argumentation, or the fact of his Greek birth to accept the Church's teaching on the sign of the cross (which as the questions indicated was very important to Sergii and the Irgiz Old Believers). Finally, he was shown a fifteenth-century shroud depicting Christ giving the sign of the cross with three fingers and he became a fervent defender of *edinoverie*.[50] Sergii returned to Irgiz and eventually to his position as head of the community in 1793 only to lose it again in 1795 because of his proclaimed intent to convert one and all to *edinoverie*. He then made his way to St. Petersburg where he prevailed upon Metropolitan Gavriil to send two Orthodox priests to Irgiz in June 1796. A community council rejected both him and the priests in October 1796. The opposition to Sergii continued to grow and eventually included his old companion Zlobin and his own wife. Finally, Sergii relented and left Irgiz for Starodub where he was ordained an *ieromonakh* and became the abbot of Uspenskii Monastery in Novorossiia.[51]

Ironically, the outcome of this particular attempt at returning Old Believers to the fold of the Orthodox Church through the means of *edinoverie*, though not especially successful in light of the fact that very few actually returned to the Church,[52] secured for Theotokis a more positive response from the Holy Synod than his first, more productive, attempt in the Znamenka case. This, of course, was due partly on account of having occurred after the Synod's own successful effort at *edinoverie* with Nikodim and the Starodub community in the early 1780s. The Synod's oblique recognition of Theotokis's contributions to the notion of *edinoverie* was its decision in September 1796 to publish his exemplary *Otvety* in book form. Archbishop Amvrosii of Kazan submitted the petition to the Holy Synod requesting publication of the *Otvety*. It was published in 1800 with the generous financial support of Theotokis's personal friend N. N. Bantysh-Kamenskii.[53] Coincidentally, the publication of Theotokis's work occurred at a time when Emperor Paul expressed a great interest in seeing a speedy resolution to the Old Believer issue. In October 1800, Paul issued a decree on the policy of *edinoverie* which was written by Metropolitan Platon with some assistance from Archbishop Amvrosii. *Ieromonakh* Sergii also emerged from the affair without having persuaded many Old Believers to join him in his accommodation with the Church but he did publish a work in 1799, *A Mirror for Old Believers*, dedicated to Archbishop Nikiforos, which admonished the Old Believers for their obduracy and general ignorance.[54]

••••

As a result of Catherine's enlightened religious policies and liberal immigration laws, the number of non-Orthodox believers in Russia increased dramatically in the last quarter of the eighteenth century. This was especially true of the southern provinces which absorbed the majority of the foreign colonists. The inhabitants of the provinces of Astrakhan and the Caucasus were for the most part Orthodox, but Old Believers, Armenian and Georgian Christians, Protestants (Lutherans, Mennonites, Moravian Brethren), Catholics, Moslems, Jews and Hindus were also represented in the population. The diocesan leadership's toleration of other religious groups, of course, reflected Catherine's wish for all of her subjects to live in harmony without the threat of persecution, harassment or proselytization. Diocesan toleration faded, however, when the diocese defended perceived attacks on its flocks' immortal souls.

By all accounts the number of Catholics in the diocese of Astrakhan and Stavropol was minuscule. Theotokis's feelings toward them, however, had not substantially altered since his experiences with a Catholic majority twenty years before. On 18 March 1788 Archbishop Nikiforos published a directive concerning Catholics in the diocese. He was troubled by the possible negative ramifications of Orthodox believers who were in the service of non-Orthodox households (and specifically of the Catholics whom he regarded as active proselytizers). The consistory wanted to determine, with the assistance of the parish priests to whom this directive was sent, whether or not these individuals were still "sons of the true Church" who attended Orthodox services, feast days, observed Lent and received the Eucharist as other Orthodox. Priests were to compile lists of all those in the service of non-Orthodox households within their parish and submit them to the consistory annually. The consistory wanted the names of any individuals prevented from doing their religious duty. This directive, it was noted, pertained to Orthodox believers who "not only live with Indians, Muslims, Armenians, Lutherans, Catholics, etc., but Schismatics, slaves or servants of merchants and other *raznochintsy*, not only in Astrakhan town, but in the whole eparchy." Most of the Orthodox in this position lived with Tatars and Armenians, and some with Old Believers and Lutherans. According to official consistory records, not one priest reported that a master had in any way impeded his Orthodox servants from participating in Orthodox services.[55] Two very different conclusions can be drawn from this: either the priests were bribed by the offending individuals and were not reported or a spirit of religious toleration pervaded these particular inter-faith situations.

There were, of course, situations in the diocese when religious toleration was noticeably absent. The largest minority community in the city of Astrakhan was the Armenian. In 1793, Parkinson reported that the city had 4000 households and 1600 (10,000 people) of those were Armenian.[56] The religious leader of the Armenian Apostolic Church and, in effect, the Armenian community in Astrakhan was Archbishop Joseph Argutinskii-Dolgorukii. He was born in 1743 in a small village near Tbilisi, entered a monastery at the religious center of Echmiadzin where he studied under Catholicos Simeon (head of the Church), who ordained him bishop in 1771.[57] In June 1774 he arrived in Astrakhan as the new archbishop and leader of the Armenians living in Russia. He was instrumental in adding to the number of Armenians in Russia when he successfully worked to have the city of Nakhichevan founded for the Armenians who were forced from the Crimea in 1779.

Joseph was, in a sense, the Armenian equivalent of Voulgaris, Theotokis and Gozadinov. The Russian government was very active in recruiting Greek ecclesiastics as a means to lend support to its foreign policy against the Turks and domestic programs in the southern Ukraine and Crimea; all of which was a part of the so-called "Greek Project." In a similar manner, Archbishop Joseph was to serve as an integral part in Russian designs in the Caucasus or what Prince Potemkin referred to as his "Armenian Project." Where Voulgaris and Theotokis played almost no role in the actual implementation of Russian foreign policy in the Balkans, Joseph was to have a more active role in Russian foreign policy in the Caucasus. All, however, had in common a very strong desire to protect and assist the communities of their countrymen in Russia.

The Armenian community in Astrakhan was under considerable pressure to convert to Orthodoxy in the early 1770s and a large number did.[58] Joseph possessed a moral strength that the secular leaders (the Armenian *sud* or court) of the community entirely lacked and he used it to his advantage in stemming the tide of apostasy. In the four years after his arrival the number of apostates diminished drastically: only seven men and one woman.[59]

Archbishop Joseph acted exceedingly harshly toward those who did convert in spite of his blandishments. In February 1790 Archbishop Nikiforos received a letter from Father Ivan Ivanov, an

Orthodox priest who had converted from the Armenian Church and was living in Mozdok. Ivanov requested that Theotokis offer him protection from an irate and malicious Archbishop Joseph. The archbishop, according to Ivanov, "does not allow Armenians to visit me at my home, publicly damned me twice in sermons in 1784 and 1788 and harasses me constantly."[60] The source of this vitriol can be found in an incident ten years earlier when the recently converted Father Ivanov and two Armenian merchants, Egor Panin and Boris Naskidov, petitioned Archbishop Antonii to place in their possession one of the Armenian churches in Mozdok, which was built by Panin, in order to attract other Armenians to Orthodoxy. Antonii informed the Holy Synod and Astrakhan Chancellery of this request, the Synod deferred to the secular authorities who reasoned that if there were no objections from the Armenian community the request would be approved. Not surprisingly, Archbishop Joseph vehemently opposed such an event and worked assiduously and fervently to prevent its realization. Archbishop Joseph correctly chose to repulse this assault on the Armenian Church by strengthening it institutionally by establishing the Astrakhan Spiritual Consistory and the Mozdok Spiritual District in 1785.[61] Joseph used the authority and offices of these institutions to discourage and punish "enemies" of the Church.

One month after receiving the letter from Father Ivanov, Nikiforos received a similar complaint from another Armenian in Mozdok who had converted to the "Greco-Russian rites" and was systematically harassed by Archbishop Joseph.[62] This individual, Andrei Ivanov, was the brother of the first complainant. He recounted how he was treated as a second-class citizen and how, at one time, a congregation, incited to violence by one of Archbishop Joseph's sermons, set upon him and chased him through the streets of Mozdok.[63] As a last resort, Andrei Ivanov went to the local military commander, Colonel Taganov, to seek his protection. The commander recognized Ivanov's precarious position and ordered the local police to protect him from his fellow citizens, but was able to provide this for only two weeks. Andrei Ivanov closed his letter with a plea for protection from the diocesan leadership.[64]

Archbishop Nikiforos sent his report to the Synod and it replied on 3 May 1790. The Synod stated unequivocally that Archbishop Joseph was in violation of the Synod's 1782 statute #202 which allowed for the practice of all beliefs without being subject to abuse, profanity or quarrels and #244 which pronounced that anyone who breached #202 could be taken to court and punished for the infraction.[65] The Synod instructed Theotokis to inform Joseph of these statutes and of the severity of the penalty for not abiding by "Her Imperial Majesty's wishes." The response also suggested that Archbishop Joseph was transgressing the intent of Catherine's Charter to the Towns and Nobility of 21 April 1785 which included sections on religious tolerance. The Synod concluded by recommending that if Archbishop Joseph continued this behavior he must be reported to Governor-General P.S. Potemkin.[66]

Archbishop Nikiforos informed the Synod in June 1790 that he had forwarded material on the case to the Astrakhan Chancellery and he had written to the Astrakhan Armenian consistory concerning the events in Mozdok.[67] In an apparent attempt to protect himself, Archbishop Joseph ordered the Mozdok Spiritual District to begin an investigation into the alleged incidents of 1784 and 1788 and collect depositions from Armenian citizens who had been harmed by the pernicious influence of the Ivanovs. These depositions were sent to the Holy Synod by the Armenian consistory in Astrakhan as evidence in defense of Joseph. The witnesses stated that they were infuriated by the turbulent life of the priest and had requested that the archbishop do something about it. The archbishop promised them that he would put a stop to the quarrels between them and the "turbulent man."[68]

The Synod issued an *ukase* on 12 August 1792 which declared that Archbishop Joseph's activities had been fully examined and found to be outrageous in their blatant disregard of Catherine's statutes on religious toleration. The Synod added that the Armenian consistory was guilty of complicity in this affair because it sent to the Holy Synod the depositions which all contained sentences taken from the archbishop's own injunction to the witnesses "in clear violation of the law." The consistory also acted in a negligent manner when it arbitrarily discredited the evidence of the local commander. The case was now to be passed on to the civil authorities of the Caucasus *namestnichestvo*.[69]

Archbishop Joseph's importance to Catherine's plans in the Caucasus and the prosecution of the war against the Ottoman Empire during this affair effectively precluded any action being taken against him by the government. In fact, his fortunes improved in the late 1780s and throughout the 1790s. In 1788, by order of Catherine, he accompanied the Russian Army and furnished it with strategically important information on conditions in the Ottoman Empire he obtained from Armenians fleeing the Turks. Those same Armenians were later settled by him in a place (recently acquired from the Turks) selected by Prince Grigorii Potemkin on the Dniester River and named Grigoriopol in honor of him in 1792. In the same year he was appointed to the Free Economic Society and moved his archiepiscopal offices to the city of Nakhichevan on the lower Don near Azov. He also established a second Georgian-Armenian press (the first was in Astrakhan) at the Holy Cross Monastery in Nakhichevan.[70] He once again served the Russian Army by accompanying it on the 1796 Caucasian campaign and the Russians expressed their appreciation for his years of service by procuring for him the office of Catholicos of the Armenian Apostolic Church in 1799 which he held until his own death in 1801.[71]

Marriage difficulties also attracted the attention of the consistories and the Synod if the difficulties involved mixed faith couples. In April 1791, Archbishop Nikiforos reported to the Holy Synod the interesting case of an Armenian man, Gavriil Manuilov, who recently had converted to Orthodoxy and wanted his estranged wife to return to live with him.[72] It seems he was singularly impossible to live with and the wife simply refused. When the wife, Tsagika Azarapetova, was questioned about her situation by the Astrakhan consistory she revealed that she and her husband already had requested a divorce from the Armenian consistory (before he converted to Orthodoxy) and added that upon receiving the divorce she was entering a second marriage. Disregarding this, Theotokis ruled in Manuilov's favor but was informed by Governor Brianchaninov that the request could not be allowed because the Armenian consistory had granted her the divorce, but was awaiting Archbishop Joseph's approval. Theotokis refused to accept this reasoning and appealed to the Holy Synod to allow his decision to stand because the Armenian archbishop had not yet responded.[73] The Synod argued against this action by Theotokis and recognized Tsagika's right to an answer from the Armenian Church. If the Armenian archbishop, however, did not confirm the consistorial decision soon then she should return to her husband. Theotokis finally received word of Archbishop Joseph's confirmation and the divorce was granted.[74]

Archbishop Nikiforos continually struggled against the forces he deemed harmful to the Orthodox believers of his diocese. He wrote sermons and sent them to the clergy in order to assist them in combating the Old Believers in Krasnii Iar or the simple superstition and ignorance found in all parishes. He traveled repeatedly around the diocese and delivered sermons in countless parishes. Theotokis even began to encounter publicly members of the minor sects such as the *molokane* or "milk drinkers." The diocesan and provincial authorities knew that the sect was spreading under the leadership of Uklein but were confident that it attracted very few Orthodox to it. In 1787, Governor-General P.S. Potemkin informed Archbishop Nikiforos of an infantry regiment quartermaster-sergeant who had become a *molokanin*. Even after *Ieromonakh* Silvester and Archbishop Nikiforos had admonished him for abandoning the Orthodox faith he "remained inexorable in his error."[75]

••••

Archbishop Nikiforos enjoyed his diocesan duties which involved education, attempting to persuade the Old Believers and members of other sects to return to the mother Church, and defending the interests and rights of Orthodox believers from competing faiths and the state. He took little if no pleasure, however, in managing the day-to-day affairs of the diocese which included staffing, disciplining clergy, and sparing with the state and Synod over legal and financial matters. Undoubtedly, these latter duties oppressed and tired him the most and led to his relatively early retirement at the age of sixty.

Not long after his arrival Theotokis sent a report to the Holy Synod in April 1789 complaining about the abysmally low number of monks and nuns in the diocese and their nearly destitute condition. He reported that the total number of monks in the episcopal house, eparchial monasteries and hermitages was only thirty-five and the number of nuns reached only nine. Most of these were old and sick, he added, and incapable of performing their duties either to the Church or to the communities they were in. Theotokis pleaded with the Synod to grant him at least one hegumen and a few monks and nuns as the Synod purportedly had promised in a 4 December 1788 *ukase*.[76]

The Synod responded in a very diplomatic fashion: satisfying Theotokis and at the same time obeying Catherine's strictures against too many churchmen. At the end of May 1789, the Synod informed Theotokis that the neighboring dioceses of Voronezh and Belgorod agreed to give him some of their supernumerary (*zashtatnykh*) monks and nuns and a *hegumen*. The Synod, with the assistance of the diocesan authorities in Belgorod and Voronezh, had determined the amount of money required to travel to Astrakhan (the hegumen, of course, was to incur greater travel expenses than either the monks or the nuns) and Theotokis was obliged to reimburse the two dioceses.[77] By the end of September 1789 Theotokis reported that one hegumen and two nuns had arrived from Voronezh and from Belgorod appeared three *ieromonakhs* and one *ierodeacon*. Theotokis was satisfied with them and noted that their travel expenses would be reimbursed from the diocesan fishery account.[78]

The number of monks and nuns was very small for a diocese the size of Astrakhan and Stavropol but the region was sparsely inhabited and inhospitable in most areas. During Theotokis's tenure the major cities were Astrakhan, Tsaritsyn, Dubovka, Kamyshin, Saratov, Petrovsk and Kizliar. The Orthodox believers were clustered in two groups along the Volga at either end of the diocese: Astrakhan in the south and Saratov in the north. The diocese had 306 churches in 1792 but only sixty-six were in Astrakhan *guberniia*; the others were in the provinces of Saratov (238) and Penza (two). The diocese counted one registered (*shtatnykh*) monastery and one registered convent but also seven unregistered (*zashtatnykh*) monasteries.[79] The consistory was constantly receiving petitions from parishioners who wanted their parish to be transferred to a diocese whose consistory was closer to them than the one in Astrakhan. Theotokis granted requests in 1787 and in 1791 for transfers: both were over 1500 *versty* or 900 miles from Astrakhan.[80] The consistory also processed petitions for church construction and the archbishop was allowed to grant these privileges without Synodal approval as it was done in Novorossiia. Soon after Theotokis's arrival he reprimanded and fined the staff of the consistory and reported them to the Holy Synod for denying a petition for church construction in the Caucasus because the consistory had not yet secured Synodal approval even though it did not need it.[81]

Although the number of churches and clergy was low, Theotokis still had to contend with charges filed against disobedient priests and to discipline priests who were harmful to the Church and state. In July 1789, Archbishop Nikiforos sent a report to the Holy Synod *po sekrety* (in secret) concerning a very strange petition he had received in January from a priest, Emelian Akimov, in Saratov *guberniia.* Akimov requested Theotokis's assistance in gaining the discharge of his two sons from state service. In the midst of his petition he used indecent language (*neprilichnye slova*) in reference to the empress. Theotokis immediately began proceedings to have him arrested and exiled. He was not able to travel to Astrakhan until spring due to his age and disabilities, but finally arrived in June 1789 and was interrogated about his intentions. "What state of mind were you in when you used these words in your petition," they asked him. The priest admitted that he had signed the petition but it was written by someone who worked for the Saratov Chancellery. Theotokis reported that he was holding Akimov in seclusion without privileges in Voskresenskaia Pustyn' until further word from the Synod.[82]

The Synod responded very quickly and instructed Theotokis to turn all the materials over to Governor-General Potemkin with the utmost secrecy.[83] Theotokis's last involvement with the case was his letter to the Synod in September in which he noted that the case was now in the hands of General Brianchaninov and that Father Akimov was to be relieved of all his duties pending further investigation.[84]

In another incident, the priest and deacon of a parish in Saratov *guberniia* were charged with the theft of church funds by the elders of the parish in late 1789.[85] Theotokis instructed the Kamyshin and Petrov spiritual districts to investigate the matter and was convinced that the charges were false. The parish, however, appealed directly to the Holy Synod in February 1790 and charged that Theotokis had done nothing about the charges or the priest and deacon. The elders must have been quite important because the Synod immediately ordered Theotokis to begin an investigation (which he already had done in March 1790). In this instance, Theotokis protected the churchmen not only from the parish members but from the Holy Synod as well. The case was finally resolved (the churchmen were innocent) six months after Theotokis left the diocese.[86]

Foreign colonists and Russian peasants were not the only people attracted to the Volga River region and the North Caucasus with offers of land and privileges. Beginning with the first colonizing attempts under Catherine in the 1760s, the nobility began acquiring land along the Volga beyond the Samara Bow. The Orlov brothers, among others, exchanged their estates near St. Petersburg and Moscow for larger tracts of land on the lower Volga.[87] In 1765 the government began selling lands in Astrakhan and the Caucasus to the nobility. Many who purchased estates were functionaries in the provinces (Khvostikov, Krivoruchkov) or were in some manner involved in its administration from the capital (Count Chernyshev, Prince A.A. Viazemskii and Count A.R. Vorontsov).[88] Given the sparse population and absence of adequate surveys disagreements occasionally arose over property or fishing rights. Prior to the colonization effort and land sales of the late eighteenth century the Church was a large landowner (even after the secularization of 1764) in the Astrakhan region and not surprisingly some of its possessions were subjected to legal challenges.

One such challenge was initiated by the procurator of the Central War Commissariat (*glavnii krigs-kommisariat*) at the request of Governor-General P.S. Potemkin against the Spaso-preobrazhesnkii Monastery in Astrakhan in the spring of 1791. Archimandrite Silvester informed Archbishop Nikiforos that the government wanted to seize a 10,000-*desiatin* estate belonging to the monastery. The estate (*dvor*) was mostly an animal farm with horses, cattle, chickens and a few peasants who maintained the estate. The legal challenge was based on Catherine's 1764 decree on the secularization of monastic lands. Silvester recounted the history of the estate's ownership and pointed out that Catherine's decree provided an exception for the monastery which was confirmed by the College of Economy in 1766.[89]

Theotokis reported these events to the Holy Synod and it moved very quickly to support the monastery in its case against the government. The Synod's own research indicated that the estate had been in the monastery's possession since 1717 and that this had been confirmed by the state in 1752 and in 1766. The Synodal staff also reconfirmed Silvester's contention that the monastery's holdings were sanctioned by Catherine's secularization decree of 1764 in point 12, which declared that all second-class monasteries had the right to possess a limited amount of property and Spasopreobrazhenskii was within that limit.[90] The Synod also directed Theotokis and Silvester to toughen their resolve in the case and not fear governmental reprisals because the *Spiritual Regulation* gave bishops and lower level churchmen the right to question the validity of any decree not originating from the Synod. The legal battle continued long after both Archbishop Nikiforos and Archimandrite Silvester had left the diocese. A letter from the Astrakhan Chancellery to the Astrakhan consistory on 9 September 1797 indicated that the case had been settled in the monastery's favor.[91]

In another incident, Archbishop Nikiforos himself was involved in a lawsuit concerning the fishing rights of the episcopal house (*arkhiereiskii dom*). He reported to the Synod in June 1791 that he had received a court opinion in the beginning of May that ordered him to relinquish the fishing rights to the plaintiff, Collegial Assessor Skripitsyn. The Lower Land Court ruled that the episcopal house also must surrender all profits from the business since the rights were first contested by the plaintiff in November 1786 (Theotokis's appointment). The counsels for the diocese, *Ieromonakh* Innokentii and consistory Chancellor Stepan Serebriakov, appealed the ruling to the Astrakhan Superior Land Court.[92] The Synod's response was not as supportive as it was in the monastery case; it counseled that if the appeal failed, the episcopal house must abide by the law. On 20 August 1791, the Astrakhan Superior Land Court ruled against the diocese.[93]

The letter Theotokis sent to the Synod on 24 June 1791 describing the legal difficulties concerning fishing rights did not reflect an individual whose complete comprehension of any issue before him was a given. He seemed totally flustered and disconnected from the events he was attempting to delineate. It is difficult to say whether he was suffering from a temporary mental diminution or that legal matters were simply beyond his understanding. Most probable, however, Theotokis was not interested in the matter and did not consider a legal action over fishing rights deserving of his full attention. Even the Synod, which was giving its fullest support to the monastery case at the same time, had resigned itself to the loss of that particular piece of land and the fishing rights attached to it. Regardless, the two cases do illustrate the tension that was present in this sparsely settled region between Church and state and between Church and nobility over any enterprise that appeared profitable in a land that showed very little profit: the cattle farm at the monastery and the land with the fishing rights attached to the episcopal house.

••••

On 16 April 1792 Catherine and the Holy Synod granted Archbishop Nikiforos's request for retirement from his position as archbishop of Astrakhan and Stavropol.[94] Theotokis served in the

Astrakhan diocese for only five years but the combined effects of the inclement weather, the constant struggles with the Old Believers, and frequent journeys through the eparchy took their toll. In an ironic turn of events, Theotokis's retirement was slightly marred by some oblique questions posed by the Synod concerning the financial affairs of the diocese. The Synod was particularly curious about the activity in accounts related to the diocesan fishery. Evidently the archbishop had direct access to this account and could use it at will. The Synodal *ukase* announcing Theotokis's retirement also ordered the consistory to bar him from any further access to diocesan accounts effective his last official day, i.e., 16 April 1792. The *ukase* continued by way of explanation to report that as of 17 July 1788 the archbishop was to keep an accurate account of receipts and expenditures relevant to the fishery. By order of the Holy Synod, a local hierarch was to examine the books to confirm that all was proper.[95]

Further examination indicates that the Synod's insinuations were not as insulting as they first appeared. A 16 December 1726 statute required that a bishop have his access to diocesan funds severed immediately upon acceptance of his resignation. The bishop was provided a salary commensurate with his former position and if the need arose, he could apply for additional funds from the consistory. In Theotokis's case, the hierarch appointed by the Synod to look into the fishery accounts was Archimandrite Silvester, who was now head of the Astrakhan consistory. He reported to the Synod on 27 October 1792 that all the accounts were completely in order and that he had dispensed to Archbishop Nikiforos 614 rubles 84 kopecks as the portion of his salary due him until 16 April 1792, another 259 rubles to cover his expenses through July and 208 rubles for provisions.[96]

On the eve of his departure from Astrakhan Archbishop Nikiforos performed his final divine liturgy in Uspenskii Cathedral on 15 June and then closed with a sermon.[97] He opened by telling of the address that Prophet Samuel delivered to the Israelites after his decision to lead them no longer because of old age (1 Samuel 12:1-5). Samuel asked the Israelites to testify against him before the Lord as witness but they could find no offense that he had committed. Theotokis remarked humbly that he too was old and needed to retire, but he dared not ask his Astrakhan flock the same question Samuel put to the Israelites. All he wanted and strived to do, he said, was to train his priests to enlighten souls through the word of God and by virtuous example. He wanted all his Christians to love one another, obey His commandments, and lead virtuous lives, and as such they would be happy on earth and blissful in heaven. But, he continued, the spirit was willing, the flesh was weak. His own sermons were hardly glorious and his life was dismal, he stated.[98]

He confessed that he never ceased, and never would for the reminder of his life, to be amazed at the love, respect, kindness, favor and obedience shown to him, a foreigner (*muzh inostrannii*), feeble and a poor speaker of their language. He then chided himself for his impertinence in comparing his situation to that of Samuel. Perhaps, he said, Paul's parting words to the Ephesians would be more appropriate: "I know that all you among whom I have gone about preaching the kingdom of God will see my face no more." Theotokis was adept at demonstrating Biblical continuity to his listeners and a trifle disingenuous: Samuel, as a prophet in the Old Testament and Paul, as one of Christ's disciples in the New Testament, were both teachers among the people and Theotokis as an inheritor of the Apostolic Succession was a continuer of their tradition. His honorable parishioners of Astrakhan were also deserving of praise for they were, in Peter's words, a "chosen race, a royal priesthood, a holy nation, God's own people." He commended them to God and spoke of their painful separation from one another. But, he asked, when and how would they meet again?[99]

Theotokis told them that two types of wings were necessary to fly beyond earthly cunning and up to heaven. One of these wings was the Orthodox faith, the other was the true belief of the virtuous man. If a man lacked either wing he would not attain heaven. But God has already given you one wing, Theotokis continued, and if you can find true virtue we will meet again in heaven. But when? He gave them hope by citing Paul's promise to the Thessalonians that they would see one another again with the final resurrection and would live in ageless and eternal happiness.[100]

NOTES

1. Platon (Liubarskii), *Ierarkhiia Viatskaia i Astrakhanskaia* (Moscow, 1848), p. 56. Archbishop Nikiforos evidently thought so much of his new residence that when informed of Prince Potemkin's upcoming visit to Astrakhan in the late summer of 1787 he wrote him a letter on 14 August 1787 claiming that "my house has the best location of the city and the air around it is purer than in any other house in Astrakhan. It would certainly be advantageous for you, it seems to me, during your stay." *RGADA*, f. 18, o. 1, d. 310, l. 1.

2. John Parkinson, an English traveler to southern Russia in the summer of 1793 told of "marshy ground" in the middle of the city of Astrakhan which could "only be in some degree unhealthy." Related to Theotokis's comment on the air, Parkinson noted that "when there is no wind here what renders the heat insupportable are the Saline Particles which rise out of the earth and load the Air. These...penetrate into the skin and cause fevers." John Parkinson, *A Tour of Russia, Siberia and the Crimea, 1792-1794* (London, 1971), pp. 161-162.

3. A.V. Fadeev, *Rossiia i Kavkaz v pervoi treti XIX v.* (Moscow, 1960), p. 37.

4. Cited in Bartlett, *Human Capital*, pp. 118-119.

5. *Ibid.*, p. 120.

6. *Ibid.*, pp. 121-122.

7. Ioann Savvinskii, *Astrakhanskaia eparkhiia, 1602-1902 g.g.*, vol. I (Moscow, 1848), p. 219.

8. These actions as well as the plague that occurred during his three-year tenure may account for the hostility that the people of Astrakhan felt toward Varlaam and their joy at his departure from the diocese in 1730. A contemporary source said about him, "because of our sins our God sent to us this haughty and unapproachable little ruler." "Astrakhanskaia eparkhiia," *Entsiklopedicheskii slovar'*, vol. 3, p. 365.

9. Schools of this nature were quite common before 1760 in areas where children were not educated in basic Russian grammar at home or if many of the students were orphans.

10. Savvinskii, I, p. 220.

11. Iaskol'skii attended the Kievan Academy and later the Slavonic-Greek-Latin Academy in Zaikonospasskii Monastery in Moscow. "Materialy dlia istorii Astrakhanskoi Dukhovnoi Seminarii," *Astrakhanskie eparkhial'nye vedomosti*, 2 (1876): 8.

12. Savvinskii, I, pp. 221-222.

13. *Ibid.*, p. 222.

14. *Ibid.*, p. 223.

15. *Ibid.*, pp. 223-224.

16. N. Leont'ev, "Kratkii ocherk istorii Astrakhanskoi Dukhovnoi Seminarii," *Astrakhanskie eparkhial'nye vedomosti*, 17 (1892): 513.

17. Savvinskii, I, p. 224.

18. "Materialy," pp. 9-10.

19. *RGIA*, f. 796, o. 71, g. 1790, d. 154, ll. 6ob-7. This is taken from the service record which *Ieromonakh* Silvester wrote at the request of the Holy Synod in 1790. The service record of the rector of the seminary, *Ieromonakh* Parfenii, was also included.

20. This, of course, was not the first time that Theotokis turned to the Kharkov Collegium as a source for teachers. Many of the seminary teachers at Poltava were either students of the Kievan Academy or the Collegium or both. See Chapter 3.

21. *RGIA*, f. 796, o. 71, g. 1790, d. 154, l. 6.

22. Savvinskii, I, p. 224.

23. *RGIA*, f. 796, o. 71, g. 1790, d. 154, ll. 6ob-7.

24. *Ibid.*, l. 10ob.

25. "Kratkaia istoriia Astrakhanskoi Eparkhii, 17. Astrakhanskii i Stavropol'skii arkhiepiskop Nikifor Theotoki (1786-1792 g.g.)," *Astrakhanskie eparkhial'nye vedomosti*, 16 (1883): 282.

26. Trofim Chudnovksii and Ivan Rubashevskii were students of the Kharkov Collegium and taught many of the first seminary students at Astrakhan who later became teachers themselves: Ivan Golubev, Nikolai Skopin, Andre Bedniakov, Semen Vasil'ev, Nikifor Sergiev and Semen Kondakov. "Materialy dlia istorii Astrakhanskoi seminarii," *Astrakhanskie eparkhial'nye vedomosti*, 4 (1879): 60.

27. Lebedinskii's career continued to progress after leaving Astrakhan in 1794. He was ordained bishop in 1799 and eventually served in his old diocese as archbishop for eleven months in 1807-8 (probably a very somber experience owing to a plague which devastated the diocese throughout his entire tenure). "Kratkaia istoriia Astrakhanskoi Eparkhii," *Astrakhanskie eparkhial'nye vedomosti*, 19 (1883): 341.

28. Leont'ev, p. 516.

29. "Materialy," *Astrakhanskie eparkhial'nye vedomosti*, 4 (1879): 60.

30. Savvinskii, I, p. 225. Theotokis was also involved in Catherine's decree of November 1788 which directed members of the Church to assist in establishing similar schools in the sixteen provinces not included in the first decree. Astrakhan was included in the statute of 1786 and the Caucasus was covered in the 1788 version. *RGIA*, f. 796, o. 69, g. 1788, d. 406, ll. 1-2.

31. The director of the schools was himself a widely traveled man of Greek background. He served as host to the English traveler John Parkinson in the summer of 1793. Parkinson witnessed one of the twice-yearly school examinations and reported that six girls were examined in the first or primary class. Parkinson, p. 177.

32. Savvinskii, I, pp. 225-226.

33. *Ibid.*, p. 226.

34. *RGIA*, f. 797, o. 1, d. 900, ll. 1-5.

35. Savvinskii, I, p. 234.

36. Ivan Golubev was possibly the instructor at the school. He was transferred to the Saratov Spiritual District in 1790 after teaching grammar at the Astrakhan Seminary for two years. Besides attending the Moscow Academy he also took classes in moral philosophy, politics and experimental physics at the University of Moscow. Savvinskii, I, p. 157.

37. "Kliucharevskaia letopis'," *Astrakhanskie eparkhial'nye vedomosti*, 10 (1887): 372.

38. Savvinskii, I, p. 242ff.

39. Sergii was the son of the Moscow merchant Iurshev, who was found guilty of inciting a crowd to riot which then killed Archbishop Amvrosii of Moscow during the plague of 1771. Smirnov, p. 135.

40. Savvinskii, I, p. 250.

41. The men's skete verkhnii Isaakiev became Uspenskii; srednii Pakhomiev – Nikolskii ; nizhnii Avraamiev – Voskresenskii and the women's sketes of Margaritin and Anfisin became Pokrovskii and Uspenskii. Smirnov, p. 135.

42. N. Sokolov, *Raskol' v saratovskom krae* (Saratov, 1888), p. 132. Citation from Theotokis's *Otvety na voprosy staroobriadtsov* (Moscow, 1834), pp. 394-395.

43. "Kliucharevskaia," p. 372.

44. Nikodim and Sergii were both inheritors of the priestly tradition of the Vetka community in Poland. Starodub was the main center of the transplanted Vetka community but it was losing its vigor and gradually was being supplanted by the Irgiz and Rogozh communes.

45. Sokolov, pp. 130-131.

46. *Ibid.*, pp. 133-134.

47. *Ibid.*, pp. 135-137.

48. *Ibid.*, pp. 137-139.
49. *Ibid.*, pp. 139-140.
50. *Ibid.*, p. 141.
51. Smirnov, p. 212.
52. Only one source claims that "a few thousand" converted to the Church but all others suggest no more than a handful.
53. Bantysh-Kamenskii was born in Nezhin in 1737. His father's mother, a cousin of the poet Dmitri Kantemir, fled to Ukraine in 1711 from Moldavia. He attended Greek school in Nezhin and later the Kievan Academy and Slavonic-Greek-Latin Academy in Moscow (where he spent his leisure hours reading Latin with the future metropolitan, Platon Levshin). His uncle, Archbishop Amvrosii of Moscow, tried to interest him in a Church career to no avail and he chose instead archival work in the College of Foreign Affairs. (Tragically, he was visiting his uncle at Donskoi Monastery in 1771 and witnessed his murder by a mob incited to riot by Sergii Iurshev's father.) In 1794, A.I. Musin-Pushkin, over procurator of the Holy Synod, requested that Bantysh-Kamenskii write a paper on the Uniates in Poland. This must have brought him into contact with Voulgaris, who was asked by Musin-Pushkin to write a position paper on the Uniates in 1793, and with Theotokis who was living at Danilov Monastery in Moscow at the time. *Russkii biograficheskii slovar'* (hereafter *RBS*), II, pp. 468-470.
54. *Ieromonakh* Sergii, *Zerkalo dlia staroobriadtsev* (St. Petersburg, 1799).
55. Savvinskii, I, pp. 261-263
56. Parkinson, pp. 164, 167.
57. *RBS*, p. 333.
58. Very little exists in the records of the consistorial archives, according to Savvinskii, which suggests that an atmosphere of hostility existed between Armenian and Orthodox, but much exists which points to the opposite. In one incident, the absence of marriage crowns (*ventsy*) prevented an Armenian couple from marrying in an Armenian church. They solved the problem by proceeding to the nearby Orthodox church and asking the priest for crowns which he gladly gave them and even accompanied the couple back to the Armenian church for the ceremony. Savvinskii, II, p. 155, n. 2.
59. Savvinskii, II, p. 154.
60. *RGIA*, f. 796, o. 71, g. 1790, d. 107, l. 2. This is the Russian translation of the original which was in Armenian.
61. Savvinskii, II, pp. 159-160.
62. *RGIA*, f. 796, o. 71, g. 1790, d. 107, l. 6.
63. That Archbishop Joseph was actually personally responsible for all the maltreatment accorded the Ivanov brothers is doubtful (his offices were in Astrakhan), but he bore indirect responsibility for not condemning the actions of others.
64. *RGIA*, f. 796, o. 71, g. 1790, d. 107, ll. 6ob-7.
65. *Ibid.*, l. 9.
66. *Ibid.*, ll. 18-18ob.
67. *Ibid.*, ll. 21-21ob.
68. *Ibid.*, ll. 31-32.
69. *Ibid.*, l. 35ob.
70. In 1793, the Nakhichevan press published two books: *Dver milostyni* (Doors of Alms), a short history of the two Armenian cities of Grigoriopol and Nakhichevan and Fenelon's *Adventures of Telemach*. Archbishop Joseph was himself a published author: in 1790 Potemkin published his history of Russian-Armenian relations during the reign of Peter the Great.
71. *RBS*, p. 333.
72. *RGIA*, f. 796, o. 72, g. 1791, d. 149, l. 1.
73. *Ibid.*, l. 2ob.

74. *Ibid.*, ll. 7-7ob.
75. Savvinskii, I, pp. 252-254.
76. *RGIA*, f. 796, o. 70, g. 1789, d. 169, l. 1.
77. *Ibid.*, l. 6.
78. *Ibid.*, ll. 27-28. The diocesan fishery account and fisheries were to cause Theotokis great difficulties during his tenure and even after his retirement.
79. *RGIA*, f. 796, o. 72, g. 1791, d. 16, l. 70ob.
80. Savvinskii, I, p. 133.
81. *Ibid.*, pp. 162-163.
82. *RGIA*, f. 796, o. 70, g. 1789, d. 250, ll. 1-1ob.
83. *Ibid.*, l. 5ob.
84. *Ibid.*, l. 9ob.
85. *RGIA*, f. 796, o. 71, g. 1790, d. 93, l. 1.
86. *Ibid.*, ll. 13ob, 33.
87. Bartlett, pp. 94-95.
88. Fadeev, pp. 38-39.
89. *RGIA*, f. 796, o. 72, g. 1791, d. 334, ll. 1-3.
90. *Ibid.*, ll. 14-14ob.
91. *Ibid.*, l. 34.
92. *RGIA*, f. 796, o. 72, g. 1791, d. 234, ll. 1-1ob.
93. *Ibid.*, l. 17.
94. *RGIA*, f. 796, o. 73, g. 1792, d. 152, l. 1.
95. *Ibid.*, ll. 7-7ob.
96. *Ibid.*, ll. 107-107ob.
97. A.A. Dmitrievskii, "Po povodu izdaniia v svet neskol'kikh traktatov i pisem arkhiepiskopa Nikifora Theotoki," *Astrakhanskie eparkhial'nye vedomosti*, 8 (1895): 241.
98. A.A. Dmitrievskii, "K voprosu o propovednicheskikh trudakh Nikifora Theotoki v bytnost' ego arkhiepiskopom astrakhanskim i stavropol'skim," *Astrakhanskie eparkhial'nye vedomosti*, 14 (1895): 366-367.
99. Dmitrievskii, "K voprosu," pp. 367-368.
100. *Ibid.*, p. 368.

7

THE LAST YEARS:
STRUGGLE FOR A FREE GREECE

No matter in which place or circumstance I find myself I will
always try to be of use to my nation. I will try to retrieve it
from the ignorance into which the inevitable fate of time has
cast it and deliver to it [nation] the keys of science so that it
can be absorbed in its [science's] most mysterious depths.[1]

– Archbishop Nikiforos

Theotokis remained in Astrakhan until 14 July 1792 awaiting
the Holy Synod's approval of his request for placement during his
retirement.[2] The Synod initially wanted Theotokis to proceed
"immediately" to the second-class Danilov Monastery in the diocese
of Suzdal in the city of Pereiaslavl in the *guberniia* of Vladimir
where he was to begin his duties as archimandrite. On his way to
Pereiaslavl he stopped in Moscow and on 9 September 1792 he requested that he be allowed to stay at a monastery in that city.
Theotokis presented a list of reasons as to why he should not be sent
to Pereiaslavl: first, it was located in the "wilderness" (*v pustom
meste*) and there was no need for him there; second, the city had no
pharmacies or doctors and his health was quite poor; and third, after
his many years of dedicated service to the Church could not the
Synod grant him this last request.[3] In late September the Synod
approved his wish to spend the rest of his life in Moscow at Danilov
Monastery, a small third-class monastery located on the southern
edge of Moscow. This monastery was founded in 1272 by the first
Prince of Moscow, Daniil (son of Alexander Nevsky), and served as
part of Moscow's southern defensive network. He sought a reprieve
from administrative duties and the solitude and quiet of a small
monastery where he could once again engage in scholarly work as
Voulgaris had done before him. In late June, the Synod had informed
Theotokis that he would receive 1000 rubles per annum as a pension
beginning 19 June 1792.[4] The low amount of the pension (Voulgaris
received 1500 r.p.a.) was possibly due to the fact that he was also to
be the abbot of Danilov Monastery. This would not pose a serious
problem for a man desiring an escape from administrative affairs, as

a third-class monastery was only allowed a budget of 900 r.p.a. and no more than twelve monks.

Although Theotokis was physically removed from Greece he still maintained contact with events there through merchants and travelers and an active correspondence with intellectuals and other clerics. He was thoroughly informed about the latest developments in theology, publishing, education, and politics (e.g., his close friend, Dorotheos Voulismas who served in the patriarchal offices, notified him about the arrest of Rigas Pheraios).[5] He also contributed to Greece's intellectual and educational development by reviewing books for publication, providing financial assistance for the establishment of schools and for book publication, and sending books to Greece for free distribution. In the late 1780s, while still in Astrakhan, he was given the opportunity to assist his native land by countering the spread of Voltaire's writings on religion. The Church leadership in Constantinople never was comfortable with the Enlightenment emanating from the West, but found it expedient to accept it in moderate doses because Catherine was an ardent admirer of French ideas and of Voltaire in particular. With the advent of the French Revolution in 1789, however, Catherine ceased to perceive the Enlightenment's notions of toleration, freedom and reason as convenient ideological pillars for her form of government but as forces utterly contrary to it. Catherine's change of opinion now provided the opportunity for many who had not agreed with all of Voltaire's writings and ideas to challenge them with impunity.

The Ecumenical Patriarchate in Constantinople was particularly concerned about a tract Voltaire had written in 1766, *Le Bible enfin expliquee par plusieurs aumoniers de S.M.L.R.D.P.*, which it feared was corrupting the minds of Greeks who had gone abroad to study and were not only attracted to the idea of freedom but infected with atheism as well.[6] Voltaire's tract was one among many that appeared in the eighteenth century which vehemently attacked all religion, but especially Christianity, as being intolerant and oppressive. In this particular tract, Voltaire combined his love for the ancients and the spirit of critical inquiry with a barely concealed repugnance for Christianity to uncover the superstitions and falsehoods found in the Old and New Testaments.[7] The Patriarchate asked Theotokis to counter Voltaire's criticisms of the Bible with a publication based on logic, reason, and a firm understanding of the sources.[8]

Theotokis agreed to assist the Patriarchate in defending Ortho-
dox Greece from atheism by translating the 1782 publication of J.G.
Clemence, *L'authentincite des livre, tant du Nouveau que de l'
Ancien Testament demontree et leur veridicite defendue*, into Greek
and appending a commentary to it. He began the translation in
Astrakhan and finished the commentary in Moscow. The work was
published anonymously in Vienna in 1794 with the assistance of
Eleftherios Mikhail as *A Proof of the Validity of the Books of the
New and Old Testaments, and a Defense of the Truths Found in
Them or a Refutation of Voltaire's Bible, Recently Called the Inter-
pretation of the Testament*.[9] Theotokis stated the objective of this
translation and commentary in the Prologue:

> Unfortunately, we hear that poisonous plants arising from
> fatal seeds have appeared in Greece. Therefore, although our
> bodies are distant, our hearts are close, we know that the
> local clergy and teachers are zealously arming themselves
> with all forces against this innovation of the ungodly ser-
> pent. We, however, also want to assist Greece and decided to
> compile and publish this book, written in a simple language.
> We hope that it will be one – a means of protection; two – of
> education; three – of confirmation; and, in general, a guide to
> salvation.[10]

Theotokis's notes comprised the final third of the book. He refuted
Voltaire's statements by whichever means seemed appropriate. He
revealed Voltaire's ignorance of Greek, Latin and Hebrew and
charged that these linguistic deficiencies precluded him from reading
the Testaments correctly. In other instances he found that Voltaire
willfully misinterpreted passages to prove a polemical point.
Theotokis's theological, philological and historical critique constituted a book in itself without the accompanying translation.
Theotokis, as usual, was very methodical and thorough in his approach. He never deviated or digressed into thoughtless polemics. In
a sense, Theotokis was disappointed with Voltaire, not because the
tract was just a polemic against the foundations of Christianity but
because he found it was superficial, puerile, and methodologically
unsound.[11]

Theotokis's attention remained firmly fixed on Greece during
his retirement and the means by which he could continue to assist it
in its struggles against the Ottoman Empire and the greater enemy,

as far as he was concerned, ignorance. Although Theotokis undoubtedly was more interested in matters affecting his native Greece
during his years in Moscow, the Russians honored him for his years
of service in their own country in 1797. At the coronation ceremony
of the Emperor Paul I on 5 April 1797, the emperor bestowed on
Theotokis the Order of St. Anne, First Class. One writer claims that
he also received four hundred souls or serfs as well.[12] Theotokis, in
a sense, was closer to the center of power during the reign of Paul
than he was during the reign of his patroness, Catherine. He was
awarded the medal because his name was included in list compiled by
his long-time acquaintance Metropolitan Platon, who had been one of
Paul's tutors. His work on the Old Believers was also first published
during Paul's reign and the policy of *edinoverie* was officially
recognized as well. In other words, Theotokis's earlier activities
were still appreciated in Russia after his thoughts turned to Greece.

Soon after arriving at Danilov Monastery Theotokis began
making preparations for the publication of his most well-known and
highly regarded work, the *Kyriakodromion* (Collection of Sunday
Sermons). Theotokis's talent for oratory and rhetoric was recognized
very early in his life and earned him the attention of the ecumenical
patriarch which, in a sense, initiated his ecclesiastical career. He took
great pride in his sermons and his parishioners responded warmly to
this "sweet tongued writer" (*sladkoglagolivii pisatel'*).[13] He
published many of his sermons separately over the years but he now
wanted to make them available in one book. The "sermons" were
actually a thorough and complete exegesis on each Sunday's Gospel
reading. The collection Theotokis was preparing consisted of one
sermon or commentary for each week of the year.

Theotokis explained in his Prologue that he was compelled to
undertake this task of collecting his previous sermons and writing
new homilies by the general level of ignorance and misunderstanding
of the Gospel passages which were read every Sunday morning for
the supposed edification of the congregation. He wanted the
Kyriakodromion to fill a needless void in the education of every
Christian. His own solid foundation in the Church Fathers and other
commentaries on the Gospels provided him with the means to
produce an interpretation of the Scriptures easily understood by all
people. Theotokis wrote the homilies in a very simple and direct
style; free from unnecessary intellectual complexities, foreign words,
archaicisms and a heavy reliance on *katharevousa* or puristic

Greek.[14] Theotokis held firmly to the conviction that the well-educated believer was not as susceptible to the dangers of heresy as the uneducated; and most priests, much to his chagrin, were not capable of explaining the meaning of the word of God and presenting it to the parishioner in a comprehensible manner. Therefore, Theotokis wrote interpretations or exegeses of the Scriptures and dispensed practical advice for daily life through the accompanying homily.

Theotokis adopted a simple, straight-forward method for each Scriptural reading. The lessons were divided into two sections, interpretive and homiletic. In the interpretive section he assiduously analyzed the evangelical passages. The text was first examined in the context of the Evangelist's or Apostle's other writings. He adeptly revealed the essence of the passage and tested it for dogmatic rectitude, and if variations existed with comparable passages he clarified them. In his analysis, Theotokis remained literal-minded and eschewed allegorical interpretations and developments.[15] Theotokis made it possible for the non-specialist to understand the subtleties of Scripture without overburdening the reader with copious notes and ponderous commentaries.[16]

The second part of the lesson was the actual homily or sermon as generally understood. The homily provided the practical applications based on the previous interpretation. In these sections Theotokis's own personality was drawn into the writing. His personal views on how to live the virtuous life based on the Gospels were reflected in the homilies. He did not shrink from addressing contemporary political and social issues. He openly and critically examined such topics as the relationship between master and servant, politics, women's position in society, the status and life of the clergy, the meaning of personal struggle, the precise mission of the pastor, justice, the meaning of the divine passion (crucifixion), inequality of citizens, the French Revolution, and ethics, to name a few. His homilies and the range of topics he addressed exhibited his broad education and vast intellect. Throughout the *Kyriakodromion* the reader is vaguely aware of the author's rhetorical skill, because it does not overwhelm the text but lightly suffuses it with a special grace. Theotokis sought to persuade the reader intellectually, not emotionally.[17]

Anastasios Zosimas of the Zosimades Brothers publishing house published *Kyriakodromion, that is, Exegeses with Accompany-*

*ing Moral Homilies on the Gospels which are Read in the Holy
Orthodox Churches on Every Sunday* in Greek in two volumes in
Moscow in 1796.[18] Zosimas covered the costs of the first printing
and produced 2000 copies. Initially, Theotokis and Zosimas
distributed copies free of charge to hierarchs and to churches in the
Greek East. D. Voulismas, a friend of Theotokis's in Constantinople
with whom he kept an active correspondence, reported that demand
for the book was so great that a second printing was planned in
Moldavia. The second printing in Moldavia did not occur but the
plans themselves were a testament to the work's true popularity.
Voulismas also proposed to Theotokis that he place the volumes in
bookshops in Constantinople to be sold at regular prices and/or send
them to school teachers for free distribution to those who requested
it. Theotokis did send 100 copies to the Ecumenical Patriarchate and
the enthusiastic response which followed obliged Voulismas even to
surrender ten of his own personal copies.

Theotokis's commentaries on the Evangelists were translated
into Russian and published in 1805 as *Tolkovanie voskresnyk
evangelii* and his collection of sermons and exegeses on the Apostles
entitled *Kyriakodromion, that is, Exegeses with Accompanying
Moral Homilies on the Acts of the Apostles which are Read in the
Holy Orthodox Churches on the Sundays from Easter until Pentecost,
and on the Pauline Epistles which are Read on the Remaining
Sundays of the Whole Year* was published in Greek in 1808 and,
later, translated into Church Slavonic and Russian and published in
1819 and 1820 respectively.[19] His work was lauded in Russia as well
as in Greece for the high quality of its exegetical sections and the
obviously sympathetic nature of the homilies.

Nikiforos Theotokis was forever the pedagogue and, as a
result, his three areas of competence and scholarly expertise were all
within the realm of education: theological, spiritual, and secular
(scientific). In the first years of his retirement he published characteristic works of theological (e.g., *A Proof of the Validity...*) and
spiritual (e.g., *Kyriakodromion*) significance which instructed his
readers to follow prescribed measures to secure their minds and
spirits from metaphysical harm. Following these publications,
requests from Greece for mathematics textbooks induced him to turn
his attention to the physical or scientific in the late 1790s. He wrote a
three-volume textbook, *Elements of Mathematics*, which was
published between 1798 and 1799 in Moscow and dedicated to the

Zosimades Brothers who subsidized the work and made it possible to send it to the schools of Greece, and especially to Ioannina.[20] The first volume contained lessons on geometry and arithmetic, the second volume covered Archimedean principles, trigonometry and conic projections, and the third described algebra.

Theotokis did not hold to the belief that science and faith were mutually exclusive in the world of the eighteenth century. This was the area of the Enlightenment which he experienced first as a student under Kavvadias and in Italy and learned to appreciate the most as an adult. His first publication in 1766 was in the sciences (*Elements of Physics*) and he now returned to that interest in his final years. He considered, quite correctly, mathematics to be the cornerstone of the sciences. It was impossible, he argued, to possess a reasonable understanding of the heavens and the earth without a solid grounding in mathematics. One can not comprehend the universe without the knowledge of astronomy, physics, optics, and mechanics and one can not comprehend those subjects without mathematics. The importance of mathematics, however, was not limited to the purely physical world. Philosophy and logic, according to Theotokis, required a diligent and well-trained mind which could be attained by "exercising" with mathematics. Therefore, mathematics should not be of interest only to the specialist but to all types of scholars and students.[21]

The third volume of *Elements of Mathematics* was published one year before Theotokis's death. He was preparing another scientific textbook in the final year of his life which he left incomplete at his death. The book was a collection of the lectures Theotokis used when he taught in Jassy. *Elements of Geography*, however, was finally completed by Anthimos Gazis and was published with the financial support of the Zosimades Brothers in Vienna in 1804.[22] Theotokis devoted the majority of his book to an analysis of the different theories on the movement of the earth. He examined the ideas of Ptolemy, Tycho Brahe, Copernicus, Kepler and Newton. He contended that the heliocentric theory was not a "discovery" of modern science because the ancient Greeks wrote of it long before the sixteenth century. In the second section of the work, Theotokis turned his attention to political geography and criticized the Ottoman Empire as an example of a despotic political system. At his death Theotokis also was preparing works on astronomy and meteorology for future publication but this was never accomplished.[23] And according to Zaviras, Theotokis produced a number of unpublished works on science as well: 1) on electrical forces, 2) on meteorological physics, and 3) on metaphysics based on the system of the Moderns.[24]

Theotokis often remarked that he was but physically removed from Greece for his heart was always there. In mid-1799, a situation arose which suddenly presented the possibility for him to return physically to Greece. Catherine's disillusionment with the French Revolution nearly convinced her to join an anti-French coalition just before her death in 1796. Her son and successor, Paul I, initially proclaimed Russia neutral in the struggle between England and France, but Napoleon's aggressive actions in the eastern Mediterranean brought an abrupt end to that neutrality. In an unprecedented departure from diplomatic routine, Russia and the Ottoman Empire along with Austria and Naples, joined forces as part of the Second Coalition which was led by England and Russia. As part of a concerted campaign to expel France from Egypt and the eastern Mediterranean, a Russo-Turkish fleet, under the command of Admiral Fedor F. Ushakov liberated the Ionian Islands.[25]

The improved fortunes of Corfu affected Theotokis directly. Antonios Maria Kapodistrias, a former student of Theotokis's and the father of the future president of Greece, had secured the support of many Corfiote people to present Theotokis as a possible candidate for the position of bishop of Corfu. In a letter from Constantinople, Kapodistrias asked Theotokis's permission to submit his name as a formal candidate. At first, Theotokis demurred but then relented and agreed to become a candidate. Kapodistrias was so entirely convinced that Theotokis would be chosen that he tried to persuade him to leave Moscow and return to Corfu before the election took place. Unfortunately, for reasons unknown, Admiral Ushakov, the Russian commander on Corfu, was opposed to Theotokis's candidacy and openly insisted on the election of Petros Voulgaris (no relation to Eugenios) for the position. Also, rumors were circulating that even if he were elected, Theotokis would not come to Corfu because of his advanced age. On 11 October 1799, Petros Voulgaris was chosen as the new bishop.[26]

Theotokis still had a possibility of returning to Corfu because the election of Petros Voulgaris was not confirmed by the patriarch because he was married. A new election date was set for 27 December 1799. On that morning, a large number people from the city of

Corfu and the surrounding communities staged a demonstration by marching through the streets of the city. The demonstrators carried Russian flags and persistently demanded that Theotokis be the first bishop of Corfu. The local commander of the Russian fortress, Borozdin, met with the demonstrators and promised that he would honor their demands and send for Theotokis. Admiral Ushakov, however, was still adamantly opposed to Theotokis and when the election was held the next day, 28 December, Archimandrite Ioannis Kigalas became the new bishop of Corfu. Thus, Theotokis was denied the possibility of returning to his native land.[27]

••••

Archbishop Nikiforos Theotokis died at three a.m. on 31 May 1800 at Danilov Monastery after a lengthy illness.[28] Three weeks earlier, on 10 May 1800 he called the treasurer of the monastery, Ieromonakh Ignatii, to his bed and gave him a sealed envelope which contained his "personally" written will. Theotokis instructed Ignatii to keep it safely with him until his death and then to deliver it to the executor of the will and his close friend, Moisei Dmitrievich Kritskii, who was a Collegial Registrar at the College of Foreign Affairs Archive in Moscow. Theotokis knew that this would not be appreciated by the Office (*Kontor*) of the Holy Synod but that was his wish.[29] Theotokis's will was in Greek and he wanted Kritskii to translate it into Russian and provide the Synod with five copies but keep the original. Theotokis was correct in that the Synod was dissatisfied with the arrangement but there was nothing it could do.

Theotokis wrote his will on 7 November 1795 at a time when he was very ill. He appointed Moisei Dmitrievich (Kritskii) as the executor of his will and entrusted him with all his money and worldly possessions. He was very generous to the monastery that was his home for the last eight years of his life. He left five hundred rubles, the interest of which was for the education of the brothers of the monastery, and in return, he asked only that they say an annual prayer for him. To Ieromonakh Mikhail he left three hundred rubles and all his books which were in Church Slavonic or Russian. He gave his gold watch to N.N. Bantysh-Kamenskii as a measure of their friendship. Greece also was a recipient of his kindness. He expressed his love for Greece by leaving it something which would have a lasting impact on it for generations. He wished that all of his books in the Greek language be sent to the school located on Mt. Athos. Any other items he might possess at the time of his death were to be disposed of as directed by Kritskii.[30]

Theotokis strongly desired that a new school should be established on Mt. Athos in place of the Athonian Academy which fell into ruin after Eugenios Voulgaris's departure in 1759. Kritskii, as the executor of his will, worked to realize this desire. When Theotokis's considerable library arrived on Athos (and according to other authors, a large sum of money) the school existed only in name due to infighting among the monastic communities of Athos. The library was stored in the *stavropigial'* monastery of Iviron on the orders of the ecumenical patriarch and Kritskii. In January 1804, a conference was held in Constantinople and attended by educators, intellectuals, clerics, merchants and presided over by Patriarch Kallinikos. This body decided to merge the inchoate Athonian school with the old Great School in the Phanar to found the Patriarchal School. This would be the new home of Theotokis's library. Iviron Monastery, however, was reluctant to surrender its prize and only after repeated Synodal letters from Patriarch Kallinikos to former Patriarch Grigorios VI, who was living in Iviron, was the library sent to Constantinople. The books finally arrived in Constantinople in May 1805 and became the nucleus of the Patriarchal School's library.[31] Thus, Theotokis did leave a physical testament of his love of Greece to the future generations of young Greeks.

NOTES

1. Cited in Solov'ev, p. 595.
2. *RGIA*, f. 796, o. 73, g. 1792, d. 152, l. 88 and f. 797, o. 1, d. 1157, ll. 1-3.
3. *RGIA*, f. 796, o. 73, g. 1792, d. 235, ll. 29-29ob.
4. *RGIA*, f. 796, o. 81, g. 1800, d. 313, l. 3. This information is from an internal Synodal communication created at the time of Theotokis's death. The two-page document briefly highlighted his career from 1792-1800.
5. Mourouti-Gkenakou, *O Nikiforos Theotokis*, p. 52.
6. Why this specific work exercised them so much is not clear.
7. Peter Gay, *The Enlightenment: An Interpretation/The Rise of Modern Paganism* (New York, 1966), p. 169.
8. Mourouti-Gkenakou, p. 53.
9. N. Theotokis, *Apodeixis tou kyrous ton tis Neas kai Palaias Diathikis vivlion, kai tois en aftois alitheias yperaspisis i anaskevi tis ek tou Voltairou vivlou, tis kaloumenis teleftaion dierminevtheisis diathikis, ek ton Gallon fonis metafrastheisa, yper prosetethisan kai tines simeioseis* (Vienna, 1794).
10. *Apodeixis*, Prologos.

11. Mourouti-Gkenakou, p. 55.

12. "Materialy k istorii Astrakhanskoi eparkhii," *Astrakhanskie eparkhial'-nye vedomosti*, 30 (1880): 475.

13. Dmitrievskii, "Po povodu," p. 240.

14. N. Theotokis, *Kyriakodromion, itoi, ermineia kai met' aftin ithiki omilia eis to kata pasan Kyriakin en tais aghiais ton orthodoxon ekklisiais anaginoskomenon Evangelion*, 2 vols. (Moscow, 1796), Prologos.

15. Whether this is done for the benefit of the reader or because Theotokis rejected allegorical interpretations of the Bible is not clear. The absence of allegorical interpretation is extremely interesting in light of Father Florovsky's condemnation of eighteenth-century Russian ecclesiastical education for its strict adherence to a scriptural fundamentalism caused by the Protestantism of Peter's reforms. Marc Raeff, "Enticements and Rifts: Georges Florovsky as Historian of the Life of the Mind and the Life of the Church in Russia," *Modern Greek Studies Yearbook*, 6 (1990): 227.

16. Mourouti-Gkenakou, p. 58.

17. *Ibid.*, p. 59.

18. N. Theotokis, *Kyriakodromion, itoi, ermineia kai met' aftin ithiki omilia eis to kata pasan Kyriakin en tais aghiais ton orthodoxon ekklisiais anaginoskomenon Evangelion*, 2 vols. (St. Petersburg, 1796).

19. N. Theotokis, *Kyriakodromion, itoi, ermineia kai met' aftin ithiki omilia eis tas praxeis ton Apostolon, tas anaginoskomenas en tais aghiais ton orthodoxon ekklisiais en tais Kyriakais apo tou Pasha ahri tis Pentikostis kai eis tas epistolas tou Pavlou, tas anaginoskomenas en tais loipais Kyriakais tou olou etous* (Moscow, 1808). The Russian translation was *Tolkovanie voskresnykh apostolov* (Moscow, 1819). See, "Nikifor," *RBS*, p. 338; and *RGIA*, f. 796, o. 81. g. 1800, d. 137, ll. 1-61. The Synod reported that the press printed 1200 copies, kept 70, and sold the remaining 1130 at four rubles each.

20. N. Theotokis, *Stoiheion Mathimatikon ek palaion kai neoteron*, 3 vols. (Moscow, 1798-1799).

21. Mourouti-Gkenakou, p. 145.

22. N. Theotokis, *Stoiheia Geografias* (Vienna, 1804).

23. Mourouti-Gkenakou, pp. 149-150.

24. G. Zaviras, *Anekdota Syngrammata: Nea Ellas i Ellinikon Theatron* (Athens, 1872), p.494.

25. On the Russian campaign in the Ionian, see A.M. Stanislavskaia, *Rossii i Gretsia: Politika Rossii v Ionicheskoi respublike, 1798-1807 gg.* (Moscow, 1976); idem, *Politicheskaia deiatel'nost' F.F. Ushakova v Gretsii v 1798-1800 gg.* (Moscow, 1983); and Norman Saul, *Russia and the Mediterranean, 1797-1807* (Chicago, 1970).

26. Solov'ev, p. 595.

27. Mourouti-Gkenakou, p. 64.

28. *RGIA*, f. 797, o. 1, d. 2062, l. 1.

29. *RGIA*, f. 796, o. 81, g. 1800, d. 313, l. 1.

30. *Ibid.*, ll. 11-12ob.

31. Koukkou, *Nikiforos Theotokis*, pp. 97-99.

8

CONCLUSION

Religious culture, as suggested by Natalie Zemon Davis, cannot be understood unless it is situated in a particular historical period and geographic location. Russia during the reign of Catherine the Great provided the historical framework, while the southern frontier offered the locale for this study of religious culture. Catherine's reign was particularly appealing because her government consciously adopted and implemented policies which reflected the Enlightenment's spirit of reform. At the most fundamental level, Catherine's reforms expanded the domain of the state into realms previously dominated or inhabited by other institutions. Her reform efforts affected all matters political, social, economic and cultural. Catherine's religious policies reflected her belief that, although the state was responsible for the material and spiritual well-being of its subjects, the Church was instrumental in assisting the state in this task. Even though Catherine had "instrumentalized" religion, she understood that religious belief and, more important, the institutions which propagated those beliefs, were essential for creating and maintaining a semblance of social harmony and control.

The Church recognized its obligations to the state and, more important, to its parishioners to promote Christian values for social and political order. The Church diligently searched for the means successfully to "Christianize" (i.e., inculcate with the "correct" rituals, beliefs, and behavior) the empire's subjects and protect them from various forms of *sueverie* or superstition. The Church sought to accomplish this task by promoting well-educated and enlightened churchmen to the ranks of bishop, archbishop, and metropolitan. These hierarchs then instituted reforms in clerical education and established successful seminaries with the intent of fashioning educated and moral priests. The prelates were also occupied with the physical creation of "sacred" space in the form of chapels, churches, cathedrals, and military field altars. The importance of this task was illustrated by Catherine's decree which exempted *only* the southern prelates from Synodal oversight in matters of parish and monastic construction. Finally, the priests, the alleged beneficiaries of the new reforms, were to lead their parishioners down the correct path of Orthodoxy and away from the false teachers and purveyors of superstition. A mission more easily assigned than accomplished in the rich and diverse lands of southern Russia.

The Church responded to this diversity by appointing hierarchs and priests of non-Russian ethnicity, such as the Greeks Nikiforos Theotokis and Eugenios Voulgaris and the Armenian Joseph Argutinskii, to these regions, particularly in the south. Theotokis came to Russia at the invitation of his fellow Corfiote Eugenios Voulgaris and the two of them held in common the belief that by promoting both Catherine's immediate domestic program in southern Russia and Russia's long-term goals in the Mediterranean they were also realizing Greece's quest for liberation from the Ottoman Turks. Theotokis was not an important political personage but he did play a direct role in Russian domestic policy as an educator, scholar, and cleric and an indirect role in foreign policy as a liaison between Russia and Greece.

This was not unique to him but was almost *de rigueur* for any high official, secular or sectarian, in southern Russia, a region where it was impossible to separate domestic and foreign policy into distinct spheres owing to the problematic nature of the so-called "double" frontier zone (i.e., a frontier region with an extremely permeable and unstable border). Catherine, of course, did not intentionally design her foreign policy to benefit Greece, but Greece was subsumed in her broader designs of Russian territorial aggrandizement at the expense of the Ottoman Empire. If, in the future, the vagaries of foreign policy demanded that Greece be abandoned or sacrificed for some singular Russian advantage there is no doubt that this would be done.[1]

Yet Theotokis, as Voulgaris, was an educated, enlightened prelate from the Greek East whose ecumenical Orthodoxy informed his world view and, in particular, his perceptions of the relationship between Church and state, confessionality and nationality, and universal and local identities. He looked to Russia, as an Orthodox state, to deliver Greece from Ottoman control and, thereby, create another Orthodox state centered on Constantinople. The Orlov expedition, although a failure from the Greek perspective, proved to many of the Greek elite that Russia was capable of greater deeds. Theotokis alluded to as much in his thanksgiving oration after his ordination on 6 August 1779 when he glorified Catherine for her role as a militant protectress of all Orthodox believers and drew explicit attention to the fact that her new grandson, Constantine

Pavlovich, shared his name with the last Byzantine emperor. Nor were his hopes ill-founded as his speech occurred only one year before Foreign Secretary A.A. Bezborodko drafted his infamous memorandum on the so-called "Greek Project."

Nikiforos Theotokis's world view coincided with Catherine's enlightened views regarding the moral and societal benefits of education and religious toleration, but foundered on her policies of secularization grounded in the inherent anti-clericalism of the French Enlightenment and German *Aufklärung*. Although Theotokis was one of Catherine's "enlightened" prelates whom she could exhibit to the *philosophes* and despots of Europe as a manifestation of her non-obscurantist Russian Church, he was no disciple of Voltaire. His appreciation of the Enlightenment was based upon its non-prejudicial precepts of science, rationality, education and toleration. These, according to Theotokis, did not preclude nor were in any way inimical to revelatory belief or traditional Orthodox tenets. In a sense, Catherine and Theotokis were engaged in acts of self-delusion: each wished to extract from the Enlightenment those ideals beneficial to them while denying those deemed "irrational," "sinful," or "revolutionary." Theotokis accepted the educational aspects with great delight but was horrified by "freethinking" and the skepticism of received religion which usually accompanied an enlightened education. Catherine, likewise, welcomed freedom of expression and religion, but was shocked by the writings of Radishchev who expressed himself too freely and behaved as if he were exercising freedom "from" religion. Catherine and Theotokis considered order and respect of tradition as absolutely essential to a healthy society and soul.[2]

The intersection of religion and politics in the last quarter of eighteenth-century imperial Russia occurred at various levels. At the Church-state level Catherine declared that religion was central to the establishment and maintenance of public and private morality and the preservation of public order. Religion and religious toleration were encouraged among and between the diverse cultures of southern Russia provided it was understood that the power and authority of the state stood supreme. Catherine's desire to colonize the southern borderlands and increase their economic productivity was the primary motivation for her invitation to the Old Believers. She promised the Old Believers religious toleration as a condition for their return and strongly suggested that the Holy Synod overcome its differences with them and bring them back to the fold. Archbishop Nikiforos did exactly what Catherine and Prince Potemkin wanted but not because religion was a social cement to be used cynically and opportunistically. Theotokis's Orthodoxy was ecumenical and he sincerely believed the Old Believers to be faithful to the one true Church. In this instance, the "tolerance" of his Orthodox ecumenical-ism and Catherine's notion of religious toleration dovetailed. He envisioned himself as the Apostle Paul who accepted many into the Church on the basis of their inner faith and not their outward appearance. Catherine believed herself to be a glorious enlightened monarch and a member of the "party of humanity."

Even though Catherine advocated religious toleration for her Empire, she did not advocate religious freedom. Toleration allows for a measure of religious variety only at the sufferance of the state. Catherine's own sense of toleration had its limits; those who professed beliefs which exceeded those limits became religious sectarians and political dissenters. The Dukhobors obviously believed that their own values and beliefs were so alien to those of the state and the Orthodox Church that no accommodation was possible. The sectarians, as well as the "wayward" Orthodox believers, kept their "enthusiasm" for religion alive by introducing minor changes into rituals and festivals or denying rituals altogether as a symbol of their faith. Even within Catherine's definition of religious toleration, these religious dissenters were beyond the pale because they failed to adopt the minimum of universal values and beliefs essential to the mainte-nance of the Russian Empire. The Orthodox Church, for its part, treated them as if they were merely ignorant children who required further church teaching or "Christianization."

The best illustration of competing identities at play on the broad field of southern Russia at the end of the eighteenth century was the multiple crossings of boundaries or of conversions from and to Orthodoxy on the part of sectarians and dissenters. Individuals certainly make spontaneous choices in all realms of their life but the act of choice is prepared by a long process which they do not neces-sarily choose for themselves. As St. Augustine suggested, this process is often imposed on individuals, against their will, by God. Power creates the conditions for experiencing the truth, even if the mind does not move spontaneously to that truth. Power takes many forms: imperial and ecclesiastical laws; the threat of sanctions; the dis-ciplinary activities of the family, school, or church; and human activities such as fasting, prayer and penance. An individual is constantly shaped or conditioned by these manifestations of power and can quite easily move from one area of influence to another dependent on their material and cultural milieu. Hence, the Orthodox Church's willingness to accept conversions without ascertaining the "sincerity" of the act, because the Church, and its agents, understood the inherent weakness of its children and, therefore, the necessity of maintaining the "correct" path through "teaching," *eruditio*, and warning, *admonitio*.[3]

Religion and politics also intersected in the complex and problematic relationship of confessionality and "national" identity. Theotokis lived with the seemingly paradoxical situation of maintaining a sense of Greek identity within the context of his Orthodox ecumenical world view, one might even label it Byzantine. Archbishop Nikiforos worked diligently to establish churches for the new Greek communities in Russia and appointed, whenever possible, Greek-speaking clergy. He actively promoted and encouraged the preservation and cultivation of Greek traditions through the construction of schools and the establishment of printing presses in the Greek settlements. In the schools, the Greek students learned two languages, Greek and Russian, so they could not only preserve their ethnic consciousness but also become loyal and productive citizens of Russia.

Theotokis served the movement for Greek liberation by contributing textbooks, sermons and his personal library to the struggle against general ignorance and for popular enlightenment. He believed the Greek nation could not escape Ottoman subjugation before it escaped intellectual and moral deprivation. He wrote textbooks on mathematics, physics and geography for students in Greece. The Zosimas brothers published them and were responsible for distributing them to the Greek schools in the Balkans. His sermons and commentaries, published in Greek and Russian, were intended to educate parishioners not only about the Bible but daily existence. His library, intended for a revived Athonite Academy, ultimately served as the nucleus for the library of the Patriarchal School in Constantinople.

While Theotokis and Voulgaris served as eloquent spokesmen and proponents of close Greek-Russian ties as well as advocates of Greek liberation in the eighteenth century, others would continue that tradition into the nineteenth century. Three prominent supporters of Greece comprised the so-called Greek lobby in Alexander I's Foreign Ministry. Aleksandr S. Sturdza (1791-1854), the member of a powerful Phanariot family that fled Constantinople during the Russo-Turkish War of 1787-1792, benefited significantly from the influence of Theotokis and Voulgaris and wrote tirelessly on behalf of the Orthodox Church and his fellow Greeks under Ottoman rule. Sturdza worked in the Ministries of Foreign Affairs and Public Enlightenment and acquired a well-earned reputation as one of Russia's leading conservatives. Although he stood adamantly opposed to constitutionalism and liberalism in Russia he was an outspoken advocate of Russian assistance to liberate Greece.[4] Ioannis Kapodistrias (1776-1831), like Theotokis and Voulgaris, was a native of the Ionian island of Corfu.[5] Kapodistrias, who was a politician on Corfu during the short-lived Ionian Republic, appreciated the importance of Russian support if Greece was to gain its independence. When France took control of the Ionian Islands in 1807, Kapodistrias emigrated to Russia and eventually became a joint minister of foreign affairs between 1815 and 1822, where he endeavored to advance Greek interests, but always within the framework of Russian interests. Another Ionian, Spyridon Iu. Destunis (1782-1848) from Cephalonia, served in the Ministry of Foreign Affairs and was consul general in Smyrna (1818-1821).[6]

Sturdza, Kapodistrias and Destunis also labored on behalf of Greece by promoting classical studies in Russia and assisting educational programs in Greece. Sturdza wrote essays on the value of teaching ancient Greek to Russians, directed charitable organizations and was instrumental in the foundation and early direction of the Odessa Society of History and Antiquities. Destunis translated Plutarch's *Lives of Great Men* for its edifying moral lessons as well as Byzantine documents into Russian. All three collected donations for the *Filomousos Etairia* (Society of Friends of the Muses), an educational and philanthropic organization founded in Vienna in 1814 to establish Greek schools in Thessaly and Athens and to support Greek students in their studies in Europe. Above all, Sturdza, Kapodistrias and Destunis were most similar to Theotokis in their belief that Greece's moral and intellectual regeneration was a necessary precondition to its political liberation. They advocated a conservative enlightened education properly grounded in Orthodoxy. Sturdza helped the Odessa Commercial Gymnasium establish a Greek-language printing press and simultaneously proposed censorship guidelines to prevent the publication of liberal or anti-clerical tracts.[7] He too wanted to circumscribe that aspect of the Enlightenment which had aggrieved Catherine so greatly: the critical spirit of inquiry and its attendant questioning of traditional authority.

Theotokis considered Orthodoxy as inextricably bound to the "nation" or *yenos*. This relationship was still considered important by most Greek intellectuals and activists at the time of Theotokis's death and Orthodoxy was construed as a *conditio sine qua non* for the creation, cultivation and preservation of a Greek national identity.[8] However, beginning in the late eighteenth and early nineteenth century, Greek merchants and intellectuals in the diaspora, Phanariots, *klephts* (Greek "bandits") and local leaders in Ottoman-occupied Greece fashioned their own diverse conceptions of what constituted the "nation," the role of Orthodoxy in it, and how this entity was to achieve liberty. These constructions differed from the more conservative ideas of Theotokis, Voulgaris, Kapodistrias, et al. A group of Greeks in Odessa sought a more activist political solution to the problem of independence when a socially diverse assembly of diaspora and Ottoman Greeks founded the *Filiki Etairia* (Society of Friends) in 1814.[9] The *Filiki Etairia* eschewed the cautious approach of the likes of Kapodistrias and promoted liberation through armed insurrection. So deep were the differences between the two outlooks that when the *Filiki Etairia* appealed to Kapodistrias to lead them, he refused.[10] The Greek War of Independence reflected the cleavages between the two groups and the disparate backgrounds of their respective members as the struggle against the Ottoman Empire was frequently eclipsed by political and military disputes among those who held conflicting visions of Greece's future.[11] Yet, the belief that to be Greek meant *inter alia* to be Orthodox was strongly held. Even Adamantios Korais (1748-1833), who spent most of his life in France, absorbing the ideas of the Enlightenment and offering critiques of the Orthodox Church, still considered Orthodoxy as central to his Greek identity.[12] After Greece gained its independence, the new state led by King Othon attempted to subdue or harness Orthodoxy to its own needs by founding an autocephalous "Greek" Church centered in Athens as opposed to the "ecumenical" Church centered in Constantinople.[13] This action on the part of the state spawned numerous popular religious movements seeking to rescue the Church from the state and restore it to its traditional place in Greek society,[14] an attitude not unlike that manifested by sectarians and dissenters in Russia.

The life and career of Nikiforos Theotokis in the last quarter of the eighteenth century reflected the transitional nature of that time for both Russia and Greece. Catherine was proceeding apace with the "secularization" of Russian culture and society begun by Peter the Great in the first quarter of the century but she still recognized the necessity of religion as not only a social bond but a central element to Russian identity. She also contended with popular beliefs that could effectively challenge her conscious development of a universal Russian identity. The relationship between the various sectarian and dissenting communities who chose to define themselves by virtue of their religious beliefs and the Russian state during the course of the imperial period was a seemingly well-rehearsed series of moves and countermoves. When the government adopted programs of religious toleration, minority groups such as Lutherans, Catholics, Old Believers, Dukhobors, Khlysty, Skoptsy, Jews, Muslims and Buddhists, flourished. Unfortunately, apart from the reign of Alexander I with his extension of toleration to the Dukhobors and Skoptsy (his support of the Russian Bible Society initially undermined his program of toleration when the society began its missionary activities), the nineteenth-century tsars, compelled in their own minds by the exigencies of state, not only retreated from toleration but actively proselytized among and discriminated against the religious and ethnic minorities of the empire. The minority groups then sought survival by drawing a veil of secrecy over themselves, migrating to a fringe of the empire and away from the central authorities, or, failing that, emigrating.

Alexander not only promoted religious toleration but continued the colonization of Novorossiia. Able governors-general such as Aleksandr F. Langeron, the Duc de Richelieu, and Mikhail S. Vorontsov nurtured Novorossiia's economic development by encouraging the influx of different ethnic groups whose business acumen and trade connections were beneficial to the south and the Empire as a whole.[15] Among the ethnic groups who continued to settle in the south were people fleeing the Ottoman Empire: Serbs, Greeks, Armenians and Bulgarians.[16] Richelieu and Vorontsov, in the furtherance of economic development successfully secured for Odessa the status of a free port and Vorontsov, during the reign of Nicholas, protected Russian sectarians, Jews and Muslim Tatars from the discriminatory policies the tsar wished implemented. The importance of capable provincial administrators was underscored by the difficulties Alexander had with the Georgians at this time owing to the incompetence of the Russian military administrators in that region.[17]

Nicholas I placed religion at the forefront of Russian identity with the adoption and implementation of the policy of Official Nationality whose three pillars were Orthodoxy, autocracy and nationality (*narodnost'*).[18] Nicholas began the process whereby the distinction between *russkii* and *rossiiskii*, as terms of individual and group identity, gradually disappeared and *russkii* became the recognized form of identity. Within this schema subject nationalities and minority religious groups (usually one and the same), no longer enjoyed Alexander I's benign neglect but confronted Nicholas's adulatory estimation of Great Russian culture and their own subsequent relegation to the periphery of imperial society, politics and life. Nicholas's attitude toward the non-Orthodox elements bore institutional consequences as well when, in 1824, he established the Directorate of Foreign Confessions to manage non-Orthodox affairs. The Roman Catholic section of the directorate presided over the western *gubernii*. The Uniate Church suffered a series of reverses after the Polish rebellion in 1831 which ultimately led to its forcible reunification with Orthodoxy in 1839. The government created distinct sections to govern the affairs of Evangelical-Lutherans, Muslims and Buddhist Kalmyks. The sectarians and dissenters did not fair as well as the non-Orthodox. The gains the Old Believers secured under Alexander I quickly eroded under Nicholas who referred to them again with sufficient opprobrium as *raskol'niki*. The government singled out Old Believer monasteries and lay communities for especially fierce attention because of their alleged subversive activities and rumored lives of sexual debauchery which threatened to undermine the Nicholaevan system.[19] In 1842, Count Protasov, the overprocurator of the Holy Synod, issued a decree which defined sectarian groups as "most harmful," "harmful" and "less harmful" to the state. The Molokane, Khlysty, Skoptsy, Dukhobors and those *bezpopovtsy* who denied the sacrament of marriage occupied the first category; the other *bezpopovtsy* were in the second category; and the *popovtsy* comprised the third. Alexander I had granted the Dukhobors land in the Crimea, the Milky Waters, where they could practice their religion freely, but their continued growth and their tendency to move out of the Crimea and into the central *gubernii* prodded Nicholas to offer them the choice of conversion to Orthodoxy or a new settlement in the Akhalkalaki district of the Caucasus in 1841. They accepted the latter and moved further from the center.

Nicholas I's explicit belief that Orthodoxy and loyalty to the tsar could alone make one a Russian had the unintended consequence of enlarging the geographical and cultural periphery of the empire. The conflation of Orthodoxy and Russian identity obliged the Russian Orthodox Church to return actively to missionary (educational) work to save souls and fashion educated citizens; something it had not done systematically since the late seventeenth and early eighteenth centuries. Nicholas particularly loathed Jews, Tatars, and Poles; a dislike born, if not nourished, during his three-month tour of central Russia, Ukraine, the Crimea, and Novorossiia in the spring of 1816.[20] After the Polish rebellion, Nicholas attempted to suppress Polish identity by closing or Russifying Polish secondary schools. He closed the University of Vilno, restructured the University of Dorpat and opened the University of St. Vladimir in Kiev to educate young Polish men correctly. Nicholas hoped to save the Jews from themselves when he put into practice much of what Catherine's administrators had suggested were the necessary steps to assimilate Jews into "Russian" society successfully.[21] The emperor took considerable pride in the integrationist character of the Russian military and was convinced that it would serve as an effective assimilationist instrument for Jews. He made them liable for military service beginning at the age of twelve. He redefined the Pale of Settlement in 1835, expelled Jews from the cities of Kiev, Kherson and Sevastopol, and legally defined them as "aliens." He forbade them to use Hebrew in public business. Most important, however, was the abolition of the *kahal* which ended Jewish local self-governance and placed them under the same government as other citizens. Nicholas called upon the Russian Orthodox Church to assist him in converting the Muslim Tatars of the Volga region to Orthodoxy and, thereby, creating good Russian subjects. This action ultimately led to a growing missionary movement within Russian Orthodoxy which spread to all the borderlands but was directed primarily at the north Caucasus, Central Asia, and Siberia.[22] The missionary movement was institutionalized with the creation of the Orthodox Missionary Society in 1865 and the Confraternity of St. Gurii in 1867 which emphasized teaching in the native language through the establishment of native primary schools.

This method was extended to the other "aliens," Muslim, animist, or Buddhist in 1906 and to all primary schools in 1914.

••••

Religious culture on Russia's southern frontier at the end of the eighteenth century was continuously in flux. The contending notions of identity held by the enlightened and "Christian" center and those maintained by the local communities and foreign colonists on the borderlands often collided, yet usually reached a level of equilibrium through accommodation and compromise. As religion was the dominant means of expressing identity beyond that associated with the family or village, it became the medium for change. In the eighteenth century, the Church was still the instrument of civilization and acculturation on the periphery. Civilization was synonymous with Christianization; and parish schools and diocesan seminaries educated thousands. In this context, resistance to Christianization or civilization, not surprisingly, was often religiously grounded. Even communities which practiced religion "enthusiastically" could collide with the center if that enthusiasm resulted in a disregard for the power of the center. The relationship between the center and periphery was not a one-way street. The imperial government did not develop a master plan sufficient to administer effectively all the borderlands, but recognized that the process of integration and assimilation could only be accomplished, paradoxically, by allowing governors-general and viceroys a measure of latitude to adopt unique methods for particular regions. The imperial government and Russian society not only influenced the borderlands as they attempted to incorporate them but were influenced in turn during that very process. Finally, this study accentuates the value of not only the southern frontier but of periphery studies in general as a legitimate and valuable means to enhance our understanding of the social, political, and religious dynamics which forged the Russian state and society.

NOTES

1. For an examination of Russo-Greek ties in the early nineteenth century, see Theophilus C. Prousis, *Russian Society and the Greek Revolution* (DeKalb, 1994).

2. For a brief analysis of Theotokis's social and political conservatism in the broader context of Church-state relations in Greece see Ioannis S. Petrou, *Ekklisia kai Politiki stin Ellada (1750-1909)* (Thessaloniki, 1990), pp. 104-111.

3. Talal Asad, *Genealogies of Religion*, pp. 34-35.

4. Theophilus C. Prousis, "Aleksandr S. Sturdza: A Russian Conservative Response to Greek Revolution," *East European Quarterly*, 26:3 (1992): 309-344.

5. On Kapodistrias see G.L. Arsh, *I. Kapodistria i grecheskoe natsional'no-osvoboditel'noe dvizhenie, 1809-1822 gg.* (Moscow, 1976); C.M. Woodhouse, *Capodistria: The Founder of Greek Independence* (London, 1973); Eleni Koukkou, *Ioannis Kapodistrias: O Anthropos-O Diplomatis (1800-1828)*, 2nd ed., (Athens, 1984); and Stephen K. Batalden, "John Kapodistrias and the Structure of Greek Society on the Eve of the War of Independence: An Historiographical Essay," *East European Quarterly*, 13:3 (1979): 297314.

6. On Destunis, see Theophilus Prousis, "The Destunis Collection in the Saltykov-Shchedrin State Public Library in Leningrad," *Modern Greek Studies Yearbook*, 5 (1989): 395-452.

7. Prousis, *Russian Society*, pp. 14-17, 167.

8. See Vasilios N. Makrides, "Orthodoxy as a Conditio sine qua non: Religion and State/Politics in Modern Greece from a Socio-Historical Perspective," *Ostkirchliche Studien*, 40:4 (1991): 281-305. For a reexamination of the standard assumptions of a "national awakening" in the Balkans and the role of the Orthodox Church as a champion of nationalism, see Paschalis M. Kitromilides, " 'Imagined Communities' and the Origins of the National Question in the Balkans," *European History Quarterly*, 19 (1989): 149-194.

9. See G.L. Arsh, *Eteristskoe dvizhenie v Rossii. Osvoboditel'naia bor'ba grecheskogo naroda v nachale XIX v. i russko-grecheskie sviazi* (Moscow, 1970); E.G. Protopsaltis, ed., *I Filiki Etairia, Anamnistikon tefkhos epi ti 150eteridi* (Athens, 1964); and Tasos Vournas, ed., *Filiki Etairia* (Athens, 1965).

10. C.M. Woodhouse, "Kapodistrias and the *Philiki Etairia*, 1814-21," in Richard Clogg, ed., *The Struggle for Greek Independence* (London, 1973), pp. 104-134.

11. On the social and ideological diversity of the *Filiki Etairia* and its ramifications in early Greek politics, see George D. Frangos, "The *Philiki Etairia*: A Premature National Coalition," in Clogg, ed., *Struggle for Greek Independence*, pp. 87-103; John Petropoulos, *Politics and Statecraft in the Kingdom of Greece, 1833-1843* (London, 1968); and Thanos Veremis, "From the National State to the Stateless Nation, 1821-1910," *European History Quarterly*, 19:2 (April 1989): 135-148.

12. Makrides, "Orthodoxy," p. 286.

13. See Charles Frazee, *The Orthodox Church and Independent Greece, 1821-1852* (Cambridge, 1969). The new organization closely resembled the Synodal system prevailing in Russia since the time of Peter the Great and included a Holy Synod and a procurator appointed by the state. The man behind the changes was Georg von Maurer, one of King Othon's regents. See N.J. Pantazopoulos, *Georg von Maurer – I pros evropaika protipa oloklirotiki strofi tis neoellinikis nomothesias* (Thessaloniki, 1968).

14. See N. Kokosalakis, "Religion and Modernization in 19th Century Greece," *Social Compass*, 34 (1987): 223-241.

15. On the southern region in the early nineteenth century, see E.I. Druzhinina, *Iuzhnaia Ukraina v 1800-1825 gg.* (Moscow, 1970); idem, *Iuzhnaia Ukraina v period krizisa feodolizma, 1825-1860 gg.* (Moscow, 1981); A.

Skal'kovskii, *Pervoe tridtsatiletie istorii goroda Odessy, 1793-1823* (Odessa, 1837); and Patricia Herlihy, *Odessa: A History, 1794-1914* (Cambridge, 1986).
    16. On the immigration of Greeks, see G.M. Piatigorskii, "Grecheskie pereselentsy v Odesse v kontse XVIII-pervoi treti XIX v.," in V.N. Vinogradov, ed., *Iz istroii iazyka i kul'tury stran Tsentral'noi i Iugo-Vostochnoi Evropy* (Moscow, 1985), pp. 33-60; Viron Karidis, "The Greek Mercantile *paroikia*: Odessa, 1774-1829," in Clogg, ed., *Balkan Society in the Age of Greek Independence*, pp. 111-136; Patricia Herlihy, "Greek Merchants in Odessa in the Nineteenth Century," *Harvard Ukrainian Studies*, 3/4 (1979-80): 399-420; and idem, "The Greek Community in Odessa, 1861-1917," *Journal of Modern Greek Studies*, 7 (1989): 235-252. On the sizable Bulgarian immigration see A. Skal'kovskii, *Bolgarskii kolonii v Bessarabii i Novorossiiskom krai* (Odessa, 1848).
    17. See Stephen F. Jones, "Russian Imperial Administration and the Georgian Nobility: The Georgian Conspiracy of 1832," *Slavonic and East European Review*, 65:1 (1987): 53-76.
    18. On the genesis of Official Nationality, see Cynthia H. Whittaker, *The Origins of Modern Russian Education: An Intellectual Biography of Count Sergei Uvarov, 1786-1855* (DeKalb, IL, 1984), pp. 86-127; Nicholas Riasanovksy, *Nicholas I and Official Nationality in Russia, 1825-1855* (Berkeley, 1959). Whittaker also treats the implications of Official Nationality for the subject nationalities. See Whittaker, pp. 189-212.
    19. Crummey, "Interpreting the Fate," pp. 150-153.
    20. W. Bruce Lincoln, *Nicholas I: Emperor and Autocrat of All the Russias* (Bloomington, IN, 1978), pp. 63-64.
    21. On the policies of Catherine and Alexander I, see John Klier, *Russia Gathers Her Jews: The Origins of the "Jewish Question" in Russia, 1772-1825* (DeKalb, IL, 1986). For subsequent developments see Michael Stanislawski, *Tsar Nicholas I and the Jews: The Transformation of Jewish Society in Russia, 1825-1855* (Philadelphia, 1983); and Hans Rogger, *Jewish Policies and Right-wing Politics in Imperial Russia* (Berkeley, 1986).
    22. These regions have only recently become the subjects of critical scholarly studies which focus on the social, cultural and religious implications of Russian imperialism and its impact on indigenous peoples as opposed to the simplistic chronicling of the inexorable advance of the Russian military with culture trailing in its wake. On the north Caucasus see Marie Bennigsen Broxup, ed., *The North Caucasus Barrier: The Russian Advance Towards the Muslim World* (New York, 1992); Michel Tarran, "The Orthodox Mission in the North Caucasus: End of the 18th – Beginning of the 19th Century," Central Asian Survey, 10:1,2 (1991): 103-117; and Moshe Gammer, *Muslim Resistance to the Tsar: Shamil and the Conquest of Chechenia and Daghestan* (Portland, 1994). On Siberia, see David N. Collins, "Colonialism and Siberian Development: A Case Study of the Orthodox Mission to Altay, 1830-1913," in Alan Wood and R.A. French, eds., *The Development of Siberia: People and Resources* (New York, 1989), pp. 50-71; James Forsyth, *A History of the Peoples of Siberia: Russia's North Asian Colony, 11581-1990* (Cambridge, 1992); and Yuri Slezkine, "Savage Christians or Unorthodox Russians? The Missionary Dilemma in Siberia," in Gayla Diment and Yuri Slezkine, eds., *Between Heaven and Hell: The Myth of Siberia and Russian Culture* (New York, 1993), pp. 15-31. On the Muslims and Central Asia, see Elizabeth Bacon, *Central Asians under Russian Rule: A Study in Culture Change* (Ithaca, 1966); Edward J. Lazzerini, "Volga Tatars in Central Asia, 18th-20th Centuries: From Diaspora to Hegemony," in Beatrice F. Mantz, ed., *Central Asia in Historical Perspective* (Cambridge, 1994), pp. 82-102; Wayne Dowler, "The Politics of Language in Non-Russian Elementary Schools in the Eastern Empire, 1865-1914," *The Russian Review*, 54 (October 1995): 516-538; and Hélène Carrère d'Encausse, *Islam and the Russian Empire: Reform and Revolution in Central Asia* (Berkeley, 1988).

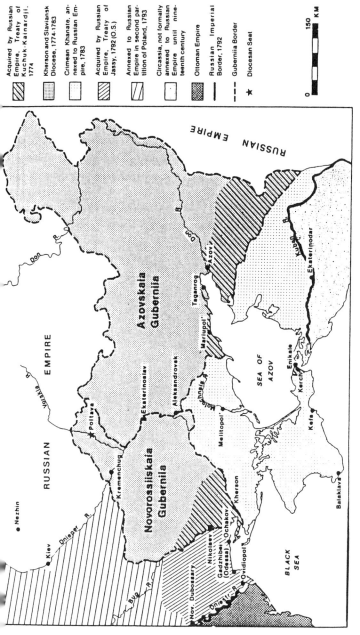

FIGURE 1

Novorossiia under Catherine the Great
(Reprinted from Stephen K. Batalden, *Catherine II's Greek Prelate:*
Eugenios Voulgaris in Russia, 1771-1806, East European Monographs, 1982).

ΑΠΟΚΡΙΣΙΣ
ΟΡΘΟΔΟΞΟΥ ΤΙΝΟΣ
πρός τινα ἀδελφὸν ὀρθόδοξον
ΠΕΡΙ ΤΗΣ
ΤΩΝ ΚΑΤΟΛΙΚΩΝ
ΔΥΝΑΣΤΕΙΑΣ,
Καὶ περὶ τοῦ·

Τίνες οἱ Σχῖσαι καὶ οἱ Σχισματικοὶ καὶ οἱ Ἐσχισμένοι·
Καὶ περὶ τῆς βαρβαρικῶς λεγομένης Οὐνίας
καὶ τῶν Οὐνίτων·
καὶ περὶ τοῦ·
Πῶς δεῖ τὰς Ὀρθοδόξες ἀπαντᾷν τῇ τῶν Κατολίκων
τυραννίᾳ.

Θεῷ ἔπαινος, ὁ δράκων νικητὴς ἐδείχθη
Γέλως δὲ τὸ μέρος αὐτὸ ἐν τῇ ἀβύσσῳ εὐλήφθη

✤✤✤✤✤✤✤✤✤✤✤✤✤✤✤✤✤✤✤✤✤✤

Ἐν Χάλλῃ, 1775.

FIGURE 2

Title page of Theotokis's anti-Latin work,
*A Reply by a Certain Orthodox Christian to an Orthodox Brother
on the Catholic Dynastic Rule*, published in Halle in 1775.

FIGURE 3

Medallion struck to commemorate the Russian naval victory at the Battle of Chesme in June 1770. The face side depicts Count Alexei Orlov-Chesmenskii and the obverse side represents the battle.

FIGURE 4

Metropolitan Platon (Levshin) of Moscow

FIGURE 5
Prince Grigorii Potemkin-Tavricheskii

FIGURE 6
Empress Catherine II (1773)

FIGURE 7

Medallion struck to commemorate the birth of
Grand Prince Constantine Pavlovich on 27 April 1779
and to allude to his association with the "Greek Project."

FIGURE 8

Medallion struck to commemorate Catherine's trip to the Crimea in 1787.
The face side depicts Prince Potemkin-Tavricheskii
and the obverse side a map of the southern provinces.

ΣΤΟΙΧΕΙΑ

ΓΕΩΓΡΑΦΙΑΣ

ΕΡΑΝΙΣΘΕΝΤΑ

ὑπὸ τῦ Ἀρχιεπισκόπη

ΝΙΚΗΦΟΡΟΥ τῦ ΘΕΟΤΟΚΟΥ

πλείςοις δὲ Σημειώμασι καὶ Σχ
μασι πλετισθέντα

ὑπὸ

ΑΝΘΙΜΟΥ ΓΑΖΗ.

νῦν πρῶτον τύποις ἐκδοθέντα, φιλοτίμῳ Δα
τῶν Αὐταδέλφων

ΚΥΡΙΩΝ ΖΩΣΙΜΑΔΩΝ

Ἰνα διανέμωνται δωρεὰν εἰς χρῆσιν τῶν Ἑλλη
Φροντιςηρίων.

Ἐπιςασίᾳ ΙΩΝΑ, τῦ ἐκ Μονῆς Κλήμεντος
τῆς ἐν Ὀλύμπῳ.

Ἐν Βιέννῃ τῆς Αὐςρίας
ἐν τῇ τυπογραφίᾳ Γ. Βεντώτη.

1804.

FIGURE 9

Frontispiece and title page of Theotokis's *Elements of Geography*
published in Vienna in 1804 with the financial support
of the Zosimades Brothers.

BIBLIOGRAPHY

Archival Sources

A. St. Petersburg
   1. Saltykov-Schedrin State Public Library, Manuscripts Division (RNB-Otdel rukopisei).
     fond 588 – Pogodinskie Avtografy
   2. Russian State Historical Archive (RGIA)
     a. *fond* 796 – Kantseliariia Sinoda
     b. *fond* 834 – Rukopisi Sinoda
B. Moscow
   Russian State Archive of Ancient Acts (RGADA)
     a. *fond* 16 – Dukhovnoe vedomstvo
     b. *fond* 18 – Vnutrennee upravlenie

Works of Nikiforos Theotokis

Apodeixis tou kyrous ton tis Neas kai Palaias Diathikis vivlion, kai tois en aftois alitheias yperaspisis I anaskevi tis ek tou Voltairou vivlou, tis kaloumenis teleftaion dierminevtheisis diathikis, ek ton Gallon fonis metafrastheisa, yper prosetethisan kai tines simeioseis (A Proof of the Validity of the Books of the New and the Old Testaments, and a Defense of the Truths Found in Them or a Refutation of Voltaire's Bible, Recently Called the Interpretation of the Testament, Translated from the French Language, Including Some Additional Notes). Vienna, 1794.

Apokrisis Orthodoxou tinos pros tina adelfon orthodoxon peri tis ton Katolikon dynasteias, kai peri tou tines oi Schistai kai oi Schismatikoi kai oi Eschismenoi kai peri tis varvarikos legomenis Ounias kai ton Ouniaton kai peri tou pos dei tous Orthodoxous apantan ti ton Katolikon tyrannia (A Reply by a Certain Orthodox Christian to an Orthodox Brother on the Catholic Dynastic Rule, and on Who are the Separatists, the Schismatics, and the Severed Ones, and on the Barbarically Called Unia and the Uniates, and on How the Orthodox Must Respond to Catholic Tyranny). Halle, 1775.

Logoi eis tin aghian kai megalin Tessarakostin, meta kaitinon Panigyrikon, Epifonimatikon kai Epitafion (Sermons for Holy and Great Lent, along with Certain Panegyrics, Proclamations, and Funeral Orations). Leipzig, 1766.

Kyriakodromion, itoi, ermineia kai met' aftin ithiki omilia eis to kata pasan Kyriakin en tais aghiais ton orthodoxon ekklisiais anaginoskomenon Evangelion (Kyriakodromion, that is, Exegeses with Accompanying Moral Homilies on the Gospels which are Read in the Holy Orthodox Churches on Every Sunday), 2 vols. Moscow, 1796.

Kyriakodromion, itoi, ermineia kai met' aftin ithiki omilia eis tas praxeis ton Apostolon, tas anaginoskomenas en tais aghiais ton orthodoxon ekklisiais en tais Kyriakais apo tou Pasha ahri tis Pentikostis kai eis tas epistolas tou Pavlou, tas anaginoskomenas en tais loipais Kyriakais tou olou etous (Kyriakodromion, that is, Exegeses with Accompanying Moral Homilies on the Acts of the Apostles which are Read in the Holy Orthodox Churches on the Sundays from Easter until Pentecost, and on the Pauline Epistles which are Read on the Remaining Sundays of the Whole Year). Moscow, 1808.

Otvety preosviashchennago Nikifora arkhiepiskopa slavenskago I khersonskago, a potom byvshago astrakhanskago I kavalera, na voprosy staroobriadtsov. Moscow, 1800.

Ponima hrysoun Samouil Ravvi tou Ioudaiou exelenghon tin ton Ioudaion planin. Proton men, ek tis Aravikis eis tin Latinida metafrasthen. Nyn de ek tis Latinidos eis tin koinin ton Ellinon dialekton (The Golden Text of Rabbi Samuel, the Jew, Scrutinizing the Deception of the Jews. First translated from Arabic to Latin and now from Latin into the Common Dialect of the Greeks). Leipzig, 1770.

Prosfonima ti evsevestati, theostepto, sevasti, trismegisti kai filanthropotati avgousti kyria Aikaterini Aleksiadi, aftokratori pasis Rosias (Address to the Most Pious, Crowned by God, Venerable, Thrice Great, and the Most Philanthropic and August Catherine of Alexeis, Empress of All Russia). St. Petersburg, 1779.

Seira enos kai pentikonta ypomnimatiston eis tin oktatefhon kai ta ton Vasileion idi proton typois ekdotheisa axiosei men tou evsevestatou kai galinotatou igemonos pasis Oungkrovlahias kyriou kyriou Grigoriou Alexandrou Gkika. Epimeleia de Nikiforou ieromonahou tou Theotokou. (A Series of 51 Commentators into the Eight-Volume Work and about the Heavenly Kingdom, Already First Published Courtesy of the Most Pious and Serene Ruler of all Ugro-Vlachia the Honorable Grigorios Alexandros Ghikas. Under the Supervision of the ieromonakh Nikiforos Theotokis). 2 vols. Leipzig, 1772-1773.

Stoiheia Geografias (Elements of Geography). Vienna, 1804.

Stoiheion Mathimatikon ek palaion kai neoteron (On the Old and New Mathematical Elements). 3 vols. Moscow, 1798-1799.

Stoiheia Physikis, ek neoteron syneranisthenta (Elements of Physics, from Recent Compilations). 2 vols. Leipzig, 1766-1767.

Tolkovanie voskresnykh apostolov. Moscow, 1819.

Tolkovanie voskresnykh evangelii. Moscow, 1805.

Tou osiou patros imon Isaak episkopou Ninevi tou Syrou, ta evrethenta Askitika axiosei men tou makariotatou theiotatou kai sofotatou patriarhou tis aghias poleos Ierousalim kai pasis Palaistinis kyriou kyriou Efraim epimeleia de Nikiforou ieromonahou tou Theotokou idi proton typois ekdothenta (The Discovered Spiritual Exercises of the Holy Father Isaac Syros, Bishop of Nineveh, Courtesy of the most Blessed, Divine and Wise Patriarch of the Holy City of Jerusalem and Palestine, the Honorable Ephraim, under the Supervision of the ieromonakh Theotokis Published for the First Time). Leipzig, 1770.

Published Primary Sources

Bantysh-Kamenskii, N.N. "Moskovskaia pis'ma v poslednie gody Ekaterininskago tsarstvovaniia OT N.N. Bantysh-Kamenskago k kniazu A.B. Kurakinu," *Russkii arkhiv*, bk. 3 (1876): 257-284, 387-413.

Bartenev, P., ed. *Osmnadtsatyi vek.* 4 vols. Moscow, 1868-9.

"Kratkoe povestvovanie o obrashchenii raskol'nikov seleniia Znamenki, kakim obrazom oni byli priniaty v pravoslavnuiu tserkov'; izlozhenie osnovanii, po kotorym im pozvoleno bylo chitat' starinnyia knigi, izdannyia v Rossii, I pet' po svoemu obychaiu, postavit' sviashchennika iz ikh sredy, esli by iavilsia dostoinyi; mezhdu prochim I razsyzhdenie o obriadakh." *Bratskoe slovo*, 2 (1892): 128-138.

Clarke, E. *Travels in Russia, Tartary, and Turkey.* Aberdeen, 1848.

Craven, E. *A Journey through the Crimea to Constantinople.* London, 1789.

Drummond. *Travels.* London, 1754.

Dukes, Paul, ed. *Catherine the Great's Instruction (Nakaz) to the Legislative Commission, 1767.* Newtonville, 1977.

Dyovouniotis, K.I. "Logoi anekdotoi kai epistolai Nikiforou tou Theotoki." *Ieros Syndesmos* (15 Sept. 1915): 4-8.

Holderness, Mary. *New Russia. Journey from Riga to the Crimea.* London, 1823.

Ioannidis Amorginos, Emmanuel. "Anekdotoi epistolai Nikiforou tou Theotoki, Arhiepiskopou Slavoniou kai Hersonos." *Ellinikos Filologikos Syllogos Konstantinoupoleos*, 18 (1861-86): 102-111.

Lentin, Antony, ed. *Voltaire and Catherine the Great. Selected Correspondence.* Cambridge, 1974.

Parkinson, John. *A Tour of Russia, Siberia and the Crimea, 1792-1794.* London, 1971.

[Potemkin]. "Pis'ma kniazu G.A. Potemkinu-Tavricheskomu." *Zapiski odesskogo obshchestva istorii I drevnostei*, 9 (1875): 227 282.

[Potemkin]. "Pis'ma svetleishago kniaza Grigoriia Aleksandrovicha Potemkina-Tavricheskago," *Russkii arkhiv*, 7 (1880): 1597.

Polnoe sobranie zakonov Rossiiskoi imperii. St. Petersburg, 1830.

Reddaway, W.F., ed. *Documents of Catherine the Great, the Correspondence with Voltaire and the Instruction of 1767 in the English Text of 1768.* Cambridge, 1931.

Richardson, William. *Anecdotes of the Russian Empire.* London, 1784; repr. London, 1968.

Sbornik imperatorskogo russkogo istoricheskogo obshchestva.. 148 vols. St. Petersburg, 1867-1916.

Secondary Sources

Adler, Philip J. "Habsburg School Reform Among the Orthodox Minorities, 1770-1780." *Slavic Review*, 33 (1974): 23-45.

Alev, Gustav. "Diaspora Greeks in Muscovy." *Byzantine Studies*, 6 (1975): 26-34.

Alexander, John T. *Bubonic Plague in Early Modern Russia: Public Health and Urban Disaster.* Baltimore, 1980.

Alexander, John T. *Catherine the Great: Life and Legend*. Oxford, 1989.

Allen, W.E.D. *The Ukraine: A History*. Cambridge, 1940.

Anderson, Benedict. *Imagined Communities: Reflections on the Origin and Spread of Nationalism*. Revised Edition. London, 1991.

Anderson, M.S. *The Eastern Question, 1774-1923*. New York, 1966.

Andreev V.V. *Raskol' i ego znachenie v narodnoi russkoi istorii, Istoricheskii ocherk*. St. Petersburg, 1870; repr. Osnabruck, 1965.

Angelou, A. *Platonos Tyhai*. Athens, 1963.

Aron, Raymond. "On the Proper Use of Ideologies," J. Ben-David and Terry Nichols Clark, eds., *Culture and Its Creators: Essays in Honor of Edward Shils* (Chicago, 1977), 1-14.

Arsh, Grigorii Lvovich. *Eteristskoe dvizhenie v Rossii. Osvoboditel'naia bor'ba grecheskogo naroda v nachale XIX v. i russko-grecheskie sviazi*. Moscow, 1970.

_____. "Grecheskaia emigratsiia v Rossiiu v kontse XVIII-nachale XIX v." *Sovetskaia etnografiia*, 3 (1969): 85-95.

_____. *I. Kapodistriia i grecheskoe natsional'no-osvoboditel'noe dvizhenie, 1809-1822*. Moscow, 1976.

_____. "Novogrecheskoe prosveshchenie v Rossiia." *Balkanskie issledovaniia*, 9 (1984): 304-313.

Asad, Talal. "Anthropological Conceptions of Religion: Reflections on Geertz." *Man*, 18 (1983): 237-259.

_____. *Genealogies of Religion: Discipline and Reasons of Power in Christianity and Islam*. Baltimore, 1993.

Atkin, Muriel. *Russia and Iran, 1780-1828*. Minneapolis, 1980.

Avouri, S. *Syntomos istoria tis Ekklisias ton Ionion nison*. Athens, 1966.

Bacon, Elizabeth. *Central Asians under Russian Rule: A Study in Culture Change*. Ithaca, 1966.

Badone, Ellen, ed. *Religious Orthodoxy and Popular Faith in European Society*. Princeton, 1990.

Baehr, Stephen L. "From History to National Myth: *Translatio imperii* in Eighteenth-Century Russia." *The Russian Review*, 37:1 (January 1978): 1-13.

_____. *The Paradise Myth in Eighteenth-Century Russia: Utopian Patterns in Early Secular Literature and Culture*. Stanford, 1991.

Bagalei, D.I. *Kolonizatsiia novorossiiskago kraia i pervye shagi ego po puti kultury*. Kiev, 1889.

Barrett, Thomas M. "Lines of Uncertainty: The Frontiers of the North Caucasus." *Slavic Review*, 54:3 (Fall 1995): 578-601.

Barth, Fredrik, ed. *Ethnic Groups and Boundaries: The Social Organization of Cultural Differences*. Boston, 1969.

Bartlett, Roger. *Human Capital: The Settlement of Foreigners in Russia, 1762-1804*. Cambridge, 1979.

Bartlett, Roger, and A.G. Cross, Karen Rasmussen, eds. *Russia and the World of the Eighteenth Century*. Columbus, OH, 1988.

Bartlett, Roger, and Janet M. Hartley, eds. *Russia in the Age of the Enlightenment*. New York, 1990.

Batalden, Stephen K. *Catherine II's Greek Prelate: Eugenios Voulgaris in Russia, 1771-1806*. East European Monographs: Boulder, 1982.

_____. "Eugenios Voulgaris in Russia, 1771-1806: A Chapter in Greco-Slavic Ties of the Eighteenth Century." Ph.D. dissertation, University of Minnesota, 1975.

_____. "John Kapodistrias and the Structure of Greek Society on the Eve of the War of Independence: An Historiographical Essay." *East European Quarterly*, 13:3 (1979): 297-314.

_____. "Metropolitan Gavriil (Banulesko-Bodoni) and Greek-Russian Conflict over Dedicated Monastic Estates, 1787-1812." *Church History*, 52:4 (1983): 468-478.

_____, ed. *Seeking God: The Recovery of Religious Identity in Orthodox Russia, Ukraine, and Georgia*. DeKalb, IL, 1993.

Belikov, V.I. *Deiatel'nost' moskovskogo mitropolita Filareta po otnosheniiu k raskolu*. Kazan, 1895.

Belliustin, I.S. *Description of the Clergy in Rural Russia: The Memoir of a Nineteenth-Century Parish Priest*. Translated with an Interpretive Essay by Gregory L. Freeze. Ithaca, 1985.

Benedicty, Robert. "Eine unedierte Rede von Nikephoros, Metropolit von Cherson," Johannes Irmscher and Marika Mineemi, eds., *O Ellinismos eis to Exoterikon* (Berlin, 1968), 289-295.

Berdnikov, I.S. *Kratkii kurs' tserkovnago prava*. Kazan, 1888.

Berger, Peter. *The Sacred Canopy: Elements of a Sociological Theory of Religion*. Garden City, NJ, 1969.

Billington, J. *The Icon and the Axe: An Interpretive History of Russian Culture*. New York, 1966.

Black, J.L. *Citizen for the Fatherland: Education, Educators and Pedagogical Ideals in Eighteenth Century Russia*. East European Monographs: Boulder, 1979.

Blackbourn, David. *Marpingen: Apparitions of the Virgin Mary in Bismarckian Germany*. New York, 1994.

Bonch-Bruevich, V.D. *Materials Concerning the History and Study of Russian Sectarianism and Schism*. St. Petersburg, 1908.

Braun, F.A. "Mariupol'skie greki." *Zhivaia starina*, 2 (1890): 78-92.

Brass, Paul. *Ethnicity and Nationalism: Theory and Comparison*. Newbury Park, CA, 1991.

Brooks, Jeffrey. *When Russia Learned to Read: Literacy and Popular Literature, 1861-1917*. Princeton, 1985.

Brown, Peter. *The Cult of the Saints: Its Rise and Function in Latin Christianity*. Chicago, 1981.

Broxup, Marie Bennigsen, ed. *The North Caucasus Barrier: The Russian Advance Towards the Muslim World*. New York, 1992.

Bruess, Gregory L. "Religious Toleration in the Reign of Catherine the Great." Menahem Mor, ed., *International Perspectives on Church and State* (Omaha, NE, 1993), 299-315.

Brükner, A. "Puteshestvie Imperatritsy Ekateriny II v poludennyi krai Rossii v 1787 godu." *Zhurnal Ministerstva Narodnogo Proveshcheniia*, pt. 2, vol. 162 (1872): 1-51.

Bushkovitch, Paul. "The Formation of a National Consciousness in Early Modern Russia." *Harvard Ukrainian Studies*, 10:3/4 (December 1986): 355-376.

_____. *Religion and Society in Russia: The Sixteenth and Seventeenth Centuries*. Oxford, 1992.

Camariano-Cioran, A. *Les Académies princières de Bucharest et de Jassy et leur professeurs*. Thessaloniki, 1974.

Cherniaev, P.N. *Rossiiu svedenii ob antichnom mire*. Voronezh, 1911.

_____. *Sledy znakomstva drevne-klassicheskoi literatury v veke Ekateriny II*. Voronezh, 1906.

Cherniavsky, Michael. "The Old Believers and the New Religion." *Slavic Review*, 25 (1966): 1-39.

_____. "Russia," Orest Ranum, ed., *National Consciousness, History, and Political Culture in Early-Modern Europe* (Baltimore, 1975), 118-143.

Chetverikov, S. *Starets Paisii Velichkovskii: His Life, Teachings and Influence on Orthodox Monasticism*. Belmont, MA, 1980.

Christian, William. *Local Religion in Sixteenth-Century Spain*. Princeton, 1981.

Clifford, James. *The Predicament of Culture: Twentieth-Century Ethnography, Literature, and Art*. Cambridge, 1988.

Clogg, Richard, ed. *The Struggle for Greek Independence*. London, 1973.

Collins, David N. "Colonialism and Siberian Development: A Case Study of the Orthodox Mission to Altay, 1830-1913," Alan Wood and R.A. French, eds., *The Development of Siberia: People and Resources* (New York, 1989), 50-71.

Conybeare, Frederick. *Russian Dissenters*. New York, 1921.

Cracraft, James. *The Church Reform of Peter the Great*. Stanford, 1971.

Croskey, R. "Byzantine Greeks in Late Fifteenth- and Early Sixteenth-Century Russia." Lowell Clucas, ed., *The Byzantine Legacy in Eastern Europe*. Boulder, 1988.

Cross, A.G. "Samuel Grieg, Catherine the Great's Scottish Admiral." *Mariner's Mirror*, 60 (1976): 251-266.

Crummey, Robert O. "Interpreting the Fate of Old Believer Communities in the Eighteenth and Nineteenth Centuries." Stephen K. Batalden, ed., *Seeking God: The Recovery of Religious Identity in Orthodox Russia, Ukraine, and Georgia* (DeKalb, IL, 1993), 144-159.

_____. "Old Belief as Popular Religion: New Approaches." *Slavic Review*, 52:4 (Winter 1993): 700-712.

_____. *The Old Believers and the World of Antichrist: The Vyg Community and the Russian, 1694-1855*. Madison, 1970.

Dakin, Douglas. *The Unification of Greece, 1770-1923*. New York, 1972.

Davies, Norman. *God's Playground: A History of Poland*. 2 vols. New York, 1982.

Davis, Natalie Z. "From ' Popular Religion' to Religious Cultures." Steven Ozment, ed., *Reformation Europe: A Guide to Research* (St. Louis, 1982), 321-341.

_____. *Society and Culture in Early Modern France*. Stanford, 1975.

Davison, Roderic. "' Russian Skill and Turkish Imbecility': The Treaty of Kuchuk-Kainardji Reconsidered." *Slavic Review*, 25:3 (1976): 463-484.

Demos, Raphael. "The Neo-Hellenic Enlightenment, 1750-1821: A General Survey." *Journal of the History of Ideas*, 19:4 (1958): 523-541.

d'Encausse, Hélène Carrère. *Islam and the Russian Empire: Reform and Revolution in Central Asia*. Berkeley, 1988.

Desan, Suzanne. *Reclaiming the Sacred: Lay Religion and Popular Politics in France*. Ithaca, NY, 1990.

Deutsch, Karl. *Nationalism and Social Communication: An Inquiry into the Foundations of Nationality*. Cambridge, 1966.

Dickinson, Sara. "Imagining Space and Self: Russian Travel Writing and Its Narrators, 1762-1825." Ph.D. dissertation, Harvard University, 1995.

Dimaras, K.Th. *La Grèce au temps des lumières*. Geneva, 1969.

_____. *Neoellinikos Diaphotismos*. 3rd ed. Athens, 1983.

Dimaras, K.Th. "Peri Phanarioton." *Arheion Thrakis*, 34 (1969): 117-140.

Dmitriev, S.S. *Chesmenskaia pobeda*. Moscow, 1945.

Dmitrievskii, A.A. "K voprosu o propovednicheskikh trudakh Nikifora Theotoki v bytnost' ego arkhiepiskopom astrakhanskim i stavropol'skim." *Astrakhanskie eparkhial'nye vedomosti*, 14 (1895) (neoffitsial'naia chast'): 365-378.

_____. "Po povodu izdaniia v svet neskol'kikh traktatov i pisem arkhiepiskopa Nikifora Theotoki." *Astrakhanskie eparkhial'nye vedomosti*, 8 (1895) (neof. ch.): 235-244.

Dowler, Wayne. "The Politics of Language in Non-Russian Elementary Schools in the Eastern Empire, 1865-1914." *The Russian Review*, 54 (October 1995): 516-538.

Druzhinina, E.I. *Iuzhnaia Ukraina v 1800-1825 gg*. Moscow, 1970.

_____. *Iuzhnaia Ukraina v period krizisa feodolizma, 1825-1860 gg*. Moscow, 1981.

_____. *Kiuchuk-Kainardzhiiskii mir, 1774 goda, ego podgotovka i zakliuchenie*. Moscow, 1955.

_____. *Severnoe Prichernomorie v 1775-1800 gg*. Moscow, 1959.

Dubrovin, N.F., ed. *Prisoedinenie Kryma k Rossii*. 4 vols. St. Petersburg, 1885-1889.

Duran, Jr., James A. "Catherine II, Potemkin, and Colonization Policy in Southern Russia." *The Russian Review*, 28 (January 1969): 23-36.

Durkheim, Emile. *The Elementary Forms of the Religious Life*. Translated by Joseph Ward Swain. New York, 1965.

Dyovouniotis, K.I. *Nikiforos O Theotokis*. Jerusalem, 1913.

Eley, Geoff and Ronald Grigor Suny, eds. *Becoming National: A Reader*. Oxford, 1996.

Eliade, Mircea. *Cosmos and History: The Myth of the Eternal Return*. Translated by William R. Trask. New York, 1959.

Entsiklopedicheskii slovar'. 43 vols. in 86. St. Petersburg, 1890-1907.

Evangelidis, T.E. *I Paideia epi Tourkokratias*. 2 vols. Athens, 1936.

Fadeev, A.V. "Grecheskoe natsional'no-osvoboditel'noe dvizhenie i russkoe obshchestvo pervykh desiatiletii XIX v." *Novaia i noveishaia istoriia*, 3 (1961): 41-52.

Floria, B.N., ed. "Greki-emigranty v Russkom gosudarstve vtoroi poloviny XV-nachala XVI v. Politicheskaia i kul'turnaia deiatel'nost'," *Russko-balkanskie kul'turnye sviazi v epokhu srednevekov'ia* (Sofia, 1982), pp. 123-43.

_____. *Sviazi Rossii s narodami Balkanskogo poluostrova. Pervaia polovina XVII v.* Moscow, 1990.

_____. "Vykhodtsy iz balkanskikh stran na russkoi sluzhbe (konets XVI-nachalo XVII v.)." *Balkanskie issledovaniia*, 3 (1978):57-63.

Feodosii. *Materialy dlia istoriko-statisticheskogo opisaniia ekaterino-slavskoi eparkhii: Tserkvi i prikhody proshedshago XVIII st.* 2 vols. Ekaterinoslav, 1880.

Fisher, Alan W. *Russian Annexation of the Crimea, 1771-1783*. Cambridge, 1970.

Fonkich, B.L. *Grechesko-russkie kulturnye sviazi v XV-XVII vv: grecheskie rukopisi v Rossii*. Moscow, 1977.

_____. "Novye materialy dlia biografii Likhudov." *Pamiatniki kul'tury: novye otkrytiia* (1988): 61-70.

_____. "Russia and the Christian East from the Sixteenth to the First Quarter of the Eighteenth Century." *Modern Greek Studies Yearbook*, 7 (1991): 439-61.

Ford, Caroline C. *Creating the Nation in Provincial France: Religion and Political Identity in Brittany*. Princeton, 1993.

Forsyth, James. *A History of the Peoples of Siberia: Russia's North Asian Colony, 1581-1990*. Cambridge, 1992.

Frangos, George D. "The *Philiki Etairia*: A Premature National Coalition," Richard Clogg, ed., *The Struggle for Greek Independence* (London, 1973), 87-103.

Frazee, Charles. *The Orthodox Church and Independent Greece*. Cambridge, 1969.

Freeze, Gregory L. "Bringing Order to the Russian Family: Marriage and Divorce in Imperial Russia, 1760-1860." *Journal of Modern History*, 62 (December 1990):709-746.

_____. "The Handmaiden of the State? The Church in Imperial Russia Reconsidered." *Journal of Ecclesiastical History*, 36:1 (January 1985):82-102.

_____. "The Rechristianization of Russia: The Church and Popular Religion, 1750-1850." *Studia Slavica Finlandensia*, 7 (1990): 101-136.

_____. *The Russian Levites: The Parish Clergy in the Eighteenth Century.* Cambridge, 1977.

_____. "The Wages of Sin: The Decline of Public Penance in Imperial Russia." Stephen K. Batalden, ed. *Seeking God: The Recovery of Religious Identity in Orthodox Russia, Ukraine, and Georgia* (DeKalb, Il., 1993), 53-82.

Galpern, A.N. *The Religion of the People of Sixteenth-Century Champagne.* Cambridge, 1976.

Gammer, Moshe. *Muslim Resistance to the Tsar: Shamil and the Conquest of Chechenia and Daghestan.* Portland, 1994.

Gasparov, Boris. "Russkaia Gretsiia, russkii Rim," Robert P. Hughes and Irina Paperno, eds., *Christianity and the Eastern Slavs. Volume II: Russian Culture and Modern Times* (California Slavic Studies XVII, Berkeley, 1994), 245-285.

Gavriil (Rozanov), Archbishop of Tver. "Otryvok poviestvovaniia o novorossiiskom kraie iz originnal'nykh istochnikov pocherpnutyi." *Zapiski odesskogo obshchestva istorii i drevnostei*, 3 (1852): 79-129.

_____. "Pereselenie grekov iz kryma v azovskuiu guberniiu i osnovanie gotfiiskoi i kafisskoi eparkhii." *Zapiski odesskogo obshchestva istorii i drevnostei*, 1 (1844): 197-204.

Gay, Peter. *The Enlightenment: An Interpretation/The Rise of Modern Paganism.* New York, 1966.

Geanakoplos, Deno J. *Byzantine East and Latin West: Two Worlds of Christendom in Middle Ages and Renaissance.* New York, 1966.

Geanakoplos, Deno J.. "The Diaspora Greeks: The Genesis of Modern Greek Consciousness." N. Diamandouros and J. Petropoulos, eds., *Hellenism and the First Greek War of Liberation (1821-1830)* (Thessaloniki, 1976), 59-78.

_____. *Greek Scholars in Venice: Studies in the Dissemination of Greek Learning from Byzantium to Western Europe.* Cambridge, 1962.

_____. *Interaction of "Sibling" Byzantine and Western Cultures in the Middle Ages and Italian Renaissance (330-1600).* New Haven, 1976.

Geertz, Clifford. *The Interpretation of Cultures.* New York, 1973.

Gellner, Ernest. *Nations and Nationalism.* Ithaca, 1983.

_____. "The Struggle to Catch Up: Russia, Europe and the Enlightenment." *Times Literary Supplement* (December 9, 1994): 14-15.

Georgiev, V.A., et al. *Vostochnyi vopros vo vneshnei politike Rossii: Konets XVIII-nachalo XX v.* Moscow, 1978.

Golubev, S.T. *Petr Mogila, Mitropolit Kievskii.* Vol. I. Moscow, 1887.

Goriuchko, Platon. "Anastasii Bratanovskii, Arkhiepiskop Astrakhanskii i Kavkazskii." *Astrakhanskie eparkhial'nye vedomosti*, 2 (1902): 61-73.

Goudas, Anastasios N. *Vioi Paralliloi.* 8 vols. Athens, 1870.

Greenfeld, Liah. *Nationalism: Five Roads to Modernity.* Cambridge, 1992.

Grekov, V.A. "Kem i kak polozheno nachalo Edinoveriiu v Russkoi tserkvi." *Bratskoe slovo*, 2 (1892): 108-128.

Griffiths, David M. "Catherine II: The Republican Empress." *Jahrbücher für Geschichte Osteuropas*, 2 (1973): 337-340.

_____. "In Search of the Enlightenment: Recent Soviet Interpretations of Eighteenth-Century Russian Intellectual History." *Canadian-American Slavic Studies* 16:3-4 (1982): 317-356.

_____. "Russian Court Politics and the Question of an Expansionist Foreign Policy under Catherine II, 1762-1783." Ph.D. dissertation, Cornell University, 1967.

Gritsopoulos, T. *Ta Orlofika.* Athens, 1967.

Gurevich, A.Ia. *Problemy srednevekovoi narodnoi kul'tury.* Moscow, 1981.

____. *Srednevekovyi mir: kul'tura bezmolvstvuiushchego.* Moscow, 1990.

Hadjiantoniou, G. *Protestant Patriarch: The Life of Cyril Lukaris (1572-1638), Patriarch of Constantinople.* Richmond, 1961.

Halecki, O. *From Florence to Brest, 1439-1596.* New York, 1958.

Hall, Stuart. "Ethnicity: Identity and Difference." Geoff Eley and Ronald Grigor Suny, eds., *Becoming National: A Reader* (Oxford, 1996), 339-349.

Hartley, Janet. "The Boards of Social Welfare and the Financing of Catherine II's State Schools." *Slavonic and East European Review*, 67:2 (April 1989): 211-227.

Henderson, G.P. *The Revival of Modern Greek Thought, 1620-1830.* New York, 1970.

Herlihy, Patricia. "The Greek Community in Odessa, 1861-1917." *Journal of Modern Greek Studies*, 7 (1989): 235-252.

____. "Greek Merchants in Odessa in the Nineteenth Century." *Harvard Ukrainian Studies*, 3/4 (1979-80): 399-420.

____. *Odessa: A History, 1794-1914.* Cambridge, 1986.

Herzfeld, Michael. *Ours Once More: Folklore, Ideology, and the Making of Modern Greece.* Austin, 1982.

Hobsbawm, Eric and Terence Ranger, eds. *The Invention of Tradition.* Cambridge, 1983.

Hunt, Lynn, ed. *The New Cultural History.* Berkeley, 1989.

Iastrebov, V.N. "Greki v Elisavetgrade, 1754-1777." *Kievskaia starina*, 8 (1884): 673-684.

Ingle, H. Larry. *First Among Friends: George Fox and the Creation of Quakerism.* New York, 1994.

Ioannidis Amorginos, Emmanuel. "Istoriki Perigrafi tis Poleos Taganrog." *Ellinikos Filologikos Syllogos Konstantinoupoleos*, 18 (1861-86): 112-119.

Isaievych, Iaroslav. "Greek Culture in the Ukraine: 1550-1650." *Modern Greek Studies Yearbook*, 6 (1990): 97-122.

Istoria tou Ellinikou Ethnous, v. IA, O Ellinismos ypo Xenokyriarhia, Tourkokratia-Latinokratia, 1669-1821. Athens, 1975.

Jelavich, B. *History of the Balkans: Eighteenth and Nineteenth Centuries*. Cambridge, 1983.

Jones, Robert E. *The Emancipation of the Russian Nobility, 1762-1785*. Princeton, 1973.

_____. "Opposition to War and Expansion in Late Eighteenth Century Russia." *Jahrbücher für Geschichte Osteuropas*, 32 (1984): 34-51.

_____. *Provincial Development in Russia: Catherine II and Jacob Sievers*. New Brunswick, NJ, 1984.

Jones, Stephen F. "Russian Imperial Administration and the Georgian Nobility: The Georgian Conspiracy of 1832." *Slavonic and East European Review*, 65:1 (1987): 53-76.

K., P.M. "Peri Marianoupoleos." *Pandora*, 16: 533-538.

Kabuzan, V.M. *Zaselenie Novorossii (Ekaterinoslavskoi i Khersonskoi gubernii) v XVIII-pervoi polovine XIX veka, 1719-1858 gg*. Moscow, 1976.

Kamenskii, A. *"Pod seniiu Ekateriny..." Vtoraia polovina XVIII veka*. St. Petersburg, 1992.

Kaplan, Herbert. *The First Partition of Poland*. New York, 1962.

Kapterev, N.F. *Kharakter otnoshenii Rossii k pravoslavnomu vostoku XVI i XVII st*. Moscow, 1885.

Kara, G. *Oi Fisikes-Thetikes epistimes ston elliniko 18o aiona*. Athens, 1977.

Karidis, Viron. "The Greek Mercantile *paroikia*: Odessa, 1774-1829," Richard Clogg, ed., *Balkan Society in the Age of Greek Independence* (Totowa, NJ), 111-136.

_____. "The Mariupol Greeks: Tsarist Treatment of an Ethnic Minority ca. 1778-1859." *Journal of Modern Hellenism*, 3 (1986): 57-74.

Kartashev, A.B. *Ocherki po istorii russkoi tserkvi*. Paris, 1859.

Katsiardi-Hering, O. *I Elliniki Paroikia tis Tergestis, 1751-1830*. 2 vols. Athens, 1986.

Kharlampovich, K.V. *Zapadnorusskie pravoslavnye shkoly XVI i nachala XVII v.* Kazan, 1898.

Khodarkovsky, Michael. *Where Two Worlds Met: The Russian State and the Kalmyk Nomads, 1600-1771*. Ithaca, 1992.

Kitromilides, P.M. *The Enlightenment as Social Criticism: Iosipos Moisiodax and Greek Culture in the Eighteenth Century*. Princeton, 1992.

_____. "' Imagined Communities' and the Origins of the National Question in the Balkans." *European History Quarterly*, 19 (1989): 149-194.

_____. *Iosipos Moisiodax*. Athens, 1985.

_____. "The Idea of Science in the Modern Greek Enlightenment." P. Nicolacopoulos, ed., *Greek Studies in the Philosophy and History of Science* (Boston, 1990), 187-200.

Klibanov, A.I. *The History of Religious Sectarianism in Russia (1860s-1917)*. Reprint, Oxford, 1982.

_____, ed. *Russkoe pravoslavie*. Moscow, 1989.

Klier, John. *Russia Gathers Her Jews: The Origins of the "Jewish Question" in Russia, 1772-1825*. DeKalb, IL, 1986.

Klingenstein, Grete. "Modes of Religious Tolerance and Intolerance in Eighteenth-Century Habsburg Politics." *Austrian Studies Yearbook*, 24 (1993): 1-16.

Kohut, Zenon. *Russian Centralism and Ukrainian Autonomy*. Cambridge, 1988.

Kokosalakis, N. "Religion and Modernization in 19th Century Greece." *Social Compass*, 34 (1987): 223-241.

Kolbasin, E. "I.I. Martynov." *Sovremennik*, 4 (1856):3-6.

Komninos-Ypsilantis, A. *Ta meta tin Alosin, 1453-1789*. Constantinople, 1870.

Kontoyiannis, P.M. *Oi Ellines kata ton proton epi Aikaterinis B' rosso-tourkikon polemon, 1769-1774*. Athens, 1903.

Korol'kov, K. *Ob otkrytii i zakrytii eparkhii v russkoi tserkvi.* Kiev, 1876.

Kostomarov, N.I. "Istoriia raskola i raskol'nikov." *Vestnik evropy* (April 1871): 496-536.

Kotzamanidou, M. "The Greek Monk Arsenios and His Humanist Activities in Seventeenth-Century Russia." *Modern Greek Studies Yearbook*, 2 (1988): 73-88.

Koukkou, Eleni. *Ioannis Kapodistrias: O Anthropos – O Diplomatis (1800-1828).* 2nd ed. Athens, 1984.

_____. *Nikiforos Theotokis, (1731-1800).* Athens, 1973.

Koumas, K.M. *Istoria ton Anthropinon Praxeon.* 12 vols. Vienna, 1832.

"Kratkaia istoriia Astrakhanskoi eparkhii. 17. Astrakhanskii i Stavropol'skii arkhiepiskop Nikifor Theotoki (1786-1792 g.g.)." *Astrakhanskie eparkhial'nye vedomosti*, 16 (1883): 279-283.

Krieger, Leonard. *Kings and Philosophers, 1689-1789.* New York, 1970.

Kselman, Thomas, ed. *Belief in History: Innovative Approaches to European and American Religion.* Notre Dame, 1991.

_____. *Miracles and Prophecies in Nineteenth-Century France.* New Brunswick, NJ, 1983.

Lang, D.M. *The First Russian Radical, Alexander Radishchev, 1749-1802.* London, 1959.

Laskaridis, Ch. *O Arsenios o Graikos kai i Mosha (17os Aionas).* Ioannina, 1988.

Lattimore, Owen. "The Frontier in History." Owen Lattimore, ed., *Studies in Frontier History: Collected Papers, 1928-1958* (Oxford, 1962), 469-491.

Latyshev, V.V. *K nachal'noi istorii g. Mariupoliia.* Odessa, 1914.

Lazzerini, Edward J. "Volga Tatars in Central Asia, 18th-20th Centuries: From Diaspora to Hegemony." Beatrice F. Mantz, ed., *Central Asia in Historical Perspective* (Cambridge, 1994), 82-102.

Leonard, Carol S. *Reform and Regicide: The Reign of Peter III of Russia.* Bloomington, IN, 1992.

Leonard, Carol S. "The Reputation of Peter III." *The Russian Review*, 47:3 (July 1988): 263-292.

Leont'ev, N. "Kratki ocherk istorii astrakhanskoi dukhovnoi seminarii." *Astrakhanskie eparkhial'nye vedomosti*, 17 (1892): 508-527.

Levin, Eve. "*Dvoeverie* and Popular Religion." Stephen K. Batalden, ed., *Seeking God: The Recovery of Religious Identity in Orthodox Russia, Ukraine, and Georgia* (DeKalb, IL, 1993), 29-52.

Lincoln, W. Bruce. *Nicholas I: Emperor and Autocrat of All the Russias.* Bloomington, IN, 1978.

Livanov, F.V. *Raskol'niki i Ostrozhniki: ocherki i razskazy.* Vols. I-IV. St. Petersburg, 1872-1873.

Lotman, Iurii M. and Boris Uspenskii, "Binary Models in the Dynamics of Russian Culture (to the End of the Eighteenth Century)." A.D. and A.S. Nakhimovsky, eds., *The Semiotics of Russian Cultural History* (Cornell, 1985), 30-66.

Lynch, Donald. "The Conquest, Settlement and Initial Development of New Russia (The Southern Third of the Ukraine): 1780-1837." Ph.D. dissertation, Yale, 1965.

Lysogorskii, N.V. *Moskovskii mitropolit Platon Levshin kak protivo-raskol'nicheskii deiatel'.* Rostov-on-the-Don, 1905.

Madariaga, Isabel de. "Catherine and the *Philosophes*," A.G. Cross, ed., *Russia and the West in the Eighteenth Century* (Newtonville, MA, 1983), 30-52.

_____. *Russia in the Age of Catherine the Great.* New Haven, 1981.

Manoussacas, M.I. "The History of the Greek Confraternity (1498-1953) and the Activity of the Greek Institute of Venice (1966-1982)." *Modern Greek Studies Yearbook*, 5 (1989): 321-94.

Makrides, Vasilios N. "Orthodoxy as a Conditio sine qua non: Religion and State/Politics in Modern Greece from a Socio-Historical Perspective." *Ostkirchliche Studien*, 40:4 (1991): 281-305.

_____. "Science and the Orthodox Church in 18th and Early 19th Century Greece: Sociological Considerations." *Balkan Studies*, 29:2 (1988): 265-282.

Mango, Cyril. "The Phanariots and the Byzantine Tradition," Richard Clogg, ed., *The Struggle for Greek Independence* (London, 1973), 41-66.

Marker, Gary. "Faith and Secularity in Eighteenth-Century Russian Literacy, 1700-1775." Robert P. Hughes and Irina Paperno, eds., *Christianity and the Eastern Slavs, II: Russian Culture in Modern Times* (Berkeley, 1994), 3-24.

_____. *Publishing, Printing, and the Origins of Intellectual Life in Russia, 1700-1800*. Princeton, 1985.

_____. "Who Rules the Word? Public School Education and the Fate of Universality in Russia, 1782-1803." *Russian History*, 20:1-4 (1993): 15-34.

Markevich, A.I. *Iuzhnaia Rus' pri Ekaterine II*. Odessa, 1893.

Markova, O.P. "O proiskhozhdenii tak nazyvaemogo grecheskogo proekta (80-e gody XVIII v.)." *Istoriia SSSR*, 4 (1958): 52-78.

"Materialy dlia istorii Astrakhanskoi Dukhovnoi seminarii." *Astrakhanskie eparkhial'nye vedomosti*, 1 (1876): 5-8; 2 (1876): 7-10.

"Materialy dlia istorii Astrakhanskoi seminarii." *Astrakhanskie eparkhial'nye vedomosti*, 4 (1879): 56-61.

Maude, Aylmer. *A Peculiar People: The Doukhobors*. Reprint, New York, 1970.

Medlin, W.K. and Christos G. Patrinelis (with forward by Sir Steven Runciman). *Renaissance Influences and Religious Reforms in Russia: Western and Post-Byzantine Impacts on Culture and Education*. Geneva, 1971.

Mourouti-Gkenakou, Z. *O Nikiforos Theotokis (1731-1800) kai I Symvoli aftou eis tin Paideian tou Yenous*. Athens, 1979.

McNeill, William H. *Europe's Steppe Frontier, 1500-1800*. Chicago, 1964.

_____. *Venice: The Hinge of Europe, 1081-1797*. Chicago, 1974.

Michels, Georg. "The Solovki Uprising: Religion and Revolt in Northern Russia." *Russian Review*, 51 (January 1992): 1-15.

Miliukov, Pavel N. "Educational Reforms." Marc Raeff, ed., *Catherine the Great: A Profile* (New York, 1972), 100-112.

Murav'ev, A.N. *Raskol', oblichaemii svoeiu istorieiu*. St. Petersburg, 1854.

Murzakevich, N.M. "Eparkhial'nye arkhierei novorossiiskago kraia: I. Eparkhiia slovenskaia i khersonskaia." *Zapiski odesskogo obshchestva istorii i drevnostei*, 9: 297-313.

_____. "Materialy dlia istorii novorossiiskoi ierarkhii." *Pribavleniia khersonskim eparkhial'nim vedomostiam*, 20 (1878): 587-602. Note: Same as *Zapiski odesskogo obshchestva istorii i drevnostei*, 9: 297-313.

_____. "Otvod' zemli grekam, v 1780 g. pereseliavshimsia iz kryma k Azovskomu moriu." *Zapiski odesskogo obshchestva istorii i drevnostei*, 4 (1860): 359-363.

Nevodchikov, N. *Evgenii Bulgaris, Arkhiepiskop Slavenskii i Khersonskii*. Odessa, 1875.

Nichols, Robert L. "Orthodoxy and Russia's Enlightenment, 1762-1825." Robert L. Nichols and Theofanis George Stavrou, eds., *Russian Orthodoxy under the Old Regime* (Minneapolis, 1978), 65-89.

Nicolopoulos, John. "From Agathangelos to the *Megali Idea*: Russia and the Emergence of Modern Greek Nationalism." *Balkan Studies*, 26:1 (1985): 41-56.

Novitskii, Orest. *Dukhobortsy: ikh istoriia i verouchenie*. Kiev, 1832; 2nd ed., 1882.

Oberoi, Harjot. *The Construction of Religious Boundaries: Culture, Identity, and Diversity in the Sikh Tradition*. Chicago, 1994.

Okenfuss, Max J. "Education and Empire: School Reform in Enlightened Russia." *Jahrbücher für Geschichte Osteuropas*, 27:1 (1979): 41-68.

_____. "From School Class to Social Caste: The Divisiveness of Early-Modern Russian Education." *Jahrbücher für Geschichte Osteuropas*, 33:3 (1985): 321-344.

Olmsted, Hugh M. "A Learned Greek Monk in Muscovite Exile: Maksim Grek and the Old Testament Prophets." *Modern Greek Studies Yearbook*, 3 (1987): 1-73.

Olmsted, Hugh M. "Maxim Grek's ' Letter to Prince Petr Shuiskii': The Greek and Russian Texts." *Modern Greek Studies Yearbook*, 5 (1989):267-319.

Omel'chenko, O.A. *"Zakonnaia monarchiia" Ekateriny vtoroi: Prosveshchennyi absoliutizm v Rossii.* Moscow, 1993.

Obolensky, D. *The Byzantine Commonwealth: Eastern Europe, 500-1453.* London, 1971.

____. *Byzantium and the Slavs: Collected Essays.* London, 1971.

____. *Six Byzantine Portraits.* Oxford, 1988.

Pallot, Judith and Denis J.B. Shaw. *Landscape and Settlement in Romanov Russia, 1613-1917.* Oxford, 1990.

Papadopoullos, Th. H. *Studies and Documents Relating to the History of the Greek Church and People under Turkish Domination.* Brussels, 1952.

Panchenko, A.M. "' Potemskie derevni' kak kul'turnyi mif." *XVIII vek*, 14 (1983): 93-104.

Pantazopoulos, N.J. *Georg von Maurer – I pros evropaika protipa oloklirotiki strofi tis neoellinikis nomothesias.* Thessaloniki, 1968.

Papmehl, K.A. *Metropolitan Platon of Moscow (Petr Levshin, 1737-1812): The Enlightened Prelate, Scholar and Educator.* Oriental Research Partners: Newtonville, MA, 1983.

Paranikas, M. "Nikiforos o Theotokis kai i en Enetia Ekklisia." *Ellinikos Filologikos Syllogos Konstantinoupoleos*, 20 (1891): 109-126.

Pascal, Pierre. *Avvakum et les débuts du raskol.* Paris, 1938.

Pera, Pia. "Edinoverie: Storia di un tentativo di integrazione del Vecchi Credenti all'interno dell'Ortodossia." *Rivista di storia e letteratura religiosa*, II (1984): 290-351.

Petropoulos, John. *Politics and Statecraft in the Kingdom of Greece, 1833-1843.* London, 1968.

Petrovich, M. "Catherine II and a False Peter III in Montenegro." *Slavic Review*, 14:2 (April 1955): 169-194.

Petrou, I.S. *Ekklisia kai Politiki stin Ellada.* Thessaloniki, 1990.

Piatigorskii, G.M. "Grecheskie pereselentsy v Odesse v kontse XVIII-pervoi treti XIX v.," V.N. Vinogradov, ed., *Iz istroii iazyka i kul'tury stran Tsentral'noi i Iugo-Vostochnoi Evropy* (Moscow, 1985), 33-60.

Pisarevskii, G.G. *Iz istorii inostrannoi kolonizatsii v Rossii v XVIII v.* Moscow, 1909.

Platon (Liubarskii). *Ierarkhiia Viatskaia i Astrakhanskaia.* Moscow, 1848.

Ploumidis, G. "Ai Praxeis Engrafis ton Ellinon Spoudaston tou Panepistimiou tis Padouis (Meros B': Legistis, 1591-1809)." *Epetiris tis Etaireias Vyzantinon Spoudon,* 38 (1971).

Pokrovskii, I.M. *Russkiia eparkhii v XVI-XIX vekakhy, ikh otkrytie, sostav i predely.* 2 vols. Kazan, 1897-1913.

Pokrovskii, N.N. *Antifeodal'nyi protest uralo-sibirskh krestian-staroobriadtsev v XVIII v.* Novosibirsk, 1974.

Polonska-Vasylenko, N.D. "The Settlement of the Southern Ukraine, 1750 till 1775." *The Annals of the Ukrainian Academy of Arts and Sciences in the United States.* Vols. 4-5. New York, 1955.

Poselianin, E. *Russkaia tserkov' i russkie podvizhniki 18-go veka.* St. Petersburg, 1905.

Protopsaltis, E.G., ed. *I Filiki Etairia, Anamnistikon tefkhos epi ti 150eteridi.* Athens, 1964.

Prousis, Theophilus C. "Aleksandr S. Sturdza: A Russian Conservative Response to the Greek Revolution." *East European Quarterly,* XXVI:3 (Sept. 1992): 309-344.

_____. "The Destunis Collection in the Saltykov-Shchedrin State Public Library in Leningrad." *Modern Greek Studies Yearbook,* 5 (1989): 395-452.

_____. "The Greeks of Russia and the Greek Awakening, 1774-1821." *Balkan Studies,* 28:2 (1987): 259-280.

_____. *Russian Society and the Greek Revolution.* DeKalb, IL, 1994.

Raeff, Marc, ed. *Catherine the Great: A Profile.* New York, 1972.

Raeff, Marc. "The Enlightenment in Russia and Russian Thought in the Enlightenment," J.G. Garrard, ed., *The Eighteenth Century in Russia* (London, 1973), 25-47.

____. "Enticements and Rifts: Georges Florovsky as Historian of the Life of the Mind and the Life of the Church in Russia." *Modern Greek Studies Yearbook*, 6 (1990): 187-244.

____. "Patterns of Russian Imperial Policy Toward the Nationalities," E. Allworth, ed., *Soviet Nationality Problems* (New York, 1971), 22-42.

____. "Pugachev's Rebellion." Robert Forster and Jack Greene, eds., *Preconditions of Revolution in Early Modern Europe* (Baltimore, 1970), 161-202.

____. "Uniformity, Diversity, and the Imperial Administration in the Reign of Catherine II." *Osteuropa in Geschichte und Gegenwart: Festschrift fur Gunther Stokl zum 60. Geburtstag.* Cologne, 1977.

____. *The Well-Ordered Police State: Social and Institutional Change Through Law in the Germanies and Russia, 1600-1800.* New Haven, 1983.

Ragsdale, Hugh. "Evaluating the Traditions of Russian Aggression: Catherine II and the Greek Project." *Slavic and East European Review*, 66:1 (January 1988): 91-117.

Ransel, David L. *The Politics of Catherinian Russia: The Panin Party.* New Haven, 1975.

Rasmussen, Karen. "Catherine II and the Image of Peter I." *Slavic Review*, 37:1 (1978): 57-69.

Riasanovsky, Nicholas V. *The Image of Peter the Great in Russian History and Thought.* Oxford: 1985.

____. *Nicholas I and Official Nationality in Russia, 1825-1855.* Berkeley, 1959.

Rieber, Alfred J. "Persistent Factors in Russian Foreign Policy: An Interpretive Essay." Hugh Ragsdale, ed., *Imperial Russian Foreign Policy* (New York, 1993), 315-359.

____. "Struggle Over the Borderlands." S. Frederick Starr, ed., *The Legacy of History in Russia and the New States of Eurasia* (Armonk, NY, 1994), 61-89.

Robson, Roy R. *Old Believers in Modern Russia*. DeKalb, IL, 1995.

Rogger, Hans. *Jewish Policies and Right-wing Politics in Imperial Russia*. Berkeley, 1986.

_____. *National Consciousness in Eighteenth-Century Russia*. Cambridge, 1960.

Roider, Karl. *Austria's Eastern Question*. Princeton, 1982.

Runciman, Sir Steven. *Great Church in Captivity*. Cambridge, 1969.

Safonov, S. "Ostatki grecheskikh legionov v Rossii ili nyneshnee naselenie Balaklavy." *Zapiski odesskogo obshchestva istorii i drevnostei*, 1 (1844): 205-238.

Sathas, Konstantinos N. *Mesaioniki Vivliothiki*. Venice, 1872.

_____. *Neoelliniki Philologia*. Athens, 1868.

_____. *Tourkokratoumeni Ellas*. Athens, 1870.

Saul, Norman. *Russia and the Mediterranean, 1797-1807*. Chicago, 1970.

Saunders, David. *The Ukrainian Impact on Russian Culture, 1750-1850*. Edmonton, 1985.

Savvinskii, Ioann. *Astrakhanskaia eparkhiia, 1602-1902 gg.* 2 vols. Astrakhan, 1905.

Segel, Harold B. "Classicism and Classical Antiquity in Eighteenth- and Early Nineteenth-Century Russian Literature." John G. Garrard, ed., *The Eighteenth Century in Russia* (Oxford, 1973), 48-71.

Shchapov, A. *Russkii raskol staroobriadchestva*. Kazan, 1859.

_____. *Zemstvo i raskol*. St. Petersburg, 1862.

Shils, Edward. *Center and Periphery: Essays in Macrosociology*. Chicago, 1975.

Sinitsa, V.I. "Vosstanie v Moree 1770 i Rossiia." *Voprosy novoi i noveishei istorii* (Minsk, 1974): 12-21.

Sinitsyna, N.V. *Maksim Grek v Rossii*. Moscow, 1977.

Skal'kovskii, A.A. *Bolgarskii kolonii v Bessarabii i Novorossiiskom krai.* Odessa, 1848.

_____.*Khronologischeskoe obozrenie istorii novorossiiskago krai, 1730-1823.* 2 vols. Odessa, 1825-1838.

_____. *Pervoe tridtsatiletie istorii goroda Odessy, 1793-1823.* Odessa, 1837.

Skvortsov, V. "Nikifor Theotoki, vtoroi arkhiepiskop slavenskii i khersonskii." *Poltavskie eparkhial'nye vedomosti*, 6-7 (1878).

Slezkine, Yuri. "Naturalists Versus Nations: Eighteenth-Century Russian Scholars Confront Ethnic Diversity." *Representations*, 47 (Summer 1994): 170-195.

_____. "Savage Christians or Unorthodox Russians? The Missionary Dilemma in Siberia," Gayla Diment and Yuri Slezkine, eds., *Between Heaven and Hell: The Myth of Siberia and Russian Culture* (New York, 1993), 15-31.

Smolitsch, Igor. *Geschichte der Russischen Kirche, 1700-1917.* Leiden, 1964.

Smirnov, P.S. *Istoriia russkago raskola staroobriadstva.* St. Petersburg, 1895.

Smirnov, Sergei. *Istoriia Moskovskoi Slaviano-Greko-Latinskoi Akademii.* Moscow, 1855.

Sokolov, I.I. "Mariupol'skie greki." *Trudy instituta slavianovedeniia AN SSSR*, 1 (1932): 297-317.

Sokolov, N.S. *Raskol' v saratovskom krae.* 2 vols. Saratov, 1886.

Solov'ev, M.M. "Nikifor Theotoki." *Trudy kievskoi dukhovnoi akademii*, 9 (1894): 78-115, 10: 248-266, 12: 569-597.

Solov'ev, S.M. *Istoriia Rossii s drevneishikh vremen.* repr., 15 vols., Moscow, 1959-66.

Soloveytchik, G. *Potemkin.* London, 1939.

Sorel, Albert. *The Eastern Question in the Eighteenth Century: The Partition of Poland and the Treaty of Kainardji.* 1898, repr. New York, 1969.

Sperber, Jonathan. *Popular Catholicism in Nineteenth-Century Germany.* Princeton, 1984.

Stadnitskii, Arsenii. *Gavriil Banulesko-Bodoni: ekzarkh moldo-vlakhiiskii, 1808-1812 gg., i mitropolit kishinevskii, 1813-1821 gg.* Kishinev, 1894.

Stanislavskaia, A.M. *Politicheskaia deiatel'nost' F.F. Ushakova v Gretsii v 1798-1800 gg.* Moscow, 1983.

_____. *Rossiia i Gretsiia v kontse XVIII-nachale XIX veka.* Moscow, 1976.

Stanislawski, Michael. *Tsar Nicholas I and the Jews: The Transformation of Jewish Society in Russia, 1825-1855.* Philadelphia, 1983.

Stavrianos, L.S. *The Balkans since 1453.* New York, 1958.

Stavrou, Theofanis G. and Peter R. Weisensel. *Russian Travelers to the Christian East from the Twelfth to the Twentieth Century.* Columbus, OH, 1986.

Stepniak, Sergei M. *The Russian Peasantry: Their Agrarian Condition, Social Life and Religion.* Westport, CT, 1977. Reprint of New York, 1888 ed.

Storozhenko, N.V. "Iz istorii nezhinskikh grekov." *Kievskaia starina,* 29:6 (1890): 540-544.

Storozhevskii, N.K. *Nezhinskie greki.* Kiev, 1863.

Stourtzas, Alexander. *Anamniseis kai eikones. Evgenios Voulgaris kai Nikiforos Theotokis....* Translated from the French by G. Soutsos. Athens, 1858.
Also translated into Russian by M. Magnitskii, "Evgenii Bulgaris i Nikifor Theotokis, predtechi umstvennago i politicheskago probuzhdeniia grekov. Iz frantsuzskoi rukopisi A. S. Sturdzy, nazvannoi: vospominaniia i obliki." *Moskvitianin,* 2 (1844): 337-367.

Strakhov, Ol'ga B. "Attitudes to Greek Language and Culture in Seventeenth-Century Muscovy." *Modern Greek Studies Yearbook,* 6 (1990): 123-156.

Subtelny, Orest. *Ukraine: A History.* Toronto, 1988.

Sugar, P. *Southeastern Europe under Ottoman Rule, 1354-1804.* Seattle, 1977.

Sukhorev, V.A. *Dokumenti po Istorii Dukhobortsev i Kratkoe Izlozhenie ikh Veroispovedaniia.* North Kildonan, Manitoba, 1944.

Sumner, B.H. *Peter the Great and the Ottoman Empire.* Hamden, 1965.

Sysyn, Frank. *Between Poland and the Ukraine: The Dilemma of Adam Kysil, 1600-1653.* Cambridge, 1985.

Tarran, Michel. "The Orthodox Mission in the North Caucasus: End of the 18th – Beginning of the 19th Century." *Central Asian Survey,* 10:1,2 (1991): 103-117.

Tarle, E.V. *Chesmenskii boi i pervaia russkaia ekspeditsiia v Arkhipelag, 1769-1774.* Moscow, 1945.

Tatakis, V.N., ed. *Skoufos, Miniatis, Voulgaris, Theotokis.* Vasiki Vivliothiki 40. Athens, 1957.

Terras, Victor. *A Karamazov Companion: Commentary on the Genesis, Language, and Style of Dostoevsky's Novel.* Madison, 1981.

Thaden, Edward C. *Russia's Western Borderlands, 1710-1870.* Princeton, 1985.

Theotokis, S. "Peri tis Ekpaidefseos en Eptaniso." *Kerkyraika Hronika,* V (1956): 9-142.

Thomas, Keith. *Religion and the Decline of Magic.* London, 1971.

Tikhomirov, M.N. "Greki iz Morei v srednevekovoi Rossii." *Srednie veka,* 25 (1964): 166-75

Titlinov, B.V. *Gavriil Petrov, mitropolit novgorodskii i sanktpeter-burgskii.* Petrograd, 1916.

Tolstoi, D.A. *Gorodskie uchilishcha v tsarstvovanie Imperatritsy Ekateriny II.* St. Petersburg, 1886.

Troitskii, S.M. *Rossiia v XVIII veke.* Moscow, 1982.

Tsoukalas, K. *Eksartisi kai Anaparagogi.* Athens, 1974.

Tsourkas, C. *Les Débuts de L'Enseignement Philosophique et de la Libre Pensée dans les Balkans: La Vie et L'Ourve de Théophile Corydalée, 1570-1646.* Thessaloniki, 1967.

Turner, Victor. *From Ritual to Theatre.* New York, 1982.

Vakalopoulos, A. *Istoria tou Neou Ellinismou*. 6 vols. Thessaloniki, 1973-1982.

Vasiliev A.A. *History of the Byzantine Empire*. 2 vols. Madison, 1952.

Vasiliev, Kyrill. "Kliucharevskaia letopis'." *Astrakhanskie eparkhial'nye vedomosti*, 10 (1887): 371-374.

Veloudis, I. *Ellinon orthodoxon apoikia en Venetia*. Athens, 1893.

Venturi, Franco. *The End of the Old Regime in Europe, 1768-1776*. Princeton, 1989.

Vranousis, Leandros I. *Athanasios Psalidas, o Didaskalos tou Yenous, 1767-1829*. Ioannina, 1951.

_____. "Post-Byzantine Hellenism and Europe: Manuscripts, Books, and Printing Presses." *Modern Greek Studies Yearbook*, 2 (1986): 1-71.

Vretos, Andreas Papadopoulos. *Neoelliniki Philologia*. 2 vols. Athens, 1854-1857.

Vrokinis, L. *Viografika Shedaria*. Vol. I. Corfu, 1884.

Vournas, Tasos, ed. *Filiki Etairia*. Athens, 1965.

Vucinich, A. *Science in Russian Culture: A History to 1860*. Stanford, 1963.

Ware, Timothy. *Eustratios Argenti: A Study of the Greek Church under Turkish Rule*. Oxford, 1964.

_____. *The Orthodox Church*. London, 1963.

Weeks, Theodore R. "Defending Our Own: Government and the Russian Minority in the Kingdom of Poland, 1905-1917." *The Russian Review*, 54 (October 1995): 539-551.

White, Richard. *The Middle Ground: Indians, Empire, and Republics in the Great Lakes Region, 1650-1815*. New York, 1991.

Whittaker, Cynthia. *The Origins of Modern Russian Education: An Intellectual Biography of Count Sergei Uvarov, 1786-1855*. DeKalb, IL, 1984.

_____. "The Reforming Tsar: The Redefinition of Autocratic Duty in Eighteenth-Century Russia." *Slavic Review*, 51:1 (Spring 1992): 77-98.

Wieczynski, Joseph, L. *The Russian Frontier: The Impact of the Border-lands upon the Course of Early Russian History.* Charlottesville, VA, 1976.

Wilson, Bryan. *Religious Sects: A Sociological Study.* London, 1970.

Woodcock, George, and Ivan Avakumovic. *The Doukhobors.* Toronto, 1968.

Wolff, Larry. *Inventing Eastern Europe: The Map of Civilization on the Mind of the Enlightenment.* Stanford, 1994.

Woodhouse, C.M. *Capodistria: The Founder of Greek Independence.* London, 1973.

____. *Gemistos Plethon: The Last of the Hellenes.* Oxford, 1986.

____. "Kapodistrias and the *Philiki Etairia*, 1814-21," Richard Clogg, ed., *The Struggle for Greek Independence* (London, 1973), 104-134.

Worobec, Christine D. "Death Ritual Among Russian and Ukrainian Peas-ants: Linkages Between the Living and the Dead." Stephen Frank and Mark Steinberg, eds. *Cultures in Flux: Lower-Class Values, Practices, and Resistance in Late Imperial Russia* (Princeton, 1994), 11-33.

Wortman, Richard. *Scenarios of Power: Myth and Ceremony in Russian Monarchy.* Princeton, 1995.

Xydis, Stephen G. "Modern Greek Nationalism." Peter F. Sugar and Ivo J. Lederer, eds., *Nationalism in Eastern Europe* (Seattle, 1969), 207-258.

Zagorovskii, E.A. *Ekonomicheskaia politika Potemkina v Novorossii, 1774-1791.* Odessa, 1926.

____. *Organizatsiia upravleniia Novorossii pri Potemkine.* Odessa, 1913.

____. *Voennaia kolonizatsiia Novorossii pri Potemkine.* Odessa, 1913.

Zakythinos, D.A. *The Making of Modern Greece from Byzantium to Inde-pendence.* London, 1976.

Zaviras, G.I. *Anekdota Syngrammata: Nea Ellas i Ellinikon Theatron.* Athens, 1872.

Zenkovsky, Serge. *Russkoe staroobriadchestvo.* Munich, 1970.

Zhakin, V. "Nachalo edinoveria." *Khristianskoe chtenie*, 12 (1900): 979-1004.

Znamenskii, I. *Polozhenie dukhovenstva v tsarstvovanii Ekateriny II i Pavla I.* Moscow, 1880.

Znamenskii, P.V. *Dukhovnye shkoly v Rossii do reformy 1808 goda.* Kazan, 1881.

Conference Proceedings

Russia's Dissenting Old Believers: An International Conference, Northfield, MN, Sept. 30-Oct. 2, 1994.